CBE STYLE MANUAL

CBE Style Manual Committee

Erwin Neter, *Chairman*
Philip L. Altman
Murrie W. Burgan
Noel H. Holmgren
Gisella Pollock
Elizabeth M. Zipf

Other Publications of the
Council of Biology Editors, Inc.

Scientific Writing for Graduate Students:
A Manual on the Teaching of Scientific Writing
(ISBN: 0-914340-01-8)

Economics of Scientific Journals
(ISBN: 0-914340-03-4)

Illustrating Science: Standards for Publication
(ISBN: 0-914340-05-0)

CBE STYLE MANUAL

Fifth Edition, revised and expanded

A Guide for Authors, Editors, and Publishers in the Biological Sciences

Prepared by
CBE STYLE MANUAL COMMITTEE

Published by

Council of Biology Editors, Inc.
Bethesda, Maryland

Council of Biology Editors, Inc.
Bethesda, MD 20814

Printed in the United States of America
All Rights Reserved

Library of Congress Cataloging in Publication Data

CBE Style Manual Committee.
   CBE style manual.

   Rev. and expanded ed. of: Council of Biology Editors style manual. 4th ed. c.1978.
   Bibliography: p.
   Includes index.
   1. Biology—Authorship. 2. Printing, Practical—Style Manuals. I. Title. II. Title: CBE style manual.
QH304.C33 1983   808'.02   83-7172
ISBN 0-914340-04-2

Correct citation:
CBE Style Manual Committee. CBE style manual: a guide for authors, editors, and publishers in the biological sciences. 5th ed. rev. and expanded. Bethesda, MD: Council of Biology Editors, Inc.; 1983.

CONTENTS

Preface

It was the aim of the present Style Manual Committee to update the 4th edition in accord with recent developments, to use much of its contents, and to consider carefully the suggestions made by the Evaluation Committee charged with critical perusal of the 4th edition. As a result, the section on Plant Sciences in the chapter "Style in Special Fields" was completely revised and expanded, and three major new chapters were added to replace previous sections. The chapter "Ethical Conduct in Authorship and Publication" was contributed by Edward J. Huth; the chapter "Application of Copyright Law" was contributed by Carol A. Risher; and the chapter "Illustrative Material" was contributed by Paul J. Anderson, chairman of the CBE Committee on Scientific Illustrations, and members of that committee.

Numerous colleagues aided in the preparation of the current edition and their contributions are acknowledged with gratitude. Individuals who provided the Style Manual Committee with significant portions of a chapter or section are listed as Contributors, and those colleagues who aided the committee with specific problems are listed as Consultants. To acknowledge the contributions of many individuals who helped in the preparation of the 4th edition, we reprint its preface and the lists of subcommittees and consultants.

The chairman would like to express his gratitude to the members of the present Style Manual Committee, who worked in a most harmonious and effective manner. Special thanks are expressed to Philip L. Altman, who served on the committee for two previous editions of the Style Manual, and whose sound judgment, knowledge, and quiet efficiency immeasurably helped the present committee in its task. Because of the location of the CBE Secretariat, the committee held all of its meetings at the Federation of American Societies for Experimental Biology; we express our gratitude to FASEB for making these facilities available. Particular thanks are due also to the Manuscript Editor, Jean C. Newman, without whose help the manuscript would not have been completed according to plan. Finally, we express our appreciation to the Board of Directors of CBE, past and present, who gave wholehearted support to the preparation of this edition. It is the hope of the committee that the present edition will be received as well as were its predecessors. We invite suggestions from readers as a guide to the committee charged with the preparation of the 6th edition.

CBE STYLE MANUAL COMMITTEE

COMMITTEE MEMBERS, CONTRIBUTORS, AND CONSULTANTS

CBE STYLE MANUAL COMMITTEE MEMBERS

ERWIN NETER, *Chairman*
Professor Emeritus of Microbiology and
Pediatrics
Department of Microbiology
State University of New York at Buffalo
and Children's Hospital
Buffalo, NY 14222

PHILIP L. ALTMAN
Executive Secretary
Council of Biology Editors, Inc.
Bethesda, MD 20814

MURRIE W. BURGAN
Technical Editor
Technical Publications Group
The Johns Hopkins University

Applied Physics Laboratory
Laurel, MD 20707

NOEL H. HOLMGREN
Curator
New York Botanical Garden
Bronx, NY 10458

GISELLA POLLOCK
Publications Consultant
American Chemical Society
Washington, DC 20036

ELIZABETH M. ZIPF
Technical Consultant to the President
BioSciences Information Service
Philadelphia, PA 19103

CONTRIBUTORS

ARLY ALLEN
Vice President and General Manager
Allen Press, Inc.
Lawrence, KS 66044

PAUL J. ANDERSON
Editor-in-Chief, *Journal of Histochemistry
and Cytochemistry*
Mt. Sinai School of Medicine
New York, NY 10029

LOUIS E. BARBROW
Consultant, Office of Weights and Measures
National Bureau of Standards
Washington, DC 20234

JUDITH P. BLOOMER
Copy Editor, *Journal of Applied Physiology*
American Physiological Society
Bethesda, MD 20814

MARGARET BROADBENT
Editorial Consultant (retired)
300 Broadway
Dobbs Ferry, NY 10522

CATHERINE B. CARLSTON
Copy Editor, *Handbooks of Physiology*
American Physiological Society
Bethesda, MD 20814

WENDELL COCHRAN
Director, Editorial Group

American Geological Institute
Falls Church, VA 22206

ARTHUR FREEMAN
Editor-in-Chief, *American Journal of Veterinary Research* and *Journal of the American Veterinary Medical Association*
American Veterinary Medical Association
Schaumburg, IL 60196

ALAN M. GITTELSOHN
Professor of Biostatistics
School of Hygiene and Public Health
The Johns Hopkins University
Baltimore, MD 21205

PHILLIP GORDON
Information Center Manager
EDP Department
Guy F. Atkinson Company
San Francisco, CA 94080

C. GRACE GURTOWSKI
Librarian, Federation of American Societies for Experimental Biology
Bethesda, MD 20814

EDWARD J. HUTH
Editor, *Annals of Internal Medicine*
American College of Physicians
Philadelphia, PA 19104

CHRISTOPHER JOHNSON
Vice President, Capital City Press, Inc.
Montpelier, VT 05602

DONALD T. KRIZEK
Plant Physiologist
Plant Physiology Institute, USDA/ARS
Beltsville, MD 20705

BARBARA A. KUHN
Managing Editor, *Journal of Heredity*
American Genetic Association
Washington, DC 20006

ERWIN F. LESSEL
Chief Editor, Professional Medical Serv-
ices
Lederle Laboratories
Pearl River, NY 10965

A. JEAN MacGREGOR
Director, Educational Services
Calgary General Hospital
Calgary, Alberta T2E 0A1
Canada

JOSEPH L. MELNICK
Distinguished Service Professor of Vi-
rology and Epidemiology
Department of Virology and Epidemiol-
ogy
Baylor College of Medicine
Houston, TX 77030

REBECCA G. NISLEY
Technical Editor
Agricultural Research Service, USDA
Beltsville, MD 20705

BYUNG H. PARK
Professor/Director of Immunology
Laboratory

Pediatrics and Microbiology
Children's Hospital/State University of
New York
Buffalo, NY 14222

CAROL A. RISHER
Director of Copyright
Association of American Publishers, Inc.
Washington, DC 20036

CURTIS W. SABROSKY
Cooperating Scientist, Systematic Ento-
mology Laboratory, USDA
U.S. National Museum
Washington, DC 20560

LAUREL V. SCHAUBERT
President, Biomed Arts Associates, Inc.
San Francisco, CA 94117

ROBERT E. STEVENSON
Director, American Type Culture Col-
lection
Rockville, MD 20852

AMIE VAN ITALLIE
Group Leader, Systems Design and De-
velopment Department
BioSciences Information Service
Philadelphia, PA 19103

NANCY VAUPEL
Head, User Services Department
BioSciences Information Service
Philadelphia, PA 19103

CONSULTANTS

CHRISTIANE ANDERSON
Editor, *Systematic Botany Monographs*
Herbarium
University of Michigan
Ann Arbor, MI 48109

WILLIAM R. ANDERSON
General Editor, *Flora Novo-Galiciana*
Herbarium
University of Michigan
Ann Arbor, MI 48109

MARIANNE BROGAN
Associate Head, Journals
American Chemical Society
Columbus, OH 43210

DAVID E. GIANNASI
Associate Professor, Department of
Botany
University of Georgia

Athens, GA 30602

RICHARD GUTHRIE
Soil Conservation Service
P.O. Box 2890
Washington, DC 20013

JAMES C. HICKMAN
Former Editor, *Madroño*
Department of Botany
University of California
Berkeley, CA 94720

PATRICIA K. HOLMGREN
Associate Editor, *Brittonia*
New York Botanical Garden
Bronx, NY 10458

JACQUELYN KALLUNKI
Associate Editor, *Brittonia*
New York Botanical Garden
Bronx, NY 10458

MANUSCRIPT EDITOR AND INDEXER

PREFACE TO THE FOURTH EDITION

The committee that wrote this style manual has been in continuous existence for almost two decades, first as the Committee on Form and Style and now as the Style Manual Committee. Its membership has changed for the preparation of each successive edition, but only in part. This continuity in the committee has helped to ensure consistent aims and policies for the manual through its four editions.

In preparing this edition, we have tried to address the same readers and users and to provide the same wide range of content as did the third edition. The sequence of chapters has been changed; most chapters have been thoroughly rewritten.

We have based our recommendations on style and format in large part on standards established by international and U.S. organizations concerned with science or with information services. In aspects of usage pertinent to all of biology for which such standards do not exist, we have either avoided making recommendations or have drawn on widely accepted practices. The greatest difficulties in deciding on the scope of the manual arose in preparing Chapter 9, "Style in Special Fields." The limits set for the length of the manual precluded our presenting usage for some specialized fields in full detail. Several fields, such as neurophysiology, are not represented because their conventions have not been established by appropriate agreement within their professional societies, national or international. We hope that all fields of science may some day agree to use the same conventions in style to facilitate communication among all scientists. Toward that end, we have adopted recommendations from the American Chemical Society, the American Geological Institute, and the American Institute of Physics that are applicable for the needs of authors in biology.

We are grateful to the subcommittee members and consultants listed at the end of this preface who contributed to, and critically reviewed, sections of Chapter 9 and parts of other chapters. Many suggestions also were received from users of the third edition.

This edition is built on the first three editions, and we acknowledge our debt to the preceding members of the committee who were authors of those editions.

Committee on Form and Style for First Edition: J. R. Porter (Chairman), Sheridan Baker, George B. Cummins, Harold Cummins, Graham DuShane, Richard H. Manville, Robert V. Ormes, A. J. Riker, William C. Steere, H. B. Vickery.

Committee on Form and Style for Second Edition: J. R. Porter (Chairman), James S. Ayars, Harold Cummins, Graham DuShane, Richard H. Manville, Robert V. Ormes, A. J. Riker, William C. Steere, H. B. Vickery.

Committee on Form and Style for Third Edition: James S. Ayars (Chairman),

Philip L. Altman, Margaret Broadbent, Edward J. Huth, David R. Lincicome, Robert V. Ormes.

Before beginning her terms as Vice-Chairman and Chairman of the Council of Biology Editors, Margaret Broadbent served as a member of the Style Manual Committee for this edition. We are pleased to acknowledge her important contributions, particularly in drafting content for Chapter 3.

Kathleen van Steenburgh served as manuscript editor from close to the beginning of work on this edition, but her assistance went beyond what is usually asked of an editor. She gathered documentary sources and prepared first versions of text for several sections. She offered astute and pertinent criticisms of many sections of text prepared by committee members. Her careful work for the Committee deserves the gratitude of members of the Council of Biology Editors and other users of the manual.

A statement in the preface of the first edition applies to this edition: "If this manual is to be useful, it must be kept up to date by frequent revision. Comments by users will be helpful." To this we add that international and national scientific organizations preparing recommendations for usage and style in their disciplines should call these to our attention to be considered for use in later editions. Comments, suggestions, and recommendations should be addressed to the Style Manual Committee of the Council of Biology Editors, in care of the American Institute of Biological Sciences, 1401 Wilson Boulevard, Arlington, VA 22209, USA [present address: Council of Biology Editors, Inc., 9650 Rockville Pike, Bethesda, MD 20814].

STYLE MANUAL COMMITTEE

Edward J. Huth, *Chairman*
Philip L. Altman
Murrie W. Burgan
Edwin H. Feinberg

Stephen R. Geiger
C. Grace Gurtowski
William H. Klein
Erwin Neter

SUBCOMMITTEES

Abbreviations and Symbols
Edwin H. Feinberg, *Chairman*
Dorothy D. Katz
Elizabeth M. Zipf

Animal Sciences
Philip L. Altman, *Chairman*

Robert M. Berne
Thomas C. Cheng
Barbara C. Kuhn
Aaron J. Ladman
Curtis W. Sabrosky
Jean D. Wilson

xviii

Microbiology
Erwin Neter, *Chairman*
L. Leon Campbell
Erwin Lessel
Joseph L. Melnick

Biochemistry
Murrie W. Burgan, *Chairman*
Paul J. Anderson
Bernard K. Forscher
Martin Gibbs
J. Stanton King, Jr.

Plant Sciences
William H. Klein, *Chairman*
Robert Aycock
Norman H. Boke
Jane T. Buckley

Word Usage
Stephen R. Geiger, *Chairman*
Bernard K. Forscher
Lois T. Hunt
Leslie W. Scattergood

CONSULTANTS

Abbreviations and Symbols
Marianne Brogan

Animal Sciences
Neva Abelson
K. Frank Austen
Denis A. Baron
Digamber S. Borgaonkar
Robert W. Bull
Samuel Charache
Stewart Clarke
John E. Cotes
Margaret O. Dayhoff
S. Fedoroff
J. L. Hamerton
W. C. D. Hare
Theodore S. Hauschka
Paul Heller
Alfred P. Krauss
Hermann Lehmann
S. M. Lewis
D. Armstrong Lowe
Paul A. Marks
John B. Miale
Arno G. Motulsky
Samuel E. Poiley
Oscar D. Ratnoff
Joseph C. Ross
Max Samter
John E. Shannon
George S. Smith
Philip W. Smith
Joan Staats
Roy L. Walford
Russell Weisman, Jr.
Alexander S. Wiener
Raymund L. Zwemer

Chemistry and Biochemistry
Marianne Brogan
Gary T. Cocks
Waldo E. Cohn
Eli Grushka
Martin A. Paul

Geology
Wendell Cochran

Indexing
Dorothy D. Katz

Microbiology
Robert A. Day
Gladys L. Hobby
Elizabeth McFall
Gisella Pollock
Robert J. Shepherd

Plant Sciences
Houston R. Baker
Richard S. Cowan
John G. Moseman

SI Units
Louis E. Barbrow

Word Usage
Catherine B. Carlston

MANUSCRIPT EDITOR
Kathleen C. van Steenburgh

INDEXER
Eleanor B. Kuljian

1

Ethical conduct in authorship and publication

Scientists build their concepts and theories with individual bricks of scientifically ascertained facts, found by themselves and their predecessors. Scientists can proceed with confidence only if they can assume that the previously reported facts on which their work is based are indeed correct. Thus all scientists have an unwritten contract with their contemporaries and those whose work will follow to provide observations honestly obtained, recorded, and published. This ethic is no more than science's application of the ancient Golden Rule: "Do unto others as you would have them do unto you." It is an ethic that should govern everyone in the community of scientists when they serve as authors, editors, or manuscript referees. The second governing ethical principle is that a scientist's observations and conclusions are his or her property until the scientist presents them to the scientific community in a published paper.

ETHICS FOR AUTHORS

This manual cannot concern itself with the conduct of scientists in their research: whether they record only that which they observe or measure, whether they treat human or animal subjects in accord with accepted standards, and whether they adequately communicate with their co-workers. It must confine itself to ethical standards for the steps in scientific publication, of which the first is writing the scientific paper.

AUTHORSHIP
The authorship of a paper should be decided, if possible, before the paper is written, even if the decision is only tentative. This decision should come from the scientist who has been most engaged in designing and executing the research. Any conflicts on authorship or content of the paper should be resolved among the co-workers. The basic requirement for authorship is that an author should be able to take public responsibility for the content of the paper (2). An author should be able

1

to indicate why and how the observations were made, and how the conclusions follow from the observations. An author should be able to defend criticisms of the paper, as, for example, in a letter-to-the-editor responding to published criticisms. These abilities should come from having participated in design of the study, in observing and interpreting the reported findings, and in writing the paper.

Claims to authorship may come from persons who have had little to do with the intellectual content of the paper, but who have provided financial support, routine technical assistance, or research space and equipment. Such contributions need not be rewarded with authorship but can be acknowledged in the appropriate section of the paper.

CONTENT OF A MANUSCRIPT

Authors have three main ethical responsibilities in presenting their research in scientific papers. A paper must report only observations actually made by one or more of its authors and must not fail to report evidence conflicting with the conclusions reached. Authors must relate their study to previously published relevant work and unpublished observations of others. A paper must indicate how the research was conducted in relation to generally held ethical standards.

Honest and full reporting, the first responsibility, calls for accurately and completely representing the observations made and data collected. At least one of the authors, preferably the principal author, should have been closely enough involved with conduct of the study to be reasonably sure that data have not been fabricated or improperly manipulated by any of the other authors or by technicians (1). If any data are excluded from the report, the exclusion should be described and justified. Unpublished data drawn from other sources should be identified as such and appropriately credited, with indication that such acknowledgment is with the consent of the person being credited.

To meet the second responsibility, the authors must honestly relate their work to that of others so that readers can objectively evaluate the present report. Conflicting evidence from the work of others should not be ignored but should be included to help readers judge the soundness of the conclusions stated in the paper.

The third responsibility is met by describing the safeguards used to meet both formal and informal standards of ethical conduct of research: approval of a research protocol by an institutional committee, procurement of informed consent, proper treatment of animals, and maintenance of confidentiality of personal data on patients.

AUTHORS' RESPONSIBILITIES TO THEIR INSTITUTIONS

Many private and governmental institutions and their departments have formal or informal requirements ethically or legally binding authors to obtain approval or clearance of a paper before it is submitted to a journal. There are various reasons for these requirements: to protect the institution's scientific reputation, to prevent publication of papers conflicting with institutional policies, or to guard against disclosure of restricted or classified information. Most authors are likely to have been made aware of such requirements at the time of employment; if not, they should inquire into their institution's policy on approval or clearance. Institutional requirements may include specified statements in papers indicating approval or clearance of the paper for publication. Such statements may include disavowal of institutional responsibility for content of a paper and acceptance of all responsibility for the content by the authors. Authors are responsible for ensuring that such statements are presented exactly as required by the institution.

Institutional policies on copyright differ. Most academic institutions allow their authors to retain copyright, which is an author's property by virtue of creating the work. Some institutions require that authors in their employ assign copyright to the institution. Works (papers, books, maps, and other works) created by persons as a duty of employment by the United States government belong to the public domain and cannot be copyrighted. (For further information, *see* chapter 8, Application of Copyright Law.)

SUBMISSION OF PAPERS TO JOURNALS

Editors, responsible to both readers and authors, expect authors to meet the ethical standards discussed above for the preparation and the content of papers submitted to their journals. They also expect full, honest disclosure (3) of other facts that may bear on acceptance or rejection of a paper. These facts should be stated in the submission, or covering, letter that accompanies the manuscript.

Many journals specify in their instructions to authors that papers will be considered for possible publication only with the understanding that the papers have not already been submitted to, accepted by, or published in, another journal totally or in part. Therefore, authors should inform editors in submission letters of any possible conflict with these policies. An editor will be helped in deciding on the extent of overlap of the submitted paper with a previously published paper or one submitted to another journal if a copy of the other paper is enclosed with the manuscript being submitted.

Some journals require that the submission letter state that each author listed on the title page has agreed to authorship. Inclusion of someone's name as an author without that person's consent is both a violation of that person's right to be responsible for his or her reputation in the world of science and, from the editor's point of view, a dishonest act.

ETHICS FOR EDITORS

The responsibility of the editor in scientific communication is broad, affecting not only authors but manuscript reviewers and readers as well. Therefore, editors must be especially sensitive to ethical conduct of their duties.

EDITORS AND AUTHORS

The author's work, as represented by the manuscript, is the author's intellectual property. Some journals require transfer of copyright from the author to the journal, with such transfer required usually before final acceptance of the paper. From the ethical point of view, however, copyright does not belong to the journal until the paper is published. Until then, the paper must be regarded by the editor as belonging to the author. This principle requires that the manuscript be treated as a confidential communication from the author to the editor at all points up to publication. Its contents must not be divulged to anyone other than persons necessarily involved in reading the paper in the editorial office or reviewing it for the editor, or persons assisting in these functions, such as secretaries and office clerks. The editor must make clear to the office staff and to reviewers the confidentiality of manuscripts. Editors can help to ensure that reviewers will treat manuscripts as confidential communications by stating this ethical standard on manuscript-review forms.

EDITORS AND REVIEWERS

The editor is obliged to authors to prevent an inappropriate judgment by a reviewer resulting in rejection of a valid and important paper. The editor is also obliged to readers to publish only valid and important papers. Both of these obligations require that the editor select reviewers with careful attention to their competence in the subject of the paper, an absence of bias, and honesty. If the author recommends reviewers, the editor may or may not follow the recommendation. If, on the other hand, the author asks that certain reviewers not be used, because of unfavorable bias, that request should be honored unless the editor has reason to believe the request is intended to eliminate all competent reviewers from examining the paper.

When the judgments of two reviewers on a paper differ greatly, the editor must take responsibility for deciding which judgment is probably the more reliable or for seeking additional reviews. Should the latter course result in excessive delay in the review process, the editor should offer the author the option of withdrawing the paper.

Excessive delays in the review process are a disservice to both authors and readers. Scientific reputations and professional advancement of authors depend, in part, on prompt publication of their research findings. New information should be made available to the scientific community without delay.

ETHICS FOR REVIEWERS

Reviewers must follow the same ethical standards as authors and editors and should serve only in their areas of competence. As anonymous judges of the work of peers, reviewers must avoid bias in making recommendations. Adverse bias may result if the author is a strong rival, or if the paper undermines the reviewer's scientific position. Favorable bias may result if the author is a friend and not a rival, or if the paper supports the reviewer's own views.

Reviewers should avoid either kind of bias and make judgments as if those judgments had to be publicly defended. A reviewer should assist an editor by informing him or her of any condition that might affect objective evaluation of the paper.

A reviewer may prefer to waive anonymity, but this choice should be subject to the approval of the editor, who may wish to maintain anonymity of reviewers. In either case, the responsibility of the editor must be preserved by preventing direct communication between reviewer and author.

The reviewer, like the editor, must treat the paper as a confidential communication. If on reading the paper the reviewer concludes that an associate would be a better reviewer, he or she should get permission from the editor to pass the paper to that associate for review; the editor may already have presented this option. An associate who reviews the paper or joins in the review must also honor confidentiality. In honoring this principle of confidentiality, reviewers accept the underlying premise that a paper's intellectual content is the property of the author until the paper is formally published; reviewers are not free to use any of the content for their own purposes.

Reviewers are responsible not only for objective critical analysis of manuscripts but also for completing their tasks within the time allowed by the editor. Should illness, vacation, or other events delay the reviewer, the editor should be notified promptly.

ETHICS FOR PUBLISHERS AND PRINTERS

Confidentiality must be maintained not only by editors and reviewers but also by the publishing office and the printing firm. No one should divulge the identity of authors or the content of papers to persons not authorized by authors. Thus information must not be given to, for example, reporters for the news media, or employees of investment or economic-analysis firms, even in response to inquiries from such sources.

A paper is accepted by an editor for publication with the implicit understanding that its content at that point is the content that will be published. The editor and the copy editor may make redactorial changes in style to correct grammatical and typographical errors and unclear details of prose but must make no changes in the substantive content of a paper. The author should accept the redactorial changes, but be alert to possible changes in meaning that can occur during copy editing for publication.

LITERATURE CITED: Ethical Conduct in Authorship and Publication

1. AAMC Ad Hoc Committee on the Maintenance of High Ethical Standards in the Conduct of Research. The maintenance of high ethical standards in the conduct of research. Washington, DC: Association of American Medical Colleges; 1982.
2. Huth, E. J. Authorship from the reader's side. Ann. Int. Med. 97:613–614; 1982.
3. Huth, E. J. The ethics of medical publishing: prior publication and full disclosure by authors. Ann. Int. Med. 94:401–402; 1981.

2

Planning the communication

It is anticipated that the readership of this manual will be scientist/authors, editors, publishers, and manuscript editors whose main interest in written communication is the primary research journal. The focus, therefore, is on the preparation of articles for publication in primary research journals. However, other types of written communications must be considered. Some of these are described briefly in this chapter and, where appropriate in later chapters, suggestions are made for handling such communications.

TYPES OF COMMUNICATIONS

RESEARCH ARTICLES

A research article for publication in a primary journal should be based on research that has been completed to the point of yielding conclusions amply supported by firm evidence. For a laboratory or clinical investigation, for example, you must begin with an appropriate study design, use adequate methods, collect sufficient data, and organize the data into tables or graphs. Use proper statistical methods for interpretation of results. If your research consisted of field observations, you must have field notes, photographs, or maps that clearly represent what you are about to report.

You must now consider whether the findings should be reported in the scientific literature. Colleagues who have not worked with you in your research but who know the subject may be able to help you decide whether your material is suitable for publication. Do not be tempted to publish more than one article reporting the same results. A widely understood and often explicitly stated condition for acceptance of an article by a scientific journal is that its content has not been submitted or published elsewhere in either identical or similar form (*see* chapter 1, page 3). Editors occasionally allow exceptions.

REVIEW ARTICLES

A review article may be prepared at the invitation of the editor or it may be initiated by the author. It is advisable for the author to discuss a proposed review with the editor before undertaking the project.

Before starting work on a review article, the editors as well as the authors should consider carefully what specific question the review will attempt to answer. A useful scientific review should provide an answer to an important question; the answer may be useful either conceptually or practically. The review may not, however, provide a definitive answer; in this case, it may indicate directions for future research.

Is the review needed? Useful reviews summarize, critically analyze, and integrate. A review may be needed when the number and content of research reports on a scientific question are such as to permit the developing of a clear, well-supported answer to that question. The author contemplating the writing of a review should search recent literature to be sure that a similar review has not been published. Colleagues may help by commenting on the need for the proposed review.

MULTIAUTHORED BOOKS

There are numerous types of multiauthored books, including those written by invitation, as well as contributions from symposia and proceedings of meetings, specialty volumes such as *Advances in . . .*, *Reviews of . . .*, *Survey on . . .*, and all manner of textbooks, monographs, and yearbooks. These publications, written by several or many authors under the guiding influence of an editor or editors, usually concentrate on a central theme, in an adequately balanced milieu. In a specific subject volume, it is the aim of the editor(s) to select appropriate authors who have demonstrated expertise in their field of study to contribute to the volume. And it is the endeavor of the editor to derive a product that is adequately unified and balanced in topic and construction.

The authors are dependent on the editor's guidelines. The editor should present the aim and scope of the book to the authors in clear, concise terminology and construct an outline of topics. The outline of topics should be utilized not only to demonstrate the scope of coverage but to maintain a balance of subject specialties. In these instructions, the authors should receive explicit instructions on the form, style, and length of the manuscript; number and types of graphics permitted; conventions to be followed; terminology; abbreviations, if any; suggestions for the construction of index terms and key words; order and manner of reference citations; deadlines for publication; and the many other details necessary for publication.

The most important function of the editor is to be able to tie together the primary and essential theme running through the volume, so that the subject flows in logical order from one contribution to another. Consistency of style is essential; unity of thought is obligatory. Although occasionally an invited author's contribution is not refereed, in deference perhaps to the researcher's professional status, it is advisable to have the chapters reviewed, even though such a contribution is not usually refused at that point. It is up to the communicative skill of the editor, who should be knowledgeable in the subject area as well, to diplomatically suggest any major or minor changes in such a document.

The role of the editor cannot be minimized. He or she has the authority to control every phase of the publication from the inception of the idea to the final printing of the volume. One of the last contributions the editor will make will be to write an introduction or preface to define the book's aims, objectives, purpose, and scope for the readers. This part of the book will influence the reader significantly, and even may be reflected in sales of the volume.

SYNOPTICS

The synoptic form of publication has been used, usually experimentally, by a limited number of publishers. Complete information regarding the synoptic form is available in the *American National Standard for Synoptics* (2), which describes this form of publication as follows:

> (A synoptic is) . . . a concise (usually two-page), first publication in a primary journal. It presents, in a directly usable form, those key ideas and results from a simultaneously available full paper on completed work which the author(s) selected as being most important and useful to others. An abstract is included in the synoptic. Use of figures, tables, and/or equations that will efficiently transmit the selected information is encouraged. Both the synoptic and the backup full paper must be reviewed before the synoptic is accepted for publication. The combination of the foregoing characteristics sets a synoptic apart from the abstract or "conclusions" section of a paper, from the Notes and Letters published in many journals, and from abridgments or synopses prepared by someone other than the author(s) . . . .

ABSTRACTS AS THE BASIS FOR ORAL OR POSTER PRESENTATIONS

Abstracts published in connection with meetings may be considered primary communications since the work reported presumably has not been published or presented previously. An abstract of this type should contain a concise statement of the problem under investigation, the experimental methods used, the essential results (in summary form), and conclusions. It should not contain any tabular material, illustrations, or references.

Program organizers provide forms that instruct authors how to prepare their abstracts. These instructions should be read and followed carefully since the rules may change from year to year or vary from organization to organization.

POSTERS

During the last few years, poster sessions have become an important addition to meetings, both national and international. They provide the opportunity of personal communication between authors and interested individuals. The sponsoring organization usually establishes the time period available for viewing a given poster and provides information on the physical features of the display. In addition to content, the author must prepare the poster with particular care so that it can be seen easily from a distance. For example, the title should be visible from a distance of 40 feet and the text from a distance of 2 feet. The heading gives the title of the poster together with the name and affiliation of each author. The subject matter usually is divided into the following parts: problem at hand or introduction; subjects, materials, and methods; results; and conclusions. Well-designed tables and figures provide the visual interest necessary for an effective poster presentation. The nomenclature appropriate for a special field should be used. The program for a meeting may include abstracts of papers to be presented in poster sessions, but more frequently poster presentations are listed only by title and author(s).

THESES

Scientific Writing for Graduate Students (3) states that "... the principles to be applied to writing a thesis are identical with those to be applied to writing a journal article. Both forms call for the same self-discipline, the same hard thinking, and clear, logical, concise writing." In general, a thesis differs from a scientific journal article in several respects: it may deal with more than one topic; it usually contains most, if not all, of the data obtained in the research conducted preparatory to writing the thesis; it is the result of individual, rather than team, effort; and it is much longer than journal articles.

The format for doctoral theses varies among institutions, and anyone facing this type of writing task should receive guidance from the major professor. In addition, students preparing to write a doctoral thesis should read the entire section in *Scientific Writing for Graduate Students* (3). Another excellent source is *A Manual for Writers of Term Papers, Theses and Dissertations* (5).

SYMPOSIA

A symposium usually deals with a single topic and may result in the preparation of from 3 to 10 manuscripts. Often the chairman of the symposium serves as editor of the publication based on the symposium. Peer review of symposium manuscripts is highly desirable, although this is not always practiced.

Symposia may be published as monographs or books or in certain journals. The symposium organizer should inform the participants in advance of the meeting of the appropriate style and format of manuscripts to be submitted for publication. Publication of the symposium is expedited if the manuscripts are available at the time of the meeting.

Nomenclature and terminology will vary among the manuscripts, and careful copy editing is therefore required. Titles of the papers should be complete without reference to the name of the symposium.

EXTENDED ABSTRACTS

Some publishers use the extended abstract form for rapid, concise publication of proceedings of conferences. Specific instructions are prepared and mailed to participants, who are expected to submit completed manuscripts to the publisher before or during the conference. The extended abstract form has a short abstract and a limited number of tables and figures (no more than two or three total); references are discouraged. The text presents the basic methodology (with little or no experimental data) and the results. In printed form, an extended abstract is usually no longer than two or three pages, depending on page and type design.

Authors are advised that, although the publisher of extended abstracts may regard this form as not constituting primary publication, other publishers may refuse to consider publication of the full report on the grounds of previous publication.

BOOK REVIEWS

Book reviews are usually prepared at the invitation of editors or publishers and are published to acquaint potential readers and purchasers with relevant features of the book. The title of the volume, the name(s) of the author(s) or editor(s), the name of the publisher, the year of publication, the International Standard Book Number (ISBN), the number of pages, and the price are commonly included in the heading. The reviewer should identify the major topics covered in the volume and provide critical, but objective, interpretation of the value, the shortcomings, or both. A comparison with other books addressing the same or related subjects can be helpful to the readers. Additionally, the reviewer should identify the particular audience interested in the volume. The name of the reviewer and his or her affiliation usually are included in the review. Book reviews may also benefit the author(s) since shortcomings may be corrected in future printings or editions.

EDITORIALS

Many biological and medical journals publish editorials, the majority being signed by the writer. These editorials may be written by editors, by members of editorial boards, or upon invitation by well-qualified colleagues. Scientific aspects of subjects related to the scope of the publication are appropriate for discussion. Editorials may be written about the contributions of individuals as authors, editors, teachers, and researchers. Editorials may also, for example, address problems of ethics or the relationship of biology and medicine to social problems. Occasionally, editorials provide a critical review of a topic related to an original article in the journal. Since editorials carry the impact of authority, they must be prepared with great care and in a scholarly manner.

GRANT PROPOSALS

A good proposal must be written in accord with the requirements of the institution or the agency to which it is to be submitted. The proposal should be as brief as possible without sacrificing the details required for completeness and clarity of presentation. Grant application packets from the National Institutes of Health, the National Science Foundation, the U.S. Department of Agriculture, and other granting agencies include instructions for preparing research grant applications.

A good research grant proposal should include the following:
1) An original, delimited idea with a measurable conclusion achievable within the time frame of the grant.
2) Demonstrated knowledge (not necessarily exhaustive) of related and antecedent work in the field.
3) A carefully outlined plan and timetable, with all procedures fully referenced or described; the results of a pilot study, if available; explicit mention of relevant facilities (including departmental or other shared resources); and explicit mention of potential problems and their solutions.
4) The relevance of any conclusions to the field as a whole, and, when appropriate, any social benefit that might reasonably accrue from them.
5) Explicitly outlined credentials of all significantly involved personnel, including technical staff, and letters of intent from collaborators outside the institution (more than a typical curriculum vitae, the credentials should detail relevant experience and education, and state specifically why the individual is particularly qualified for this project).
6) Mention of other commitments of the professional personnel, especially to active and pending grants.
7) A complete, realistic budget.

The National Institutes of Health, many years ago, rejected proposals for reasons (1) that are as timely today as they were in the past:
1) The applicant lacked scientific and technical competence.
2) The problem at hand was not important enough or was too complex for the proposed study.
3) The approach to the problem lacked coordination between methodology and objectives or was poorly designed, lacking attention to statistics or adequate controls.

At the present time many grant applications are approved and considered worthy of study but are not funded because of financial restrictions. Thus it is even more important that proposals be prepared with utmost care. Hasty preparation because of an unrealistically planned schedule (requiring approval of department chairmen, financial officers, program directors, or institutional directors) must be avoided. Inexperienced applicants may benefit from consultation with senior colleagues.

GENERAL PLANNING

Whatever type of communication you are planning to write, certain basic procedures need to be followed. This section deals with preliminary planning that should be done before the actual writing begins, from assembling the data through selection of a journal.

ASSEMBLING THE EVIDENCE

Whether you will write the first draft of the article from a detailed outline or from cards bearing notes corresponding to outline headings, collect the evidence to be presented in support of the conclusions before the first draft is written so that this evidence can be in front of you as you write. This evidence may include, for example, tables of quantitative data (such as the results of chemical analyses), graphs showing relations between two variables, photographs or drawings that illustrate or exemplify observations, and references to literature consulted in planning the research and interpreting its findings.

Examine your supporting evidence with objectivity. Put aside any that is not clearly and directly relevant to your purpose in writing the article. Prepare preliminary versions of tables, graphs, and other supporting evidence that will probably be used and arrange them in the order called for by your outline. Reexamine each unit of evidence and question its form and suitability. For example, would the data in a graph be more useful to the reader if presented as exact numerical data in a table? Would the data in a small table convey as much information in less space if placed in the text? Would the data on the relation between two variables that you thought at first should be in a table be more clearly presented in a graph?

Examine your illustrations to decide which should be discarded because they are not sufficiently relevant to your central thesis and which should be replaced by illustrations of better quality or more suitable kinds. Remember that various media are available for figures—photographs, wash or continuous-tone drawings, line drawings. A photograph might be better than a line drawing to convey the appearance of a piece of laboratory equipment, whereas a line drawing might be better than a photograph to show essential differences between pieces of equipment or to suggest how to build equipment. The same data should not be presented in both graphic and tabular form; graphic presentation is likely to be more effective if relations of variables are more important than their exact numerical values. Consider whether additional illustrations could help the reader to a clearer understanding of your methods, evidence, or conclusions. Arrange to have any new or modified illustrations completed by the time you have finished writing the article.

If any illustration shows identifiable persons, be sure that you have written permission for publication of their pictures.

If you believe color illustrations should be used, be sure that the journal's instructions to authors indicate that they may be acceptable. Some journals require that authors pay the costs of color illustrations. Transparencies are usually preferred to color prints for preparation of color-separation plates, but the editor may be willing to accept prints. For further information on illustrative material, *see* chapter 6, Illustrative Material.

USING OTHER SOURCES

Decide which passages you want to quote and which illustrations you may want to reproduce from other sources. To use material that is protected by copyright, you must secure written permission from the holder of the copyright. Because of the many legal implications of an infringement of copyright statutes, you must know which works are protected by copyright and which are in the public domain. For a complete discussion of copyright in regard to scientific publication, *see* chapter 8, Application of Copyright Law.

ASSEMBLING THE REFERENCES

Sources to be cited in an article may be published or unpublished documents. Published documents include journal articles, books, technical reports, cataloged theses and dissertations, patents, maps, recordings, and other similar matter available to the public and to libraries, by subscription, purchase, lease, or free distribution. Unpublished documents include handwritten or typewritten documents (such as letters, diaries, or field notes) held by individuals or libraries in single copies or distributed primarily to limited segments of the scientific community.

Complete bibliographic data for each reference should be written or typed on a separate card. The cards with references to be listed at the end of the article should be grouped together and placed in the sequence in which they are to be first cited in the text, even if the references will have to be listed in alphabetical order in the final draft. Numbers assigned to the references at this stage should be tentative. The cards carrying references to be given in footnotes on text pages, rather than in the reference list at the end of the article, should be grouped separately and in probable order of citation (*see* chapter 5, References).

ACKNOWLEDGING ASSISTANCE _____

Even before you begin the first draft, make a list of persons and agencies whose help in research or writing should be acknowledged. Keep accurate and complete records of such assistance.

IDENTIFYING THE AUTHORS _____

Decide who will be named as authors before you begin to write the first draft. Do not list as an author any person who has not participated in planning, executing, or analyzing the research. An early decision about authorship may prevent later misunderstanding and embarrassment. The practice of including in the by-line (author designation) the name of a person who has not actually engaged in the reported research is considered by many scientists to be unethical. One of the chief offenders in this practice is the institutional superior who insists that his or her name appear in the by-line of every article produced in the department he or she supervises (*see* chapter 1, page 1).

SELECTING THE JOURNAL _____

Careful, early selection of the journal to which the planned article will be submitted may help in getting it accepted and may save time in getting it into print. Journals differ in their audience, prestige, speed of publication, and other characteristics. The most eminent journals have relatively high rates of rejection. Delay in publication of your article may be avoided by submitting it to a less prestigious journal more likely to accept it. Whatever journal is chosen, the article is more likely to be accepted without extensive revisions if it has been prepared carefully in accord with the journal's characteristics and requirements.

In matching the planned article with a particular journal, consider these questions: Is the subject within the scope of the journal? What is the format (length, structure, tables, and figures) of articles acceptable to the journal, and can the research you have to report be presented within this format? The answers may be found in information for prospective authors published by the journal (either in each issue or in the first issue of each volume). In some cases you may have to consult the editor. Careful examination of some recent issues may give you an ample view of the journal's scope of subjects and the length and structure of the articles it publishes.

After you have selected the journal, carefully prepare the manuscript in accord with the journal's style and requirements, such as specific forms for bibliographic references. Manuscript requirements for journals published by a scientific society or for a group of journals that have agreed on such requirements may be available in separately published handbooks for authors (*see* chapter 17, Useful References with Annotations). For example, certain biomedical journals follow *Uniform Requirements for*

Manuscripts Submitted to Biomedical Journals (4). If you publish in this field, you may receive a free copy of the Uniform Requirements by sending a stamped, self-addressed envelope (no smaller than 105 by 220 mm) to: Publications Manager, *Annals of Internal Medicine*, 4200 Pine Street, Philadelphia, PA 19104, USA.

LITERATURE CITED: Planning the Communication

1. Allen, E. M. Why are research grant applications disapproved? Science 132:1532–1534; 1960.
2. American national standard for synoptics, Z39.34-1977. New York: American National Standards Institute; 1977.
3. CBE Committee on Graduate Training in Scientific Writing. Scientific writing for graduate students: a manual on the teaching of scientific writing. Bethesda, MD: Council of Biology Editors, Inc.; 1968 (reprinted 1983).
4. International Committee of Medical Journal Editors. Uniform requirements for manuscripts submitted to biomedical journals. Ann. Int. Med. 96 (part 1):766–771; 1982.
5. Turabian, K. L. A manual for writers of term papers, theses and dissertations. 4th ed. Chicago: Univ. of Chicago Press; 1973.

3

Writing the article

This chapter presents guidelines for preparation of manuscripts in a format that will be acceptable for most biological journals. However, journals differ in their specific requirements, as noted on page 15, and authors should consider these guidelines as general rather than specific. Consult a recent issue of the journal to which you plan to submit the article. If further guidance is needed, consult the editor for scientific questions or the publisher for questions of style and format.

In the fourth edition of the *CBE Style Manual* (4), authors are taken step by step through several drafts. A summary is given in table 3.1 (*see* page 25). In the present edition, emphasis is placed on style and conventions that will help to make your manuscript acceptable for publication. Detailed, specific information on the literature section, illustrative material, and prose style is given in later chapters. Additional sources of information include *How to Write Scientific and Technical Papers* (7), *How to Write and Publish a Scientific Paper* (5), and the CBE book *Scientific Writing for Graduate Students* (3). *See also* chapter 17, Useful References with Annotations.

ORGANIZING THE CONTENT

Most scientific journal articles are arranged in four main sections: introduction; subjects, materials, and methods; results; and discussion. If this format is suitable for your report, you may begin by organizing your material under these headings. You will then have the beginning of an outline.

A fully developed outline will have secondary and tertiary headings that will correspond to paragraphs within the article. Secondary headings under "Subjects, Materials, and Methods" might include "Study design," "Experimental animals," "Drug dosage," "Chemical analyses," and "Statistical methods." The secondary outline headings for "Results" might include "Findings in control animals" and "Findings in treated animals." Other primary and secondary outline headings (corresponding to divisions of text) may be more appropriate for other types of research articles, such as reports of field observations and taxonomic descriptions, for review articles, or for even simpler articles such as editorials. The journal for which the article is being prepared should be examined closely for examples of the kind of article you intend to write; these

17

examples will indicate the structure likely to be acceptable in that journal and hence the kind of outline that should be written. The outline headings can serve as headings and subheadings for the text in the first and later drafts of the article.

Some authors may be able to write the first draft from the outline. Others might find it helpful to prepare an expanded version of the outline by writing brief notes on the content of planned paragraphs.

After you have outlined the article and assembled the supporting evidence, you should be ready to write the first draft. Choose the place, time, and method that suit you best. You may prefer to dictate or to write in longhand, with little regard for sentence structure and other details of prose style, or you may prefer to revise as you proceed. The article may have to be revised at least twice before the final draft is typed, so do not go back and revise earlier parts of the first draft each time that you sit down to write. Have the first draft typed double or triple spaced to allow enough room for revision. If you are an author for whom English is a second language, the first drafts of an article to be published in English may be more efficiently written in your native language. If you have a thorough knowledge of English, you may then be able to prepare the revisions of the manuscript in English. If you prefer to write in your native language, have the English translation for the final draft prepared by a translator competent in English scientific idiom.

PARTS OF THE MANUSCRIPT

TITLE

Just as the content of a scientific article can be condensed stepwise into successively shorter summaries—outline, abstract, and then title—so an article can be prepared by using the reverse steps—title, abstract, and outline. The simplest way to start to write is to prepare a title that represents the article's proposed content. Conventional titles are usually indicative rather than informative; they state the subject of the article rather than its conclusions: "Effect of Radar Electromagnetic Fields on Migrating Birds." An informative title gives instead the article's main point, or conclusion, in a concise statement: "Migrating Birds Respond to Radar Electromagnetic Fields."

Attempting to write an informative title is an effective test of whether the research to be reported has led to a definite conclusion; if you cannot write a clear and specific informative title, you may not be sure of what you have to say. An informative title may have to be revised later to an indicative title, since many journals do not use informative titles.

After you have written the first draft of your paper, examine the title you have tentatively chosen. It should identify precisely the main topic of your article, as it may be used later for information retrieval by abstracting and indexing services. It should be specific and concise. If appropriate, it should include the name of the organism used. (For taxonomic papers, *see* chapter 13, Style in Special Fields, pages 157, 170, and 185). Phrases such as "studies on," "preliminary studies on," or "contributions to" are superfluous and should not be used in titles. The following titles are unsatisfactory:

Further Studies on the Erythrocyte Anti-Inflammatory Assay
Notes on Amphibian Parasites
Opuscula miscellanea nematologica IX
LDH-Isoenzymes in Infarcted Heart Muscle.

The first two titles contain superfluous words. The second and third are so general that they have insufficient meaning for a reader searching the literature. The fourth, from a nonclinical journal, fails to specify the host or the animal involved.

Many journals have special requirements or limitations regarding titles, such as length, use of abbreviations, and series numbers. All of these should be considered before making final decisions about the title.

BY-LINE

Use the by-line style in a recent issue of the journal. The by-line normally has two elements: the name(s) of the author(s)—that is, the person (or persons) who contributed materially to the research being reported; and the name(s) of the institution(s) where the research was done. The use of authors' full names rather than initials will prevent confusion in the literature. Otherwise, problems may arise in bibliographic data bases. Omit academic degrees unless the journal includes them. Give the name of the department and institution in which the research was done, and add the mailing address of the institution, including the postal code. If you are no longer at the institution where the research was done, include your current address for correspondence and requests for reprints. If the article has several authors from different institutions, list their names and respective institutions so that readers can associate each author with his or her institution. Do not give credit in the by-line for technical assistance (*see* Acknowledgments, this chapter). A person thus credited may be mistakenly cited as an author. Before naming a present or former co-worker as an author, let the individual review your manuscript, and then obtain permission for use of his or her name.

ABSTRACT

An abstract is a very important portion of an article and is best placed before the text of the manuscript so that the reader might comprehend the essence of the author's research. The formulation of an abstract into a short paragraph forces the author to express precisely the most important information of the research. The American National Standards Institute recommends that abstracts be included with every journal article.

According to *BIOSIS Guide to Abstracts* (2), "An abstract is a noncritical, informative digest of the significant content and conclusions of the primary source material. It is intended to be intelligible in itself, without reference to the paper, but not a substitute for it."

An abstract differs from an annotation, extract, summary, and synoptic. The *American National Standard for Writing Abstracts* (1) defines these in the following manner:

> An *annotation* is a brief comment or explanation about a document or its contents, usually added as a note after the bibliographic citation of the document. An *extract* is one or more portions of a document selected to represent the whole. A *summary* is a brief restatement within the document (usually at the end) of its salient findings and conclusions and is intended to complete the orientation of a reader who has studied the preceding text. A *synoptic* is a concise first publication in a directly usable form of key results selected from an available but previously unpublished paper. It differs from an abstract (which it contains) in that it is often a combination of text, tables, and figures, and may contain the equivalent of 2000 words.

An abstract should contain about 250 words and should include such information as:

1) The objectives and purpose of the study.
2) The materials, methods, techniques, and apparatus, and their intended use, as well as new items and new applications of standard techniques and equipment.
3) Scientific and common names of organisms (if given in the article) with special emphasis on new taxa or new distribution records.
4) Specific drugs (generic names preferred) and biochemical compounds, including the manner of use and route of administration.
5) New theories, terminology, interpretations, or evaluations concisely stated.
6) New terms and special abbreviations and symbols defined.

An abstract generally excludes:

1) Additions, corrections, or any information not contained in the manuscript.
2) Tables and graphs and direct references to them.
3) Detailed descriptions of experiments, organisms, standard methods, techniques, and apparatus.
4) References to the literature.

When mentioning names of chemicals and drugs in an abstract, colloquial terminology and trade names should be avoided; generic names are preferred. Chemical formulas and compounds should be defined. Registered proprietary names are always printed with an initial capital;

e.g., Levanil is a proprietary name for ectylurea, the generic name for (2-ethyl-crotonoyl)urea.

In abstracts mentioning geographic locations, the state (province, prefecture, or republic) and country should be indicated; e.g., Moscow, Russian SFSR, USSR; Berlin, New Jersey, USA.

In abstracts mentioning Latin names of organisms, the author should remember that the specific epithet of an organism is never used without its accompanying generic name (which may be abbreviated if first given in full), e.g., *Escherichia coli*, *E. coli*.

Distribution data, such as new records, new localities, maps, range changes, faunistic or floristic changes, and epoch or period of fossils, are included in the abstract. For information on presenting plant, animal, and microbiological taxonomic information, *see* chapter 13, pages 157, 170, and 185.

Common abbreviations and symbols should be used sparingly in abstracts; less common abbreviations should be avoided. For units of measurement, the International System of Units (SI) is preferred. Many journal guidelines for authors include a list of abbreviations that may be used without definition. However, long substantives used repeatedly, such as compounds, hormones, or enzymes, are abbreviated after first mention; e.g., "succinate dehydrogenase (SDH)," or "pollen mother cell (PMC)."

INTRODUCTION

Begin the article by clearly identifying its subject. State the hypothesis or define the problem your research was designed to solve. Orient the research you are reporting to previous concepts and research, possibly by a brief and concise review of the literature that is unmistakably relevant to the specific aims of your research. Do not use the introduction to try to convince the reader of the importance of your research. If the reader knows the field, the importance of the research should be evident.

SUBJECTS, MATERIALS, AND METHODS

Describe subjects, materials, and methods used, including experimental design, in sufficient detail to enable other scientists to evaluate your work or to duplicate your research procedure. The usual sequence for experimental studies is design of the experiment, subjects (plant, animal, human), materials, procedures, and methods for observations and interpretation.

Avoid unnecessary details. If you used well-known methods without modification, simply name the methods or, at most, cite the papers in which they are described. If you used modifications of previously described methods, describe the modifications. Give details of unusual experimental designs or statistical methods, and precisely describe experimental animals used (*see* pages 150 and 211).

Human subjects should be characterized appropriately (sex, age, ethnicity, disease) to assure the reader of the homogeneity of control and experimental groups. Experimental studies should meet appropriate ethical standards; describe the precautions taken (for example, anesthesia, review of experiments by institutional committees, informed consent from human subjects) to ensure that these standards were met. When appropriate, include a statement verifying that the care of animals followed accepted standards.

RESULTS AND OBSERVATIONS

Present the results of your research in a sequence that will logically support (or provide evidence against) the hypothesis or answer the question stated in the introduction. For example, in reporting a study of the effect of an experimental diet on the skeletal mass of the rat, consider first giving the data on skeletal mass for the rats fed the control diet and then give these data for the rats fed the experimental diet. In an article on the mendelian pattern of inheritance of an enzyme deficiency in humans, describe first the characteristics of the index case that led to study of the family and then describe findings in the study of family members, proceeding first to siblings, and then to other generations.

Include only the data and illustrative material that are pertinent to the subject of the article. Numerical data presented in tables usually need not be restated in detail in the text, but mean values for group data may be restated to emphasize the evidence on which conclusions are based. Conclusions drawn from numerical data should be supported by brief statements of the statistical criteria applied. Do not omit important negative results. Present the data that validate methods used in the study in the subjects, materials, and methods section, not in the results section, if the validation was an incidental product of the study, not its major object.

DISCUSSION

Interpret the data presented in the results section, giving particular attention to the problem, question, or hypothesis posed in the introduction. Do the data provide answers to the questions that led to the design and execution of the study? Is your evidence adequate? Relate your findings to previous observations or experiments. Include discussion of previous findings, both yours and those of other investigators, that do or do not agree with yours; consider reasons that might account for differences in findings. State the conclusions that can be drawn from your data, in the light of these considerations. Present briefly any logical implications of your findings for practical application or future studies. Some journals allow use of a conclusions section, as well as a discussion section.

ACKNOWLEDGMENTS

Some journals include an acknowledgments section in which you may give credit for grants-in-aid, and to persons (if you have their permission) who have helped you with research or in writing your article. If the journal does not carry such sections, you can acknowledge assistance in the introduction or possibly in one or more footnotes (if the journal permits them). Examine articles in the journal for the proper placement of acknowledgments. If your article is based on your dissertation or thesis, state this either in the acknowledgments section or as a footnote to the introduction.

Acknowledgments that are to appear as a special section at the end of the article should be typed on a separate page. Type them at the bottom of the title page if that is the style of the journal. Recheck accuracy of names and supply full information for grants-in-aid: number of grant and name and location of institution or organization.

LITERATURE CITED

The list of references cited in the body of an article (including tables and figures) is usually placed in a separate section at the end of the text. While writing the first draft, insert into the text the appropriate citations of published literature and unpublished documents, using parenthetical notes of author and date. These notes can be converted to a number system in a later draft when the content of the article is closer to final form.

Complete bibliographic data for each reference should be written or typed on a separate card. The cards with references to be listed at the end of the article should be grouped together and placed in the sequence in which they are to be first cited in the text, even if the references will have to be listed in alphabetical order in the final draft. Numbers should not be assigned to the references at this stage, even if the style of the journal calls for text citation of references by number rather than by authors and year.

In some journals, certain references may be given in footnotes on text pages. Cards carrying such references should be grouped separately and in probable order of citation. Full information and guidance for handling bibliographic data are given in chapter 5.

THE FIRST AND LATER DRAFTS

In recent years, most institutions have acquired word-processing equipment that is especially useful in facilitating the preparation of manuscripts. No longer is it necessary to proofread the same material in successive drafts. With the advent of word processing, only the new or altered sections of a manuscript need to be retyped and proofed. Other portions should, however, be checked for dropped lines. A number of publishers are requiring authors to submit "camera ready" copy for rapid and inexpensive publication; for this type of manuscript, word processing is particularly helpful. It permits the author to see how space will be used and to make numerous changes quickly and easily. For all manuscript preparation, authors are urged to make use of such equipment if it is available to them.

In writing the successive drafts of your article, give attention to different aspects at each stage (*see* table 3.1). A useful scheme in reviewing the first draft is to concentrate on major aspects of the article: defects in content and the sequence of content within each section of the text.

At the writing of the second draft, you may have been involved too long in your research and in preparing the first draft to have an objective view of the article. You may be better able to find defects with the help of one or more colleagues in the same field who have not been involved in your research or in writing the article. Experienced scientists will know the criteria by which the article will be judged. For questions likely to be considered by those who will review the final manuscript for the journal, *see* chapter 7, page 83.

The second draft should be typed with wide margins (4 to 5 cm on each side) in which colleagues reviewing the article can make notes. Provide your colleagues with photocopies of the original manuscript, and ask them to review the second draft within a specific period. Shortly before this deadline, reread the second draft closely. If you have not read the article for several weeks, major defects in content or sequence may now be more apparent. This second reading should be carried out before your colleagues return their comments so that their criticisms will not influence your own evaluation.

Defects in content, length, and sequence found by you and your colleagues should be corrected in the third draft. Experienced writers may also correct defects in prose style when they prepare the third draft, but if you are not an experienced writer, consider using additional drafts beyond the third. Frequent defects in prose style are discussed and illustrated in chapter 4. You will improve your ability to identify these defects by reading the text of the third or later draft of the article a number of times, allowing an interval of several days between each reading, and each time looking for only one kind of defect.

PREPARING THE FINAL DRAFT

The manuscript that you will submit for review must conform in all respects to the specific requirements of the journal. In preparing the final draft for typing, check carefully the conventions discussed in this section and in chapters 5, 12, and 13.

Table 3.1. Steps in revising first and later drafts

FIRST DRAFT

Review:
Is all of the text needed?
Is the content of each section appropriate to that section?
Is the sequence of paragraphs proper?
Should any paragraphs be divided?
Are headings and subheadings appropriate to their sections and is their heirarchy clear?
Is the title informative, specific, and concise?
Does the abstract represent all elements of the article, within the length allowed by the journal?
Should any tables or figures be eliminated?
Is each table and figure cited in the text?
Are footnotes, table headings, and figure legends precise and concise? Are they redundant with the text?
Have you acknowledged assistance received up to this point?
Have you checked quotations and references against original sources?
Is each reference cited in the text?

Correct: Make the necessary changes and have the manuscript retyped (second draft).

SECOND DRAFT

Review: Ask appropriate colleagues to read this draft and criticize its content and style.

Rewrite: Consider criticisms of colleagues and rewrite sections as necessary. Add to acknowledgments, as appropriate, names of colleagues who made substantive criticisms.

THIRD DRAFT

Review: Is the text clear and concise? *See* chapter 4, Prose Style for Scientific Writing.

Correct: Make corrections in prose style. Prepare additional drafts to refine further the content and style.

FINAL DRAFT

KEY WORDS, INDEX TERMS, OR DESCRIPTORS

Many journals publish with each article index terms (or descriptors) suitable for information retrieval systems. Select words that reflect the central topics of the article. These words may be from the title, abstract, or text and are often used as main entries in cumulative indexes. Criteria for selection of main entries (key words) are given in chapter 11, Indexing. Key words may be typed on the page carrying the abstract.

Some biomedical journals use descriptors from the structured system of Medical Subject Headings (MeSH) used by the National Library of Medicine for its Medical Literature Analysis and Retrieval System (MED-LARS), including *Index Medicus* (6). Indexes are the responsibility of the editors of the journal. Sources for information on indexing are cited in chapter 11.

RUNNING HEAD OR RUNNING FOOTLINE

Authors may be required to provide a shorter version of the title to be set as a running head at the top of each right-hand page of the published article or as a footline at the bottom of the page. The running head for an article titled "Morphologic Differentiation and Adaptation in the Galápagos Finches" might be "Galápagos Finches." Determine the maximum length by counting characters and spaces in running heads or footlines in an issue of the journal.

HEADINGS AND SUBHEADINGS

Most journal articles contain headings and subheadings of two or three levels, each level with its distinctive typography and position with relation to the text. If the headings and subheadings are readily understood and effectively placed, they help the reader to discern quickly and fully the structure and content of the paper. Reproduce as closely as possible the style of the headings in the journal you have selected; if this cannot be reproduced on a standard typewriter, distinguish three descending orders of headings by their location: 1) centered between the margins of the text, with space above and below; 2) placed flush left (at left margin) on a page; 3) placed at the beginning of a paragraph of text (run-in sidehead). A copy editor will later mark headings for the position and type faces used by the journal, but the order of headings should be clear from the style used in the manuscript.

Read your tentative headings and subheadings critically, first individually in relation to the text that follows and then in relation to each other. Are they concise, pertinent to the text, and similar in tone and grammatical construction? Does each describe the text that follows? A common fault is to follow a subheading directly with a pronoun referring to a word or phrase in the subheading.

Enzyme Purification. This was done by . . .

A less serious fault is to repeat the subheading in the sentence after the subheading.

Laboratory Animals. Laboratory animals were selected . . .

FOOTNOTES TO TEXT

Use footnotes to the text only when they are needed to present documentary or explanatory material—that is, when the material is important but its inclusion in the text would be distracting. Do not use footnotes to abstracts. Some journals do not sanction footnotes to titles; others permit them only in tables. A quick inspection will reveal the preferred style.

Unless the journal for which you are writing follows a different system of annotation, indicate a footnote to the text by a superscript number, shown in typescript by an inverted caret: ⌄ ⌄ ⌄ . . . . Some journals use a series of symbols or reference marks (*, †, ‡, §, ||, ¶, #, **, †† . . .) to identify footnotes. Treat each footnote as a paragraph by indenting the first line, which should begin with the superscript number or character that relates to the citation in the text.

In revising your manuscript, you may delete or add footnote references. In the final draft, be sure that each footnote number or symbol in the text has a corresponding footnote at the bottom of the page and that the series of reference marks begins anew with each page containing footnotes.

QUOTATIONS AND PARAPHRASES

Copies of letters granting permission to use material from other sources should be included with the manuscript when it is submitted for publication. Absolute accuracy is imperative in quoting or paraphrasing published or unpublished authority. Check against the original of each published reference for names of authors, date of publication, title of article (or book), name of journal (or publisher), and other bibliographic detail (*see* chapter 8, Application of Copyright Law).

To be sure that your quotation or paraphrase is accurate, compare it with the original source and not with another author's quotation or paraphrase of the material. In paraphrasing, be objective in selecting data and unbiased in interpreting statements; respect the intent of the original author. Quote exactly—spelling, italics, and punctuation—or indicate that you have made changes (for example, by inserting words within brackets). To assure the reader that quotations are accurate, write *sic* within brackets immediately after misspelled words or other inaccuracies or irregularities in quoted material.

"The plant had prulep [*sic*] leaves."

Or you may suggest a correction and place it within brackets.

"The plant had prulep [purple?] leaves."

If you make an insertion in a quotation, enclose it within brackets.

". . . by Van Slyke's [manometric] method."

Do not substitute parenthesis signs for brackets. Parenthesis signs falsely identify your words as those of the original writer. Add brackets by hand if they are not available on your typewriter. If you change the emphasis of all or part of a quotation—for example, by using italics—indicate this within parentheses.

"Omit *useless* words" (italics added).

Note that the parentheses are outside the closing quotation mark but before the period. If you omit a word or words from a quotation, indicate the omission by spaced periods or ellipsis marks (*see* chapter 12, page 127). Type all quotations and paraphrases double spaced. Follow the rules for quotation marks given in chapter 12, page 137.

MATHEMATICAL FORMULAS AND EQUATIONS

In preparing mathematical copy for typesetting, be precise in aligning numerals, letters, and symbols; hand-letter any that cannot be typewritten. Some letters, numerals, and other characters may be ambiguous to a printer, especially when they stand alone. In typewritten copy, ambiguity may occur in the use of 1 (one or el), 0 (zero or oh), X (multiplication sign or ex), Greek letters, script letters, diacritical marks, and prime. Some handwritten capital letters (especially C, K, O, P, S, U, V, W, X, Z) are difficult to distinguish from lowercase letters. Identify any possibly ambiguous character by a circled notation in the nearest margin.

Although the editor is responsible for instructing the printer about the use of italics in mathematical equations, every author should know accepted practices. With certain exceptions, single letters in equations are italicized. Chemical symbols, abbreviations of more than a single letter (ln, avg, max), and numbers are not italicized. If you use an abbreviation that is not standard, explain it in the text or legend. See chapter 9 for instructions for marking capital and lowercase letters, italics, and superscript and subscript characters.

Simplifying equations   Use the simplest form of equation that can be made by ordinary mathematical calculation. Although a bar fraction (cross-rule) is acceptable in a centered (displayed) equation, avoid using this form of fraction in a line of text. Substitute a slant line for the bar. This will enable the printer to fit the fraction within the text line without its projecting above or below it. Each of the recommended forms of notation in figure 3.1 can be set on one line; any of the forms not recommended requires more than one line and is difficult and expensive to set in type.

Presenting complex equations   Center (display) complex equations between left and right margins of the manuscript page; leave generous space above and below. Number each equation; place the number in parentheses near the right margin of the page.

The editor or the printer will decide how to break equations that exceed page or column width in the journal. The printer may extend to page width an equation that exceeds the width of a single column. If one of your equations exceeds the width of a manuscript page, break it before a sign of operation, which should begin the runover line. When several

Form of notation	Not recommended (typewritten)	Recommended (typewritten)	Recommended (in type)
One-line fraction	$\dfrac{a + b}{2}$	$\frac{1}{2}(a + b)$ or $0.5(a + b)$	$1/2(a + b)$ or $0.5(a + b)$
Fractional exponent	$a\sqrt{bc}$	$a(bc)^{\frac{1}{2}}$ or $a(bc)^{0.5}$	$a(bc)^{1/2}$ or $a(bc)^{0.5}$
Slant line (solidus)	$\dfrac{a + b}{x + y}$	$(a + b)/(x + y)$	$(a + b)/(x + y)$
Negative exponent	$\underline{a = \dfrac{2g\ \sin B}{3R}}$	$a = 2/3(R^{-1}g)\ \sin B$ or $a = 0.66R^{-1}g\ \sin B$	$a = 2/3(R^{-1}g)\ \sin B$ or $a = 0.66R^{-1}g\ \sin B$
Pointed bracket instead of bar to designate average	$\overline{a + b}$	$\langle a + b \rangle$	$(a + b)/2$
Exponential function	$Ae^{\frac{1}{2}(V_o/D)}$	$A \exp \frac{1}{2}(V_o/D)$ or $A \exp 0.5(V_o/D)$	$A \exp 1/2\ (V_o/D)$ or $A \exp 0.5\ (V_o/D)$
Superior over inferior	X_a^2	X_a^2	X_a^2

Figure 3.1. Mathematical formulas. Forms in the first column are not recommended; they are difficult and expensive to set in type. The recommended equivalents in the second column require only one line each.

breaks are necessary and the equation contains few signs of operation, arrange the components in logical sequence.

If an equation cannot be reproduced entirely by typewriter, you may type the characters that are available and complete the equation with lines, symbols, and other characters drawn with black ink. The editor or the printer will usually decide whether the equation can be set entirely in type or whether it can be better rendered as a cut made from a combination of typeset letters and hand-drawn symbols and lines. For long, complicated equations, it is best to supply professional-quality camera-ready copy sized to the correct page or column width for the journal. This will avoid printer's errors in setting the equations.

TYPING THE FINAL DRAFT

Many of the following suggestions are addressed to the person who will type the manuscript. That person should also read the instructions to authors for the journal and examine a recent issue.

PAPER AND TYPING

Use 215 by 280 mm (8½ by 11 in.) or standard international paper, ISO A4 (212 by 297 mm) white bond paper. Do not use onionskin paper or erasable bond. A typewriter with standard characters is preferred to one with unusual characters, such as only capital letters or capitals and small capitals, or script letters. Double space the entire manuscript, including text, quotations, footnotes, table titles, legends, and references. Use more space above and below equations and formulas. *Do not single space any part of the manuscript.*

Type on one side of the paper only, keep lines approximately uniform in length, and leave margins of 25 to 40 mm (1 to 1½ in.) at top, bottom, and sides for editors' markings and queries. Avoid hyphenating a word at the end of a line. Do not type the title of the paper and headings entirely in capital letters; a copy editor can easily mark them to conform to the journal's typographic style.

Start a new page for each of the sections listed below and arrange them in the following order:
1) Title, by-line, name and address of corresponding author, running head
2) Abstract and key words
3) Text
4) Acknowledgments
5) References or Literature Cited
6) Footnotes to text (if allowed)
7) Tables (separate page for each table)
8) Legends for figures.

Number pages consecutively, starting with the title page, each in the upper right-hand corner.

READING COPY

The final draft should be read first by the typist, for typographic errors and omissions. The author should then read the entire manuscript at least twice, paying particular attention to accuracy of quotations and citations, spelling of technical terms and names of persons and places, and correctness of data. One of these checks should be made with another person reading aloud the pages from which the final draft was typed, while the author checks the final manuscript for accuracy.

CORRECTIONS AND INSERTIONS

Insert corrections or additions *above* the lines to be changed, not in margins or on slips of paper attached to the pages. Show by a caret (∧) the exact place for each insertion. Retype any page with lengthy insertions. If the retyping results in a page only partly filled, draw a line from the end of the text diagonally to the lower right-hand corner of the page to indicate that additional material follows.

MARKING POSITIONS FOR FIGURES AND TABLES

To guide the editor and printer in making up pages, indicate by circled marginal notes where tables or figures are first cited in the manuscript. Their placement on the printed page will depend on the amount of space they occupy in relation to the amount of text and on the style of the journal.

SUBMITTING THE MANUSCRIPT

CHECKLIST

Before submitting a manuscript to a journal for review, check each item in the following list to make certain that the manuscript is complete.

1) Text pages of final draft are numbered consecutively, beginning with the title page.
2) Figures and tables, in separate series, are numbered consecutively according to order of citation in the text, and each text citation is to the appropriate figure or table.
3) Marginal notes are added to indicate the point where each table or figure is first cited in the text.
4) The figure number and the author's name(s) are written lightly in pencil on the reverse side of each figure.
5) There is one suitable copy of each figure for each copy of the manuscript.
6) Each reference cited in the text, tables, and legends is also listed in the bibliographic section.
7) All references listed in the bibliographic section are cited at least once in the text, tables, or legends.
8) Accuracy of all references in the bibliographic section, as retyped in the final draft, is confirmed by comparison with the *original* article or book or with a previous draft that has been carefully checked against the *original* source.
9) Each footnote symbol or number in text or tables has a corresponding footnote.
10) The final draft has been carefully read at least twice, once against the pages from which it was typed.

11) Letters granting permission to publish material borrowed from other sources and permissions from persons to use their photographs are ready to be sent with the manuscript.

12) The address to which letters and proof should be sent is on the title page of the manuscript.

MULTIPLE COPIES

Make enough photocopies of the final manuscript to satisfy all requirements. All copies should be on good-quality white paper; the characters must be clear and black. Send one copy to each coauthor for approval before the paper is submitted for publication. Most journals require at least one copy with the original manuscript to expedite editorial review. Retain for your file a complete copy of the final manuscript and the accompanying material (figures, tables, permissions) to ensure against loss in the mail.

TRANSMITTAL

The manuscript should be sent to only one journal. Be sure to use the address given in the instructions to authors; in some cases this will be the editor's office and in others it will be the editorial office of the publisher. Enclose with the manuscript a short covering letter containing information that may be helpful to the editor, such as reference to enclosed copyright permission form, institutional approval, reference to previous correspondence or a previous submittal of the same work, and appropriate subject category.

If you have an unusually large number of tables or figures, tell the editor whether you are willing to have some of them held out of the article and sent to a repository such as The National Auxiliary Publications Service of the American Society for Information Science (ASIS/NAPS, c/o Microfiche Publication, P.O. Box 3513, Grand Central Station, New York, NY 10163, USA). The publisher can arrange for deposit of the excess material and announce in the published article where such material may be obtained for study.

Some organizations require payment of a handling charge before considering a submitted manuscript. Requirements for such charges may be found in the instructions to authors in a recent issue of the journal.

Do not fold, staple, or bind the manuscript. Mail the manuscript, together with the illustrations, in a sturdy envelope or as a package, by first class surface mail or airmail. For special instructions regarding the mailing of illustrations, *see* chapter 6, page 74.

LITERATURE CITED: Writing the Article

1. American national standard for writing abstracts, Z39.14-1971. New York: American National Standards Institute; 1974.

2. BioSciences Information Service. BIOSIS guide to abstracts—1978. Biol. Abst. 65(1): Jan. 1; 1978.

3. CBE Committee on Graduate Training in Scientific Writing. Scientific writing for graduate students: a manual on the teaching of scientific writing. Bethesda, MD: Council of Biology Editors, Inc., 1968 (reprinted 1983).

4. CBE Style Manual Committee. Council of Biology Editors style manual: a guide for authors, editors, and publishers in the biological sciences. 4th ed. Bethesda, MD: Council of Biology Editors, Inc. 1978.

5. Day, R. A. How to write and publish a scientific paper. Philadelphia: ISI Press; 1979.

6. National Library of Medicine. Medical subject headings; (number 1, part 2 of each January issue of *Index Medicus*). Washington, DC: U.S. Government Printing Office.

7. Trelease, S. F. How to write scientific and technical papers. Cambridge, MA: MIT Press; 1969.

4

Prose style for scientific writing

A scientific article should hold the attention of its readers by the importance of its content, not by a presentation calculated to impress the reader with the author's intellect and scientific status. The meaning should be clear, not obscured by imprecision, verbosity, or obvious rhetorical devices. Generally, details of prose style are best considered after the basic structure of the manuscript is complete to the author's satisfaction. This is usually done in the third or later draft (*see* table 3.1, page 25). Chapter 17, Useful References with Annotations, includes references to sources that can help you to develop more skill in improving or correcting prose style.

The article should be rewritten as often as necessary to achieve logical order and maximum clarity of expression. At a late stage of revision, the manuscript should be reviewed sentence by sentence and word by word. Incorrectly used words should be recast until they are so clear that they cannot be misunderstood.

SENTENCE LENGTH AND STRUCTURE

An excessively long sentence makes it difficult for the reader to connect the opening words with the closing words and to grasp the point of the sentence at first reading. Excessive length cannot be defined simply, but a sentence of more than four or five typed lines should be examined to see whether it can be rewritten to form two sentences. Consecutive sentences of like structure can make monotonous reading; changing the word order will add variety to sentence structure. Helpful discussions can be found in *Simple and Direct: A Rhetoric for Writers* (4) and in *On Writing Well* (10).

VERBIAGE

Review the text of the manuscript to eliminate phrases and words that are not needed. Although writing can be too compact and terse, wordiness is the more common fault. For example, a phrase such as "it is interesting to note that" adds no information and only delays getting to the point of the sentence. Change expressions such as "It was reported by Smith that ..." to "Smith reported that ...." Below are some frequently used wordy phrases and their more concise equivalents.

Wordy	*Concise*
a number of	few, many, several
an innumerable number of tiny veins	innumerable tiny veins
as far as our own observations are concerned, they show	we observed
ascertain the location of	find
at the present moment, at this point in time	now
bright green in color	bright green
by means of	by, with
(We) conducted inoculation experiments on	inoculated
due to the fact that	because
during the time that	while
fewer in number	fewer
for the purpose of examining	to examine
for the reason that	because, since
from the standpoint of	according to
goes under the name of	is called
if conditions are such that	if
in all cases	always, invariably
in order to	to
in the course of	during
in the event that	if
in the near future	soon
in the vicinity of	near
in view of the fact that	because
it is often the case that	often
it is possible that the cause is	the cause may be
it is this that	this
it would thus appear that	apparently
large numbers of	many
lenticular in character	lenticular
masses are of large size	masses are large
necessitates the inclusion of	needs, requires
of such hardness that	so hard that
on the basis of	from, by, because
oval in shape, oval-shaped	oval
plants exhibited good growth	plants grew well
prior to (in time)	before
serves the function of being	is
subsequent to	after
the fish in question	this fish
the tests have not as yet	the tests have not
the treatment having been performed	after treatment
there can be little doubt that this is	this probably is
throughout the entire area	throughout the area

throughout the whole of the experi-	
ment	throughout the experiment
two equal halves	halves

ABSTRACT NOUNS

The frequent use of nouns formed from verbs and ending in *-tion* produces unnecessarily long sentences and dull prose. Examples of such nouns are "production" from "produce" and "interpretation" from "interpret." The excessive length results in part from the length of the *-tion* nouns and in part from the need to use unnecessary verbs with them. The dullness results from the abstract nature of these nouns and the usually passive, weak verbs that accompany them. In reviewing your manuscript look for the *-tion* nouns that can be replaced in rewritten sentences by their more direct and forceful verb equivalents.

> If we interpret the deposition of chemical signals as initiation of courtship, then initiation of courtship by females is probably the usual case in mammals. (*25 words*)
> If courtship is initiated by depositing chemical signals, then it is likely that courtship in mammals is usually initiated by females. (*21 words. The noun "deposition" is replaced by the present participle "depositing," the noun "initiation" by the verb "initiated"; other words not needed have been dropped.*)

Changes that shorten a sentence may also put its elements into a clearer sequence.

> A direct correlation between serum vitamin B_{12} concentration and mean nerve conduction velocity was seen. (*15 words*)
> Mean nerve conduction velocity correlated directly with serum vitamin B_{12} concentration. (*11 words*)

Below is another example, with a revised version.

> It is possible that the pattern of herb distribution now found in the Chilean site is a reflection of past disturbances. (*21 words*)
> The pattern in which herbs are distributed in the Chilean site may reflect past disturbances. (*15 words*)

Replacing an abstract noun (*-tion*) with a verb may bring the agent into the sentence and make it more vivid and specific.

> Following termination of exposure to pigeons and resolution of the pulmonary infiltrates, there was a substantial increase in lung volume, some improvement in diffusing capacity, and partial resolution of the hypoxemia. (*31 words*)
> After the patient stopped keeping pigeons, his pulmonary infiltrates partly resolved, lung volume greatly increased, diffusing capacity improved, and hypoxemia lessened. (*21 words*)

EXCESSIVE USE OF NOUNS AND RELATIVE PRONOUNS

Avoid habitual use of nouns and relative pronouns where adjectives, adverbs, or participles would be more concise or give variety to sentence structure. The term, "the tube, *which is 3 m long*," or "the tube, *3 m long*," is preferable to "the tube, *which has a length of 3 m*"; "a process for *avoiding waste*" is better than "a process for *the avoidance of waste.*"

EXCESSIVE USE OF *THAT* AND *OF*

Below is a passage modified from one cited by Baker (3) in which "of" and "that" are overused; *that* and *of* are italicized for emphasis.

> Many biological journals, especially those *that* regularly publish new scientific names, now state in each issue the exact date *of* publication *of* the preceding issue. In dealing with journals *that* do not follow this practice, or with volumes *that* are issued individually, the biologist often needs to resort to indexes ... in order to determine the actual date *of* publication *of* a particular name.

By eliminating half of the *of*'s and the nouns they bring in, replacing *that* phrases with participles, and making a few other changes, you can reduce the length of the passage without changing its sense.

> Many biological journals, especially those regularly *publishing* new scientific names, now give the exact date of the preceding issue. In using journals, and some books, not *adhering* to this practice, the biologist must turn to indexes ... *to date* the publication of a particular name.

ACTIVE VOICE OR PASSIVE VOICE

The active is the natural voice, the one in which people usually speak or write, and its use is less likely to lead to wordiness and ambiguity. The "passive of modesty," a device of writers who shun the first-person singular, should be avoided. "I discovered" is shorter and less likely to be ambiguous than "it was discovered." The use of "I" or "we" ("we" for two or more authors, never as a substitute for "I") avoids dangling participles, common in sentences written in the third-person passive voice (*see* Dangling participles, below).

Although frequently misused and abused, the passive voice has proper uses in scientific writing. It may serve when the agent of action (the discoverer and the publisher in the examples below) is irrelevant in the context.

> Penicillin was discovered in 1929.
> Darwin's *Origin of Species* was published in 1859.

The passive voice can be used to emphasize something or someone other than the agent. Whether one writes "antibiotics are produced by fungi" or "fungi produce antibiotics" may depend upon where the emphasis is to be placed, on antibiotics or on the agent, fungi.

TENSE

Properly used verb tenses not only indicate the time relation of past events to each other and to the present but indicate the completion or continuation of events. Completed observations and procedures are described in the past tense (*was*, *were*); directions, conclusions, generalizations, and references to stable conditions are stated in the present tense (*is*, *are*). The past perfect tense is used to describe events completed before a time in the past—for example, "Jones *had completed* his studies of anerobic metabolism when he started his investigation of copper toxicity." Events repeated or continued from the past to the present are described with the present perfect tense—for example, "viral infections of tomatoes *have been studied* in numerous climatic conditions."

AGREEMENT OF SUBJECT AND PREDICATE

Most nouns are either singular or plural in both form and sense and require a verb of the same number (the *insect is*, the *insects are*). Some are plural in form but usually singular in sense (*kinetics is*). Some are collectives that are singular in form but may be either singular or plural in sense (*school*, *herd*, *family*). When a collective noun is used as a subject, its verb is singular when you believe that the subject acts as a unit, but its verb can be plural if the subject is thought of as individuals: The *committee resolves* that . . .; the *committee believe* that . . . . Units of measure (*grams*, *litres*) are often used in a collective sense: "Ten millilitres of serum was added to the mixture." Be alert for nouns that have plural forms not ending in *s*, such as *data* (singular, *datum*) and *media* (singular, *medium*).

DANGLING PARTICIPLES

In scientific writing, dangling participles are distressingly frequent. They are most likely to occur in sentences written in the passive voice—sentences in which the agent of the action suggested by the participle is not named. Hence the action is attributed to an agent that cannot perform the action.

Judging by present standards, these *trees* are . . . .

The present participle should be changed to the past participle, *judging* to *judged*, and the subject brought forward in the sentence.

These trees, judged by present standards, are . . . .

JARGON

The technical vocabulary or typical idiom of specialists or workers in a particular discipline is considered jargon. Jargon that meets standards of good etymological practice has a place in formal reports. To be avoided, however, is a vocabulary or jargon so peculiar to a discipline that it inhibits rather than promotes the interchange of ideas beyond that discipline. For example, a fisheries biologist may write that he "stocked trout in the stream" when he means that he "stocked the stream with trout." A pathologist may write that "no pathology was found in the lung," using *pathology* as a jargon term for *abnormality* when its formal, widely accepted meaning is a discipline within the medical sciences.

Some statements in a jargon that may be the normal acceptable idiom in a particular discipline are amusing to readers unfamiliar with that jargon. For example, a surgeon may write in a case description that "The patient left the operating room in good condition." This sentence does not mean that the patient cleaned up the operating room and went out of it but that when the patient was taken from the operating room at the end of the operation, his or her physical condition was satisfactory.

Jargon that is informal, slangy, confusing, or ambiguous should be replaced by formal and accurate equivalents. One form of jargon is the euphemistic term or phrase used to soften or disguise a harsh reality, as in "Some in the population suffered mortal consequences from the lead compound in the flour" for "Some people died as a result of eating bread made from the lead-contaminated flour."

INAPPROPRIATE SEX REFERENCES AND DEHUMANIZING TERMS

Careful writers will choose nouns and pronouns referring to men, women, or children of either sex as carefully as they select other words for precise meaning. The use of *man* or *men* as generic terms for human beings can lead to ambiguity that is unacceptable in scientific writing. For example, in "The high incidence of renal disease in the American black is probably related to *his* susceptibility to hypertension," is the reference only to adult male blacks or to male and female adult blacks? Other problems in sex reference and problems in sex stereotyping are discussed in detail, with examples, in guidelines issued by the American Psychological Association (2).

Similar care should be taken to avoid use of terms that dehumanize the persons to whom they refer. Errors of this kind frequently occur in clinical journals in which *patients* (persons under medical care) may be referred to as *cases* (instances of disease) or *persons with hypertension* designated by the jargon shorthand as *hypertensives.*

CONFUSING PAIRS

Many words are used erroneously because they resemble other words with similar meaning, sound, or appearance. Even experienced writers may fail to distinguish clearly between the meanings of the words in such pairs. For example, *varying* and *various* are not synonymous. *Varying* is used incorrectly in the sentence, "Light intensity was controlled by cheesecloth shades of *varying* thickness," because no shade changed its thickness during the experiment; the shades were of *various* thicknesses. To *infer* is to derive by implication or reasoning; to *imply* is to intimate or suggest a meaning not expressed. A list of frequently confused pairs of such words is given in chapter 15, Word Usage.

THAT AND *WHICH*

Precise usage favors *that* to introduce a restrictive (defining, limiting) clause and *which* to introduce a nonrestrictive (nondefining, descriptive) clause. Maintaining the distinction between these relative pronouns contributes to clarity and understanding. In the sentence, "The fish that survived the treatment developed tumors," the defining clause, "that survived the treatment," is needed to identify the fish being discussed. In the sentence, "The third fish, which survived the treatment, developed tumors," the nondefining or descriptive clause, "which survived the treatment," merely gives additional information about its subject, which has already been identified by the adjective "third." Each of these pronouns signals the function of the words it introduces—defining or merely describing.

WHILE, ALTHOUGH; SINCE, BECAUSE

While has long been used with the concessive connotation expressed by *although*, and *since* in the meaning expressed by *because* or *for the reason that*. Both *while* and *since* have a strong sense of time, and either one at the beginning of a sentence may be ambiguous. Each of the two sentences below has two possible interpretations; one interpretation of the first is absurd.

> While the peanuts are grown in Georgia, most of them are eaten in New York.
> Since snow fell yesterday, the roads have been slippery.

A sentence in which any of these words might be ambiguous should be revised by the use of words or phrases such as *although, but, whereas, even though, even if* instead of *while*; *because, for, inasmuch as* instead of *since*. Alternatively, two coordinate clauses separated by a semicolon may be used.

> The peanuts are grown in Georgia; most of them are eaten in New York.
> Because snow fell yesterday, the roads have been slippery.

NEW WORDS

A word that is not listed in a dictionary should not be used unless it is widely accepted in formal communications in a given field or unless a need for such a word exists. Scientists coin technical words—especially nouns and verbs—in several ways. Some of the new words are self-explanatory and fill a need; others are vague or pretentious substitutes for well-established terms. If scientists are to interchange ideas successfully from discipline to discipline, they must exercise restraint in coining new words as well as in creating new meanings for old words.

Many nouns in acceptable usage have been formed by adding the suffix *-ate* (indicating the result of a process or action) to a stem implying action. Nouns of this kind include: *exudate, eluate, diffusate, homogenate*. Such neologisms as the following are not acceptable: *grindate, shockate, pressate, washate*.

Many acceptable verbs have been constructed from the stem of a noun or adjective and the suffix *-ize*, meaning to make into or cause to be or resemble: *colonize, oxidize, stabilize, lyophilize*. Reckless extension of the practice of forming new verbs by adding *-ize* to nouns or adjectives is to be avoided: *inoculize, blenderize, rigidize*.

Although many verbs with the suffix *-ate* (*concentrate, propagate, fractionate*) are widely accepted, use of an invented verb, such as *sedimate*, that lacks etymological or scientific justification should be limited.

EXCESSIVE USE OF ABBREVIATIONS

Abbreviations should be used primarily for the convenience of the reader, and thoughtful authors will avoid using abbreviations not likely to be understood readily without explanation. In general, use only those abbreviations that are widely understood because they have been sanctioned by international and national scientific organizations or they have become conventional through long use in one or more scientific disciplines. Abbreviations with international sanction as well as many approved by the publishing services of major American scientific organizations are listed in chapter 14.

If the article is to be published in a highly specialized journal with a small audience, abbreviations well known in that discipline may be understood even if they do not have the sanction of official organizations or wide usage. If the article is to be published in a journal with a very large audience in diverse disciplines, frequent use of abbreviations not listed in chapter 14 may impede understanding of the article for most of the audience.

Confusion can arise with abbreviations having two or more meanings in different fields. For example, MS can mean mitral stenosis in cardiology, multiple sclerosis in neurology or virology, morphine sulfate in therapeutics, and manuscript in an editorial office. Abbreviations used as modifiers can often be omitted. An article, for example, about systemic lupus erythematosus might contain this sentence:

> Most of the SLE patients were treated with prednisone before the diagnosis of SLE had been firmly established.

Because the article is solely about systemic lupus erythematosus, this sentence does not need the modifying abbreviations.

> Most of the patients were treated with prednisone before the diagnosis of SLE had been firmly established.

For details on the use of abbreviations, see chapter 12, pages 142–145.

NOUNS AS MODIFIERS

Although many nouns properly can be used as modifiers (*horse* fly, *tree* house), confusing clusters of such nouns should be avoided: "a new *type motor skills college performance* test"; "a *percentage transmission* recording *ultraviolet light adsorption* meter." When a noun is used as a modifier, an adjectival ending must be added if the noun form more correctly expresses the meaning. Consider the meanings of these noun and adjectival forms: a *science* writer, a *scientific* writer; *nerve* ending, *nervous* ending; *insecticide* application, *insecticidal* application.

EPONYMS

Standard, descriptive, equivalent terms are preferable to eponymous terms (those derived from the names of persons) when they are available. A term such as "citric acid cycle" is preferable to "Krebs cycle"; "osteitis deformans" is preferred to "Paget disease" (which can refer either to a bone disease or to a lesion of the female breast).

SIMILES AND METAPHORS

A simile compares one thing to something of a different kind, class, or quality; the comparison is usually illustrative and introduced by *like, as, if,* or *as when*: "The water is as blue as the sky." A mixed figure shows confused thought: "Your contribution will seem like a drop in the bucket of this great bundle of red tape." In metaphor, a word or phrase denotes one kind of object or idea in place of another by suggesting a likeness or analogy: "The professor *punctured* my excuses with a question." "A mad bull is a *demon of energy.*" Metaphors are to be used sparingly; mixed comparisons can lead to absurdity.

> Already there are indications that astronautics is upsetting the familiar apple-cart in which for generations we have piled our most precious ideas and rationalizations that protect and comfort us in the midst of the sea of ignorance that is our true cosmic environment.

HEDGING

Many careful researchers in biology have some degree of doubt about their observations and conclusions. To convey their uncertainty, they hedge—that is, they "arrange a way of escape from any positions taken." They use such nouns as *view, supposition, idea, notion, speculation, conjecture, surmise, thought,* and even *guess*; such qualifying adverbs as *probably, possibly,* and *apparently*; and such verbs as *indicate, suggest, appear, seem,* and *feel* (for *believe* or *conclude*). When disciplined hedging seems necessary, select the word that precisely describes the situation, but do not overdo the hedge. The following sentence contains a triple-barreled hedge.

> The fact that the active enzyme system is found only in the chlorophyllous plant *may* be *suggestive* of a *possible* function in the photosynthetic reactions.

FAULTS IN EUPHONY

Prose that sounds right when read aloud is not likely to contain elements that would distract readers. Excessively long sentences, rhymes, and conspicuous alliteration are apparent when the article is read aloud.

> The experimental subject suffered uninterrupted strain from unintended pain. The syndrome seen in seven starved siblings seemed startlingly severe.

AMERICAN AND BRITISH USAGE

The most conspicuous differences in the American and British varieties of English are in vocabulary and spelling. For an article being prepared for a journal published in the United States, follow American usage. If the article is for British publication, follow British usage. Canadian journals tend to use terms of American English (*gasoline* rather than *petrol*) but British spellings (*programme* rather than *program*). Journals published in other Commonwealth countries tend to use British terms and spelling.

British and American vocabularies differ mainly in common terms (*windscreen, windshield*) and less in scientific terms. Authors uncertain of terms preferred in either vocabulary should consult standard dictionaries: the *Shorter Oxford English Dictionary* (7) or *Chambers Twentieth Century Dictionary* (5) for British terms; the Merriam-Webster dictionaries (8, 9), *The American Heritage Dictionary* (1), or *Random House Dictionary* (6) for American terms. (Differences in drug names, both generic and proprietary, are shown in chapter 13, pages 214 and 215.) Some differences in spelling are listed below:

	American	British
Nouns ending in -or, -our	color	colour
Nouns ending in -er, -re	center	centre
Nouns ending in -se, -ce	license	licence
Words with double or single consonants	woolen	woollen
	program	programme
Verbs ending in -ise, ize,	rationalize	rationalise
and nouns derived from them	rationalization	rationalisation

In scientific vocabulary the commonest differences in spelling are in terms with diphthongs. British English retains *ae* and *oe* in many scientific nouns.

estrus	oestrus
hemoglobin	haemoglobin

Regardless of the country in which an article is to be published, retain the original spelling in bibliographic references and quotations.

LITERATURE CITED: Prose Style for Scientific Writing

1. The American heritage dictionary of the English language. New college edition. Boston: Houghton Mifflin Co.; 1981.

2. American Psychological Association. Publication manual. 3rd ed. Washington, DC: American Psychological Association; 1983.
3. Baker, S. Scholarly style, or the lack thereof. Am. Assoc. Univ. Professors Bull. 42:464–470; 1956.
4. Barzun, J. Simple & direct: a rhetoric for writers. New York: Harper & Row, Publishers; 1975.
5. Chambers twentieth century dictionary. New York: Hippocrene Books, Inc.; 1978.
6. The Random House college dictionary. Revised ed. New York: Random House, Inc.; 1975.
7. Shorter Oxford English dictionary on historical notations. Oxford: Oxford Univ. Press; 1973.
8. Webster's new collegiate dictionary. Springfield, MA: G. & C. Merriam Co.; 1981.
9. Webster's third new international dictionary of the English language. Unabridged. Springfield, MA: G. & C. Merriam Co.; 1976.
10. Zinsser, W. On writing well: an informal guide to writing nonfiction. New York: Harper & Row, Publishers; 1980.

References

References to be cited in an article include both published and unpublished documents. Published documents include journal articles, books, technical reports, cataloged theses and dissertations, patents, maps, recordings, and other similar matter available to the public, and to libraries, by subscription, purchase, lease, or free distribution. Unpublished documents include handwritten or typewritten documents (such as letters, diaries, or field notes) held by individuals or libraries in single copies or distributed primarily to limited segments of the scientific community. The placement of references to such documents within articles differs among journals, but references to published documents are usually listed in a bibliographic reference section at the end of the article. References to articles accepted for publication but not yet published and to unpublished documents held in a library or archival collection accessible to the public are often listed in this section. Other unpublished materials not accessible to the scientific public (such as letters, private tape recordings, data to be published, preliminary drafts of reports) are identified in most journals in footnotes to the text or in statements within the text.

CITING REFERENCES IN THE TEXT

Literature cited in the text should refer to well-documented sources of additional background information for readers who may find the subject pertinent to their own fields of interest and wish to know more about it. No reference should be included in the article unless it can be verified against the original document. The accuracy of all reference material is the responsibility of the author, not the copy editor. Practices for citing references in the text vary widely, but most editors endorse one of the systems described below.

NAME-AND-YEAR SYSTEM
For the name-and-year system (sometimes known as the Harvard System), cite the name(s) of the author(s) and the year of publication in the text. The placement of parentheses depends on sentence structure.

One author: Dawson (1976) or (Dawson 1976)
Two authors: Dawson and Glenn (1976) or (Dawson and Glenn 1976)
Three or more authors: Dawson et al. (1950) or (Dawson et al. 1950); Dawson and others (1950) or (Dawson and others 1950); Dawson and co-workers (1950) or (Dawson and co-workers 1950)

If the author(s) and the year are identical for more than one reference, insert lowercase letters (in alphabetical succession) after the year.

Dawson (1976a) or (Dawson 1976a)
Dawson (1976b) or (Dawson 1976b)
Dawson et al. (1960a) or (Dawson et al. 1960a)
Dawson et al. (1960b) or (Dawson et al. 1960b)

To cite an article, report, or monograph issued by a committee, institution, society, or government agency, cite the sponsoring organization or, if named, a chairman or editor(s) as the author(s).

(CBE Style Manual Committee 1983)

In some journals the page numbers of the references as well as the author(s) and year of publication must be included in the text citation.

(Benson 1967, p. 16–25)
(Talbot and Seagram 1971, p. 119)
(Wilson et al. 1974, p. 44a–49a)

NUMBER SYSTEM
Number references in the order of their first mention in the text; cite only the number assigned to the reference. However, in some journals, both the assigned number and the name of the author(s) are included.

Two new species of the genus *Aristida* are described (7).
Two new species of the genus *Aristida* are described (Caro and Sanchez 7).

NUMBER SYSTEM WITH REFERENCES ALPHABETIZED
The entire list of references is alphabetized by author(s), then numbered and cited in the text as in the number system above. With this system, the references listed in the bibliographic section will not be in the order of their first mention in the manuscript, and the numerical citations in the text will not be seriatim.

ENTIRE REFERENCE IN TEXT
In the format for some publications, there is no separate reference section; bibliographic data are given only in the text. Author(s) may or may not be named. Abbreviate the journal title only if you enclose it in parentheses; give inclusive page numbers and the date of publication.

CITING UNAVAILABLE PUBLISHED MATERIAL
The need to cite references not readily available or no longer in existence

presents a problem to some biologists, particularly taxonomists. If you must cite such a reference, indicate in some way, possibly in a footnote or a notation in parentheses, that you have not read the reference in the original. The citation "Powell (1858, cited by Forbes, 1872)" would indicate that you have depended on an article written by Forbes and published in 1872 for information originally in an article written by Powell and published in 1858. You should include both articles in your list of references and add in parentheses at the end of the Powell entry that you have been unable to see the article and are depending on Forbes (1872) for the information from Powell. Similar candor is desirable in citing articles published in foreign languages. Indicate either in the text or in the list of bibliographic references whether you are citing the original article, a translation, or an abstract.

LIST OF REFERENCES

Because a reference list is also a form of scientific communication, it should be prepared with great care according to the rules established by the editor of the publication to which you will submit the article. If a recent issue is not available for use as a style guide, prepare the list of references according to the *American National Standard for Bibliographic References* ANSI Z39 29-1977 (2). This standard (*see* Examples of bibliographic references, page 55) is recommended because it 1) provides guidelines for the cataloging of usual and unusual references to both print and nonprint materials, 2) encompasses many of the concepts being developed at the international level, 3) ensures that all references are consistently formatted and structured, 4) requires a minimum of copy editing, 5) provides sufficient information to enable a reader to retrieve an item with a minimum of effort, and 6) permits certain options in placement and punctuation of the bibliographic elements. With respect to item 6, for example, editors may choose to place the date of publication either after the name of the author(s) or before the volume of a journal, or to use no periods after authors' initials or a journal abbreviation.

The list of the references cited in the body of an article (including tables and figures) is usually placed at the end of the text in a section titled "Literature Cited," "References Cited," "References," or a similar term. Select the heading used in the journal for which you are writing.

The arrangement of references in the bibliographic section depends on how they are cited in the article. In the number system each entry appears in the order of its first mention in the text and is then numbered sequentially. For the name-and-year system, the entries are arranged alphabetically by author and then chronologically when the authors of two or more entries are the same. In a combination of the above systems, references are alphabetized by author, numbered sequentially, and cited in the article by number or author, or both. For publications other than journals, if no system is recommended or indicated, authors should follow the name-and-year system.

The information for a bibliographic reference should be taken from the original of the work being cited. Group together related bibliographic elements. The main parts of a complete entry for an article in a journal are authorship; title of article and subtitle; name of journal, usually abbreviated; part or supplement number when pertinent; volume number; inclusive page numbers; year of publication; and month of issue or number when pagination is not consecutive throughout the volume. Components for a reference to a book include author(s); title of book and subtitle; number of edition after the first; family name and initials of editor or translator, or both, if applicable; place of publication; name of publisher; year of publication; volume number; and page number(s), if specific pages are cited. Each of these components is discussed below.

AUTHORS

Initials are usually substituted for given names. To avoid confusion when family names and initials are identical for different authors, write out the first given name for each author. In biological journals the initials and family name for at least the first author listed in a reference are reversed.

J. C. Smith	Smith, J. C.
F. W. Day, Jr.	Day, F. W., Jr.
A. B. Toll III	Toll, A. B., III

Insert a comma or semicolon after Jr. and III if the name of another author follows. In reversing the normal order of a given and family name it is necessary to determine the family name. Below are examples of American practice in inversion of given and family names.

Name as in byline	*Name as in reference*
E. C. Bate-Smith	Bate-Smith, E. C.
Richard C. De Long	De Long, R. C.
A. J. de Lorenzo	de Lorenzo, A. J.
James M. van der Veen	van der Veen, J. M.
John Edward Vanderveen	Vanderveen, J. E.

In many countries—Canada, Czechoslovakia, Denmark, England, Finland, Italy, Norway, Poland, Sweden, and the USSR, for example—given and family names follow the order used in the United States, and most of them are similarly transposed for alphabetical listing. However, Western practice (3, 7, 10) in citing and alphabetizing authors' names in languages in which the family name is not always apparent varies with the authority followed by the journal. Examples of the system used in this manual are listed below in alphabetical order by nationality.

Arabian   *See* Egyptian.

Brazilian   *See* Portuguese.

Burmese   Burmese names, for the most part, contain only one element. The "U" that often accompanies a name is a term of respect, but should be retained.

U Thant	Thant, U
U Nu	Nu, U

Chinese   In Chinese publications the family name precedes the given names (usually hyphenated).

Chan Tai-chien	Chan, T.
Lin Ke-sheng	Lin, K.

In American and British journals, however, a Chinese name is usually anglicized and transposed.

C. Ying Chang	Chang, C. Y.
Hsi Fam Fu	Fu, H. F.

Dutch   In a transposed Dutch name, the particle or particle phrase precedes the family name.

Hugo de Vries	de Vries, H.
L. W. van Horts van Bing	van Horts van Bing, L. W.
Adriaan D. de Groot	de Groot, A. D.

Egyptian   An Egyptian or other Arabic family name follows the given name.

Hassan Fahmy Khalil	Khalil, H. F.
Mohammed Metawali Naguib	Naguib, M. M.

When a prefix or its variant (el, ibn, abdel, abd-el, abdoul, abu, abou, aboul) or the particle el alone precedes a name, it is hyphenated to the name it precedes when the name is transposed.

Aly Abdel Aziz	Abdel-Aziz, A.
Youssef Abou-el-Ezz	Abou-el-Ezz, Y.
Aziz Ibn Saud	Ibn-Saud, A.
Kamel el Metwali	el-Metwali, K.

French   In a transposed compound French name, the definite article (le, la, les) alone or in combination with the preposition de (du, de la, des) precedes the family name.

Jules LeBeau	LeBeau, J.
René L'Epee	L'Epee, R.

Charles de Gaulle	de Gaulle, C.
Bertrand d'Aubiac	d'Aubiac, B.

German   A particle (im, von, zu, zum, zur) or its abbreviation in a German name precedes the family name.

Kurt von Holt	von Holt, K.
Hans zur Horst-Meyer	zur Horst-Meyer, H.

Hungarian   The family name precedes the given name; transposition is unnecessary.

Farkas Karoly	Farkas, K.
Szent-Gyorgyi Albert	Szent-Gyorgyi, A.

Indian   If Sen or Das precedes an Indian name, it is included with the family name. In modern Indian usage, the family name appears as the last element.

Bimal C. Sen Gupta	Sen Gupta, B. C.
Natoobhai J. Das Gupta	Das Gupta, N. J.

Indonesian   There is only one element in most Indonesian names.

Sukarno	Suharto

Japanese   Family names are always given first when written in Japanese, but usually appear in Western form (given name first) in translated journals.

Sessue Hayakawa	Hayakawa, S.
Shigeru Yoshida	Yoshida, S.

Korean   The same system as that used for Japanese names is used for Korean names.

Tak Joon Lee	Lee, T. J.
Min-Hong Choi	Choi, M.-H.

Portuguese   In a transposed Brazilian or Portuguese name the particle (do, da, dos, das) precedes the family name.

Silvio do Amaral	do Amaral, S.
Alfredo C. dos Santos	dos Santos, A. C.

Spanish   Some Spanish names and names of Spanish origin include the maternal after the paternal family name. In the transposed name, the paternal name precedes the maternal name.

Casimir Gomez Ortega	Gomez-Ortega, C.
Juan Perez y Fernandez	Perez y Fernandez, J.

The Spanish word hijo (h.) means son; it is equivalent to junior and should be so translated. Gonzalo Ley (hijo) becomes, Ley, Gonzalo, Jr., or Ley, G., Jr., in a bibliographic list published in an English-language journal.

Thai   The given name precedes the family name and must be transposed for alphabetization.

Somsokdi Duangjai	Duangjai, S.
Anake Serimontrikul	Serimontrikul, A.

Vietnamese   In Vietnamese names the family name precedes the given name; but the first name, which is the last element, must be transposed with the middle name.

Ngo Van Hai	Ngo, H. V.
Nguyen Lam Tiep	Nguyen, T. L.

No Personal Author   Articles, reports, or books that are issued by committees, government agencies, or other organizations may carry the name of the organization as the corporate author. If an editor is cited, the name of the editor, followed by the word "editor" or the abbreviation "ed.," may be used. If authorship cannot be determined, an article may be listed under the title, or the word "Anonymous," depending on which citation system is used. Encyclopedias, dictionaries, manuals, and similar works without personal authors are better known, and may be cited, by their titles rather than by the names of their editors or publishers.

Webster's third new international dictionary of the English language. Unabridged. Springfield, MA: G. & C. Merriam Co.; 1976.

In the text citation the above title may be shortened to *Webster's Third New International Dictionary* or, after the first mention, to *Webster's Third*.

ALPHABETIZATION

Names of authors are alphabetized on a letter-by-letter basis. The particle, definite article, or preposition precedes the family name. Compound family names may be transposed if the person is most widely known by the second element.

Abdel-Aziz, A.	Macaboy, D. M.
Beethoven, L. van	Mac Adams, P. W.
Chang, C. Y.	Perez y Fernandez, J.
d'Aubiac, B.	Sen Gupta, B. C.
de Gaulle, C.	Szent-Gyorgyi, A.
Delmont, P. K.	van der Veen, J. M.
LaPorte, P. H.	von Holt, K.
Lavoisier, A.	zur Horst-Meyer, H.

TITLE AND SUBTITLE OF ARTICLE OR BOOK _____

In listing the title of an article or book, copy the wording (transliterated, if necessary), spelling, and punctuation as they appear on the first page of the article or on the title page of the publication. Follow the style of capitalization used in the journal for which you are writing. Observe the conventions of capitalization for the language in which the title is written.

Book or article titles that depend for understanding on differences in type size, arrangement of type on the title page, or subtitles may need additional punctuation when cited in bibliographies.

COMPLEMENT
Mechanisms and Functions

HISTORY OF GENETICS
From Prehistoric Times to the Rediscovery of Mendel's Laws

Punctuate such titles as follows, and list them according to the style of the journal.

Complement: mechanisms and functions
History of genetics: from prehistoric times to the rediscovery of Mendel's laws

TITLE OF JOURNAL OR OTHER SERIAL PUBLICATION ____

Many scientific journals abbreviate the names of serials in accordance with the recommendations in the *American National Standard for Abbreviations of Titles of Periodicals* (1). Lists of abbreviated journal titles are the *Chemical Abstracts Service Source Index (CASSI)* (5), *BIOSIS List of Serials* (4), and the engineering index (9). For a clinical journal in medicine, see the latest January issue of *Index Medicus* (8). Abbreviations for specific words are given in the *International List of Periodical Title Word Abbreviations* (6). Spell out every word for which you can find no abbreviation. Titles consisting of one word, such as *Phytopathology*, *Science*, or *Biochemistry*, are not abbreviated. In a few scientific journals all words in the titles of cited publications are spelled out because the editors believe that the cost of checking abbreviations is greater than the printing costs saved by abbreviating.

VOLUME, ISSUE, AND PAGES OF JOURNAL _____

Use arabic numerals to indicate the volume number of a periodical, even if the original volume numbers are roman numerals. If the pages of the journal cited are numbered by issue rather than by volume, include the issue, supplement, or part number in parentheses after the volume number.

3(5):61–69   42 (suppl. 2):13–21   51(3, pt. 2):6–14

In listing an article in a special series, precede the volume number with the number or letter designating the series.

Ser. 3, 5:118–131   Ser. D, 3:19–25

VOLUME AND PAGES OF BOOK

In an entry for a book title that covers more than one volume, include only the number (arabic) of the volumes containing the material you cite in the text. Some journals include in each entry for a book the total number of pages; others designate specific pages cited; some do not include page references.

YEAR OF PUBLICATION

The year on the cover or title page of the journal is the publication date. For the publication date of a book, use the year on the title page, or, if no date is shown there, the latest copyright date on the reverse side of the title page. If no date is given in either place, a date may be determined from library records or other sources and given in brackets. If no date of publication can be determined, use the letters n.d. An approximate date should be followed by a question mark, and enclosed in brackets. For a book that has been reprinted or has had more than one edition, use the date of the reprinting of the edition you have used (determined usually by the last copyright date). An appropriate notation [first published in 1859] may be added in brackets at the end of the entry.

To show the chronology of publication, some authors using the name-and-year system include in the text citation the date of first publication, as well as the date of the edition or printing cited. If both dates are helpful, include them as in the following:

(Darwin [1859] 1971)

This citation will indicate to the reader that the passage referred to can be found in a 1971 reprinting of a work first published in 1859.

In a bibliography arranged alphabetically, if two or more cited articles or books by the same author, or authors with names in the same order, have the same publication year, list the entries with lowercase letters (a, b, c) after the dates.

Johnson, M. A.; Adams, G. N.; Nelson, V. A. . . . 1971a.
Johnson, M. A.; Adams, G. N.; Nelson, V. A. . . . 1971b.

EXAMPLES OF BIBLIOGRAPHIC REFERENCES

The *American National Standard for Bibliographic References* (2) presents rules, rationale, principles, definitions, and examples to assist in formulating bibliographic references for a wide variety of materials (print and nonprint). These guidelines group bibliographic material in several hierarchical subdivisions (levels). A general guideline is to reference bibliographic data at the "lowest" level appropriate to the material to be cited and include reference to the pertinent "higher" level(s).

1) *Analytical (or lowest) level.*   For example, an article in a journal, a chapter of a book, a paper in conference proceedings. Citations at this level must include reference to either of the two higher levels of which they are a part.

2) *Monographic level.*   For example, a report, book, or filmstrip, unrelated to any other publication; if it is part of a series (collective level), that information should be included in the reference.

3) *Collective level.*   For example, a series of monographs, an entire journal (as in a union list of serials) or issue of a journal, or a multivolume work.

The American National Standard also categorizes bibliographic elements in three classes to indicate their degree of importance. In an abbreviated bibliographic style, the reference consists only of the *essential* bibliographic elements, whereas a comprehensive style also includes *recommended* and sometimes *optional* elements.

1) *Essential data.*   Required to provide unique identification of a work (author of a book, volume number of a periodical, or year of publication, for example).

2) *Recommended data.*   Needed to provide valuable redundancy that helps to identify a work more easily (such as the issue number of a periodical) or to provide aids for the use and reproduction of nonprint material (width of a motion picture film, or speed at which a sound recording is played, for example).

3) *Optional data.*   Aid the user by supplying such information as the affiliation of an author of a journal article.

The following bibliographic citations are examples of most of the data levels and types of references you may encounter. They also illustrate the punctuation, style of capitalization, and abbreviations recommended by the *American National Standard for Bibliographic References* (2).

JOURNALS

Standard journal article
1. Steele, R. D. Role of 3-ethylthiopropionate in ethionine metabolism and toxicity in rats. J. Nutr. 112:118–125; 1982.
2. White, H. B., III. Coenzymes as fossils of an earlier molecular state. J. Mol. Evol. 7:101–104; 1976.
3. Livanou, Th.; Nikas, A. A quick test of protein bound iodine based on the dry ash method. Folia Biochim. Biol. Graeca. 9:116–123; 1972.

Corporate author of article
1. The Committee on Enzymes of the Scandinavian Society for Clinical Chemistry and Clinical Physiology. Recommended method for the deter-

mination of γ-glutamyltransferase in blood. Scand. J. Clin. Lab. Invest. 36:119–125; 1976.

2. Fujian Institute of Microbiology. [Studies on antibiotics 104: I. Identification of *Micromonospora roseopurpurea* n.sp.] Acta Microbiol. Sin. 15:271–274; 1975. (In Chinese; English summary.)

Article with no identifiable author

1. Anonymous. Epidemiology for primary health care. Int. J. Epidemiol. 5:224–225; 1976.
2. Anonymous. Food allergy and intolerance. Lancet 2:1344–1345; 1980.

Article with author affiliation

1. Norton, E. M.; Boe, A. A. (Dept. of Plant and Soil Sciences, Univ. of Idaho, Moscow). *In vitro* propagation of ornamental rosaceous plants. HortScience 17:190–191; 1982.
2. Rosen, B. P. (Section of Biochemistry and Molecular Biology, Cornell Univ., Ithaca, NY, and Dept. of Biological Chemistry, Univ. of Maryland, School of Medicine, Baltimore). Basic amino acid transport in *Escherichia coli*: properties of canavanine-resistant mutants. J. Bacteriol. 116:627–635; 1973.
3. Halberg, F. (Chronobiology Laboratories, Dept. of Pathology, Univ. of Minnesota, Minneapolis); Katinas, G. S. (Dept. of Histology, Pavlov Medical Institute, Leningrad). Chronobiologic glossary of the International Society for the Study of Biologic Rhythms. Int. J. Chronobiol. 1(1):31–63; 1973.

Article with subtitle

1. Johnson, L. A. S.; Briggs, B. G. On the Proteaceae: the evolution and classification of a southern family. Bot. J. Linn. Soc. 70:83–182; 1974.
2. Scheller, R. H.; Anderson, D. M.; Posakony, J. W.; McAllister, L. B.; Britten, R. J.; Davidson, E. H. Repetitive sequences of sea urchin genome: II. Subfamily structure and evolutionary conservation. J. Mol. Biol. 149:15–39; 1981.

Title-first journal reference

1. Interferon: preparing for wider clinical use. Med. World News 23(9):51–54; 1982.
2. Rates of synthesis and source of glycolate in intact chloroplasts. Kirk, M. R.; Heber, U. Planta 132(2):131–141; 1976.

Article in translated journal

1. Mokul'skaya, T. D.; Smetanina, E. P.; Mychko, G. E.; Mokul'skii, M. A. Secondary structure of DNA from phages T_4 and T_6. Mol. Biol. (USSR) 9:446–449; 1976. Translation of Mol. Biol. (Moscow) 9:552–555; 1975.

Single page of an article

1. Tatemoto, K. Neuropeptide Y: complete amino acid sequence of the brain peptide. Proc. Natl. Acad. Sci. USA 79:5485–5489; 1982 (p. 5487, table 2).

Article on discontinuous pages
1. Saperstein, S.; Spiller, G. A.; Amen, R. J. Nutritional problems and the use of special dietary foods. Food Prod. Dev. (April):58, 61–64; 1974.
2. Crews, D.; Gartska, W. R. The ecological physiology of the garter snake. Sci. Am. 245(5):158–164, 166–168; 1981.

Entire issue of journal
1. Weiss, B., Chairman. Current status of behavioral pharmacology: a symposium. Fed. Proc. 34(9); 1975.

Journal paginated by issue
1. Oppenheimer, S. B. Causes of cancer: gene alteration versus gene activation. Am. Lab. (Fairfield, CT) 14(11):40, 43–46; 1982.
2. Eliel, E. L. Sterochemistry since LeBel and van't Hoff: Part II. Chemistry 49(3):8–13; 1976.

Unpaged periodical
1. Evans, J. How many botany books did Thomas Jefferson own? Bot. Garden Bull. 64(6):[8p] 1976.

Article in parent journal and in subdivision
1. Merriam, G. R.; Wachter, K. W. Algorithms for the study of episodic hormone secretion. Am. J. Physiol. 243(4):E310–E318; 1982.
2. Merriam, G. R.; Wachter, K. W. Algorithms for the study of episodic hormone secretion. Am. J. Physiol. Endocrinol. Metab. 6(4):E310–E318; 1982.

Article in issue published in more than one part
1. Cochrane, C. B. Mechanisms involved in the deposition of immune complexes in tissues. J. Exp. Med. 134(3, pt. 2):75_s–89_s; 1971.

Article in issue with special volume designation
1. Thamer, C.; Karlson, P. Nachweis der Proteinbindung von Ecdyson bei der Schmeissfliege Meizen *Caliphora erythrocephale.* Z. Naturforsch. 27B:1191–1195; 1972.

Item within another periodical
1. Bertolo, L.; Novakovic, L.; Penna, B. S. M. Les effets antirhythmiques du Dropéridol. Anesth. Analg. Réanim. 31:155–156; 1974. Condensed from: Anesthesiology 37:529–535; 1972.
2. Etienne, M.; Henry, Y. [Apparent digestibility and metabolic utilization of nutrients and reproductive performances in pregnant gilts as affected by the energy supply] Ann. Zootech. 22:311–326; 1973. Taken from: Biol. Abstr. 59:1273; 1975 (abstract no. 11904).

Article on computer-readable magnetic tape
1. Poglazov, B. T.; Levshenko, M. T. Bacteriophage T_4D-induced proteinase. J. Mol. Biol. 84:463–467; 1974. In: Chemical Abstract Condensates [Data

base]. Columbus, OH: Chemical Abstracts Service. 1974 September 30(81)13: abstract no. 74715f. Magnetic tape; 9 track, 800 and 1600 bpi, CAS standard distribution format, ASCII.

Journal published in microform
1. Osborn, E. C.; Rigby, C. V. The radioimmunoassay of angiotensin: further studies. IRCS Library Compendium [Microform]. 1974 May; 2(5):1294. 1 microfilm reel; 16mm; 24X reduction ratio.

BOOKS AND MONOGRAPHS

Personal author(s)
1. Osler, A. G. Complement: mechanisms and functions. Englewood Cliffs, NJ: Prentice-Hall, Inc.; 1976.
2. Altschul, S. von R. Drugs and foods from little-known plants; notes in Harvard University herbaria. Cambridge, MA: Harvard Univ. Press; 1973.
3. Eason, G.; Coles, C. W.; Gettingby, G. Mathematics and statistics for the bio-sciences. West Sussex, England: Ellis Horwood Limited; 1980.
4. De Robertis, E. C. P.; Saez, F. A.; De Robertis, E. M. F., Jr. Cell biology. 6th ed. Philadelphia: W.B. Saunders Co.; 1975.

Corporate author
1. AMA Department of Drugs. AMA drug evaluations. 4th ed. New York: John Wiley & Sons; 1980.
2. ASTM Committee E-8 on Nomenclature and Definitions. Compilation of ASTM standard definitions. 3d ed. Philadelphia: American Society for Testing and Materials: 1976.
3. International Anatomical Nomenclature Committee. Nomina anatomica. Amsterdam: Excerpta Medica; 1972.

Editor, compiler, chairman as author
1. Wood, R. K. S., editor. Active defense mechanisms in plants. New York: Plenum Press; 1982.
2. Rhodes, A. J.; Von Rooyen, C. E., compilers. Textbook of virology: for students and practitioners of medicine and other health sciences. 5th ed. Baltimore: Williams & Wilkins Co.; 1968.
3. Padilla y Padilla, C. A.; Padilla, G. M., compilers and editors. Amebiasis in man: epidemiology, therapeutics, clinical correlations and prophylaxis. Springfield, IL: Charles C Thomas; 1974.

Section, selective pages, or chapter in a book
1. Strauss, J. H.; Strauss, E. G. Togaviruses. Nayak, D. P., ed. The molecular biology of animal viruses. New York: Marcel Dekker, Inc., 1977:111–166.
2. Kirkpatrick, C. H.; Sohnle, P. G. Chronic mucocutaneous candidiasis. In: Safai, B.; Good, R. A., eds. Immunodermatology. New York: Plenum Medical Book Co.; 1981:p. 495–514. (Good, R. A.; Day, S. B. Comprehensive immunology; vol. 7).
3. Schenider, B. H.; Flatt, W. P. Stage of maturity terms to describe foods.

The evaluation of feeds through digestibility experiments. Athens, GA: Univ. of Georgia Press; 1976:198–200 (Table II).

Reprint
1. Willis, J. C. The course of evolution: by differentiation or divergent mutation rather than by selection. Cambridge, England: University Press; 1940. New York: Hafner Press Reprint; 1974.

Author as publisher
1. Dimon, J. American horses and horse breeding: a complete history of the horse from the remotest period in his history to date. Hartford, CT: J. Dimon; 1895.
2. Sommer, H. H. Market milk and related products. Madison, WI: Hugo Sommer; 1938.

Book in preparation
1. Westley, J. W., editor. Polyether antibodies: naturally occurring acid ionophores. Vol. 2. Chemistry. New York: Marcel Dekker; [1983].
2. McDougald, L. R.; Long, P. L. Handbook of poultry parasitology. New York: Praeger Publications; [1983]:256 p.

Better known by title
1. American men and women of science. 15th ed. Jacques Cattell Press, ed. New York: R. R. Bowker Co.; 1982. 7 vol.
2. Harrison's principles of internal medicine. 9th ed. Isselbacher, K. J.; Adams, R. S.; Braunwald, E.; Petersdorf, R. G.; Wilson, J. D., eds. New York: McGraw-Hill Book Co.; 1980.
3. Bergey's manual of determinative bacteriology. 8th ed. Buchanan, R. E., Gibbons, N. E., eds. Baltimore: Williams & Wilkins Co.; 1974.

All volumes of multivolume work
1. Colowick, S. P.; Kaplan, N. O. Methods in enzymology. New York: Academic Press; 1955–1963. 6 vol.
2. Handbook of psychopharmacology. Section I: basic neuropharmacology. Iversen, L. L.; Iversen, S. D.; Snyder, S. H., eds. New York: Plenum Press; 1975. 6 vol.

Translation
1. Stubbe, H. History of genetics: from prehistoric times to the rediscovery of Mendel's laws. Cambridge, MA: MIT Press; 1972. Waters, T. R. W., translator. Kurze Geschichte der Genetik bis zur Wiederentdeckung der Vererbungsregeln Gregor Mendels. 2d ed. rev. 1965.
2. Vol'kenshtein, M. V. Molecules and life: an introduction to molecular biology. New York: Plenum Press; 1970. Translated from the Russian by S. N. Timasheff.

TECHNICAL REPORTS

Personal author

1. Brill, R. C. The TAXIR primer. Occasional paper—Institute of Arctic and Alpine Research. 1971; 71 p. Occasional paper no. 1. Available from: Univ. of Colorado, Boulder, CO.
2. Zavitkovski, J., editor. The Enterprise, Wisconsin, radiation forest: radio-ecological studies. Oak Ridge, TN: Energy Research and Development Administration, Technical Information Center; 1977; 211 p. Available from: NTIS, Springfield, VA; TID-26113-P2.
3. Tierney, J. T.; Larkin, E. P. Potential sources of error during virus thermal inactivation. Selected Technical Publications. No. 28, July–December 1978. Washington, DC: U.S. Dept. of Health and Human Services, Food and Drug Administration; 1981: p. 300–305. (Reprinted from Appl. Environ. Microbiol. 36:432–437). Available from: U.S. Government Printing Office, Washington, DC.

Corporate author

1. World Health Organization. WHO Expert Committee on Specifications for Pharmaceutical Preparations. 28th rep. WHO Tech. Rep. Ser. 681; 1982. 33 p.
2. U.S. Congress, House of Representatives. The international narcotics control community. A report on the 27th session of the United Nations Commission on Narcotic Drugs to the Select Committee on Narcotics Abuse and Control. Ninety-fifth Congress, first session. 1977 Feb. 37 p. Available from: U.S. Government Printing Office. Washington, DC: SCNAC-95-1-10.

Title first

1. World food and nutrition study: enhancement of food production for the United States. Report—Board of Agriculture and Renewable Resources, Commission on Natural Resources, National Research Council. 1975. 174 p. Available from: National Academy of Sciences, Washington, DC.
2. Chemical plant taxonomy. Mears, E. J., ed. Newsletter No. 27, 1977 Jan. [15 p.] Available from: The Academy of Natural Sciences of Philadelphia.

In microform

1. Baker, F. T.; Williams, J. H., Jr. Research on automatic classification, indexing and extracting; annual progress report [Microform]. Washington, DC: U.S. Office of Naval Research, Information Systems Branch; 1968 August; NONR 4456(00). 2 fiche; 24X reduction ratio. Available from: NTIS, Springfield, VA; AD 673428.

CONFERENCE PROCEEDINGS

Entire proceedings

1. Giesey, J. P., editor. Microcosms in ecological research. DOE symposium

series 52; 1978 November 8–10; Augusta, GA. 1110 p. Available from: NTIS, Springfield, VA; CONF-781101.

Page(s) in a proceedings

1. Weber, D. J.; Hess, W. M. Diverse spores of fungi. Gerhardt, P.; Costilow, R. N.; Sadoff, H. L., eds. Spores VI: selected papers from the sixth international spore conference; 1974 October 10–13; Michigan State University, East Lansing, MI. Washington, DC: American Society for Microbiology; 1975: 97–111 (p. 102–103).
2. Singh, S.; Rebischung, J. Intervention de la science dans l'augmentation des rendements en agriculture [Rebischung]; intervention of science in the increase of production of agriculture [Singh]. Galperine, C., ed. Biology and the future of man: proceedings of the international conference; 1974 September 18–24; Sorbonne, Paris. Universities of Paris. c1976: 239–272.

Unpaged paper in a proceedings

1. Merker, H. J., Körtge, P. Elektronemikroskopische Untersuchungen an menschlichen Lebern bei Virushepatitis. Beck, K., ed. Ikterus: International symposium; 1967 October 27–29; Freiburg i Br. Stuttgart: Schattauer; c1968: [Section] 12.

AUDIOVISUAL MATERIALS

Filmstrip with sound recording

1. Separation of plasma and serum from blood [Filmstrip]. American Institute of Biological Sciences. Communication Skills Corporation; 1975. 29 fr.; color; 35 mm. Accompanied by: phonotape; 1 reel; 7½ ips; approx. 15 min. (Allied Health Skills Series).

Motion picture

1. Rapid frozen section techniques [Motion picture]. U.S. Public Health Service Audiovisual Facility and St. Joseph's Infirmary. Washington, DC: National Medical Audiovisual Center and National Audiovisual Center; 1966. 6 min.; sd; color; super 8 mm; loop film in cartridge; magnetic sound track.

Slide set

1. Rare and endangered birds and reptiles [Slides]. Northbrook, IL: Hubbard Scientific Co.; 1974. 20 slides; color; 2 × 2 in. Accompanied by: descriptive material.

Videorecording

1. Mammals of Australia [Videorecording]. Hamburg, Germany: Teldec; 1972. 1 disc; 5 min; sd; b&w; 1500 rpm; 9 in.

PATENT DOCUMENTS

United States
1. Harred, J. F.; Knight, A. R.; McIntyre, J. S., inventors; Dow Chemical Co., assignee. Epoxidation process. U.S patent 3,654,317. 1972 April 4. 2 p. Int Cl² C07D 1/08, 1/12.
2. Titcomb, S. T.; Juers, A. A., inventors; International Telephone and Telegraph Corp., assignee. Reduced calorie bread and method of making same. U.S patent 3,979,523. 1976 Sept. 7. 4 p. Int. Cl² A20D 2/00.

Foreign
1. Yabutani, K.; Yanai, I.; Harado, T.; Kurono, H., inventors; Nikon Nohyaku Co., Ltd, assignee. Phthalanilates as herbicides. Japan. Kokai 76,133,420. 1976 Nov. 4. 5 p. Int. Cl A01N9/20; Appl. 75/55,494.
2. Cooke, A. N., inventor; New Zealand Inventions Development Authority, assignee. Blood albumin from blood, blood serum or blood plasma. German (Fed. Rep.) Offenlegungsschrift 2,537,123. 1977 March 3. 16 p. Int. Cl² C07G7/00; Appl. 1975 Aug. 20.

NEWSPAPER ARTICLES

Signed article
1. Bishop, J. E. Do flies spread ills or is that claim merely a bugaboo? The Wall Street Journal. 1982 Nov. 4:1 (col. 4), 23 (col. 1).

Signed article with dateline
1. Burnham, D. 1 in 4 Americans exposed to hazards on job, study says. The New York Times. 1977 Oct 3: 1 (col. 2), 22 (col. 1): Washington, DC. Oct. 2.

Unsigned article in special section
1. Puffin, a rare seabird, returns to where many were killed. The New York Times. 1977 Sept. 6; Sect. C:28.

MISCELLANEOUS PUBLICATIONS

Chart
1. British Drug Houses, Ltd. Poole, England: BDH Laboratory Chemicals Division. Laboratory first aid [chart]; n.d.; 76 × 96 cm.

Map
1. World [Political]. Washington, DC: National Geographic Society; 1957 March. 1: 39,283,200; Van der Grinten projection; 41 × 29 in.; colored. Prepared for the National Geographic Magazine.
2. Antarctica [Topographic]. R. McDonald, cartographer. Rev. [ed.] Washington, DC: U.S. Geological Survey; 1972. 1: 250,000; 80 × 44.5 cm; colored. English. (Reconnaissance Series; [sheet] ST 57-60/6).

Trade catalog

1. Eastman Kodak Company. Eastman organic chemicals. Rochester, NY: 1977; Catalog No. 49. 180 p.
2. Cole-Parmer Instrument Company. Selected instruments, equipment and supplies for industrial research, health sciences, biological studies, chemistry, agriculture, environmental and pollution control. Chicago, IL; 1979–1980 catalog. p. 106.
3. Calbiochem-Behring. 1982 Biochemical and immunochemical catalog. San Diego, CA. 256 p.

UNPUBLISHED WORKS

Dissertation or thesis

1. Spangler, R. Characterization of the secretory defect present in glucose intolerant Yucatan miniature swine. Fort Collins: Colorado State Univ.; 1980. Dissertation.
2. Maurer, M. Biochemische und mikrobiologische Untersuchungen der Bildung und der Reversion von Sphäroplasten einer diaminopimelinsäure-auxotrophen Mutante von *Escherichia coli* K12. Zurich, Switzerland: Univ. Zurich; 1974. 82 p. Dissertation.
3. Jager, F. C. Linoleic acid intake and vitamin E requirement. Vlaardongen, Holland: Unilever Research; 1973. Thesis. 1–80.
4. Ritzmann, R. E. The snapping mechanism of Alpheid shrimp. Charlottesville, VA: Univ. of Virginia; 1974. Available from: University Microfilms, Ann Arbor, MI; Publication no. 74-23, 317. 59 p. Dissertation.

Letter

1. Darwin, C. [Letters to Sir J. Hooker]. Located at: Archives, Royal Botanic Gardens, Kew, England.
2. Ruckelshaus, W. D., Administrator of EPA. [Letter to Senator E. S. Muskie, Subcommittee on Public Works, U.S. Senate]. 1973 April 25.

Document or manuscript

1. MS D.c. 2-392; Novum organum botanicum. 1 leaf. Located at: University Library, Edinburgh, Scotland.
2. Marcianus document 299. [Greek symbols for chemical substances and technical works. 10th century]. Located at: San Marco Library, Venice, Italy.

Unpublished paper

1. Lewis, F. M.; Ablow, C. M. Pyrogas from biomass. Paper presented to Conference on capturing the sun through bioconversion. Washington, DC; 1976. Available from: Stanford Research Institute, Menlo Park, CA.
2. Smith, J. New agents for cancer chemotherapy. Paper presented at 3d annual meeting of the American Cancer Society. New York; 1975 June 3–4.

Unpublished supplemental material

1. Clementi, E. Tables of atomic function. Tables supplementing the author's paper in IBM J. Res. Dev. 9:2;1965 are available from the author on request.

LITERATURE CITED: References

1. American national standard for abbreviation of titles of periodicals. Z39.5-1969 (R 1974). New York: American National Standards Institute; 1974.
2. American national standard for bibliographic references, Z39.29-1977. New York: American National Standards Institute; 1977.
3. Anglo-American cataloging rules: North American text. Chicago: American Library Association; 1970.
4. BIOSIS list of serials: with CODEN, title abbreviations, new, changed and ceased titles. Philadelphia: BioSciences Information Service; [published annually each January].
5. Chemical Abstracts Service Source Index (CASSI), 1907–1974 cumulative and its 1975–1979 quarterly supplements. Columbus, OH: Chemical Abstracts Service; 1975–1979 and supplements.
6. International standard documentation—international list of periodical title word abbreviations, ISO 833-1974. Available from: American National Standards Institute, 1430 Broadway, New York, NY 10018.
7. Jordan, L., editor. The New York Times manual of style and usage. New York: Times Books; 1982.
8. National Library of Medicine. Index medicus. Washington, DC: U.S. Government Printing Office; [published monthly].
9. Publications Indexed for Engineering (PIE). New York: Engineering Index, Inc.; [published annually].
10. University of Chicago Press. The Chicago manual of style. 13th ed. rev. Chicago: Univ. of Chicago Press; 1982.

6

Illustrative material

The advantages and limitations of tables, graphs, drawings, and photographs must be considered in planning a manuscript. Successful illustrations enhance written material, neither taking the place of text nor requiring complex and lengthy legends to ensure understanding. Illustrative material should augment written information, clarify concepts, and provide visual orientation. These criteria must always be carefully considered by the author, artist, and editor during the planning and preparation of any manuscript.

ILLUSTRATIONS

The type of information to be conveyed will often determine the medium to be used. Properly constructed graphs, like tables, are the best way to present statistical comparisons of data sets, but graphs are especially effective for illustrating trends and the relation between variables in experimental data. Tables, on the other hand, are preferred when precise numerical information is required. Drawings may be used to emphasize, subtract, and combine selected details of the subject and thus may be the choice for rendering equipment schemes, relations between structural components, and the descriptive morphology of botany and zoology. Photographs may provide the most precise subject detail and may be the best means to demonstrate the experimental observation in some morphological disciplines.

Color illustrations may be desirable to show differences in various components of the subject, but their reproduction is costly. Not all journals will accept them and many that do require that the author meet this cost. Examine the journal's instructions to determine the specifications for color (such as number of copies, transparencies or prints) and consult with the editorial office on matters of suitability and cost.

The maximum number of figures per article that a journal will accept is sometimes stated in the instructions to authors. Preparation of a textbook, on the other hand, requires development of an "art manuscript," which defines the precise number, location, content, size, and rendering technique of each illustration and provides a preliminary legend for each.

The illustrations should be tentatively identified during the earliest planning stages of the manuscript. An artist may be consulted. Resist the impulse to over-illustrate; each figure should be an essential part of the manuscript. Avoid duplicate presentation of the same data in both tabular and graphic form.

If previously published illustrations are to be used, obtain the necessary permissions and copyright releases before the manuscript is submitted for publication. Permission is obtained by writing a request to the copyright holder of the published work (usually the journal publisher). This is required even if the copyrighted illustration is from one of the author's own previously published papers. Acknowledgement of permission to reproduce the illustration must be included in the manuscript. The acknowledgement is often part of the figure legend and should identify the source (authors, title, publisher or periodical name, volume, page, and year). If any illustrations show identifiable persons, written permission must be obtained for publication of their pictures, and copies of the permission should be included with the letter of transmittal.

Drawings and graphs should be made by a professional artist. As a rule, artwork that has been poorly prepared will significantly diminish the credibility of the manuscript, the author, and the publication. If the message is important enough to warrant publication, it surely deserves competent artwork.

LINE COPY

Line copy is black-and-white artwork (drawings and graphs) that contains no shades of gray. It is prepared on a white background with black lines or portions of lines such as dots and dashes.

Line drawings are rendered in black India ink, with pens or brushes. Lines may be evenly weighted or may vary in width, depending on the type of pen or brush used and the requirements of the illustration. Graphs, charts, diagrams, chemical structures, apparatus assemblies, and hardware are usually depicted with evenly weighted lines drawn with technical pens.

Flexible pens produce thick and thin lines and generally are used in rendering soft materials and anatomic, surgical, or figure studies. A brush is occasionally used with ink to produce smooth, tapered lines or dry-brush, fuzzy effects.

Line tone   The effect of gray areas in a line drawing can be achieved with stippling, cross-hatching, or contoured lines. These techniques help define light and shadow, form and texture. If handled well by the artist, a line rendering can be pleasing and informative, and economical to reproduce; it will appear clean and sharp even when printed on a poor grade of paper.

Preprinted line tones   Patterned screens, also referred to as Benday patterns, shading mediums, or line tints, are manufactured and sold in a variety of textures and patterns. They consist of a slightly adhesive printed film mounted on a transparent backing sheet. A piece of film, slightly larger than the area of the drawing it will cover, is cut and peeled away from the backing sheet, placed on the drawing, and trimmed with a sharp blade to exactly fit the desired space. The leftover film is removed and the film on the drawing is burnished down for maximum adhesion. These materials can be applied quickly and are useful when large areas of a drawing require uniform tone or texture.

Graphs   Preparation of graphs for publication requires the same skill and care employed in rendering all types of line art. A clean, white, opaque background should be used and all lines should be drawn with black India ink. The work must be prepared for the appropriate reduction (33⅓ to 50%).

Successful graphs are simple and contain no more information than is necessary to make a point. If further data are important for comparisons, additional graphs should be prepared to appear on the same or adjacent pages, or as a set contained within one plate.

Titles are used only on graphs that will be used as slides. Graphs appearing in print should contain the title information in a legend. If a graph is prepared for use in both slide and printed form, the printer should be instructed to mask out the title when making the plate for the printing press.

Data points must be accurately plotted and should not extend beyond the axes. Connecting curves or lines must be drawn cleanly and with an even, unvarying weight. Ideally, the number of curves plotted should be limited to four or five. Symbols commonly used for data points are ○, ●, △, ▲, □, ■, ◇, ◆. Occasionally ◑ is used when data points overlap. X and * should be avoided because they do not reproduce well.

Axes should end at the level of the final data points or one increment beyond, and should be drawn cleanly with an evenly weighted line. Interval marks along the axes should be accurately placed and should not cross the axes. They may extend into or out of the data area but should not crowd the data within the graph. Each axis should be labeled, with the numbers appearing outside the graph. Intervals should not be too numerous and every one need not be numbered.

Curves may be labeled if the label is brief, or a key may be included within the confines of the axes where no data appear. If identification of the curves requires lengthy explanation, it is best written out in the legend. Explanations of symbols should be avoided in legends, since special symbols used in the illustration may not be available to the printer.

Line weights should be selected according to the importance of the information in the graph. Curves and data points should be most prominent, with the boldest lines. Axis labels are next in importance and slightly less bold, interval numbers and curve labels or keys still less bold, and axis lines and intervals even less bold. As a rule of thumb, the curves should be about twice as wide as the axis lines. Lines indicating the mean of a number of observations are the least bold of any on the graph. They are drawn vertically through the centers of the points or bars and a very short line is drawn horizontally at each end to indicate the magnitude of the variable. The legend should state whether the variability indicated is standard deviation or standard error.

COMPUTER GRAPHICS

Computers, available at an increasing number of institutions, are capable of receiving raw laboratory data and, with appropriate programming, of producing conventional camera-ready graphs with corresponding legends. These graphs may contain labeled axes, interval marks, and symbols as well as curves or histograms. The author should discuss the publication requirements with the computer programmer *in advance*, so that the computer can be adjusted to turn out graphs that meet such reproduction needs as reasonable overall size, size of lettering, and intensity of "ink." Technological advances are also being made in reproduction of continuous-tone illustrations (color as well as black and white), three-dimensional subjects, and animation.

PHOTOGRAPHS AND CONTINUOUS-TONE DRAWINGS

In the printing process, a photograph or continuous-tone drawing must be photographed through a halftone screen onto a negative. A halftone screen is a sheet of film containing an emulsion of silver salts arranged as a grid of lines made up of dots. The grid, which may have 65 to 300 lines per inch, determines the density of the screen. Screens used for biomedical reproduction are usually 133, 150, 175, 200, or 300. Dots are available in square, round, or elliptical shapes for different reproductive qualities. The greater the number of lines per inch, the closer the halftone approaches continuous tone. The emulsion of grid lines permits varying amounts of light to pass through it; thus the printed halftone will have a small dot in the light (highlight) areas and a large dot in the dark (shadow) areas.

The halftone screen is placed between unexposed film and the original photograph; light is reflected off the photograph through the lens and halftone screen onto the film and the film is chemically developed. It is then placed in close contact with a light-sensitive, flexible, anodized aluminum plate. The film–plate combination is exposed to light and the plate is processed to develop the image. The processed plate is affixed to an "offset" press cylinder on the printing press. After ink is applied to the plate, the image is transferred to a rubber blanket and thence to the printing paper.

Photographs selected for reproduction must be glossy with sharp focus, suitable contrast, and a full range of tonal values. Photographs that appear slightly gray (low in contrast) are better suited to the tonal range of the reproduction process than a high-contrast photograph. Prints should be at least 12.5 by 17.5 cm but not larger than 22 by 28 cm. Illustration sizes should conform to those commonly used in the journal. Enlargements of photographs should not be requested; the reproduction tends to lose contrast with no additional gain in detail, and a moiré pattern may occur. Photographs reproduced at one-quarter of original size or less tend to lose detail and to darken. Photomicrographs and electron micrographs should include an appropriate scale on the photograph or on an overlay; this practice will avoid the necessity of modifying magnification data if the micrograph is reduced for publication.

It is essential that the areas of the photograph that carry the message be identified. Tissue or Mylar overlays are useful for indicating important areas or suggested crop marks. Exercise care to avoid scratching, marking, or impressing any image on the area of the original photograph to be reproduced. Clear overlays should be employed for conveying information to be added to the original photograph, e.g., arrows or labels. Photographs to be grouped for sequence or comparison should be accompanied by a diagram suggesting favored positioning. Consult the editor, publisher, or instructions to the author for specific handling of photographic materials, special photographic processes, number of photographic sets required for the review process, and sizes of photographs.

DIMENSIONS AND SCALING

Illustrations, including their supporting or mounting material, should be no larger than 22 by 28 cm. Examine the journal's instructions to note any specifications on size. Some journals require that illustrations be reproduced at one, one-and-one half, or two column widths. This requirement means that either the illustration will be reduced to conform to these widths or that the illustrations must be prepared within these dimensions if they are to be reproduced without reduction. The size requirement can often be met for a photograph by cropping (trimming away) unessential segments of the figure at the margins. Cropping should be done before lettering or symbols are applied to the figure surface.

The journal's page length may also limit the size of illustrations. Although the horizontal width of a figure may conform to the journal's page width, further reduction (or cropping) of the figure may be necessary to meet the vertical dimension of the printed page. If the proportions of an illustration (whether a single figure or a composite of multiple figures) are kept at the ratio of 2:3 in either a vertical or horizontal format, they will meet the requirements of most journals.

A line or continuous-tone drawing should be prepared 33⅓ to 50% larger than its final size on the printed page. The artist should be provided with the dimensions of the space available in the publication in order to plan the artwork for proportional reduction. The correct dimensions of the reduction ratio can be calculated quickly with a proportional scale. A reducing lens held at different distances from the artwork is a useful tool for quick visual inspection of various degrees of reduction.

Reducing artwork more than 50% will generally cause thin lines and light areas to weaken or disappear and the darker areas to block up. The resulting loss of detail can totally compromise the information depicted.

Drawings should not be enlarged for reproduction. Even though the original work may appear clean and sharp to the naked eye, enlargement reveals flaws, fuzzy edges, blobs, and glitches that can distract the reader and diminish comprehension.

During the makeup of journal pages before they are typeset, the editorial office or the publisher will scale the illustrations. Scaling is the specification of the final dimensions of the reproduced figure. These dimensions may be specified by actual measurement (usually in picas) or by calculating a percentage of the original dimensions through the use of a proportional scale. The latter is an inexpensive device, resembling a circular slide rule, that allows direct reading of the percentage of reduction (or enlargement) by matching the measured width or height of the original illustration with that of the desired final reproduction. Proportional scales, useful for planning the dimensions of illustrations, are available in art supply stores.

LETTERING AND LABELING

Labels and interval numbers should be clean and crisp. They should contrast well with their background. On white illustrations or light photographs, use jet-black ink or black dry transfer letters; on dark photographs, use opaque white water color or dry transfer letters, or use a white dry transfer square with a black letter on top.

Letters and numbers may be typeset and pasted up on the copy, burnished on from a preprinted transfer sheet, or hand lettered with a stencil or mechanical lettering device such as Leroy or Wrico. Any of these methods requires skill and experience on the part of the artist in order to look professional.

When using dry transfer letters, note that they are fragile and, unless properly burnished and fixed with a chemical fixative, may rub off. Do not use fixative spray on photographs, however. Do not use dry transfer lettering on illustrations to be dry mounted because heat used in this process will remove the lettering. For lettering photographs, preburnish the dry transfer letters over the backing sheet, then lightly burnish on the photograph. This will prevent pressure damage to the photograph.

The numbering of intervals on each axis begins with zero. A single zero should be used to indicate the start of both axes. If a number is less than 1, a zero should be placed before the decimal point, e.g., 0.1. The numbers are placed outside the axis lines and the axis labels are placed outside the numbers. Axis labels should be centered along each axis and should be in upper and lower case. The greatest readability is obtained with the use of a sans serif, medium weight alphabet.

On final reduction, the height of a lowercase "x" should be no less than 1.5 to 1.75 mm on line drawings or 2.5 to 3 mm on photographs.

If the widths of both the original artwork and the final reduction are known, the desired height of lettering for the original artwork can be calculated:

$$x = \frac{\text{width of original} \times 1.5 \text{ mm (desired "x" height of final reduction)}}{\text{width of final reduction}}.$$

Labels for curves or keys should be a smaller point size than that used to label the axes. However, all lettering used on any type of illustration must be planned to print no smaller than 8 points after reduction.

STYLE

Simplicity is said to be the essence of good taste, and although this is a subjective statement, the reader usually responds subjectively to the style and refinement of artwork in print. Negative responses are inevitably elicited by sloppy rendering, over reduction, inconsistent reduction, too much information crammed into one figure, or artwork that has been "lifted" from a variety of sources, each appearing in a different style and in various degrees of blackness. Economic and time restrictions may dictate the author's selection of these lesser pieces, but the result can be a significant loss of reader interest.

Ideally, all artwork submitted with an article should be prepared by the same artist. The line work, labeling, selection of screens, and reduction must be consistent. The information conveyed must address only one main point per illustration. Decorative frames, nonessential arrows, exclamations, cartoons, and other visual flourishes should be avoided in scientific illustration. The purpose of the drawing must be readily apparent, and the information should be depicted clearly, concisely, and accurately.

REPRODUCTION AND INSTRUCTIONS

Each time artwork is reproduced there is an approximate loss of 5% in detail and contrast. Therefore, to insure optimal results on the printed page, only original artwork or first-generation glossy prints should be submitted to the printer for reproduction. If photocopies of drawings or graphs are submitted with duplicate copies of the manuscript, each should be plainly marked "Not For Reproduction." Each piece of artwork submitted for reproduction must be identified in the lower left corner of any overlays, on the back of the mount, or on an adhesive tab at the top of unmounted work. Each identification must state the author's name, title of the article or the book and chapter, and the figure number. Frequently, instructions for grouping illustrations are specified in an accompanying sketch or diagram.

The copy editor should provide instructions to the printer stating the percent of required reduction and the line size of screens or the percent of tone value. Instructions for reproduction of unmounted photographs should never be written on the back, but rather on an adhesive tab affixed to the top of each photograph.

The publisher should provide proofs for the inspection of the artist and author before final printing so that any necessary modification can be requested.

DELIVERY
Artwork should be protected with clean paper and placed between two or more slightly larger pieces of corrugated cardboard, with corrugations at right angles to each other to minimize bending. These are then wrapped with heavy wrapping paper and strong mailing tape, labeled, insured, and mailed.

TABLES

Tables are concise compilations of data, often so arranged and labeled that their interrelationships or trends are evident with little or no textual explanations. In scientific writing, the data presented are most often results of research—numerical values or case histories—or summaries of previous findings. Tables are also useful for succinctly presenting background information, e.g., the steps in a protocol, the constituents of a diet, the characteristics of experimental subjects. Conversion tables and some reference works consist solely of tables.

The following three general principles should be considered as you construct and revise the tables for an article.

1) A table should be complete in itself. The title, headings, and footnotes should contain all the information needed by the reader to understand the table without consulting the text.

2) Data should be pertinent and meaningful as well as accurate and consistent with the text and the other tables of the article. Data for display must be chosen carefully, for not all experimental results

need or deserve publication; the author should present data justifying the important conclusions. If data can be described in one or two sentences in the text, do not present them in a table. If values within a column or row are all the same, present them in the text or in a footnote to the table. Data that have been mathematically manipulated (e.g., averaged or extrapolated) should not be presented with more significance than warranted by the sensitivity with which the raw data were obtained.

3) The format should be clear, simple, and well organized, so that any trends and relationships can be recognized easily and space is not wasted. Undue complexity, awkward word choice, cryptic abbreviations, and large masses of raw or only partially digested data are common problems that slow or puzzle the reader. Tables of similar information should have similar or parallel formats, styles, and titles. Readers should not be asked to compare data presented in tables with data presented in graphs.

PARTS OF A TABLE

There are specific conventions for constructing tables (figure 6.1). Most tables have four main parts: the *number and title*; the *box* (with column headings); the *stub* (with side headings); and the *field* (or body) of the table, with its vertical columns and horizontal rows. Many tables also have footnotes, and some have a headnote under the title. With good spacing and organization, only three major horizontal lines, or rules, running across the entire table are needed. Some journals use vertical and horizontal rules to separate values; such lines clutter the tables, detract from the data, and are expensive to set. Thinner, shorter lines called straddle rules are used to organize the subheadings over the columns.

Table number, title, and headnote   Tables are numbered in arabic or roman numerals (as designated by the journal style sheet) in the order of their citation in the text. The title describes the topic or the general trends shown in the table. The species of experimental organisms and a brief description of the experimental conditions can often be put in the title instead of in the headings or footnotes. The title should be succinct, but not so terse that it is uninformative. The terms used in the title should correlate with the column headings, but the title should not consist solely of a list of the column headings if a general descriptive term can be used.

Some journal editors prefer that experimental conditions relating specifically to the data in a table be described in detail in its title, headnotes, or footnotes.

①   ②

Table 1. Growth of *Campylobacter fetus* after incubation for 0 to 72 h in brucella broth modified with 0.025% each $FeSO_4 \cdot 7H_2O$, $Na_2S_2O_5$, and sodium pyruvate

③ ⑤ ⑥ ④ ⑦ ③

C. fetus ssp./strain	Growth ($\log_{10}$ no. cells/ml broth)					
	0 h	6 h	12 h	24 h	48 h	72 h
⑨ Incubated at 25° C ⑩			⑪			
intestinalis	4.00	4.33	4.61	4.44	4.45	4.55
jejuni ⑩						
29428	3.99	3.77	3.76	3.70	2.11	2.40
MB99	3.95	3.91	3.70	3.66	3.26	1.65
3871	2.57	2.38	2.52	2.28	2.41	1.72
Incubated at 35° C						
intestinalis	4.34	5.36	5.81	6.78	8.03	8.33
jejuni						
29428	4.65	5.15	5.37	5.95	8.83	8.32
MB99	4.65	4.97	5.37	6.46	8.80	9.73
3871	5.12	5.09	6.66	6.46	9.45	10.08
Incubated at 42° C						
intestinalis	4.25	4.32	<3	<3	<3	<3
jejuni						
29428	2.28	3.62	5.11	7.51	6.92	6.15
MB99	3.28	2.85	4.13	8.24	8.68	8.53
3871	5.13	5.90	4.91	6.73	9.56	7.58

⑧   ③

⑫
Values are means of number of colonies on duplicate VPTK plates from duplicate growth flasks.

Figure 6.1. The parts of a table. 1 = table number, 2 = table title, 3 = rules, 4 = box, 5 = column heading, 6 = straddle rule, 7 = subheading, 8 = stub, 9 = stub heading, 10 = subheading, 11 = field, 12 = footnote. (Adapted from the *Journal of Food Science* 46(2):661, 1981.)

Headings   The column headings, or box headings, identify the entries (either variables or data) in the columns below them. The row headings, or stub headings, identify the entries in the rows to their right. When designing a table, keep in mind that it is easier to compare data down columns than across rows and it is simpler to include subheadings in the stub than under the column headings. A table is more likely to be printed close to the corresponding text if it is kept narrow so that it will fit into one column of a journal with a two-column format.

Make headings brief and substantive, i.e., with no phrases ending in colons or prepositions leading on to the subheadings. Each column or row should have its own heading, unless some space-saving device is used (*see* Tips for condensing large tables, below). Abbreviations not allowed elsewhere in an article are often acceptable for words and units in headings—for example, % for percentage, conc for concentration, avg for average. Abbreviations that are not common need to be explained in a key (*see* Footnotes, below).

List stub headings and subheadings in a logical order, and make them grammatically and logically consistent with each other and their column headings. Indent subheadings in the stub to set them apart from the headings. Cut-in heads, which are centered across the entire table, are sometimes useful for avoiding excessive levels of subheadings (figure 6.2). However, they must have subheadings underneath them and, thus, cannot be used to label rows of totals, means, or other averages. Stub headings for such rows should be indented more than the greatest indentation above. Experimental variables should be described entirely in the stub, rather than in the stub and several columns of the body (figure 6.2).

Place subheadings for column headings under straddle rules, but use no more than two levels of subheadings. The box headings should describe the data, not the subheadings under the straddle (figure 6.1).

Field of the table   The field, or body, of the table contains the data generated by the experiment. In columns, align the decimal points of numbers, the en dashes of ranges, and ± signs. Leave space on each side of ± signs. Place a zero before the decimal point of numbers less than 1. Center numbers in columns under their headings; align rows with the last line of a stub heading that contains additional lines (called runovers or turnovers). Capitalize only the initial letter of words or of phrase entries and indent any runovers. Avoid brackets, braces, and typographical devices such as boldface and italics for indicating statistical significance. Avoid the excessive use of footnote marks in the field; save them for directing the reader to footnotes indicating statistical significance or exceptions.

If data are missing because they could not be obtained (i.e., the box heading and stub heading do not apply), leave the data entry spaces blank. If data are missing because they were not obtained, use a dash or ND and define it in an explanatory footnote (ND can stand for *no data*, *not determined*, *not done*, or *not detectable*). Do not use ditto marks.

Table 3. Effects of storage time and temperature on pressure test readings and malic acid content of 'Golden Delicious' and 'York Imperial' apple cultivars

Temperature	Time in storage	Magness-Taylor	Malic acid content
°C	mo.	lb.	%
'Golden Delicious'			
0	0	14.4	0.46
0	2.5	7.4	0.33
0	5	7.0	0.20
5	0	14.4	0.46
5	2.5	7.0	0.26
5	5	6.5	0.19
10	0	14.4	0.46
10	2.5	4.0	0.19
10	5	3.6	0.17
'York Imperial'			
0	0	17.8	0.48
0	2.5	12.6	0.37
0	5	11.5	0.31
5	0	17.8	0.48
5	2.5	11.7	0.33
5	5	11.2	0.29
10	0	17.8	0.48
10	2.5	11.7	0.30
10	5	11.2	0.28

Table 3. Quality of two apple cultivars stored in air

Time (mo.)/temp (°C)	Pressure test reading (N)*	Malic acid content (%)†
'Golden Delicious'		
0/0	64	0.46
0/2.5	33	0.33
0/5	31	0.20
5/0	64	0.46
5/2.5	31	0.26
5/5	29	0.19
10/0	64	0.46
10/2.5	18	0.19
10/5	16	0.17
'York Imperial'		
0/0	79	0.48
0/2.5	56	0.37
0/5	51	0.31
5/0	79	0.48
5/2.5	52	0.33
5/5	50	0.29
10/0	79	0.48
10/2.5	52	0.30
10/5	50	0.28

Values are averages of three replicates of 10 apples each. * Magness-Taylor pressure tester.   † Titratable acid.

Figure 6.2. Poorly laid out table (left) and a revised version (right) showing the use of cut-in headings, proper placement of units, and proper organization of the stub.

Footnotes   Footnotes allow you to construct a succinct, uncluttered table. Units too long for inclusion in headings; keys to abbreviations and symbols; indications and explanations of statistical significance; qualifications, exceptions, and limitations in the data; sources of data and permissions—all these can be put into footnotes. However, footnotes should not be too numerous or longer than the table itself, unless the table is for a journal that allows extensive descriptions in its table titles and footnotes.

General notes, which apply to all the data in the table (such as details of experimental conditions, descriptions of data, number of experimental subjects, permissions and sources of already published material, keys to abbreviations), should be given first, in a footnote without a citation. Specific notes, which need to be attached to a particular part of the table (qualifications, exceptions, and limitations; units or descriptions too long for a heading; indications and explanations of statistical significance), are cited in order from left to right and top to bottom as superscripts.

There are several citation systems in use: the standard footnote symbols (*, †, ‡, §, ‖, ¶, #), lowercase letters, and numbers. Use of the identical system both for regular specific footnotes and for indicating statistical significance is confusing. Number citations can also be confusing when they refer to data in the field. Thus, use two systems (symbols and letters), one for indicating significance and one for other specific footnotes.

There is no need to include a footnote mark for each new abbreviation, to explain a dash, or to give units for numbers. Abbreviations and dashes can be explained in an overall key in a general footnote. Units should be given in the headings or in footnotes to the headings, not in footnotes to the values in the columns.

UNITS IN TABLES

The units of measure for the data in the field are usually best put with the box headings, not repeated in the columns or placed under the second rule just above the data (figure 6.2). Sometimes the units are best put in the stub headings, as for example in lists of the ingredients of special diets. Although some journals do put units under the second rule, this style tends to clutter up the table and confuse the reader, especially when units pertain to several columns. Units can be supplied in footnotes to headings if the words are large and space is limited; do not cite such footnotes to the data in the field.

Choose units that eliminate excess or nonsignificant zeros. For example, 159 kg and 12 μm are preferable to 159 000 g and 0.000012 m. Except in rare instances, avoid numbers ($\times 10^6$, $\times 10^{-6}$) as multiplying factors in column headings; they have caused much confusion in biological literature because of uncertainty as to whether the data beneath are to be, or have been, multiplied by these factors. Avoid ambiguity by using, for example, *No. of bacteria, millions*, in a column heading. Values for the reader to compare should be presented in comparable units.

TYPING OF TABLES

Put no more than one table on a single sheet. Double space the entire table, including the title, headings, and footnotes. If the table must be continued on another page, repeat the table number, then put the word *Continued*; repeat the boxheadings. The size of a typed table can be estimated by matching the number of characters and spaces horizontally and the number of lines and line spaces with an already printed table in the journal.

TIPS FOR CONDENSING LARGE TABLES

1) Make sure that all the columns and rows are really necessary. Could the information be put in a footnote, in the title of the table, or in the text of the article? When several columns contain values needed for calculating the values in another column, not all the columns need to be presented.

2) If columns just to the right of the stub describe the experimental variables, could they be rearranged so that they are included in subheadings in the stub? Or are they short enough to be combined? Note how efficiently space is used in the following column entry:

No. inocu-
lated /
no. dead

10/3
10/2
20/12
20/3

3) Information related to the data, such as ranges, standard errors and deviations, and numbers of experimental subjects or tests, can often be put in parentheses beside or beneath the data themselves and then explained in a footnote.

CRITERIA FOR EVALUATING TABLES

Before preparing the final draft of a manuscript, consider the following:

1) Have all the data been checked and rechecked for accuracy?
2) Are all the tables really necessary? Are any of the data already presented in the text?
3) Are the data grouped logically? Are values that need to be compared placed in the same table? Can related information in several small tables be put together in one table? Does the reader have to compare data from a table and a figure?
4) Are the style elements of the tables (units and abbreviations) and formats (wordings of title and headings, layout of tables) consistent with those of the text and with each other? Would switching row and column headings improve readability?
5) Are tables as simple and brief as possible? Can any elements of a table be eliminated, simplified, combined, or put into a footnote? Would large tables be improved by being split up?
6) Is statistical significance properly indicated?
7) Have the tables been typed neatly, with double-spacing throughout? Will they fit the format and page size of the journal?

7

Editorial review of manuscripts

Editors of most biological journals will not accept a manuscript for publication without the advice of reviewers (also known as referees or consultants), scientists qualified to judge manuscripts in their fields. The reviewers may be members of the editorial board or may serve as consultants. The identity of reviewers may or may not be revealed to authors of the articles; some journals state in their instructions to authors which policy they follow. The editor informs reviewers regarding the confidentiality of manuscripts, which are privileged communications. These directives may concern photoduplication of any part of the manuscript or consultation with colleagues. The editor informs the author regarding copyright of the article and the possible transfer of copyright from author to publisher (*see* page 91).

Reviewers provide valuable help to editors and editorial boards in maintaining high standards of publication. In recommending that articles be accepted or rejected, or returned to be modified, they can point out errors in fact or interpretation, call attention to inaccurate or ambiguous statements, advise condensing or enlarging sections, and suggest how to strengthen the presentation and clarify the writing style. An author should assume that a reviewer's criticisms and comments are constructive and should consider them objectively. A reviewer may misunderstand parts of a manuscript because they are unclear.

The editor is responsible not only for the form of published articles but also for the selection of articles that meet high scientific standards. Although the author is ultimately responsible for the accuracy of information and for statements in his or her article, the editor should challenge statements that appear illogical or are not borne out by data. Few manuscripts are accepted for publication without being revised.

Usually, editors acknowledge the contributions of consultant reviewers by listing their names in a given issue, e.g., December issue, of the journal. Courtesy suggests that reviewers of a given manuscript should be informed by the editor of the final decision regarding acceptance or rejection. Some editors even provide a reviewer of a given paper with the comments of the other reviewer(s).

Articles invited by editors are sometimes not sent to reviewers before they are accepted, but editors may reserve the right to seek reviewers' critical comments for such articles. An author who does not wish to accept an invitation to write an article if the article will be reviewed should negotiate this condition with the editor, or decline the invitation.

GOOD PRACTICE FOR REVIEWERS

Read, evaluate, and return each manuscript to the editor promptly. Inform the editor if you cannot meet the deadline. Follow closely instructions from the editor on how to prepare your critique. Some journals provide special forms for manuscript evaluations.

Be careful in your reading; authors frequently complain that reviewers' critiques give evidence of careless reading. Be objective in evaluating a manuscript and in writing comments. Avoid acrimony. Test the critique for fairness and objectivity by asking yourself if you would be willing to sign it and send it to the author.

Do not consider prevailing opinion infallible; you could reject an important manuscript because its conclusions are not in accord with current scientific orthodoxies. On the other hand, do not be misled by persuasive writing when an article lacks adequate data and proper statistical controls.

Consider not only an article's scientific merit, but also its suitability for readers of the journal and the quality of presentation. The editor may ask, however, that comments on suitability be kept separate from those intended for the author.

Be specific in your suggestions. The author of an excessively long manuscript will not be helped by a comment such as "This manuscript is too long. Condense it to half." Give specific directions for eliminating unimportant parts or for condensing others. Indicate errors in grammar or rhetoric. Call attention to verbose or unclear writing.

The contents of a manuscript are the property of the author. Treat the manuscript as a confidential communication. Do not discuss it with anyone except the editor unless you have been given the option of seeking opinions from your colleagues. Do not make photostatic copies of the manuscript (*see* chapter 1, page 5).

Do not make corrections and comments directly on the manuscript pages unless instructed to do so by the editor. The editor will stipulate the number of copies of your critique that will be needed and whether you should sign them. If the critique is not to be signed, be sure that it is identified as yours in an accompanying letter. Keep a copy of the critique for later reference or to replace copies lost in the mail.

CHECKLIST FOR REVIEWERS

1) Is the purpose of the article made clear in the introduction?
2) Is the objective of the experiment or of the observations important for the field?
3) Are the experimental methods described adequately?
4) Are the study design and methods appropriate for the purposes of the study? Have the procedures been presented in enough detail to enable a reader to duplicate them?
5) Do you find errors of fact or interpretation? Scan and spot-check calculations. Are the statistical methods appropriate?
6) Is all of the discussion relevant?
7) Has the author cited the pertinent, and only the pertinent, literature? If the author has omitted important references, cite them; if he or she has included inconsequential or not pertinent references, suggest deleting them.
8) Have any ideas been overemphasized or underemphasized? Suggest specific revisions.
9) Should some sections of the manuscript be expanded, condensed, or omitted?
10) Do you find any content repeated or duplicated? A common fault is repetition in the text of data in tables or figures. Suggest that tabular data be interpreted or summarized, not merely repeated, in the text.
11) Are the author's statements clear? Challenge ambiguous statements. Suggest by examples how clarity can be achieved, but do not merely substitute your style for the author's.
12) Is the title of the article appropriate and clear?
13) Is the abstract specific, representative of the article, and in the correct form?
14) Have key words been provided by the author? If so, do they represent the paper adequately?
15) Are the form and arrangement of illustrations and tables satisfactory? Call attention to graphs and tables that are hard to read because they are crowded with too much information or to those that could save space if they were combined with other illustrations.
16) Can the illustrations be improved? Note whether letters, numerals, or symbols may be illegible if they are reduced and whether photographs have superfluous areas that might be cropped. Are there captions or symbols that may be better included in the legend? Do illustrations show what they purport to show?
17) Should all parts of the manuscript be published? Extensive supple-

mentary tables or long reference lists may merit publication but are costly to print and interest only a few readers. You may suggest to the editor that material of this kind be deposited with the National Auxiliary Publications Service or other repository (*see* chapter 3, page 32).

18) Has material in the manuscript been published previously? If you know that any of the material in the manuscript has already been published, inform the editor of the fact and give details.

19) What are your recommendations to the editor on revision and publication of the article? Of course, it can be assumed that, if asked by the editor, you will be willing to review the revised manuscript. What priority for publication do you suggest?

20) Is the manuscript more suitable for some other journal? If you believe it is, explain the reasons and suggest to the editor, but not to the author, a more suitable journal.

AUTHOR'S RESPONSE

After the editor has received the reviewer's critiques, he or she decides whether to accept the article for publication (and what conditions should be attached to the acceptance), or to reject it. The use of the reviewers' critiques by the editor differs among journals. Critiques may be sent to the author regardless of whether the article is rejected or accepted, or they may be sent only with articles that must be revised before final acceptance.

REVISIONS

Articles are sometimes accepted in the form in which they were submitted, but most are revised at least once between the initial editorial review and publication. The revisions requested may be only those specified by reviewers, but the editor may add further comments on what is expected in response to reviewers' critiques or may add editorial requirements.

Authors should revise articles carefully in accord with the requests of the reviewers and the editor. The revised version returned to the editor should include a letter indicating the changes made in response to comments of the reviewers and the editor, points at which the article has not been changed, and why changes were not made (invalid criticisms, data not available, and other justifiable reasons).

REJECTIONS

If the article is rejected you will have to decide what step to take next.

1) Hold the manuscript, and read it again after your disappointment or anger over rejection has abated. You may then see shortcomings

in the article you did not see before and can revise it effectively for submission to another journal. Additional experiments or observations may be needed. Your colleagues may be able to help you with this reassessment. Do not, in a moment of pique, rush to submit an unrevised version to a second journal unless you are sure that the reviewers' criticisms are entirely unjustified; authors can usually profit from the reviewers' critiques, even if they were the basis for an apparently unjustified rejection. Unfair criticisms sometimes arise from a reviewer's misreading of an unclear passage.

2) Revise the article in accord with criticisms returned with the rejection, and resubmit it to the editor. You should not take this step without getting the editor's agreement to reconsider the revised version; the editor may believe that the editorial review was adequate and that further review by the previous, or new, reviewers would be an unjustified burden. If the editor agrees to consider a revised version, it should be sent with the kind of explanatory letter described in the section on revision, above. Alternatively, the revised manuscript may be sent to another journal. It is important that it be prepared in the style of the chosen publication.

8

Application of copyright law

Authors may wish to include in their work quotations, illustrations, charts, or graphs from other sources, including their own publications. Some of these materials are not protected by the copyright law and are therefore public property (in the public domain) in the United States. All works prepared by officers or employees of the U.S. government as part of their official duties are in the public domain in the United States and may be used without further permission. Works whose term of copyright has expired are also available for reprinting in this country.

Use of materials not in the public domain is subject to the U.S. copyright law. This chapter provides a brief summary of the relevant portions of the law governing such use.

SCOPE OF COPYRIGHT PROTECTION

The U.S. copyright law (Public Law 94-553, 94th Congress, 2nd Session; codified in Title 17 of the U.S. Code) provides federal copyright protection for both published and unpublished works. Publication is no longer required for a work to be protected by copyright. Unpublished works and even works published without valid copyright notice are eligible for protection (*see* section on Notice, below). Copyright protection is available for "original works of authorship fixed in any tangible medium of expression," and includes works embodied in a wide range of media, e.g., printed pages, machine-readable computer tapes, and audio and visual recordings. Copyright protection does not extend to ideas, procedures, processes, concepts, or the discoveries contained in such works.

The law specifies copyright protection for compilations ("works formed by the collection and assembling of pre-existing materials or of data that are selected, coordinated, or arranged in such a way that the resulting work as a whole constitutes an original work of authorship"). This protection is limited to the compilation and does not cover the preexisting material. Thus charts and tabular arrangements of data are protectible subject matter. Hence, permission to reprint copyrighted charts and tables should be sought.

DURATION OF COPYRIGHT

The terms of copyright protection under the copyright law for works created after 1 January 1978 are as follows: life of the author plus 50 years except in the cases of anonymous and pseudonymous works and "works made for hire" (*see* Works for hire, below) where the term of protection is 75 years from publication or 100 years from creation, whichever is shorter.

For works created prior to 1 January 1978, the duration depends on a number of factors. Was a work in its first term of copyright protection before 1 January 1978 and has a renewal been filed? Was a work in its second term of copyright on 1 January 1978? Is the work published or unpublished?

Because there are so many possibilities, it is difficult to generalize any rule of thumb. Instead authors are advised to investigate the copyright status of a given work.

The U.S. Copyright Office provides a search service that, for a fee, will investigate its records with respect to a given work. The Copyright Office will identify the copyright holder of registered works and indicate whether a first-term copyright was renewed. Transfers of copyright ownership are also frequently recorded with the Copyright Office. Consult the official *Catalogue of Copyright Entries* (found in many major libraries), or write to the U.S. Copyright Office, Library of Congress, Washington, DC 20559. However, it must be noted that the absence of a Copyright Office registration does not mean that a work is in the public domain. Registration is not required as a condition of copyright.

NOTICE

In the case of works published prior to 1978, omission of a valid copyright notice (the word "Copyright," abbreviation "Copr.," or symbol ©; the name of the copyright owner; and in most cases the year of publication) generally placed the work in the public domain. The Copyright Act of 1976 changed this provision. Although the law still requires notice on published works, its absence does not remove protection. Steps can be taken to remedy the absence of a notice. For this reason, authors are advised not to assume that a work without a notice is unprotected.

FAIR USE

If a work is protected by copyright, in most cases permission must be sought by the prospective user prior to use of that work in a subsequent document. However, certain uses of copyrighted materials are permitted by law as "fair uses" without the need to seek specific permission. In essence, the doctrine of fair use considers the purpose and character of the use of the copyrighted material, e.g., whether for commercial gain or for nonprofit educational purposes, and the effect of the use on the value of the original copyrighted work. The pertinent section (17 USC 107) states:

> ... the fair use of a copyrighted work, including such use by reproduction in copies or phonorecords or by any other means specified by that section, for purposes such as criticism, comment, news reporting, teaching (including multiple copies for classroom use), scholarship, or research, is not an infringement of copyright. In determining whether the use made of a work in any particular case is a fair use the factors to be considered shall include—
>
> (1) the purpose and character of the use, including whether such use is of a commercial nature or is for nonprofit educational purposes;
> (2) the nature of the copyrighted work;
> (3) the amount and substantiality of the portion used in relation to the copyrighted work as a whole; and
> (4) the effect of the use upon the potential market for or value of the copyrighted work.

The language of the law on this point is purposely vague about what is and what is not a fair use and suggests that each use be considered on its own merits. However, some publishers provide their own word counts to assist authors in establishing fair use of brief quotations and small excerpts. A general rule of thumb is "When in doubt, seek permission."

SECURING PERMISSIONS

Efforts to obtain permission to use materials from other sources should begin before the first draft of the article is written. Delay in obtaining permission might delay publication of the article. Journal editors and book editors usually expect their authors to obtain permissions themselves and to include evidence of such permissions with submitted manuscripts.

A request for permission is addressed to the holder of the copyright in the document from which a previously published excerpt is to be taken or an illustration or table reproduced. Requests for permission (figure 8.1) should state exactly the material to be used, including a full reference to the source and specifying such details as the table number, document title, page number, exact text to be quoted, and the intended use. Where possible, send a photocopy of the actual material for which permission is sought. If published data are to be adapted or modified, include a copy of the intended modification. A return address must accompany the request. The copyright holder will usually stipulate what information should be given in a credit line and whether a fee is required.

Even when the publisher is not the copyright holder, the publisher often can be of assistance in locating the copyright holder. Requests should be sent, together with a self-addressed return envelope, to the permissions department of the publisher in question. Current addresses for the publisher may be found in either of two publications by the R.

Date_____

To:

   I am writing an article entitled:_____

_____

to be submitted to_____

   I wish to have your permission to include in my article the following material:

_____

_____

_____

Volume_____Page(s)_____Year_____from the article___

_____

written by_____

   If permission is granted for the use of this material, the author(s) and your journal will be credited as the source. I am sending a copy of this request to (publisher or author).

                              Sincerely yours,

                              _____
                              (Signature)

Permission Granted:

_____
(Signature)

_____
(Date)

Figure 8.1.   Typical form for requesting permission to reproduce material from another source.

R. Bowker Company, *The Literary Market Place* (1) for books, and *Ulrich's International Periodicals* (2) for journals. Of course, if the address for the copyright holder is available, write directly.

TRANSFER OF COPYRIGHT

Since copyright protection begins upon creation and hence no additional step is necessary to provide that protection, an author owns the copyright upon completion of the article. Some journal publishers request that authors transfer their copyright to the publisher. This facilitates many publishing functions. A publisher who holds copyright in the individual contributions to a collective work is able to include the work in the Copyright Clearance Center (*see* the following section), to bring out a new edition, to authorize foreign language editions or other derivative works, to respond to requests for reprints, and to grant permission to other authors to use portions of the original article in newer works on the subject. Publishers can ease the administrative burden to authors by handling transactions of subsidiary rights, including new uses in electronic format.

The law specifies that the transfer of ownership must be in writing:

> A transfer of copyright ownership, other than by operation of law, is not valid unless an instrument of conveyance, or a note or memorandum of the transfer, is in writing and signed by the owner of the rights conveyed or such owner's duly authorized agent.

A simple letter will suffice.

COPYRIGHT CLEARANCE CENTER

The ability to photocopy copyrighted works when and where needed is an expanding, legitimate, widespread requirement in today's world. The Copyright Clearance Center (CCC) is an autonomous, not-for-profit organization that conveys to users permission to photocopy and collects and distributes royalties for photocopying that exceeds exemptions provided under the copyright law. The CCC aids both users and copyright holders. Information may be obtained from the Copyright Clearance Center, 21 Congress Street, Salem, MA 01970.

WORKS FOR HIRE

In the copyright law, a "work made for hire" is either "a work prepared by an employee within the scope of his or her employment" or a work "specially ordered or commissioned for use as a contribution to a collective work, . . . as a compilation, as an instructional text, ..." This second category of works can be works made for hire if the parties (the author/creator and the employer) expressly agree in a written instrument signed by them that the work shall be considered a work made for hire. If a work is a work made for hire, the "author" is the employer and not the individual hired by the employer to create the work.

COPYRIGHT FOR COLLECTIVE WORKS _____

The law provides that

> copyright in a separate contribution to a collective work is distinct from copyright in the collective work as a whole and vests initially in the author of the contribution. In the absence of an express transfer of the copyright or any rights under it, the owner of copyright in the collective work [i.e., the journal publisher] is presumed to have acquired only the privilege of reproducing and distributing the contribution as part of that particular collective work, any revision of that work, and any later collective work in the same series.

AUTHORS AND PUBLISHERS OUTSIDE THE UNITED STATES _____

This chapter has focused on the copyright law of the United States and its relevance to authors and publishers operating in the United States. The United States is a party to the Universal Copyright Convention (UCC) and therefore agrees to protect the copyright status of works emanating from other countries party to the UCC. The UCC countries agree to protect works according to the doctrine of "national treatment." In the United States foreign works are protected according to U.S. law. Other member countries protect works according to their own laws. A U.S. author wishing to use materials that appeared in a copyright publication from another country that is party to the UCC must go through the same steps to obtain permission to use the materials as if the material were published in the United States under the U.S. copyright law. For authors in other countries the general principles expressed here are germane, but it is desirable to consult the copyright laws of the respective country.

LITERATURE CITED: Application of Copyright Law

1. Literary market place, 1982: the directory of American book publishing. 42nd ed. New York: R. R. Bowker Co.; 1982.
2. Ulrich's international periodicals directory. 20th ed. New York: R. R. Bowker Co.; 1982.

9

Manuscript into print

Before the manuscript is set in type, it is carefully reviewed by a copy editor (or manuscript editor), who may be employed by the editorial office of the journal or by the publisher or printer. The copy editor checks the manuscript for consistency of capitalization, abbreviations, and punctuation and for accuracy of spelling, citations, and references. The copy editor may also call attention to ambiguous or inconsistent statements. If the editorial office has a policy that includes substantive editing, the edited manuscript is usually returned to the author for approval before it is set in type.

The copy editor marks the manuscript pages for the typesetter in accordance with a set of specifications, examples of which are discussed below. An author can do much to assure the accuracy of the printed article by indicating appropriate typographic notations relating to scientific conventions, such as those given in chapter 13, and by carefully reading the final draft for errors (*see* chapter 3).

TYPOGRAPHIC SPECIFICATIONS

The editor and the editorial board, perhaps with the aid of a professional designer, establish a set of specifications for the journal: its physical dimensions; the kind and weight of paper on which it is to be printed; and the typefaces and sizes, leading (spacing between lines of type), measure (length of line), and arrangement (including indentions) for the text, headings, abstract, tables, legends, footnotes, references, formulas, and equations, and for any other material that is to be set in type.

The typeface chosen must be suitable for the subject matter, adaptable for special kinds of typography that may be needed, and pleasing to most readers. A typeface suitable for biological publications must be available in roman lightface, in which most text matter is set, and in italics, small capitals, and boldface.

The present tendency is for a journal to use only two or three faces: possibly a display face for titles of articles and a body type in its various forms (lightface, boldface; roman, italic; capitals, lowercase, and small capitals) for all other matter.

In the United States, the weight of the paper is usually stated in pounds and the overall size of the page in inches. Other specifications are stated in the special units of the printing industry and are based on the point system. A point is 0.0138 (about $\frac{1}{72}$) in., or 0.35 mm. Units of the point system and their approximate English and metric equivalents are as follows:

1 point = $\frac{1}{12}$ pica = $\frac{1}{72}$ in. = 0.35 mm
1 pica = 12 points = $\frac{1}{6}$ in. = 4.2 mm
6 picas = 72 points = 1 in. = 25.4 mm.

The em is a linear unit of variable measurement that had its origin in the width of the capital letter M. In type of any size, it is equal to the height of the type, including ascenders and descenders; in 10-point type it is 10 points, and in 8-point type it is 8 points. Among the many phototypesetting systems now in use, there are often exceptions to this rule; e.g., the em might be slightly more or less than the type size, depending on the design of the particular type face. An en is theoretically half an em; in some phototypesetting systems it is $\frac{5}{9}$ of an em. Ems and ens are used as units of horizontal measurement, such as indentions, sentence-, word-, and letter-spacing, and dashes (1). One em is a common paragraph indention and a common indention for a runover or turnover line; it is the paragraph indention in this manual.

Whereas the overall size of a page in a journal or book is expressed in inches, the dimensions of a type page (the printed part of the book), an illustration, or an engraving are stated in picas. Spacing between characters, between words, and between lines of type is specified in points. Spacing between columns on a page of text may be specified in ems or in picas. The thickness of rules used in printing is stated in points, the length in picas.

Body type is available in several sizes and in many faces. Most articles in journals are set in 8-, 9-, or 10-point type, usually with 1- or 2-point leading. This paragraph is set in 10-point type with 2-point leading (10 on 12 or 10/12).

<small>This sentence (except the first letter) is set in lowercase 6-point roman (not italic).</small>
This line, in 8-point type, contains CAPITALS and SMALL CAPITALS.
This line, in 10-point type, contains *italic* and **boldface**.
This line is in 12-point type.

This line is in 18-point type.

The chapter titles in this manual are in 24-point Helvetica, initial capital and lowercase. Type for the text, headings within chapters, legends for illustrations, tables, and other matter is Baskerville, set on an APS5 typesetter. The size of type for most of the text is 10 point, with 2-point leading (specified as "10 on 12 Baskerville"). The measure is 27 picas. The submatter (examples, quotations, etc.) is set 9 on 11.

The first two levels or grades of headings within chapters are 10 point capitals and are distinguished by rules and by indention of the second level. The third level is a run-in sideheading in boldface.

Legends for figures and most tables are set in 9 on 11 Baskerville. Rules in tables are ½ point thick; their length varies with the number of columns they cover.

The running heads for the verso or even-numbered pages are set in 9 on 11 Baskerville, small capitals; for the recto or odd-numbered pages the heads are initial capital and lowercase Baskerville italic. Folios (page numbers) are in 10 on 12 Baskerville. The depth of the standard type page, including the running heads, is 46 picas.

TYPOGRAPHIC CONVENTIONS

Many typographic conventions relating to capital and small capital letters and to italic, roman, and boldface type have special meanings in science. Anyone writing for publication should know the common as well as the specialized conventions (*see* chapter 13) and how the kinds of type are marked for the printer. Although the copy editor usually marks the manuscript pages for sizes of type, measure, leading, and other specifications, the author is responsible for marking italics, small capitals, and other technical style conventions peculiar to his or her area of research.

Typesetters are trained to follow copy scrupulously, and a manuscript is set as typewritten and marked. For example, unmarked typewritten lines are set in lightface roman, the capital letters as capitals, the lowercase letters as lowercase, and the words as they have been typed, unless a copy editor shows, by marks the printer understands, that they should be otherwise. Each correction mark should be in or directly above the line being corrected, and not in the nearest margin as on proof (*see* chapter 10). The most common typographic conventions understood and accepted by editors and printers are outlined below.

ITALICS (marked by single underlining)

Depending upon the style of the publication, the following common conventions for the use of italics should be used (see also *The Chicago Style Manual*, ref. 2):

1) The title of a book, journal, or other published work mentioned in the text. In some journals, and in most books, such titles are italicized in bibliographic lists.

2) Most foreign words and phrases and their abbreviations, but not proper names. Many words and abbreviations of foreign origin are no longer regarded as foreign and are not italicized: a priori, in vitro, in vivo, i.e., et al.

3) A letter or number used in the text or in a legend to refer to a corresponding character in an illustration.

4) A word or term introduced for specific discussion (its first occurrence only).

5) A word or phrase to be emphasized (overuse of italics destroys the emphasis).

6) A title for a table or a legend for a figure (in some journals).

7) A cross-reference expression: *see* and *see also*.

The following specialized conventions are not subject to style changes in different publications; however, use in specialized fields may vary somewhat, and the specific citations in chapter 13 should be consulted.

1) An unknown or a constant in mathematical matter.

2) The scientific name of a genus, species, subspecies, or variety. The name of a higher taxon is usually not italicized.

3) Letters and numbers used to designate mutant viruses.

4) A letter used as a symbol for a gene or allele in most coherent systems of gene symbolization (*see* chapter 13, pages 181, 189–193, 198.)

5) A letter used as a symbol for a physical quantity in European symbol systems for respiratory physiology (*see* chapter 13, page 207).

6) A prefix to a biochemical name identifying the position of a labeled element (*see* chapter 13, page 217).

7) Prefixes that identify configurational relationships in organic compounds (*see* chapter 13, page 218).

8) The designations *dextro* and *levo* for optical rotation (*see* chapter 13, page 218).

9) The symbols of elements that occur as locants in the names of many organic compounds (*see* chapter 13, page 218).

10) The letters used as symbols for certain chemical and physical properties of chemical compounds, such as n for specific refractive index, A for absorbance, s for sedimentation coefficient (*see* chapter 13, page 220).

SMALL CAPITALS (marked by double underlining) _____

Use small capitals:

1) For certain abbreviations to help distinguish them from other abbreviations having identical letters—for example, D and L in configurational prefixes.

2) In combination with capitals to give typographic variety in some journals, as for headings, FIG. in legends, TABLE in titles, or authors' names in bibliographic lists.

3) For some symbols in respiratory physiology (*see* chapter 13, pages 207–210).

CAPITALS (marked by triple underlining) _____

A letter typed as a capital need not be underlined to indicate capitalization. Use an initial capital or initial capitals for:

1) A proper noun and usually for an adjective based on a proper noun. Some words that have been derived from proper nouns but have become part of common usage are not capitalized.

petri dish	roman type	bunsen burner
paris green	italicize	pasteurize

2) The first word of each complete sentence except when it is in parentheses or brackets within another sentence.

3) The first word after a colon if the following words form a complete independent clause that is not logically dependent on the preceding clause.

4) Proper names of stars or other astronomical bodies (*earth*, *moon*, and *sun* are capitalized only when used in connection with the names of other planets).

5) A trade name.

6) Certain words in the titles of articles and books: a) all words except coordinating conjunctions, prepositions, and articles that are not the first words; or b) the first word and all proper nouns and adjectives. The second style is common in bibliographic lists.

7) A professional, civil, military, or religious title of nobility that immediately precedes a personal name.

    Senator Kennedy   Captain Hamilton

8) The official name of a private or government organization or institution.

    Stanford University   the City of Tucson

9) A generic geographic name that is part of a proper name.

    Lake Michigan   White Mountain
    Columbia River   Red Sea

10) The name of a formal historical epoch, geologic age or stratum, zoogeographic zone, or other term used for convenience of classification (*see* chapter 13, page 227).

    Stone Age   Ice Age   Pleistocene Epoch

11) The scientific name of a phylum, class, order, family, or genus and their subdivisions, but not of a specific or subspecific taxon except where permitted by international codes (*see* appropriate section in chapter 13).

12) The complete vernacular or common name of a species of birds in accordance with the checklist of the American Ornithologists' Union.

agents, transmembrane potentials and concentrations of the test species in the bathing solution on E, r_A and r_A may be elevated.

B. APPLICATION TO LEVEL FLOW

Level flow of a test species in the stationary
state that occurs when $X = 0$. Accordingly, in
this case Eq. (19) reduces to the following:

$$\frac{s\phi}{1 - EXP(-s\phi)} = 1 - A\phi s\phi \qquad (22)$$

8 pt #238

?A: Figure 2 meant?

The graphical solution of the above equation
is shown in Figure 3. Note that $s\phi = 0$ is always a
solution. However, it is a physical solution of
the equation only when $A\phi = -0.5$ since the slope
of the exponential curve is $=0.5$ at $s = 0$.

?A: Delete?

?A: $\leq$, not a?

The slope of the exponential curve approaches
1.0 as a approaches $=$ infinity. Thus -1.0 is the
minimum permissible value of $A\phi$. The active transport process must be properly oriented to correspond
to the direction of the virtual level-flow influx.
Thus, if the unidirectional fluxes are chosen so
that J_{v1} is negative then E must also be negative.

?A: Sp ok?

It is obvious then that there is a degree of arbi-
L'hospital's rule has been used to obtain this slope.

8 pt #238

Figure 9.1 A page of edited manuscript with queries from the copy editor to the author (A) and directions to the printer (circled).

13) The common name of an insect *only* when in accordance with the list approved by the Entomological Society of America (*see* chapter 13).

14) Many gene, chromosome, blood-group, and other symbols (*see* appropriate sections in chapter 13).

BOLDFACE (marked by wavy underlining) ———————————

Use boldface for:

1) The name proposed for a new taxon (some journals).
2) A vector in mathematics.
3) Some symbols for rodent and cat chromosome designations (*see* chapter 13, page 191)
4) Serologic specificities in the Rh blood group system (*see* chapter 13, page 200).

EDITED AND MARKED COPY

Most of the various kinds of marks used by copy editors (figure 9.1) resemble standard proofreaders' marks (*see* chapter 10). Copy editors make corrections on the manuscript, on or above the line of type, whereas proofreaders make corrections in the margins of the proof and use a mark in the line of type to indicate the location and nature of the correction.

Directions to the printer and queries to the author should be circled, enclosed in boxes, or written in a color of ink different from that used for editorial changes. The printer usually knows from the specification sheet the type face(s) and the measure(s) to be used. Manuscript prepared for computer composition may carry special codes.

LITERATURE CITED: Manuscript into Print

1. Lee, M. Bookmaking: the illustrated guide to design, production, editing. 2nd ed. New York: R. R. Bowker Co.; 1980.
2. The University of Chicago Press. The Chicago manual of style. 13th ed. Chicago: Univ. of Chicago Press; 1982.

Proof correction

Most publishers provide authors with galley proof of their articles, including printer's proofs of any illustrations. These proofs are usually accompanied by the original manuscript, showing changes made by the editor or copy editor. The author is responsible for checking the proof of the typeset article and illustrations against the originals and for making any corrections on proof. Usually this is the last time the author sees the article and its illustrations before it is published, so thoroughness is essential. Proof must be returned to the printer, editor, or publisher by a specific deadline. Editors should inform authors when to expect receipt of proof so that if an author will not be available at that time he or she can ask a colleague to check proof. The form of proof of text and composed tables depends on the method of composition, and that of illustrations on the nature of the illustrations and the kind of printing process used. Manuscripts prepared in "camera-ready" form for offset printing must be proofread carefully before being submitted to the publisher, because authors will not see proofs of papers prepared for this type of publication.

KINDS OF PROOF

TEXT AND COMPOSED TABLES

The text portion of the manuscript and tabular material may be set in type by one of a variety of systems, including hot metal, strike-on composition (such as the magnetic-tape Selectric typewriter), or one of the modern phototypesetting systems. Interested readers may find a description of several of these systems in *The Chicago Manual of Style* (4). Most scientific journals are now being set by one of the processes in which characters are made by a typewriter, photocomposer, or cathode ray tube. In these systems, a copy made from a master copy or from a photographic print of the text serves as the proof. Such proof does not represent the quality of the final printed page as closely as does proof of hot metal composition. In hot metal composition, type is cast from molten metal with a Linotype or Monotype machine. The metal lines of type that are produced are placed in long trays called galleys, and proof is produced by direct impression of the inked type onto paper.

ILLUSTRATIONS

The kinds of proof provided for continuous-tone (halftone) illustrations and line drawings (*see* chapter 6) depend on the printing process used.

For illustrations that are to be printed by letterpress, images are photographically transferred and engraved onto metal plates. Proofs are made by direct transfer onto paper from the inked engravings. You may receive a set of *engraver's proofs* separate from the text or you may receive galley proof that shows the engravings assembled, with the legends below the illustrations to which they apply. Galley proofs of halftone illustrations show less contrast and detail than the illustrations show on the printed page. The engraver's proof, on coated or glossy paper of high quality, is better evidence of the quality of a halftone. Do not expect the impression on the journal page to have the brilliance of the engraver's proof, however, unless the paper used in the journal is of equally fine quality.

For illustrations that are to be printed by offset, prints of negatives that will be used to prepare the press plates serve as proof. The quality of such proof varies since it may be carefully prepared prints or merely photocopies. With halftones, the author is usually sent a print of quality close to that of the illustration that will appear in the journal.

CHECKING PROOF

TEXT AND COMPOSED TABLES

Do not mark the original manuscript. It is the record of what the printer was asked to set and is the basis for the billing to the journal of author's and editor's alterations. To lower costs and to speed publication, some publishers send authors copies of the manuscript after it has been copy edited, instead of proofs of the typeset article. Other publishers omit the galley proof stage and have type set directly into pages, a procedure that limits changes to the correcting of printer's errors.

On each sheet of galley proof are letters and numerals that include the number of the galley and other information needed by the printer. Do not cross them out or cut them off; they will be deleted when the pages are made up. In the margins of the galley proofs there may be queries, suggestions for changes, and corrections by the editor or a proofreader; do not erase or change any of these marks (*see* Marking proof, later in this chapter). Read the galley proof at least twice. Follow the text of the proof the first time while another person reads the manuscript aloud. Read the proof the second time alone. Correct errors but do not regard proof as the place for making trivial changes, for improving your prose style, for adding new material, or for making deletions. Corrections cost more than initial composition, and errors may be introduced. Correcting a photocomposed line usually necessitates recomposing at least the line with the error. With some photocomposition systems, even small changes require that entire paragraphs be rehyphenated and a new set of prints prepared. Correcting a line set on a Linotype machine requires setting the entire line on a slug of metal, removing the incorrect slug by hand, and replacing it with the new one. Correcting a line set on a Monotype machine also requires hand work—pulling out characters and replacing them with others. Adding or deleting a word— sometimes even a character—may require that several lines be reset.

Printer's errors (PE) are corrected at no cost to the journal or author, but author's alterations (AA) are charged to the journal and ultimately may be charged to the author. Indicate printer's errors by marking PE near the correction. Cooperate with the editor in his efforts to keep the cost of alterations low. If you must revise text, delete as many characters as you add (count each space as a character). If you delete material, consider adding the equivalent in number of characters and spaces. In computer-assisted systems, character-for-character replacement is less critical. The text is corrected on a text-editing terminal and paragraphs are rerun.

If since submitting your manuscript you have made or learned of observations so important and pertinent that you believe they should be reported in or with your article, add this material only if you receive permission from the editor. Adding new material in an article under an old "received" date is unethical. The editor may suggest including a dated addendum containing the new material, which will obviate the need for changes in the text.

Accuracy   Carefully check the proof against the original text for accuracy of equations and numerical data (especially in tables) and proper spelling and punctuation; separation of paragraphs; order of headings; and citation of references, figures, and tables. Some publishers require that you indicate where tables and figures are first mentioned in the text.

Typography   Check to see that letters or paragraphs are not repeated or transposed. Defective characters occur less frequently with photocomposition than with hot metal composition; remember, photocopies may not be clear reproductions of the original impression. Copy editors at the printer or publisher are responsible for correcting poor typography and alignment, but authors should verify the proper alignment of statistical or chemical data and equations. Symbols should be checked for agreement with recognized conventions (*see* chapters 12 and 13).

Word divison   End-of-line breaks on proof should be checked carefully; they may not be the same as in the typescript. With some photocomposition and cathode ray tube equipment, words are hyphenated by a computer. The extent to which computers are programmed to handle exceptions to general rules differs, so special care should be given to text prepared in this way. In the American system, word division is based on pronunciation, not on derivation of words as in the British system. In checking divided words, pay particular attention to Latin words and scientific terms. For division of Latin words, *see* the paragraph below and the rules given in *Words into Type* (3). For division of English words, consult a standard dictionary or a style manual, often specified in the journal's instructions to authors. (*See also* chapter 17, Useful References with Annotations.)

Every Latin word is divided into as many syllables as it has separate vowels and diphthongs. The consonant *h* between two vowels always joins the second vowel (*mi-hi, co-hors*); *x* between two vowels always joins the preceding vowel (*sax-um, ax-il·la*); *ch, ph,* and *th* are never separated (*Te-thys*); *gl, tl,* and *thl* are always separated (*Ag-la·o·ne·ma, At-las, ath-let·i·cus*). A single consonant between the last two vowels of the word or between any two unaccented vowels joins the final or second vowel (*pa-ter*); but a single consonant before or after an accented vowel joins the accented syllable (*i-tin'·e·ra, dom'-i·nus*). Two consonants between vowels must be separated (*cor-pus, for-ma*); for three consonants between vowels, the last joins the vowel that follows (*emp-tor*); for four consonants between vowels, two are joined to each vowel (*trans-trum*). When a compound word is divided into syllables, the component parts are separated if the first part ends with a consonant (*su·per-est, sub-i·tus, trans-i·tur*); otherwise it is divided as if it were a simple word (*dil·i-gens*). As in other aspects of Latin grammar, there are exceptions to these rules, but they are too technical or unusual to merit treatment here.

ILLUSTRATIONS

Examine the proof of each line drawing for the absence of numerals, letters, lines, or parts of lines that may unintentionally have been routed out by the engraver. Look for letters or numerals that have been "filled in" with ink. Indicate clearly on the proof any correction you believe should be made in a halftone or a line drawing. Certain kinds of flaws in a line drawing can be easily corrected by the engraver; superfluous dots and lines can be tooled or routed out; some slightly broken lines and characters can be repaired. The amount of contrast in some halftone engravings can be improved without remaking the engraving. Adding to or otherwise revising an illustration necessitates making a new cut. Corrections on illustrations for offset printing usually involve rephotographing the original rather than correcting the master print. Check that the identifying figure number appears near each illustration. Write "Top" above the upper margin of the proof of each figure. Some journals require that magnifications for figures be adjusted to accommodate any reduction or enlargement that occurs during the printing process.

MARKING PROOF

Use standard proofreaders' marks. These differ slightly in the American (1) and British (2) systems (*see* pages 106–109, this chapter), but most printers recognize both systems. There is no standardized system for European proofreaders' marks, many of which differ from those of the American and British systems; however, most European printers recognize American and British marks or provide authors with lists of marks they prefer.

Make the corrections in colors different from any already on the proof or in the colors specified on instructions that accompany the proof. For example, if the printer's proofreader has marked corrections in green, indicate the printer's errors in red and alterations in blue.

For each correction, you must make at least two marks on the proof: one or more in the text (*in-line*) and one or more in the nearer margin (*marginal*), as in figure 10.1. One of the in-line marks may be a caret (∧) to show where an addition is to be made; another may be a line drawn through a character or a word to be deleted. A marginal mark indicates what the change is to be. It may be one or more characters or words to be inserted, or a proofreader's symbol, such as a space or deletion sign. Each mark should be made on an imaginary extension (left or right) of the line to which it applies. To indicate several corrections for a single line, arrange them in sequence from left to right in the nearer margin, and separate adjacent corrections by a slash line.

European proofreaders use a series of symbols to indicate several corrections in a single line of type: ⌈ ⌊ ⌊⌈ ⌊⌈ ⌊⌈ . The symbol is placed through the type to be corrected in the proof, and the same symbol is placed before the correction that is in the margin.

Remember, corrections made on a typed manuscript are made above the line of type, but *proof corrections are made in the margins of the page*. In correcting galleys, the typesetter or compositor scans the margins of proof and makes only the alterations that are indicated there. Standard American proofreaders' marks have been used to make the corrections on the proof in figure 10.1.

If the correction or insertion consists of more than one or two lines, type it on a separate sheet and attach the sheet to the proof at the appropriate place with tape, never with a paperclip or pin. Show clearly where the new copy is to be inserted. Mark each insert with a letter and the number of the galley to which it belongs, for example, "A for galley 2." Make all corrections neatly and legibly. If a blanket order such as "set *Rosa* in italics throughout" is called for, also mark each occurrence of the change on the galley; do not expect the printer to make corrections that are indicated only in an accompanying letter.

Proofreaders' marks and symbols

Instruction	American National Standards Institute marks	
	Marginal mark	In-line mark
Delete	ℰ	the red book
Close up	⌒	the bo ok
Delete and close up	ℰ	the bøook
Restore deletion	stet	the red book
Insert in line	red	the‸book
Substitute in line	red	the black book
	e	tha book
Insert space in line	#	thebook
Equalize spacing	eq #	the ⌄yellow⌄book
Lead (space) between lines	# or ld	The red book >was lost
Remove leads between lines	ℰ# or ℰ ld	The red book was found
Insert hair space or thin space	hr # or thin #	100/000
Begin new paragraph	¶ or L	The red book was lost.⫽The black book was found.
Run paragraphs together	no ¶	The black book was lost.⌒ ⌐The red book was found.
Insert 1-em quad (indent)	☐	‸The red book
Insert 2-em quad (indent)	☐☐ or ②	‸was found
Insert 3-em quad (indent)	☐☐☐ or ③	‸at night.
Move to left	[	⌐ the book
Move to right	]	the] book
Center	ctr	] the book[
Move up	⌐ ⌐	the book˥
Move down	⌣ ⌣	the book/
Align vertically	‖ or align	‖The book ‖ was lost ‖ in the fog.
Align horizontally	= or straighten	The book was read
Transpose	tr.	The found book was.
		The book was found.
Spell out	SP	The ② books came.
Push down quad (spacing material)	⊥	the book

Proofreaders' marks and symbols

British Standards Institution marks		Corrected type
Marginal mark	In-line mark	
	the red book	the book
	the bo ok	the book
	the book	the book
	the red book	the red book
	the book	the red book
	the black book	the red book
	tha book	the book
	the book	the book
	the / yellow/book	the yellow book
extend text mark	The red book was lost	the red book was lost.
extend text mark	The red book was found	the red book was found.
thin Y	100/000	100 000
	The red book was lost. The black book was found.	The red book was lost. The black book was found.
	The black book was lost. The red book was found.	The black book was lost. The red book was found.
	[The red book [was found [at night.	The red book was found at night.
	the book the book the book	the book the book the book
[ ]	the book the book	the book the book
‖	The book was lost in the fog.	The book was lost in the fog.
	The book was read.	The book was read.
	The found book was.	The book was found.
	Teh book was found.	The book was found.
two	The 2 books came.	The two books came.
	the book	the book

Proofreaders' marks and symbols

Instruction	American National Standards Institute marks	
	Marginal mark	In-line mark
Reset broken letter	×	the book
Turn right side up	9	the book
Lowercase letter	lc	the Green book
Capitalize as marked	cap	the good book
Set in small capitals	sc	am, PM
Set in italic type	ital	The Good Book
Set in roman type (Br.: upright type)	rom	the *book*
Set in boldface type	bf	The Good Book
Set in lightface type	lf	The **book**
Set in capitals and small capitals	c&sc	A Style Manual
Set in boldface italics, capitals and lowercase	bf ital c&lc	a style manual
Wrong font; reset	wf	body type
Reset as superscript (Br.: superior)	⋎2	the book2
Reset as subscript (Br.: inferior)	⋏2	H2S
Insert as superscript	⋎6	1203
Insert as subscript	⋏2	HO
Period (Br.: full stop)	⊙	Read the book
Comma	⋏,	leaves, buds and branches
Semicolon	;	Think then decide
Colon	:	Read the following
Hyphen	=/=	up and down career
Apostrophe	⋎'	Lands End
Double quotes	⋎"/⋎"	He said book.
Single quotes	⋎'/⋎'	"Don't cry Fire!"
Question mark	?	Can you write
1-en dash (Br.: rule)	1/N	pages 10 15
1-em dash	1/M	The book find it
3-em dash	3/M	Ito, R. I. The
Parentheses	(/)	the book a manual
Brackets (Br.: square brackets)	[/]	the book
Slant line (Br.: oblique)	/	5 ms

Proofreaders' marks and symbols

Marginal mark*	In-line mark	Corrected type
		British Standards Institution marks
	the book	the book
	the book	the book
	the Green book	the green book
	the good book	the Good Book
	am, PM	AM, PM
	The Good Book	*The Good Book*
	the book	the book
	The Good Book	**The Good Book**
	the book	the book
	A Style Manual	A STYLE MANUAL
	a style manual	***A Style Manual***
	body type	body type
	the book	the book²
	H₂S	H_2S
	1203	1230^b
	H₂O	H_2O
	Read the book	Read the book.
	leaves, buds and branches	leaves, buds, and branches
	Think then decide	Think; then decide.
	Read the following	Read the following:
	up and down career	up-and-down career
	Lands End	Land's End
	He said book.	He said "book."
	"Don't cry Fire!"	"Don't cry 'Fire'!"
	Can you write	Can you write?
	pages 10 15	pages 10–15
	The book find it	The book—find it
	The	_____. The
	the book a manual	the book (a manual)
	the book	[the book]
	5 m s	5 m/s

* British usage requires that an oblique (slant line) be placed after each marginal mark, to indicate that the correction is concluded—for example, ⊙/

Fawns Versus Food

It is basic in animal biology that more young are produced than are necessary to carry on the species. This is true of ants, elephants, people, and deer. The better nourished a doe is, the more fawns she produces, and the better chances her fawns have for survival after birth. One of the principles of deer herd management, or livestock raising, can be stated briefly: If, on a given amount of food, we carry a smaller number of bred females over winter, each one will be better fed. Ten well-fed does will produce at least as many fawns as 15 half-starved ones. This has been proved beyond question.

Michigan is no exception to this rule. In the Upper Peninsula the average rate of fawn production is 14 or 15 fawns per year from every 10 breeding does . . . and in southern Michigan fawn production jumps up to 20 per 10 does.

—MICHIGAN WHITETAILS, 1959.

Fawns Versus Food

It is basic in animal biology that for more young are produced than necessary to carry on the species. This is true of ants, elephants, people, and deer. The better nourished a doe is, the more fawns she produces, and the better chances her fawns have for survival after bith. One of the principles of deer herd management, or livestock raising, can be stated briefly if on a given amount of food, we carry a smaller number of bred females over winter, each one will be better fed. 10 well fed does will produce at least as many fawns as 15 half-starved ones. This has been proved beyond question. Michigan is no exception to this rule. In the upper peninsula the average rate of fawn production is 14 or 15 fawns per year from every 10 breeding does . . . and in Southern Michigan fawn production jumps up to 20 per 10 does.

—Michigan Whitetails, 1959.

Figure 10.1. Galley proof. The left column shows a block of proof marked for corrections using the American National Standards Institute marks. If more than one instruction must be written in the margin next to a line of type, the instructions are separated by slash lines. The right column shows the proof after the corrections have been made.

There may be queries from the editor or the printer in the margins of the proof. If you wish the line to remain as set, draw a line through the query, but do not erase it. If the editor or a proofreader has indicated a change you cannot accept, draw a line through the suggested change and write in the margin "OK as set" or write "stet" in the margin and put dots below the material you want retained (*see* page 110). Circle any notations you add that you do not want set in type, such as a note to the printer.

RETURNING PROOF

Most publishers include with the proof their instructions stipulating to whom the proofs are to be returned. Remember, if illustrations are to be remade the printer must have the original artwork. Follow the instructions for mailing illustrations and manuscripts given in chapters 3 and 6.

LITERATURE CITED: Proof Correction

1. American National Standard proof corrections, Z39.22-1974. New York: American National Standards Institute; 1974.
2. British Standard copy preparation and proof correction, BS 5261. Part 2. Specifications for typographic requirements, marks for copy preparation and proof correction, proofing procedure. London: British Standards Institution; 1976. Available from: American National Standards Institute, 1430 Broadway, New York, NY 10018.
3. Skillin, M. E.; Gay, R. M.; and other authorities. Words into type. 3d ed. Englewood Cliffs, NJ: Prentice-Hall, Inc.; 1974:319–320.
4. University of Chicago Press. The Chicago manual of style. 13th ed. rev. Chicago: Univ. of Chicago Press; 1982.

11

Indexing

Primary research journals usually contain two kinds of indexes, sub-ject and author. In the last issue of the volume or the first issue of the ensuing volume, many journals include a cumulative title and author index, or a subject index and separate author index. Some publishers include an alphabetical listing of authors' names and appropriate page numbers at the back of each issue of a journal, but such a list is found only in journals publishing large numbers of articles. The publisher may also incorporate separate indexes for taxonomic entries or create special indexes for ancillary topics, such as letters to the editor, notes, errata, and book reviews.

In recent years, editors of many primary journals have been taking advantage of opportunities presented by secondary services or abstract-ing and indexing publishers who use computers to capture the journal title, add key word phrases, and alphabetically permute the entries in list form. In a comparatively short period of time, the computer can compose a KWIC (key word in context) or a KWOC (key word out of context) index of an entire volume, so that the cumulative index may be published with the last issue of the journal, thus offering the reader quick access to the information included in the volume.

Conventional subject indexes for journals are usually prepared by a professional indexer who may incorporate into the index key words and phrases that have been supplied by the author at the publisher's request. Scientific or technical books tend to be indexed in greater depth than journal articles, and authors are often expected to prepare, or assist in preparing, the index for such books. Additional information on various types of indexes can be found in several other sources (1–3).

SUBJECT INDEX

The following procedures for preparing a subject index apply to both journals and books. They will help in creating a logical, consistent, and concise index, but ultimately the indexer must depend on common sense, a retentive memory, a capacity for attention to detail, and familiarity with the vocabulary of the discipline.

MECHANICS

The first task of the indexer who is not the author is to determine the principal emphasis and orientation of the material to be indexed. This will aid in selecting key words and in manipulating entries so that the reader will be led quickly to the information sought.

The preliminary reading of the work may be of galley proof, but the actual indexing should be done from page proof. Words or phrases that should be indexed are printed or typed on file cards, along with the numbers of the pages on which the items appear. To show that a term has been indexed, underline it on the page proof.

After the last card for the last page has been prepared, arrange the cards alphabetically by main entry (*see* below). Arrange the subentries alphabetically within the category of each main entry, with the number of indentions clearly indicated. Discrepancies in terminology that cannot be resolved should be noted for the author. Insert cross-references and recheck the alphabetization and punctuation.

MAIN ENTRIES

The key word or phrase on the card is an *entry*, the basic unit of the index. Avoid terms that are nonspecific or that may be broadly interpreted. Thus, in the phrase "development of mouse carcinoma," the word "development" is too vague to be indexed except as a subentry or sub-subentry. In a permuted series of entries—desirable for most articles and particularly for books—write separate cards for "mouse" and "carcinoma," with "development," if necessary, as a sub-subentry.

Mouse	Carcinoma
carcinoma	mouse
development, 229	development, 229

SUBENTRIES

Since it is difficult to determine in advance how many page numbers will be recorded for a key word or phrase, time can be saved by including subentries when writing the main entry. Later deletion of unneeded information is easier than rereading pages of the article or book to locate meaningful terms to use as subentries.

Although some journal and book editors permit as many as five page numbers for one entry, it is preferable to cite no more than three. Therefore, main entries with more than three page numbers usually are divided into subentries and, where necessary, sub-subentries. Consider numbers connected by a hyphen (one-en dash) as one number.

Unacceptable	*Acceptable*

Carcinoma, 182–183, 221, 229, 305–306, 310–314, 423, 427, 469	Carcinoma
	  development, 229
	  genetic manipulation, 182–183, 221, 469
	  occurrence
	    monkey, 305–306
	    mouse, 310–314, 423, 427

A main entry should not be followed by a single subentry; a subentry should not be followed by a single sub-subentry.

Unacceptable	*Acceptable*

Carcinoma, 120, 211, 417
  radiation-induced, 106
    mortality rate, 118
	Carcinoma
	  animal longevity, 211, 417
	  drug therapy, 120
	  radiation-induced, 106, 118

If a key word appears on only one page of the text, either delete the subentry or make it part of the main entry. Space limitations and a prior decision on how much detail should be included in the index will determine whether supplemental information should be omitted.

Carcinoma, 229
Carcinoma, mouse, 229
Carcinoma, mouse: development, 229

PREPOSITIONS

Some indexers still favor including prepositions, but the use of computers for indexing has started a trend towards entries without prepositions. In the third example above, the meaning is clear without adding "of" after "development." Most entries can be manipulated to preserve clarity without the inclusion of a preposition.

INDENTIONS

Indent subentries under the main entry, and indent sub-subentries under the subentry. Most indexes are restricted to two indentions—rarely is it necessary to include three—and each indention must be easily distinguishable from runover lines. All indentions must follow a uniform pattern (*see* first "Acceptable" example under Subentries).

INVERSION OF COMPOUND TERMS

An adjective is usually inverted in main entries unless it is part of an anatomic term or a disease name or the noun it modifies is nonspecific. In the following list the noun is too vague for the entry to be inverted.

Cardiac output
Clotting time
Oral cavity
Pulmonary disease
Uric acid
White matter

An adjective, however, may occur as the first word in a subentry or sub-subentry.

Unacceptable	*Acceptable*
High carbohydrate diet	Carbohydrate diet, high
Pregnant mouse	Mouse, pregnant
	high carbohydrate diet
	or
	Mouse
	pregnancy
	high carbohydrate diet

When the noun in an anatomic term or a disease name is significant by itself, the entry may be listed either under the adjective or the noun, or under both. The choice should be determined by a prior decision on permutation of compound entries.

Arteriovenous blood	Blood, arteriovenous
Mitral stenosis	Stenosis, mitral
Oculomotor hypotonia	Hypotonia, oculomotor

Index compound Latin names as they are normally written: the noun and then the adjective, with no comma between.

Musculi abdominis
Rattus norvegicus

When a compound term consists of more than two words, decide which word is most significant. If permutation is desirable, ignore those elements that would be meaningless as the first word of an entry.

Cholesterol side-chain cleavage enzyme
or
Enzyme, cholesterol side-chain cleavage
or both

ABBREVIATIONS

Main entries   Do not use an abbreviation at the beginning of an entry unless:

1) A cross-reference to the written term accompanies the abbreviation. If the abbreviated term has been used in the text, the abbreviation may be added to the spelled-out entry.

ATP (*see* Adenosine triphosphate)   Adenosine triphosphate [ATP]

2) The abbreviation is part of an enzyme name.

> ATP:3-phospho-D-glycerate 1-phosphotransferase
> NADPH-cytochrome *c* reductase

3) More than one species is listed for a genus.

Ambystoma maculatum, 15	or	*Ambystoma*
A. mexicanum, 17		*maculatum*, 15
		mexicanum, 17

If confusion would result from using the abbreviated form, the genus name should be repeated.

> *Aotus dariensis* (see *Ateles fusciceps*)
> *Aotus trivirgatus*, 47

Capital letters that were once abbreviations but are now the accepted designation may be at the beginning of an entry.

> ECHO virus
> T cells

Subentries   If space is an important factor, an abbreviation may appear at the beginning of a subentry. If the abbreviation is used, it should not stand alone.

Unacceptable	*Acceptable*
Infants	Infants
CNS, 14, 17	CNS disorders, 14, 17
radiation exposure, 81, 322	radiation exposure, 81, 322

Abbreviations (or symbols) in the main entry and in subentries can be used when the abbreviation falls *within* the entry and the symbol or abbreviation has been used in the text.

> Acetyl-CoA acyltransferase deficiency
> lowered RBC count
> pulmonary CO_2 pressure

CROSS-REFERENCES

Use cross-references to lead the reader to related information and to avoid repetition of page numbers for synonymous terms. For cross-references, write "see" or "see also" in italics if the following word is in roman type, or in roman type if the following word is italicized.

> Hypophysis (*see* Pituitary)
> Mouse, 49 (see also *Mus musculus*)
> *Mus musculus*, 27, 29 (*see also* Mouse)
> Pituitary, 17, 36

Never insert a "see" cross-reference after an entry having a page number.

A "see also" cross-reference directs the reader to additional information; the entries involved should have at least one page number that is not common to both.

Adipose tissue, 13, 150, 167 (*see also* Fat cells)   Fat cells, 99, 150, 324 (*see also* Adipose tissue)

If all the numbers for one entry are included in the numbers of the referral entry, omit reciprocal cross-reference to the entry with the fewer page numbers.

Adipose tissue, 13, 150 (*see also* Fat cells)   Fat cells, 13, 74, 150

When an entry has subentries, insert the cross-reference after the main entry or after the appropriate subentry.

Adipose tissue (*see also* Fat cells)
    adrenal hormones, 330–331
    prostaglandins, 279
    water content, 190

Acromegaly
    anterior pituitary hormones, 117
    diagnosis, 125 (*see also* Pigment metabolism)
    glucose intolerance, 418

List alphabetically and separate by semicolons two or more cross-references for a single entry.

Extremities, 130 (*see also* Arm; Leg; Limb)

Where it is impractical to list multiple cross-references, insert a nonspecific referral.

Cancer cells, 361 (*see also* type of cancer)

If the cross-reference is to a specific entry or entries, the wording should be identical with the wording of the entry or entries to which the reader is referred.

CAPITALIZATION

Main entries   In indexes in which the typographic convention is to capitalize the first word of the main entry, some first words are not capitalized:

1) A compound surname in which the prefix is customarily lowercase.

de Quervain thyroiditis
van't Hoff equation
von Willebrand disease

2) The name of a chemical compound having an italicized prefix.

p-Aminobenzoic acid
tert-Amyl isovalerate
sec-Butyl alcohol
cis-2,*trans*-4-Decadienoic acid
dl-Norisoephedrine

3) A standard symbol or abbreviation that begins with a lowercase first letter.

> pH
> pK′
> mRNA

Chemical names preceded by an italicized symbol for another chemical compound are always capitalized.

> *N′*-Bromoacetamide
> *O*-(2-Naphthyl)glycolic acid

In indexes in which it is important that the reader distinguish common nouns from proper nouns, main entries are not capitalized unless style conventions require that they be capitalized in the text. For example, in an index of microbiologic names, capitalize family and generic names but do not capitalize specific epithets and common names.

> spirochetes
> Sporotrichinaceae
> *Sporotrichum schenkii*
> streptococcal infections
> *Streptococcus*

Subentries and sub-subentries   Write the first letter as lowercase unless the subentry begins with a proper name, or the first letter is a capital letter in an abbreviated term.

> Immunodeficiency
>   cytomegalovirus pneumonia
>   T cells
>   IgA defect
>   mucocutaneous candidiasis
>   Wiskott-Aldrich syndrome

PUNCTUATION

Use a comma after the last word of the entry to separate it from the accompanying page number(s), and in the inversion of compound terms.

> Ultraviolet radiation, 187   Radiation, ultraviolet, 187

Use a colon to separate supplemental information from the rest of the entry.

> Radiation, ultraviolet: abnormal pigmentation, 169

There is no punctuation after an entry that is followed by subentries, after the final page number, and before a cross-reference.

> Ultraviolet radiation
>   abnormal pigmentation, 169 (*see also* Pigmentation)
> DNA repair, 45, 49, 67

ALPHABETIZATION

The two methods of alphabetizing are the word-by-word system, frequently used in nontechnical publications, and the letter-by-letter or dictionary system, which is almost imperative for an index containing acronyms, letters and symbols with technical meanings, and expressions involving typographic conventions in special fields.

Word-by-word	Letter-by-letter (dictionary system)	
Acid chloride	Acid chloride	Crossbill
Acid number	Acidemia	Cross dating
Acid test	Acid-fast stain	Cross-fertile
Acidemia	Acidic mine drainage	Cross hair
Acid-fast stain	Acid number	Cross-reference
Acidic mine drainage	Acidosis	Cross section
Acidosis	Acid test	Crossvein

In either system of alphabetizing, respect the conventions of the nomenclature in a specific field.

Chemical compounds   Chemical names frequently contain arabic numerals; greek letters; italicized expressions such as *d*, *l*, *m*, *meta*, *n*, *o*, *ortho*, *para*, *s*, *sec*, *sym*, *syn*, *t*, and *tert*; a capital letter that is a symbol for a chemical element and that has a special meaning when capitalized; and the small-capital letters D and L. Disregard these modifiers when alphabetizing, unless they constitute the only difference in the entries.

> 3-Ethyl-4-picoline   *N*-Acylneuraminic acid
> 4-Ethyl-α-picoline   *O*-Acylneuraminic acid

When there is doubt about the order of such modifiers, consult the "Cross Index of Names" in *The Merck Index* (4).

Disregard the prefix for "cyclic" and the prefixes used to designate fractions or functions of ribonucleic acids (for example, "m" for messenger and "t" for transfer).

> Ameba   Ritalin
> cAMP (*see* Cyclic AMP)   mRNA (*see* Ribonucleic acid,
> Amputation   messenger)
>   Romberg disease

The term "bis" at the beginning of, or within, a chemical name is considered part of the name.

> Acetyl benzoyl peroxide   Biliary obstruction
> 1-Acetyl-3,3-bis(*p*-hydroxy-   *N*,*N*-Bis(2-chloroethyl)benz-
>   phenyl)oxindole diacetate   enamine
> Acetylcarbromal   Bivalvia

Anatomic terms   Disregard numbers unless they constitute the only difference in entries.

BeWo cells
B14FAF28-G3 cells
BF-2 cells
B-group chromosomes
BHK cells
BHK-21 cells
Bile duct

TA3 ascites cells
T-antigens
Tb 1 Lu (NBL-21) cells
3T3 cells
3T12 cells
TCMK-1 cells
3T3M T20 cells

Scientific names of animals and plants   When species of the same genus are alphabetized, abbreviate the generic name after the first entry and alphabetize by the specific epithet. The exception to this rule is when "sp." or "spp." is given instead of a specific epithet. The nonspecific term then becomes the first entry, with the identified species following in alphabetical order.

>*Triticum* sp.
>*T. aestivum*
>*T. durum*

Plural entries   When it is expedient to combine related entries to form a single plural entry, consider the added -*s* or -*es* in alphabetizing.

2-Methyl-1-butanol, 193
2-Methyl-2-butanol, 193, 195
2-Methyl-2-butanol carbamate, 197

2-Methyl-2-butanol carbamate, 197
→2-Methylbutanols, 193, 195

When a term has been used in the text in both the singular and the plural, (s) or (es) may be added but should be disregarded in alphabetizing.

>Protein(s) (*see also* specific proteins)
>   antigenic determinants
>   liver cell identification
>   synthesis
>Proteinate
>Protein-bound iodine

FIGURES, TABLES, HEADNOTES, FOOTNOTES _____

If it is necessary to include an indication that an entry refers to an illustration or graph, table, headnote, or footnote, set the page number in italic or boldface type or add an appropriate notation after the page number. On the first page of the index, explain any notations that are included with page numbers.

>*   indicates diagram or graph
>fn   indicates footnote material
>hn   indicates headnote material
>Carbohydrates
>   citric acid cycle, 325 hn, 329*
>   metabolic interrelationships, 210 fn

AUTHOR INDEX

Honor the author's spelling of his or her name. List the family name first. Given names are usually indicated by their initials. However, when family name and initials are the same for two authors, spell out the first given name of each.

> Glover, L. M.
> Goldsmith, R. K.
> Hamilton, James F.
> Hamilton, Joseph F.
> Henry, B. D.
> Lyons, N. S.

If two names are alike except that one is followed by "Jr." or a roman number, include both names unless it is clear that they refer to the same individual.

> Hamilton, J. F.
> Hamilton, J. F., III

When "Jr." and a roman numeral occur with otherwise like names, the name with the "Jr." is given precedence. (Note: A comma *always* precedes "Jr." but precedes a roman numeral only when the name is inverted.)

> Hamilton, J. F., Jr.
> Hamilton, J. F., II

ALPHABETIZATION

The letter-by-letter method of alphabetization is preferred, even when the index contains compound family names, as in the list below.

de Blois, L. T.	Macaboy, D. M.
Dela Rosa, C. M.	Mac Adams, G.
De La Rosa, R. E.	MacAdams, P. W.
De Lave, J.	Macpherson, J. R.
de la Viez, L. M.	Mac Pherson, K. W.
Dell'Aria, D. P.	McKay, F. D.
Delmont, P. K.	Mc Kay, N. E.
Del Solar, D. V.	Merrill, R. S.
De Luca, A. R.	
Dent, C. E.	VandenHuevel, P.
d'Epagnier, E.	VanDen Huevel, T. A.
des Cognets, J. P.	vanDer Burgh, K.
Du Pont, F. I.	van der Tak, B. P.
du Pont, M.	van Schaick, H. G.
Dupont, T. M.	Van Suteren, A. N.
	Vogel, A. H.
La Porte, P. H.	von Hoffmann, A. H.
Lavoisier, A.	vonHoffmann, R.
Le Nard, G. R.	Von Hoffmann, T. D.
L'Esperance, J. M.	

TRANSPOSITION

The prefix, or particle, in a few compound surnames may be transposed by the indexer: the French "de" (or "d' "), the Dutch "van," and the German "im," "von," "zu," "zum," and "zur."

L. van Beethoven	Beethoven, L. van
L. T. de Blois	Blois, L. T. de
E. d'Epagnier	Epagnier, E. d'
H. G. van Schaick	Schaick, H. G. van
T. D. Von Hoffmann	Hoffmann, T. D. Von

In other compound names, the position of the prefix(es) is never changed.

R. E. De La Rosa	De La Rosa, R. E.
J. P. des Cognets	des Cognets, J. P.
F. I. Du Pont	Du Pont, F. I.
P. H. La Porte	La Porte, P. H.
G. Mac Adams	Mac Adams, G.
F. D. McKay	McKay, F. D.

For information on transposition of other compound names of arabic or oriental origins, *see* chapter 5, pages 50–53.

LITERATURE CITED: Indexing

1. American National Standards Institute. Basic criteria for indexes, Z39.4-1968(R1974). New York: American National Standards Institute; 1974.
2. Anderson, M. D. Book indexing. London: Cambridge Univ. Press; 1971.
3. Knight, G. N., editor. The art of indexing. Winchester, MA; Allen & Unwin, Inc; 1979.
4. The Merck index. 9th ed. Windholz, M., ed. Rahway, NJ: Merck & Co., Inc.; 1976.

General style conventions

Many conventions in punctuation, word structure, abbreviations, and for reporting numbers are common to all scientific and nonscientific fields. These conventions are presented here, with emphasis on those with special importance for scientific writing. Additional guidance can be found in chapter 13, Style in Special Fields, and in the sources described in chapter 17, Useful References with Annotations.

PUNCTUATION

The following rules for punctuation are based on widely accepted practices. The present tendency is to avoid unnecessary punctuation; however, in scientific writing it is better to over-punctuate than to risk misinterpretation. Proper punctuation signals the relationship among words or word groups; it does not substitute for logical word order. A writer who has trouble punctuating a sentence should examine its construction; the sentence may need to be rewritten or divided into two or more sentences.

PERIOD

The period ("full stop" in British usage) has two principal functions: to indicate a full stop, when placed after a group of words, or to indicate an abbreviation, when placed after letters or part of a word. Other functions include its use as ellipsis marks, raised period, superscript period, and as a decimal point with numerals.

Use a period
1) After a declarative sentence.

   The titmouse is common in Illinois.

2) After an imperative sentence.

   Filter the solution.

3) With an abbreviation for the name of a state (but not with official

zip code abbreviations for states, *see* table 12.2, page 143), month, day of the week, or a person's given name(s).

N.C.   Jan.   Thurs.   S. A. Forbes

4) With an abbreviation in which omission of the period(s) might cause confusion.

fig.   ed.   c.o.d.   anon.   no.

5) With an abbreviation for a Latin term.

e.g.   i.e.   no.   sp.nov.   et al.

6) With an abbreviation for nontechnical words commonly abbreviated.

Jr.   Sr.   Ave.   St.   B.C.

7) At the end of a run-in sideheading (in some publications).
8) After elements of abbreviations for academic degrees and honors.

B.Sc.   Ph.D.   F.R.S.

9) At the end of certain groups of elements in bibliographic references (*see* chapter 5, References).

Place the period (special situations)

1) Inside the closing double quotation marks in a sentence ending with a quoted word, even though the period is not part of the quotation.
2) Outside single quotation marks.
3) Inside the closing parenthesis or bracket when the parenthetical matter is an independent sentence.

   The first rat died. (It had refused to eat.)

4) Outside the closing parenthesis or bracket when the parenthetical matter is a dependent element at the end of a sentence.

   The first rat died (the one that had refused to eat).

5) After ellipsis marks when the omitted material is at the end of a sentence (*see* below).

Do not use a period

1) With the capital-letter abbreviation of the formal name of the United States or the Soviet Union, a U.S. government agency, a society, an international agency, or a compass direction.

USA   NIH   CBE   WHO   N

USSR   FDA   AAAS   UNESCO   SE

2) With the symbol for a chemical element or the letters of a contraction for a chemical, biological, or medical expression.

> Ar ACTH CNS
> B DNA EEG
> Cl tRNA RBC

3) With a lowercase contraction or abbreviation (except Latin) commonly acceptable in scientific or technical writing.

> concn diam exp log
> sin satd mol mol wt

4) With an abbreviation for a unit of measure.

> Å cm °C mg g nm

5) After a period that follows an abbreviation at the end of a sentence.
6) After a title, heading, subheading, equation, or formula standing separate from the text.
7) After an entry in a table (unless the entry is, or ends with, an abbreviation that requires a period).
8) After an item in a list (unless the item is a complete sentence, completes a sentence whose beginning is the heading of the list, or ends with an abbreviation that requires a period).

ELLIPSIS MARKS

Use three ellipsis marks (spaced periods)

1) To indicate omission of a word or group of words within quoted material.

> "Laboratory findings . . . were similar in three patients."

2) To indicate that words have been omitted from the end of a sentence within quoted material; place the ellipsis marks before the period.

> "Platelet serotonin release is only one manifestation . . . ."

3) To indicate the omission of one or more paragraphs from quoted material; use an entire line of spaced periods.

Do not use ellipsis marks

1) If you have implied by use of quotation marks that you have omitted words.

> Smith characterized the outbreak as "the heaviest infestation" he had seen in 1975.

2) If the context indicates that some of the words have been omitted.

Morgan stated that a science writer "must consider whether his meaning will be clear to students of literature."

Use of the lowercase *m* in *must* implies that the first part of the sentence has been omitted. If "to students of literature" were omitted, the sentence should end thus: will be clear . . . ."

RAISED PERIOD

Use a raised (centered) period

1) To indicate multiplication if space does not permit use of the multiplication sign or if closed-up or thin-spaced symbols are unsatisfactory.

$$k \cdot g(a + 2) \quad \text{instead of} \quad k \times g(a + 2)$$

2) For water of hydration in a chemical formula.

$$Na_2B_4O_7 \cdot 10H_2O$$

3) For associating base pairs of nucleotides—for example, guanine and cytosine.

$$G \cdot C$$

4) For an ellipsis in mathematical matter (to align with a sign of operation).

$$x_1 + x_2 + \cdots x_n \qquad x_1, x_2, \cdots, x_n$$

5) To indicate multiplication when necessary to show the product of two or more units of measure. For example, the unit of electric charge, the coulomb (C), is the product of the units of current (ampere, A) and time (second, s):

$$1 C = 1 A \cdot s$$

Similarly, the unit for work, energy, and quantity of heat, the joule (J), is the product of the units for force (newton, N) and length (metre, m).

$$1 J = 1 N \cdot m$$

In preparing the typescript, do not space before or after a raised period in chemical or mathematical matter except when ellipsis is indicated. The copy editor may instruct the printer to center the period between the nearest characters, with a small amount of space (hair space, thin space) before and after it.

SUPERSCRIPT PERIOD

In some systems of symbols, a period is placed over a symbol to convert the symbol to a unit of rate. For example, in the system of symbols for respiratory physiology (*see* chapter 13, pages 208–209), V, for volume of gas, becomes V̇, volume of gas per unit of time; Q, for volume of blood, becomes Q̇, blood volume per unit of time.

COMMA

The comma separates elements of a sentence and helps to group words, phrases, and clauses for clarity and for ease and speed in reading. Placed at the end of a long introductory phrase or clause, it helps locate the subject, which usually follows closely.

Use a comma

1) To separate two independent clauses joined by a coordinating conjunction (and, but, neither, nor, or), except as in item 1 under Do not use a comma. *See also* item 2 under Use a semicolon.
2) To set off an introductory clause begun with a subordinating conjunction (if, although, since, when, where, while, because), except as in item 2 under Do not use a comma.
3) To set off an introductory phrase, to prevent misreading.

   In all, eight experiments were performed.

4) To separate a nonrestrictive (nondefining) clause or phrase from the rest of the sentence. (A nonrestrictive element gives information that is not essential for identification of the subject; *see also* That and which, chapter 4, page 41.)
5) To separate a nonrestrictive appositive from the rest of the sentence.

   Raymond Turner, a mammalogist, described the species.

6) To separate the elements (words, phrases, or clauses) of a simple series of more than two. (A comma precedes the *and* or *or*.)

   The tomatoes, beans, and peppers were planted in April.
   The weather was not favorable in the spring, in midsummer, or even in the early fall.
   The tomatoes wilted, the beans died in August, and the peppers bore no fruit.

   If any of the elements contain internal punctuation, separate them with semicolons; *see* item 3 under Use a semicolon.
7) To set off a conjunctive adverb (therefore, thus, still, however, accordingly, moreover, nevertheless, consequently) or a transitional phrase (on the contrary, on the other hand, in fact, after all, in the first place) that introduces a distinct break in continuity of thought.
8) To introduce a short quotation. (A colon is preferable before a long quotation.)

9) To set off contrasted expressions or interdependent antithetical clauses.

> It is orange, not red.
> The greater the risks, the more gratifying will be the result.

10) To set off words, phrases, or clauses placed out of their natural position for emphasis or clarity.

> Keys provide, except in the most specialized works, a useful means of identification.

11) To separate adjacent sets of numbers.

> In 1935, 100 experiments were completed.

12) To separate certain elements within grouped elements of bibliographic references; *see* chapter 5, References.
13) To separate some elements in symbolic descriptions of human chromosome aberrations; *see* chapter 13, page 196.
14) To separate amino acid symbols in amino acid residues of unknown sequence; *see* chapter 13, page 224.

> Gly,Phe,Tyr

Place the comma
1) Inside the closing double quotation marks when a sentence continues beyond the end of the quoted matter, even when the comma is not part of the quotation.
2) Outside single quotation marks.
3) After a period that follows an abbreviation if the sentence requires a comma. (Do not expect the period to do its own work and substitute for the comma also.)
4) Outside a closing parenthesis or bracket.

Do not use a comma
1) Between two independent clauses joined by a coordinating conjunction if the clauses are not complex or unusually long and if absence of the comma does not result in ambiguity.
2) After a short introductory phrase or clause if the comma does not contribute to clarity or speed of reading.
3) Before or after a restrictive (defining) appositive.

> The species *Bombyx mori* was described later.

4) Between digits in a page number, an address, or a year number.

> page 6984   1933 Glenwood Avenue   1066 A.D.

5) To separate digits in groups of threes. Use a thin space (*see* page 128, this chapter).

6) After a title, heading, subheading, equation, or formula standing separate from the text.
7) To separate subject and predicate, except when they are separated by phrases or clauses requiring balancing commas. Punctuate a sentence containing a noun clause or noun phrase as if the clause or phrase were a single word. In the first example below, a noun clause is the object of a verb. No comma separates verb from object or verb from subject except in the third example, in which a prepositional phrase intervenes.

> He said that the bird was a flicker.
> Where the plant grew was fertile ground.
> Where the plant grew, at the bottom of a narrow ravine, was fertile ground.

SEMICOLON

The semicolon is a mark of coordination and therefore should not be used immediately after or before a dependent clause.

Use a semicolon (or semicolons)

1) To separate coordinate clauses not joined by a conjunction.

> I came; I saw; I conquered.

2) To separate coordinate clauses joined by a conjunctive adverb.

> No physician was available; however, the patient recovered.

3) To separate the elements of a complex series, that is, elements containing internal punctuation.

> The tomatoes wilted; the beans, which had been planted early, died in August; and the peppers, a late variety, bore no fruit.

4) To separate certain elements of bibliographic references; *see* chapter 5, References.
5) To separate chromosome numbers in symbolic designations of chromosomal aberrations; *see* chapter 13, pages 191 and 196.
6) To separate symbols for mutant genes in nonhomologous chromosomes of the fruit fly; *see* chapter 13, page 197.

Place the semicolon

1) Outside a closing quotation mark (single or double), parenthesis, or bracket.

Do not use a semicolon

1) After a title, heading, subheading, equation, or formula standing separate from the text.

COLON
Use a colon
1) To introduce a long quotation (use a comma to introduce a short quotation).
2) To introduce a list or enumeration not immediately preceded by a verb or preposition.
3) To emphasize a close relationship in thought between two independent clauses.
4) To separate a complete clause from a following illustrative word, phrase, or clause.
5) To separate the parts of a ratio (equal space before and after colon).
6) To separate certain elements of bibliographic references; *see* chapter 5, References.
7) To symbolize breaks in human chromosomes; *see* chapter 13, page 194.

Place the colon
1) Outside a closing quotation mark (single or double), parenthesis, or bracket.

Do not use a colon
1) After a title, heading, subheading, equation, or formula standing separate from the text.

QUESTION MARK
Use a question mark
1) At the end of a direct question, even if the question is in declarative form.
2) As a mark indicating questionable identification of a chromosome or chromosomal structure; *see* chapter 13, page 195.

Place the question mark
1) Inside a closing double quotation mark if it is part of the quotation, outside if it is not; always outside the single quotation mark.

Do not use a question mark
1) After an indirect question.

EXCLAMATION MARK
The exclamation mark is rarely justified in scientific writing. It is used as a factorial symbol in mathematics.

$$(x - 2)/6!$$

It is also used in botanical writing to indicate specimens that have been examined by the author, *see* chapter 13, page 165.

(BM!, K!, NY!)

DASHES

The three kinds of dashes most often used in printed matter are the em dash (equal to the height of the type, in any type size), the en dash (half the length of the em dash), and the three-em dash. A three-em dash is used in some journals for names of authors in a bibliographic entry if the names are identical to those of a previous entry. In typescripts, however, the names should be repeated. Authors should use hyphens to indicate dashes; a copy editor will mark them appropriately for the printer.

Use an em dash (two hyphens with no space on either side in typescript)
1) To indicate an abrupt break in thought (use sparingly).
2) To isolate parenthetical matter.
3) Within brackets that are within parentheses, for a third level of interpolation.

> (The house sparrow [common in bushes—shun this cumbersome construction—as well as in trees] is a bird.)

Use an en dash (one hyphen with no space on either side in typescript)
1) To indicate range.

> 10–20 mm   pages 6–10   33.9–140.2

Do not use a minus sign or the word *from* with an en dash.

> −4 to −6° C (not −4−−6° C)
> from page 6 to 10 (not, from page 6–10)

PARENTHESES

Use parenthesis marks
1) To enclose comment or explanation that is structurally independent of the sentence (parentheses indicate a greater independence than dashes or commas).
2) To group mathematical expressions.
3) To enclose text citations of references, except in journals using superscript numbers for citations.
4) To enclose the name of the author of the original taxonomic description when a species is transferred to a genus other than the one to which it was originally assigned; *see* chapter 13, pages 159, 174, and 186.

5) To enclose back reference numbers in reversible (bracket) keys; *see* chapter 13, page 161.

6) To enclose chromosome numbers in symbolic representations of animal chromosomal aberrations; *see* chapter 13, page 191.

7) To enclose designations of potential new subclasses of immunoglobulins; *see* chapter 13, page 198.

8) To enclose numerical designations of genetic factors for Gm and Inv; *see* chapter 13, page 198.

9) To enclose elements in inorganic chemical names that must be followed by subscript numbers applying to the entire radical—for example, $(COOH)_3 \cdot 2H_2O$.

10) To enclose roman numerals representing oxidation numbers; *see* chapter 13, page 215.

11) To enclose nonstandard abbreviations that follow the written-out term; *see* page 142, this chapter.

12) To enclose herbarium abbreviations in plant specimen citations; *see* chapter 13, page 164.

Use a closing parenthesis mark

1) To set off the numeral or letter of an enumerated phrase, paragraph, or other element that begins a line, as on this page.

2) In text to set off enumerations so they will not be confused with reference citations or parenthetical absolute values.

   The analytical methods (1, 8, 12) use these steps: 1) . . . , 2) . . . , 3) . . . , 4) . . . .

   Do not label enumerations unless labels are necessary for ease and speed of reading.

Do not use parentheses

1) Within parentheses (*see* Dashes, above, and Brackets, which follows) except for a scientific name and its authority that are in parenthetical matter.

   (*Fryxellia pygmaea* (Correll) Bates)

BRACKETS _____

Use brackets

1) To enclose any matter, including bibliographic details, you have inserted in a quotation.

   "A major concern [for NSF] must be technology assessment."
   "The average seeding effect in the entire region [comprising 100 000 km^2] is a 21% loss of rain."
   "The results of an analysis by Neyman, Scott, and Smith [Science 163:1445–1449] of one carefully conducted experiment were released to the press."

2) To enclose parenthetical material inserted within parentheses.
3) To enclose symbols representing absolute values.
4) To enclose isotopic prefixes in the names of isotopically labeled chemical compounds; *see* chapter 13, page 216.
5) To enclose certain specific properties in descriptions of physical properties of chemical compounds; *see* chapter 13, page 220.

APOSTROPHE

A primary function of the apostrophe is to show possession in nouns. Authors and editors who feel that an inanimate object cannot possess something may wish to change "the leaf's color" to "the color of the leaf" or "leaf color."

Use an apostrophe

1) And *s* to form the possessive of most singular nouns or indefinite pronouns, even if they end in *s* or another sibilant.

> man's   deer's   Mendel's   ibis's   fox's   one's

Exceptions to this rule occur when the addition of an apostrophe and *s* (creating a new syllable) would result in a word that is difficult or awkward to pronounce. Some authors would write "Yates's meteorological studies" and "for conscience's sake"; some would drop the final *s*. The following possessive forms are acceptable to most authors and editors.

> | | |
> |---|---|
> | Charles's law | Archimedes' principle |
> | Berlioz's operas | Euripides' plays |
> | Marx's followers | Jesus' disciples |

If the final *s* or its equivalent in a noun is silent, as in many French names, add an apostrophe and *s* to form the possessive.

> Descartes's essays   Agassiz's lectures

Add the apostrophe to the final element of a compound word.

> someone's pen   someone else's proposal

2) And *s* to form the possessive of a plural noun not ending in a sibilant.

> | | | |
> |---|---|---|
> | men's | children's | addenda's |
> | media's | deer's | brothers-in-law's |

3) Alone (not followed by an *s*) to form the possessive of a plural noun ending in a sibilant.

> | | |
> |---|---|
> | eyewitnesses' accounts | old wives' tales |
> | the Adamses' papers | scientists' opinions |

4) And *s* to form the plural of a letter, numeral, symbol, a word used as an example word, and abbreviations that retain periods.

i's   A's   B's   7's   ♂'s
the *which*'s and *that*'s   D.Sc.'s   I.Q.'s

5) To indicate the omission of a letter or letters in some common contractions (most of them undesirable in scientific writing).

ass'n   att'y   cont'd   rec'd
you're   he's   she's   it's

Do not use an apostrophe
1) With a personal pronoun in the possessive case.

her   hers   their   theirs   its

2) With a possessive *s* in the first element of a well-established geographic name in the United States (a British geographic name is likely to retain the apostrophe).

Buzzards Bay   Pikes Peak   Woods Hole
Land's End (England)   St. John's (Newfoundland)

3) In the name of an organization in which the qualifying term is treated as an adjective rather than as a possessive noun.

Authors League of America (*but* Showmen's League of America)
Teachers College (*but* Woman's Christian Temperance Union)

4) With eponyms, in some journals.

Raynaud disease   Babinski sign

HYPHEN
Use a hyphen
1) Between the numerator and the denominator of a spelled-out fraction, unless either is already hyphenated.

one-third   five thirty-seconds   thirty-two hundredths

2) To indicate range in typescripts (a copy editor will mark the hyphen for an en dash; *see* Dashes, this chapter).
3) To represent single bonds in chemical or molecular formulas or names.
4) Between C (for carbon) and the numeral designating a particular carbon atom, as in C-3; *see* chapter 13, page 216.
5) Between amino acid symbols in amino acid residues of known sequence; *see* chapter 13, page 224.
6) Between a prefix that specifies molecular configuration, or that serves as a locant, and the name of the chemical compound; *see* chapter 13, pages 217 and 218.
7) In certain compound words; *see* Compound terms, this chapter.

QUOTATION MARKS

The rules given below are those of American usage. Many British authors and editors use single quotation marks to enclose primary quotations and double quotation marks to enclose secondary quotations.

Use double quotation marks

1) For a direct, primary quotation (never indirect quotations).
2) To set off a tertiary quotation (a quotation within a quotation within a quotation).
3) For the title of an article, the title of a chapter or other part of a book, or the title of a series, except when the title is in a bibliographic list.
4) For a new technical term, or an old term applied in a new or unusual sense, unless the journal style calls for italicizing such a term.

Place quotation marks

1) At the beginning of each paragraph of quoted text; if the quotation is of more than one paragraph, close the quotation by a quotation mark at the end of the last paragraph only. (Long quotations may be set in smaller type or narrower measure, or both, in which case quotation marks may not be needed.)
2) Outside of a comma or a period, even if it is not part of the quotation.
3) Inside of a semicolon or colon.
4) Outside of any other punctuation mark if it is part of the quotation, inside if it is not.

Use single quotation marks

1) To enclose a secondary quotation (quoted matter within a quotation).
2) For the names of plant cultivars; *see* chapter 13, page 158.

All punctuation belongs outside the single quotation mark.

SLANT LINE

The slant line (also called solidus, virgule, diagonal, stroke, slash, or shilling mark) is a mathematical sign of operation (meaning "divided by") as well as a substitute for *per* (a preposition that means "for each").

Use a slant line

1) As a mathematical sign for division ($1/4 = \frac{1}{4}$).
2) To show rates (5 m/s) or concentrations (20 mol/litre). Observe the rules of mathematics if more than one slant line or *per* occurs in an expression; *see* Raised period, this chapter.

3) To indicate division when necessary to show the quotient of two or more units of measure.

m/s   metre per second
kg·m/s²   kilogram-metre per second squared (≡ newton)
lm/m²   lumen per square metre (≡ lux)
N/m²   newton per square metre
N·s/m²   newton-second per square metre

4) To separate symbols for mutant genes on homologous chromosomes of the fruit fly; *see* chapter 13, page 190.
5) To separate the two symbols of female genotype designations for glucose-6-phosphate dehydrogenase; *see* chapter 13, page 203.

Do not use a slant line
1) To express a ratio, as in a description of a buffer solution.
2) As shorthand for *per* if more than one occurs in a measurement. The expression "1.5 pCi/km²/yr" is mathematically ambiguous. To abbreviate with mathematical correctness the measurement 1.5 picocuries per square kilometre per year, use one of the following forms.

$$1.5 \text{ pCi} \cdot \text{km}^{-2} \cdot \text{yr}^{-1}$$
$$1.5 \text{ pCi}/(\text{km}^2 \cdot \text{yr})$$

DIACRITICAL MARKS

Write on your typescript any required diacritical mark not easily available on a typewriter. Identify any mark that might be misinterpreted; write its name, with a circle around it, in the nearest margin. Several common diacritical marks (diacritics) are shown in table 12.1.

A foreign word accepted into English may or may not lose its diacritic; *facade* has lost its cedilla, but *garçon* retains it. The spelling of some adopted words has been adjusted to reflect the accepted pronunciation: *canyon* for *cañon*. If a foreign place name containing a diacritic has an English equivalent, use it: *Cologne* (not *Köln*); *Nuremberg* (not *Nürnberg*).

Because few printers have type for all the characters with diacritics, substitutes may be needed. For the umlaut in a German word, but not a family name, substitute the plain letter followed by *e*: Write *ueber* for *über* and *Blaetter* for *Blätter*.

In Scandinavian languages, the ringed *Å* and *å* were once *Aa* and *aa* and are sometimes so spelled today. An umlaut over an *o* is sometimes substituted for the stød, but in a proper name it is often omitted: *Sørensen* may be spelled *Sörensen* but more often it is spelled *Sorensen*.

SERIES AND ENUMERATIONS

A series consists of three or more items that range in complexity from

Table 12.1. Diacritical marks used in European languages

Mark	Name	Example*
°	circled *or* ringed	Ångstrom
´	acute accent	beauté
`	grave accent	le congrès
،	cedilla	garçon
؛	inverted cedilla	Dąbrowa
^	circumflex	bâtir
ˇ	inverted circumflex	Čechoslovaca
¨	dieresis	naïvement
˘	kratkaya *or* breve	Omskiĭ
⁻	macron	Kyūshū
'	soft sign	Krasil'nikov
/	slash *or* stød	København
/	stroke	społka
·	superior dot	Skarżysko
~	tilde	español
¨	umlaut	für Anfänger

* Any word from a language not based on the Latin alphabet has been transliterated.

single words to phrases, sentences, or paragraphs. The elements in a series or enumeration must have parallel construction. The following sentence is not properly constructed because the last element is not part of the series.

> The mixture was heated, shaken, centrifuged, and the supernatant fluid frozen.

The sentence can be corrected by making the last element a coordinate clause.

> The mixture was heated, shaken, and centrifuged; the supernatant fluid was frozen.

The elements in a series may be kept in proper order by punctuation; indicative words such as *and, then, when, afterward,* and *finally*; ordinals (*first, second* . . .); or numerals, letters, or both.

  1) Use commas to separate the elements of a simple series (the lowest level of complexity).

> The mixture was heated, shaken, and centrifuged.
> The mixture was heated at 40° C, shaken at 30 Hz, and centrifuged at 18 000 *g*.

  2) Use semicolons to punctuate a series at the second level of complexity, as in a sentence with clauses that contain internal punctuation.

> The mixture was heated, shaken, and centrifuged; the pellet was discarded; and the supernatant fluid was quick-frozen and stored for 3 days at −10° C.

3) To differentiate between levels of complexity in a series, enumerate
the main elements (which may be either independent clauses or
sentences) with lowercase roman numerals, arabic numerals, or
lowercase letters (italic or roman) in single parentheses or in accordance with the style of the journal.

1), 2), 3)   i), ii), iii)

a), *b*), *c*)   a), b), c)

The use of numerals or letters in complex series does not preclude
their use in simple series if they are deemed necessary for clarity
or for ease or speed of reading.

4) For a complex series in which paragraphs are the elements, begin
each paragraph with an arabic numeral and a closing parenthesis
mark.

1)   2)   3)

COMPOUND TERMS

A compound term is a combination of two or more words that through
use together have acquired a special meaning.

bluebird (a bird of the genus *Sialia*)

The words *blue bird* written separately have no special meaning. They
might refer to a blue jay, an indigo bunting, or a kingfisher.

Not all compound terms are written as one word—for example, wood
duck, half-cell. A few compound words that would otherwise be written
as one word are hyphenated to prevent a confusing sequence of letters
or a confusion of ideas (freeze-dry, red-ear sunfish). Compound common
names of plants and animals may be hyphenated, run together, or written
as two words according to rules governing taxonomy (*see* chapter 13,
pages 156 and 187). Consult an appropriate dictionary.

General rules for writing compound words are given below. For more
detailed information, *see* pages 30a and 31a under "The Writing of
Compounds" in *Webster's Third New International Dictionary* (9) and pages
176–179 of the *Chicago Manual of Style* (7).

1) A compound term derived from two or more nouns is usually
written as two words if the elements are accented equally (buffalo
fish, oak wilt, subject matter), is one word when one of the elements
has lost its accent (northwest, pineapple, paperback), and is hyphenated when one or both elements are terms of measurement (gram-
centimetre, light-year, but gram atom, gram molecule).

2) A compound term in which the second element (noun or pronoun)
is the direct object of a verb is usually one word (killjoy, lockjaw,

carryall) unless confusing combinations of letters result, when a hyphen is indicated (cure-all). A compound consisting solely of verbs is usually hyphenated (has-been, might-have-been).

3) A phrase containing a participle (present or past) or an adjective may be hyphenated as a compound when it precedes the word modified and written without a hyphen when it follows.

> A well-known method was followed.
> The method followed was well known.
> He began the small-bird study in 1969.
> He began the study of small birds in 1969.

4) A compound modifier containing a numeral or spelled-out number is usually hyphenated.

> two-thirds majority   two 30-mm rods
> a can of 10-ml pipettes   a 1-min exposure

5) An open compound noun that is well established and widely known in its field is usually not hyphenated even when it functions as an adjective preceding the word it modifies. In this category are names of many chemicals, diseases, animals, insects, and plants.

> amino acid sequences   stem rust control
> blue jay migration   chinch bug damage

6) A two-word modifier containing an adverb ending in -*ly* is not hyphenated.

> a naturally occurring substance
> a carefully preserved specimen

7) Many compounds derived from an adverb and a verb, or from a preposition and a noun, are written as one word, particularly those that might cause confusion if written as two words.

> underdeveloped   feedback   everblooming
> undercurrent   input   afterpotential
> downstream   uphill   overdosage

DERIVATIVES

A word formed from a base element and one of many prefixes (*anti, non, pre, re, semi, un*) or suffixes (*ful, ize, less, like*) usually is written as one word. More detailed information is given on pages 23a to 25a under "Derivatives" in *Webster's Third* (9). Exceptions to the general practice are derivative terms:

1) That if written as one word might have a confusing juxtaposition of letters (anti-icer, intra-abdominal, semi-independent).

2) In which the base element begins with a capital letter (mid-March, trans-Ural)—but transatlantic and Precambrian.
3) Containing a prefix that governs two or more words (pre-Ice Age)—the editor may mark the hyphen for an en dash.
4) Containing a prefix that, if written as one word with the base element, would be confused with another word (re-strain, restrain; un-ionized, unionized).
5) Containing a suffix that with the base element forms a succession of three identical letters (cell-like, hull-less).

ABBREVIATIONS AND SYMBOLS

An *abbreviation* is a shortened version of a word or phrase formed by the omission of letters or words. An *acronym* is a word formed from the initial letter, or letters, of each of the successive parts, or major parts, of a compound term. No distinction is made between abbreviations and acronyms in this manual, and they are collectively termed abbreviations. A *symbol* is an arbitrary or conventional sign related to a particular field and used to represent operations, quantities, elements, relations, or qualities.

TEXT
Abbreviations and symbols save space and, when used with discretion in text, simplify complex expressions. If overused they slow down the rate of reading or make an article unintelligible. Use symbols that are standard for units of measure, with attention to the requirements of the particular journal. In many fields such as immunology, numerous abbreviations have been introduced in recent years and have gained acceptance in the science. Abbreviations not accepted without explanation by the journal should be defined at first mention by following the written-out term with the abbreviation enclosed in parentheses.

lactate dehydrogenase (LDH)

Use only widely accepted forms for abbreviations (*see* chapter 14). Do not start a sentence with a nonacronymic abbreviation or a symbol.

TITLES, ABSTRACTS, FIGURES, TABLES
It is best to avoid using abbreviations in titles and abstracts because of the indexing difficulties that result from this practice. However, some publishers now accept a limited number of specific abbreviations in titles (e.g., DNA, RNA). In the abstract, any abbreviations that seem necessary to use should be defined just as in the main text (*see* preceding paragraph). Abbreviations and symbols not sanctioned by the editorial policy of the

journal but that are used in tables and figures must be defined in footnotes or legends.

GEOGRAPHIC AND GEOLOGIC NAMES ────────────

Abbreviate the name of a state, territory, province, or district (but not a county) only when it is preceded by the name of a city or town. The two-letter state and territory abbreviations of the U.S. Postal Service (8) are now widely used, with or without zip codes; older conventional abbreviations are given in *Webster's Third International Dictionary*. Abbreviations of state and territory names in U.S. postal addresses must be those approved by the U.S. Postal Service for use with zip codes (table 12.2).

Philadelphia, Pa. Philadelphia, PA Philadelphia, PA 19104
Philadelphia County, Pennsylvania Mexico City, D.F.
Victoria, B.C. St. Thomas, VI

The names of countries are usually spelled out in text, with the exception of USSR for the Soviet Union. When used adjectivally as in government

Table 12.2. U.S. Postal Service state and territory abbreviations

Alabama AL	Montana MT
Alaska AK	Nebraska NE
American Samoa AS	Nevada NV
Arizona AZ	New Hampshire NH
Arkansas AR	New Jersey NJ
California CA	New Mexico NM
Canal Zone CZ	New York NY
Colorado CO	North Carolina NC
Connecticut CT	North Dakota ND
Delaware DE	Ohio OH
District of Columbia DC	Oklahoma OK
Florida FL	Oregon OR
Georgia GA	Pennsylvania PA
Guam GU	Puerto Rico PR
Hawaii HI	Rhode Island RI
Idaho ID	South Carolina SC
Illinois IL	South Dakota SD
Indiana IN	Tennessee TN
Iowa IA	Texas TX
Kansas KS	Trust Territories TT
Kentucky KY	Utah UT
Louisiana LA	Vermont VT
Maine ME	Virginia VA
Maryland MD	Virgin Islands VI
Massachusetts MA	Washington WA
Michigan MI	West Virginia WV
Minnesota MN	Wisconsin WI
Mississippi MS	Wyoming WY
Missouri MO	

agencies, departments, organizations, or possessions, United States may be abbreviated.

U.S. Postal Service   U.S. Geological Survey

Do not abbreviate an English translation of a foreign geographic name: Bonn, B.R.D. (Bundesrepublik Deutschland), *not* Bonn, F.R.G. (Federal Republic of Germany). Do not abbreviate the name of a division of the earth's surface, a continent, region, mountain or a mountain range, ocean, sea, lake, or river.

Arctic Circle	Africa	Sahara
South Pole	South America	Middle West
Mount Killington	Pacific Ocean	Lake Michigan
the Himalayas	Red Sea	Hudson River

To indicate stratigraphic and time divisions on maps, use the symbols of the U.S. Geological Survey; *see* chapter 13, page 227.

UNITS OF MEASUREMENT

Use the abbreviation or symbol for a unit of measurement in text only if the unit is preceded by a number; the same abbreviation or symbol is used for the singular and for the plural form of the unit (*see* Metric and decimal systems, this chapter; and chapter 14, Abbreviations and Symbols). Spell out the name of a unit of measurement that follows a spelled-out number, as at the start of a sentence.

Ten milligrams is the lethal dose.

Use the decimal system, or multiples of 10, for units of concentration.

0.1 M or 0.1 mol/litre (not M/10)

Conventional signs and symbols are permitted in the text with units of measurement; thus, the slant line (/) can substitute for *per* (*see* Slant line, this chapter) and % for percent when preceded by a numeral. Do not use such ambiguous symbols and terms as "20 milligrams percent" (20 mg %). Use instead, as appropriate:

20 mg/100 ml *or* 20 mg/dl *or* 0.2 kg/m^3
20 mg/100 mg *or* 200 g/kg
20 mg/100 g *or* 200 mg/kg

TAXONOMIC NAMES

A scientific name usually consists of a generic name followed by a specific epithet. A generic name is abbreviated only when it is followed by a specific epithet; spell out a generic name in a title and on first mention in text; thereafter it may be abbreviated, if the context makes it clear. Specific epithets should not stand alone, except in special circumstances (as in tables of species of a single genus) and are never abbreviated. For examples of proper forms for abbreviating taxonomic names, *see* chapter 13, page 174.

WRITING ABBREVIATIONS

Do not letterspace the capital-letter abbreviation (acronym) of, for example, a chemical expression, organization or governmental group, or the name of a time zone.

> CBE for Council of Biology Editors
> CDC for Centers for Disease Control
> EST for Eastern Standard Time
> NIH for National Institutes of Health

Space the parts of a lowercase abbreviation of a compound term only if no period is between them.

> mol wt   sp gr   et al.
> e.g.   i.d.   o.d.

Lowercase abbreviations of many compound terms are written without periods and without spaces between the parts:

> bp dpm emf ppm rem

REPORTING NUMBERS

In reporting a number, the number of significant digits must be commensurate with the precision of your experimental method. If the quantity must be converted to SI units (*see* page 149, this chapter), multiply the quantity by the exact conversion factor and then round to the appropriate number of significant digits. Use the following procedure for rounding a number in which, for example, four significant digits are to be retained.

1) If the digit to the right of the fourth digit is less than 5, leave the fourth digit unchanged.

> 4.1282 rounds to 4.128

2) If the digit to the right of the fourth digit is greater than 5, increase the fourth digit by 1.

> 4.1286 rounds to 4.129

3) If the digit to the right of the fourth digit is exactly 5, followed only by zeros, and the fourth digit is even, leave the fourth digit unchanged.

> 4.1285 rounds to 4.128
> 4.12850 rounds to 4.128

If the fourth digit is odd, increase the fourth digit by 1.

> 4.1275 rounds to 4.128
> 4.12750 rounds to 4.128

4) If the digit to the right of the fourth digit is 5 and there is at least one digit other than 0 to the right of the 5, increase the fourth digit by 1.

> 4.12851 rounds to 4.129
> 4.12751 rounds to 4.128

For rounding an inconveniently large number, follow a similar procedure. The number 2 645 381, for example, can be expressed as 2.6 million. For additional discussion of how to report numbers, see the CODATA publication, *Biologists' Guide for the Presentation of Numerical Data in the Primary Literature* (4) and the *Standard for Metric Practice* (1) issued by the American Society for Testing and Materials.

WRITING NUMBERS

Unless otherwise stipulated in the journal, follow the rules given below for writing numbers in text.
1) In numbers consisting of two to four digits, the numerals are run together: 1000, 2568.
2) In numbers consisting of more than four digits, leave one space between each group of three, going in either direction from the decimal point (5). A copy editor will insert a mark for a *thin space*.

> 26 000   423 000 000   1 000 523

3) Use a numeral or numerals:
For expressing any number that immediately precedes a standard unit of measure (abbreviated).

> 3 g   18 mm   300 m^2

For a date, an expression of time, a page number, a percentage, a decimal quantity, or a numerical designation.

> 7 January 1971   the time is 0815   27 percent *or* 27%
> page 1079   37.6   a magnification of 50

For a number implying arithmetical manipulation.

> 18 multiplied by 2   a factor of 2

For numbers grouped for comparison or having statistical implications.

4) In most situations not mentioned above, use words for numbers one through nine and numerals for larger numbers:

two dogs   nine rabbits   14 parts   29 trees

In a series containing some numbers of 10 or more and some less than 10, use numerals for all (in the example below, the series is trees).

The 7 apple trees, 9 peach trees, and 20 plum trees were given six applications of dust.

5) Treat ordinal numbers as you would cardinal numbers.

third   fourth   33rd   54th

6) In writing a large number ending in several zeros, either substitute a word for part of the number or add an appropriate prefix to a basic unit of measurement.

1.6 million (*not* 1 600 000)

23 μg (*not* 0.000 023 g)

7) Do not begin a sentence with a numeral; spell out the numeral, reword the sentence, or end the preceding sentence with a semi-colon.

REPORTING TIME

Two time systems are in common use throughout the world. In one, the hours of the day (the period of the earth's rotation on its axis) are numbered consecutively, 1 through 24. In the other, they are divided into two periods of 12 hours each, the first numbered 1:00 through 12:00 (before noon, a.m.) and the second 1:00 through 12:00 (after noon, p.m.).

Scientists should adopt the 24-hour time system, which is indicated by four digits—the first two for hours and the last two for minutes. The day begins at midnight, denoted 0000, and the last minute of the day is 2359. Thus, 0830 is the same as 8:30 a.m., 1230 the same as 12:30 pm., and 2315 the same as 11:15 p.m. The notation *2400 of 10 June* designates the same instant of time as *0000 of 11 June*.

The 12-hour a.m. and p.m. time system sometimes leads to confusion. The term *12:00* can mean noon or midnight. The term *midnight of 10 June* is also ambiguous, since it could refer either to midnight of 9–10 June or to midnight of 10–11 June.

METRIC AND DECIMAL SYSTEMS

The metric system for measurements and weights is recommended in scientific writing because of its worldwide acceptance. Metric equivalents of weights and measures commonly used in the United States and Canada are given in table 12.3. In accordance with action taken by the Twelfth General Assembly of the International Union of Biological Sciences in Rome, 12 to 14 April 1955, the decimal system rather than fractions should be used in scientific publications.

Although there are several metric systems of measure, including the centimetre-gram-second system and the metre-kilogram-second system, these systems are gradually being replaced by a modernized metric system, the Système International d'Unités (SI). The new system provides unambiguous symbols, standard in all languages. Adoption of the system is advocated by most scientists.

The SI is constructed from seven base units for independent quantities plus two supplementary units for plane and solid angles (table 12.4). Other units in the SI are derived from these base and supplementary units. Some of the derived units have been assigned special names and symbols (table 12.5).

Table 12.3. Units of measurement and weight commonly used in the United States and Canada, and metric equivalents

Common	Metric	Common	Metric
inch	2.54 cm	calorie	4.1868 joule
foot	30.48 cm	pint, U.S. liquid	
yard	0.914 m	(16 oz)	0.473 litre
fathom (2 yd)	1.829 m	quart	
rod (5½ yd)	5.029 m	U.S. liquid (32 fl oz)	0.946 litre
furlong		U.S. dry (2 pt)	1.101 litre
(220 yd)	201.17 m	imperial (40 U.K. fl oz)	1.136 litre
mile		gallon	
statute		U.S. (4 qt)	3.785 litre
(1760 yd)	1.609 km	imperial	4.546 litre
nautical		peck, dry	
(2026 yd)	1.853 km	U.S. (8 qt)	8.810 litre
knot	1.853 km/h	imperial	9.092 litre
square inch	6.452 cm^2	bushel, dry	
square foot	0.093 m^2	U.S. (4 pk)	35.24 litre
square yard	0.836 m^2	imperial	36.37 litre
square rod	25.29 m^2	pound	
square mile		avdp (16 oz)	453.592 g
(640 acres)	2.59 km^2	troy (12 oz)	373.24 g
acre	0.4047 hec-	ounce	
	tares	avdp (16 dr)	28.35 g
cubic inch	16.387 cm^3	troy (480 gr)	31.103 g
cubic foot		dram, avdp	1.772 g
(1728 in^3)	0.028 m^3	grain	0.065 g
cubic yard		carat (precious stones)	0.200 g
(27 ft^3)	0.7646 m^3	ton	
board foot		long (2240 lb)	1.016 t
(144 in^3)	0.0024 m^3	short (2000 lb)	0.907 t
cord			
(128 ft^3)	3.625 m^3		

Table 12.4. SI units and symbols

Units	Quantity	Name	Symbol
Base	Length	metre	m
	Mass	kilogram	kg
	Time	second	s
	Electric current	ampere	A
	Thermodynamic temperature	kelvin	K
	Amount of substance	mole	mol
	Luminous intensity	candela	cd
Supplementary	Plane angle	radian	rad
	Solid angle	steradian	sr

Table 12.5. Derived SI units with special names and symbols

Quantity	Name of unit	Symbol for unit	Formula and definition of unit in terms of base or supplementary units
Frequency	hertz	Hz	$(\text{cycle})/s = s^{-1}$
Force	newton	N	$m \cdot kg \cdot s^{-2}$
Pressure, stress	pascal	Pa	$N/m^2 = m^{-1} \cdot kg \cdot s^{-2}$
Energy, work, quantity of heat	joule	J	$N \cdot m = m^2 \cdot kg \cdot s^{-2}$
Power, radiant flux	watt	W	$J/s = m^2 \cdot kg \cdot s^{-3}$
Quantity of electricity, electric charge	coulomb	C	$s \cdot A$
Electric potential, potential difference, electromotive force	volt	V	$W/A = m^2 \cdot kg \cdot s^{-3} \cdot A^{-1}$
Capacitance	farad	F	$C/V = m^{-2} \cdot kg^{-1} \cdot s^4 \cdot A^2$
Electric resistance	ohm	Ω	$V/A = m^2 \cdot kg \cdot s^{-3} \cdot A^{-2}$
Conductance	siemens	S	$A/V = m^{-2} \cdot kg^{-1} \cdot s^3 \cdot A^2$
Magnetic flux	weber	Wb	$V \cdot s = m^2 \cdot kg \cdot s^{-2} \cdot A^{-1}$
Magnetic flux density	tesla	T	$Wb/m^2 = kg \cdot s^{-2} \cdot A^{-1}$
Inductance	henry	H	$Wb/A = m^2 \cdot kg \cdot s^{-2} \cdot A^{-2}$
Luminous flux	lumen	lm	$cd \cdot sr$
Illuminance	lux	lx	$lm/m^2 = m^{-2} \cdot cd \cdot sr$
Activity (of a radionuclide)	becquerel	Bq	s^{-1}
Absorbed dose	gray	Gy	$J/kg = m^2 \cdot s^{-2}$
Dose equivalent	sievert	Sv	$J/kg = m^2 \cdot s^{-2}$
Temperature units			
Celsius temperature		°C	$T_{\cdot C} = T_K - 273.15\ K$
Celsius temperature difference or interval		°C	$1\,°C = 1\ K$

Standard prefixes should be used with the SI units to denote quantities larger or smaller than the base and derived units. These prefixes are listed in table 12.6. Use of prefixes denoting multiples of 10^3 or 10^{-3} is recommended. Compound prefixes should be avoided: 1 nm (*not* 1 mμm or 1 μmm). When a prefix is required to provide manageable numbers

Table 12.6. Metric system prefixes, with pronunciation and symbols

Multiple or submultiple		Prefix and pro-nunciation		Symbol
10^{18} =	1 000 000 000 000 000 000	exa	ex'a	E
10^{15} =	1 000 000 000 000 000	peta	pet'a	P
10^{12} =	1 000 000 000 000	tera	ter'a	T
10^{9} =	1 000 000 000	giga	ji'ga	G
10^{6} =	1 000 000	mega	meg'a	M
10^{3} =	1 000	kilo	kil'o	k
10^{2} =	100	hecto	hec'to	h*
10 =	10	deka	dek'a	da*
The unit =	1			
10^{-1} =	0.1	deci	des'i	d*
10^{-2} =	0.01	centi	sen'ti	c*
10^{-3} =	0.001	milli	mil'i	m
10^{-6} =	0.000 001	micro	mi'kro	μ
10^{-9} =	0.000 000 001	nano	nan'o	n
10^{-12} =	0.000 000 000 001	pico	pe'co	p
10^{-15} =	0.000 000 000 000 001	femto	fem'to	f
10^{-18} =	0.000 000 000 000 000 001	atto	at'to	a

*All acceptable in the SI; recommended by SI are only multiples of 10^3 and 10^{-3}.

to express a derived physical quantity, the prefix should usually be attached to the symbol in the numerator: 1 MN/m^2 (*not* 1 N/mm^2). When a prefix is attached to a symbol, in effect a new unit is constituted: 1 km^2 = 1 $(km)^2$ *or* 10^6 m^2, *not* 1 $k(m^2)$ *or* 10^3 m^2. For additional sources of information on SI, *see* Metric and other units, in chapter 17.

STATISTICS

Statistical methods commonly used in the biological sciences (2, 3, 5, 6) do not require presentation of mathematical formulas or bibliographic references. Those infrequently used need not be described in detail, but adequate references should be given. Standard designs are adequately described by name and size—for example, "a 6 × 6 Latin square." For a factorial set of treatments, an adequate description might be:

Tryptophan at 0.05 or 0.10% of the diet and niacin at 5, 10, or 20 mg/kg of diet were used in a 2 × 3 factorial plan arranged in a 6 × 6 Latin square with six animals per plot.

For the report of a drug study having a completely randomized design, the following description of the design might suffice.

Two hundred male patients were assigned to a control group or a treatment group on a random basis. The division was determined by the last digit of the hospital admission number; patients whose numbers ended with an even digit were assigned to the control group and those with numbers ending in odd digits to the treatment group. Each treatment patient was given 2.0-g aspirin tablets every 4 h; each control patient was given the same number of lactose tablets, identical in appearance to the aspirin tablets, in the same schedule.

Emphasize biology, not statistics. A simple statement of the results of statistical analysis should justify the interpretations and conclusions. Do not report a number of similar experiments separately. Adequate reporting may require only the number of data, n; the arithmetic mean, $\bar{x}$; and the standard deviation or the standard error of the mean. Such information may be included in text or table—for example, 324 ± 5.8 (27), in which the first two numbers show the mean plus or minus the standard deviation or standard error (indicate which), and the third number (in parentheses) represents the number of data. If the mean is presented with plus or minus two standard deviations, this information should be given.

Standard deviation refers to the variability in a sample or a population. Standard error (calculated from error variance) is the estimated sampling error of a statistic such as the sample mean. When a standard deviation or standard error is given, the number of degrees of freedom on which it rests should be stated. When any statistical value (as mean or difference of two means) is mentioned, its standard error or confidence limits should usually be given.

For analyses of variance and covariance, a statement of subclass means and their standard errors is insufficient. A table of sources of variation presents concisely many additional items such as mean squares attributable to blocks or to treatment main effects or interactions, and the error mean square(s), with their respective numbers of degrees of freedom.

Give only meaningful digits. A practical rule in statistics is to round so that the change caused by rounding is less than one-tenth of the standard error. Such rounding increases the variance of the reported statistic by less than 1%, sacrificing less than 1% of the relevant information the data contain. This rule is exemplified in the third preceding paragraph, for the statistic and for its standard error.

Conventions in statistical abbreviations vary among authorities. Table 12.7 presents some of the most frequently used symbols and abbreviations. Greek letters (table 12.8) are used for population parameters and roman or italic letters for sample statistics (the estimates of parameters obtained from samples of the populations).

Computer printout of data and pertinent statistical analyses may be suitable as manuscript or typesetter's copy and, if properly planned, may be adequate for photographic reproduction and printing. Use of such printout may reduce errors in transcription of data into typescript.

Authors and editors should cultivate close professional ties with an experienced statistician. Statistical review, requested by an author before

Table 12.7. Symbols and abbreviations currently used in statistics

Population parameters	Sample statistics	Explanation
	n, N	Total number of individuals or variates
μ		Mean of the population
	$\bar{x}$	Arithmetic mean of the sample
σ		Standard deviation of the population
	s, SD	Standard deviation of the sample
σ^2		Variance of the population
	s^2	Sample variance
	$s_{\bar{x}}$, SE	Standard error of mean of sample
	C.V.	Coefficient of variation
	t	Statistical datum derived in Student's t test
	χ^2	Statistical datum derived in the chi-square test
	p, P	Probability of wrongfully rejecting the null hypothesis (level of significance)
β		Regression coefficient of population
	r	Coefficient of correlation, sample
	R	Coefficient of multiple correlation
	F	Variance ratio

Table 12.8. Greek alphabet with Latin and English equivalents

Name of letter	Capital	Lowercase	Latin and English equivalent
alpha	A	α	a
beta	B	β	b
gamma	Γ	γ	g (*or* n)
delta	Δ	δ	d
epsilon	E	ϵ	e
zeta	Z	ζ	z
eta	H	η	$\bar{e}$
theta	Θ	θ	th (*or* t)
iota	I	ι	i
kappa	K	κ	k (*or* c)
lambda	Λ	λ	l
mu	M	μ	m
nu	N	ν	n
xi	Ξ	ξ	x
omicron	O	o	o
pi	Π	π	p
rho	P	ρ	r (*or* rh)
sigma	Σ	σ, s	s
tau	T	τ	t
upsilon	Υ	υ	y (*or* u)
phi	Φ	ϕ	ph (*or* f)
chi	X	χ	ch (*or* kh)
psi	Ψ	ψ	ps
omega	Ω	ω	$\bar{o}$

submission or by an editor afterwards, can improve a majority of papers that present numeric results of research studies.

LITERATURE CITED: General Style Conventions

1. American Society for Testing and Materials. Standard for metric practice. ASTM E 380–79. Philadelphia: American Society for Testing and Materials; 1979.
2. Campbell, R. C. Statistics for biologists. 2d ed. London and New York: Cambridge Univ. Press; 1974.
3. Cochran, W. G.; Snedecor, G. W. Statistical methods. 7th ed. Ames, IA: The Iowa State Univ. Press; 1980.
4. CODATA Task Group on the Presentation of Biological Data in the Primary Literature. Biologists' guide for the presentation of numerical data in the primary literature. CODATA Bulletin 25, Paris: CODATA; 1977. Available from CODATA Secretariat, 51 Boulevard de Montmorency 75016 Paris, France.
5. Colton, T. Statistics in medicine. Boston: Little, Brown and Co.; 1974.
6. Dunn, O. J.; Clark, V. Applied statistics: analysis of variance and regression. New York: John Wiley & Sons; 1974.
7. The University of Chicago Press. The Chicago manual of style. 13th ed. Chicago: The Univ. of Chicago Press; 1982.
8. U.S. Postal Service. 1982 National five digit zip code and Post Office directory. Washington, DC: U.S. Postal Service; 1982.
9. Webster's third new international dictionary of the English language. Unabridged. Springfield, MA: G. & C. Merriam Co.; 1976.

13

Style in special fields

The conventions described in this chapter have been published by international and national scientific associations. A few of these conventions do not have international sanction, but are structurally coherent systems that are widely used. Authors and editors are obligated, by general agreement, to accept the rules governing nomenclature as established by international committees and commissions. The rules for several fields differ in certain basic principles and practices (1) because of usage, and because of inherent differences among plants, microorganisms, and animals. For the convenience of readers, the references to literature cited in each main section of this chapter are listed by section at the end of the chapter.

PLANT SCIENCES

The format for research articles in most branches of botany needs very little explanation here. Taxonomic articles require special forms of presentation for keys to taxa, nomenclatural bibliography, descriptions, and specimen citations.

GENERAL STYLE

Most botanical articles, taxonomic or not, are concerned with certain taxa, and for accuracy in communication the following points may be applicable.

Article titles   The title of a taxonomic article should include the family name of the group under discussion; it may be given within parentheses. Author citations of scientific names should be omitted from the title.

Typographical style   Use italic type for scientific names of genera, species, and their subdivisions. Use roman type for the names of higher rank. Boldface type is often used for a new name (nomen novum) or new combination in the text where it is followed by its validating Latin description or diagnosis or by the bibliographic reference to its basionym (original name applied to the type) or a replaced synonym. Cultivar names are in roman type.

Vernacular names   Many plants are known by their vernacular or common names, as well as by their scientific ones. Most common names are not capitalized, although a name derived from a proper noun may retain the initial capital letter, whether hyphenated or set as two words (Cupid's-dart, Dutchman's-pipe, English ivy). A generic name used as a vernacular name is neither italicized nor capitalized (*Camellia*, camellia; *Iris*, iris; *Rhododendron*, rhododendron), and is pluralized as though English (crocuses, not croci).

The following rules were established by Rickett (22) to bring some consistency to the hyphenating and running together of English names.

1) Words of one or two syllables referring to plants in general or to some part of a plant are joined to a preceding word without a hyphen, unless the resulting word is long and unwieldy or it brings together a collection of consonants that are not readily grasped by a reader (bladderwort, redbud, dogberry, but unicorn-plant, carpenter-weed, partridge-berry).

2) If a second word is itself taxonomically correct, it is not joined or hyphenated to the preceding word (wood lily [because it is a lily], moth mullein, water cress).

3) If a second word is not taxonomically correct it is hyphenated to the preceding word (water-lily [because it is not a lily], skunk-cabbage, poison-oak). Names beginning with "false" are a special case and provide an exception to this principle; "false" indicates that the name is misapplied and therefore a hyphen is not used (false foxglove, false dandelion). "Indian," in its usual application in plant names, is equivalent to "false" (Indian bean is not a bean, Indian cherry is not a cherry).

4) A hyphen is used when the second word is a purely fanciful name (lady's-slipper, cat-tail, shooting-star).

5) Names composed of more than two words are generally hyphenated throughout (star-of-Bethlehem, Jack-in-the-pulpit, Queen-Anne's-lace). The name of a color need not be joined by a hyphen to an already hyphenated name (yellow star-grass is preferable to yellow-star-grass).

Citation of voucher specimens   Cytological, anatomical, or chemical information taken from plant material should be documented by depositing a voucher specimen in a recognized herbarium or culture collection so that future workers can check the determination. The scientific or cultivar name of the organism and the source or collection site should be included in the publication. When several specimens are used in a study they should be listed in a table with the scientific name, locality, collector, collector's identification number, and place of deposit for each specimen (*see* Citation of specimens, below).

NOMENCLATURE

The *International Code of Botanical Nomenclature* (32) provides a precise, stable, and universally accepted system for the application of scientific names to the categories of classification. It covers all plants, both living and fossil, but not bacteria. It consists of 85 articles (including 10 on naming of hybrids) with numerous recommendations, notes, and examples; a guide for the determination of types; and lists of conserved family and generic names. The Code also provides detailed rules governing form and grammar of names at various ranks. Additional information may be found in *An Annotated Glossary of Botanical Nomenclature* (16) and in systematic botany textbooks (7, 20, 24). Major responsibility for adherence to the Code rests with the author.

Scientific names   The scientific names of all taxa are treated as Latin, regardless of their derivation. Names in higher ranks are identified by their endings. Table 13.1 lists the principal ranks of plant taxa and gives the endings for names above the rank of genus.

Names of genera and higher ranks may stand by themselves (monomials), but categories below the rank of genus must be given in combinations consisting of the generic name and an epithet. The epithets of combinations other than species must be preceded by the word (often abbreviated) indicating their rank (e.g., *Aster* sect. *multiflora*, *Erigeron pumilus* subsp. *intermedius* var. *gracilior*, or *E. pumilus* var. *gracilior*). There is only one infraspecific category for cultivated plants, the cultivar (cv.).

Table 13.1. Principal ranks of plant taxa, their endings and abbreviations

Division, *-phyta*, *-mycota* (Fungi)	Genus
Subdivision, *-phytina*, *-mycotina* (Fungi)	Subgenus (subg.)
Class, *-opsida*, *-mycetes* (Fungi),	Section (sect.)
-phyceae (Algae)	Subsection (subsect.)
Subclass, *-idae*, *-mycetidae* (Fungi),	Series (ser.)
-phycidae (Algae)	Subseries (subser.)
Order, *-ales*	Species (sp., spp.)
Suborder, *-ineae*	Subspecies (subsp.)
Family, *-aceae**	Variety (var.)
Subfamily, *-oideae*	Subvariety (subvar.)
Tribe, *-eae*	Form (f.)
Subtribe, *-inae*	Subform (subf.)

* The Code allows the option for using eight family names not ending in *-aceae*. The families are: Compositae (Asteraceae), Cruciferae (Brassicaceae), Gramineae (Poaceae), Guttiferae (Clusiaceae), Labiatae (Lamiaceae), Leguminosae (Fabaceae), Palmae (Arecaceae), and Umbelliferae (Apiaceae).

Infraspecific categories for hybrids use the prefix "notho-" with the terms designating their rank, e.g., nothosubspecies and nothovariety (32).

The names of taxa above the rank of species are always spelled with an initial capital letter, whereas specific and infraspecific epithets usually have an initial lower case letter. Although the Code allows the option for initial capitalization if the epithet is based on the name of a person (whether actual or mythical), a vernacular name (in any language), or a former generic name, this practice is becoming obsolete.

A generic name that is followed by a specific epithet must be spelled out the first time it is used in the text; subsequently it may be abbreviated to its initial letter unless confusion would arise. Specific epithets must not be abbreviated. A specific epithet is part of the binomial and should not appear as a monomial, except perhaps when used in a key or table devoted to a single genus. A subspecific or varietal epithet can appear alone with its rank designation if the binomial to which it belongs is apparent.

Interspecific and intergeneric hybrids can be designated by a formula consisting of the names of two parents connected by the multiplication sign (e.g., *Agropyron trachycaulum* × *A. dasystachyum* or *Agropyron spicatum* × *Sitanion hystrix*) or they can be given binary names (*Agropyron* ×*pseudorepens* or ×*Agrositanion saxicola*; these names are based on parentage of the formulas in the preceding examples). In the binary name of an interspecific hybrid the epithet is preceded by the multiplication sign and in the binary name of an intergeneric hybrid the multiplication sign precedes the "generic name" of the bigeneric hybrid. Notice that the multiplication sign is placed against the word following. The naming of the interspecific and intergeneric hybrids is subject to the same rules as that of species and genera with only a few modifications. For hybrid infraspecific categories the prefix notho- is used instead of the multiplication sign, with terms designating the rank, e.g., nothosubspecies, nothovariety, and nothoform.

Plants that have arisen as a result of deliberate crossing or selection are termed cultivars (cv.) to distinguish them from natural or wild varieties. Nomenclature of cultivated plants is governed by the *International Code of Nomenclature of Cultivated Plants* (5). Most of these rules are the same as for wild plants and are taken from the Botanical Code. The main difference is the recognition of only one rank, the cultivar. The cultivar epithet must follow the name of a genus, subspecies, or hybrid and is treated like an infraspecific name. It usually takes a vernacular rather than a latinized form. It is written in roman type with an initial capital letter and is either enclosed in single quotation marks (*Syringa vulgaris* 'Mont Blanc') or preceded by the abbreviation "cv." (*Chamaecyparis lawsoniana* cv. Silver Queen).

For correct spelling, authorship, reference to place of publication, and typification of all validly published generic names the most reliable source is *Index Nominum Genericorum* (8). For family names and additional information on genera, Willis's *Dictionary of the Flowering Plants and Ferns* (33) is an accepted source. In Willis's dictionary the estimated number of species and the general geographic distribution are given for each accepted genus, and an attempt is made to indicate the taxonomic placement of synonyms. For each family the estimated total number of genera and species is given with a short description.

Authorship   Authors of validly published names of specific and in-fraspecific taxa should be cited, but only when the name is first used in the text. This rule should be followed even in a paper emphasizing physiology, embryology, or other aspects of the taxon. The names of authors are often abbreviated; for the sake of consistency in abbreviation, consult either *Draft Index of Author Abbreviations* (17) or *Taxonomic Literature* (25).

When an epithet is transferred from its original position (e.g., a specific epithet to another genus or an infraspecific epithet to another species) and when one epithet is changed in rank (e.g., from subspecies to species or from genus to subgenus) the original author's name is placed in parentheses followed by the name of the author(s) responsible for the change, as in the following examples: *Haplopappus radiatus* (Nutt.) Cronq. from *Pyrrocoma radiata* Nutt.; *Pinus contorta* var. *murrayana* (Balf.) Engelm. from *Pinus murrayana* Balf. If the author of a name ascribed it to another person who may have merely suggested the name or published it as a nomen nudum, the name of that person, followed by the connecting word "ex," may be inserted before the name of the publishing author (e.g., *Castilleja miniata* Dougl. ex Hook.). If format calls for an abbreviated form only the publishing author's name (Hook.) is given. When the validating author's description or diagnosis is published in a work by another author, the word "in" should be used to connect the name of the two authors (e.g., *Myriophyllum brasiliense* Camb. in St. Hilaire). In this case the name of the author who supplied the description or diagnosis (Camb.) should be retained when its citation is abbreviated.

SPECIAL FEATURES OF TAXONOMIC TREATMENTS ⸺

Regardless of the kind of taxonomic treatment, it likely includes keys and descriptions and possibly nomenclatural bibliography, illustrations, distribution maps, discussion of taxonomic relationships, and citation of specimens. Particular forms of presenting these data are described below and more information can be found in Leenhouts' *Guide to the Practice of Herbarium Taxonomy* (14).

Dichotomous keys   Dichotomous keys consist of pairs (couplets) of contrasting statements (leads) that offer the user a choice depending on the material being identified (figures 13.1 and 13.2). Each lead of a couplet leads to a further couplet or, if it is an ultimate lead, to a name of a taxon. Strictly dichotomous keys are the rule in modern-day systematics and an occasional diversion from them (e.g., a trichotomy) could lead to confusion.

Consecutive numbering of the couplets aids in clarity and is preferable to alphabetic lettering. It is not necessary to distinguish the first lead from the second in each couplet, as some authors do with the letters "a" and "b" or the prime sign (') on the second lead. Introduce those groups with variable character states in a key more than once when necessary. Start both leads of a couplet with the same word, usually the plant part, and follow with contrasting descriptive phrases. This facilitates orientation of leads of any one couplet. Insofar as possible phrase the leads to read as positive statements, especially the initial lead of a couplet. When more than one character is used in a couplet, give priority to the one most differentiating or easiest to assess. Geographical distribution and habitat data, when used in a key, should always be placed last in a couplet.

Structurally there are two basic types of keys, indented (figure 13.1) and bracket (figure 13.2), both of which incorporate the same data, differing only in organization. Most botanists prefer the indented type and most zoologists and typesetters prefer the bracket type.

A well-organized indented key (figure 13.1) can be rapidly scanned

---

Pedicularis of Nevada

1 Corolla 16-42 mm long, the galea blunt-tipped.
  2 Stems short, less than 1 dm long, surpassed by the leaves; leaves pinnatifid or bipinnatifid; calyx lobes 5.
    3 Corolla 30-42 mm long, pale violet; leaves pinnatifid; valleys and foot hills in northern two-thirds of the state . . . . . 1. *P. centranthera*
    3 Corolla 16-25 mm long, yellow; leaves bipinnatifid; Charleston and Sheep mountains of Clark Co. and Carson Range of Douglas, Ormsby, and southern Washoe Cos. . . . . 2. *P. semibarbata*
  2 Stems elongate, over 1.5 dm long, much exceeding the leaves; leaves simple, crenate; calyx lobes 2; wet valley bottoms of northeastern Lincoln Co. and eastern White Pine Co. . . . . 3. *P. crenulata*
1 Corolla 3.5-5.5 mm long, the galea extended into a narrow, curved beak, contributing to the elephant's head appearance.
  4 Inflorescence glabrous; corolla violet to purple, the beak 7-18 mm long; mountains of western and northern parts of the state . . . . 4. *P. groenlandica*
  4 Inflorescence villous; corolla white to pink, the beak 4-5 mm long; Carson Range of Douglas, Ormsby, and southern Washoe Cos. . . . . .5. *P. attollens*

Figure 13.1. Example of an indented key based on the species of *Pedicularis* (Scrophulariaceae) of Nevada.

Pedicularis of Nevada

1 Corolla 16-42 mm long, the galea blunt-tipped (2).
1 Corolla 3.5-5.5 mm long, the galea extending into a narrow, curved
  beak, contributing to elephant's head appearance (4).
2(1) Stems short, less than 1 dm long, surpassed by the leaves;
  leaves pinnatifid or bipinnatifid; calyx lobes 5 (3).
2 Stems elongate, over 1.5 dm long, much exceeding the leaves;
  leaves simple, crenate; calyx lobes 2; wet valley bottoms of northeastern
  Lincoln Co. and eastern White Pine Co. .... 3. *P. crenulata*
3(2) Corolla 30-42 mm long, pale violet; leaves pinnatifid; valleys
  and foot hills in northern two-thirds of the state .... 1. *P. centranthera*
3 Corolla 16-25 mm long, yellow; leaves bipinnatifid; Charleston
  and Sheep mountains of Clark Co. and Carson Range of Douglas,
  Ormsby, and southern Washoe Cos. .... 2. *P. semibarbata*
4(1) Inflorescence glabrous; corolla violet to purple, the beak 7-18
  mm long; mountains of western and northern part of the state ......
  .... 4. *P. groenlandica*
4 Inflorescence villous; corolla white to pink, the beak 4-5 mm long;
  Carson Range of Douglas, Ormsby, and southern Washoe Cos. .....
  .... .5. *P. attollens*

Figure 13.2. Example of a bracket key based on the same data as figure 13.1.

and worked backwards when one goes astray. It has the advantage of
making the relationships of the groups more apparent to the eye and can
easily be read in both directions. Its disadvantages, which are minor,
arise in long keys. Successive shifts of leads to the right result in waste
of space, and the members of a principal couplet may become separated
by more than one page. These problems can be avoided if printers are
clearly instructed to use minimal indention or if long keys are broken
into groups, the first key being a key to the groups.

In constructing an indented key the leads of the first couplet begin at
the left margin and each successive subordinate couplet is indented
beyond the one preceding (leading to) it. When the lead runs more than
one line the "run-over" lines should, for the sake of clarity, be indented
slightly farther than the next subordinate lead. It often happens that one
section of an indented key contains a smaller number of leads than the
other. In a key intended for identification it is desirable to have the
smaller division precede the larger so that the leads of the dividing
couplet are closer together. An effort should be made to construct a
balanced key, i.e., one in which each lead of each couplet accounts for
approximately one-half the remaining number of taxa. This construction
requires fewer choices for most taxa in the key and has fewer levels of
indention.

The bracket key (figure 13.2) requires less space on a page, and some prefer to see the opposing leads in juxtaposition (bracketed). It does not readily show relationships and it is difficult to scan backwards and forwards. Typesetting is easy because all couplets or alternate couplets begin flush left. To facilitate backtracking within the key the number of the antecedent lead can be inserted parenthetically at the beginning of the first lead of a couplet (as shown in figure 13.2).

Descriptions and diagnoses   A description is composed of adjectival phrases separated by punctuation. One method is to set off the account of each part by semicolons, using the period only at the end of the description. Another method is to describe each organ in a separate phrase each of which begins with a capital letter and ends with a period, semicolons being used to mark off its parts. Each segment of the description begins with a noun (the subject), followed by adjectives separated by commas. Selective reading of a description is made easier by italicizing the name of each plant part.

When describing a plant part that occurs only once on the plant or on an organ it is treated as a singular noun, and if it occurs more than once it is plural. A typical flower has one calyx, one corolla, and one pistil, but it has sepals, petals, and stamens.

Measurements are by the metric system, the units of which are abbreviated without periods (mm, cm, dm, m). Ranges of measurement are connected by en-dashes and exceptional measurements are placed in parentheses, e.g., 15–20 (25) mm long or 15–20 (−25) mm long. In order to save space, measurements of plane figures can be given as length by width, e.g., 8–15 × 5.5–15 cm, those of solid figures as length by width by diameter, e.g., 10 × 8 × 2 cm.

Examples of descriptions and diagnoses are given by Stearn in his *Botanical Latin* (26). A useful reference for writing descriptions is the *Guide for Contributors to Flora North America, Part II* (19). This includes a morphological outline consisting of more than 30,000 character states and a glossary of morphological terms arranged in such categories as apex and base shapes, branching patterns, dehiscence, and odor, to name only a few. For correct application of terminology describing types of indumentum and trichomes *see* Payne (18), for describing leaf shape *see* the article in *Taxon* by the Systematics Association Committee for Descriptive Terminology (27), and for describing leaf architecture *see* Hickey (9).

A brief diagnostic description states only the characters that distinguish a taxon from related taxa (key characters). A diagnosis should contain no superfluous information, only that which is peculiar to the taxon. It should be as brief as possible, yet sufficiently complete to distinguish the taxon.

In writing a Latin diagnosis, as prescribed by the Code for valid publication of a name of a new taxon, Stearn's *Botanical Latin* (26) is recommended for syntactic, grammatical, and vocabulary assistance. A Latin diagnosis is preferred to a longer Latin description. The ideal protologue (the term given to everything associated with a name at its first publication) includes a definitive Latin diagnosis and a detailed description in the language of the journal.

Nomenclature citation   In monographic and revisional studies the listing of pertinent published names should include author(s), place of publication, and the citation of the nomenclatural type and where deposited. This includes the accepted names of all synonyms, both nomenclatural and taxonomic. Nomenclatural (homotypic) synonyms are different names or combinations based on the same type, and taxonomic (heterotypic) synonyms are names based on different types, but considered to belong to the same taxon.

Citation of nomenclatural bibliography can be dealt with in two ways. In that most commonly used, each name or combination begins a new line and is listed in chronological order whether nomenclatural or taxonomic (figure 13.3). The other method is to group related nomenclatural synonyms in a paragraph beginning with the basionym, followed by subsequent combinations in chronological order, and ending with the citation of the type (figure 13.4). The name of the author of the basionym need not be repeated in parentheses following each subsequent name change because it is already apparent. The basionym paragraph method,

---

Penstemon thompsoniae (A. Gray) Rydb.

Pentstemon caespitosus var.? *incanus* A. Gray, Proc. Amer. Acad. Arts 8:395. 1872. Type: U.S.A. Nevada. [Lincoln Co.]: Pahranagat Mountains, *Miss Searles s.n.* (Holotype: GH!). Gray wrote "very likely a distinct species," hence his question mark after "var."

Pentstemon pumilus var. *incanus* (A. Gray) A. Gray, Syn. Fl. N. Amer. 2(1):269. 1878.

Pentstemon pumilus var. *thompsoniae* A. Gray, Syn. Fl. N. Amer. 2(1):269. 1878. Type: U.S.A. Utah. Kanab Co.: Kanab, in 1872, *Mrs. Thompson s.n.* (Holotype: GH!)

Pentstemon thompsoniae (A. Gray) Rydb. Bull. Torrey Bot. Club 36:690. 1909.

Pentstemon incanus (A. Gray) Tidestrom, Contr. U.S. Natl. Herb. 25:495. 1925.

Penstemon caespitosus var. *thompsoniae* (A. Gray) A. Nels. Univ. Wyoming Publ. 3:104. 1937.

Penstemon caespitosus subsp. *thompsoniae* (A. Gray) Keck ex A. Nels. Univ. Wyoming Publ. 3:104. 1937; as synonym of *P. caespitosus* var. *thompsoniae* (A. Gray) A. Nels.

Figure 13.3. Example of the chronological method of citing nomenclatural bibliography for *Penstemon thompsoniae* (A. Gray) Rydb. Some authors and editors prefer to include the place of publication with the accepted name, used here as a heading.

Penstemon thompsoniae (A. Gray) Rydb.
  Pentstemon caespitosus var.? *incanus* A. Gray, Proc. Amer. Acad. Arts 8:395.
  1872. *Pentstemon pumilus* var. *incanus* A. Gray, Syn. Fl. N. Amer.
  2(1):269, 1878. *Pentstemon incanus* Tidestrom, Contr. U.S. Natl. Herb.
  25:495. 1925. Type: U.S.A. Nevada. [Lincoln Co.]: Pahranagat Mountains, *Miss Searles s.n.* (Holotype: GH!). In the protologue Gray wrote
  "very likely a distinct species," hence his question mark after "var."
  Pentstemon pumilus var. *thompsoniae* A. Gray, Syn. Fl. N. Amer. 2(1):269.
  1878. *Pentstemon thompsoniae* Rydb. Bull. Torrey Bot. Club 36:690.
  1909. *Penstemon caespitosus* var. *thompsoniae* A. Nels. Univ. Wyoming
  Publ. 3:104. 1937. *Penstemon caespitosus* subsp. *thompsoniae* Keck ex A.
  Nels., loc cit., pro syn. Type: U.S.A. Utah. Kanab Co.: Kanab, in 1872,
  Mrs. Thompson s.n. (Holotype: GH!).

Figure 13.4. Example of the basionym-paragraph method of citing nomenclatural bibliography for *Penstemon thompsoniae* (A. Gray) Rydb., based on the same
data as figure 13.3.

which has the advantage of taking less space, unambiguously indicates
the basionym and its type.

Journal titles are abbreviated according to *Botanico-Periodicum-Huntianum* (13) and book titles according to *Taxonomic Literature* (25).

Names previously applied to a group but excluded from it by the
monographer should be listed in a section titled "Excluded Species"
(species exclusae). In this list the name, author, place of publication,
nomenclatural type, and accepted identity are given.

Citation of specimens   In describing a new taxon, the citations of all
specimens of that taxon known to the author are usually appropriate. In
studies where many specimens of a taxon have been examined it may be
sufficient to cite only representative collections, in which case the choice
of specimens should preferentially include: 1) those of the author,
indicating his or her familiarity with the plant in the field; 2) those
identified by a collector's serial number; 3) those represented by dupli-
cates in many herbaria and more accessible for examination; 4) those
documenting the geographical extremities of the range; and 5) those of
possible historic value.

Specimen citation may range from a mere reference by collector's
name and number to quotation of all field data. The data in specimen
citations are preferably arranged in the following order: country, state
or province, locality, elevation, date, phenology, collector's name and
number, and herbaria of deposit cited according to the abbreviation
system of *Index Herbariorum* (10). The author may state that all the
specimens cited have been examined or, by tradition, may indicate
specimens examined by an exclamation mark (!) following the herbarium
abbreviation. Figure 13.5 shows an example of minimal specimen citation
data for specimens of *Castilleja arvensis*.

Representative specimens examined: COSTA RICA: ALAJUELA: Colinas de San Pedro de San Ramón, 3 Jul 1925, *Brenes 592* (F); Cacao de Alajuela near Río Poás, 13 Nov 1932, *Brenes 61* (NY); road between the Alajuela-Grecia road and the gorge of the Río Rosales, 8 Dec 1933, *Brenes 12* (F, NY); region of Zarcero, *Smith H119* (F), *A629* (F). CARTAGO: 3 km W of Jicotea on road to Moravia, *Almeda 551* (DUKE); edge of Cartago, *Stork 1232* (F); above Río Grande de Orosí, 10-20 km SE of bridge at Tapantí, *Wilbur & Luteyn 18038* (DUKE). HEREDIA: Vera Blanca de Sarapiquí, N slope of Central Cordillera, between Poás and Barba volcanoes, *Skutch 3545* (NY); about 2 km S of Vara Blanca and 7.8 km N of La Concordia, *Wilbur et al. 15775* (DUKE). PUNTARENAS: 2 km SE of Monteverde, *Burger & Gentry 8793* (F); Lourdes de Montes de Oca [Osa], *Orozco 57* (F). SAN JOSÉ: along Río Virillo, about 1 km S of Santo Domingo, *Taylor 17525* (DUR); near La División, N of San Isidro de El General, *Williams et al. 24439* (F, NY). PANAMA: CHIRIQUÍ: 1 mi E of Cañas Gordas, near Costa Rican border, *Croat 22317* (MO); S of Alto Respinga, *D'Arcy 10728* (MO, NY); 2.5 km SE of Cerro Punta, *Mori & Kallunki 5642* (MO). VERAGUAS, *Seemann s.n.* (US).

Figure 13.5.   An example of format for citation of specimens for *Castilleja arvensis* (from *Brittonia* 30:185; 1978). The states and collectors are listed in alphabetical order. If a geographical sequence is used, the order should be explained. Punctuation in this example is as follows: A colon follows the political division or subdivision when more than one subdivision or collection follows; if only one of a category follows, it is a comma. Semicolons separate collections within a political division or subdivision. Periods end collections within a political division or subdivision.

The inclusion of an appended "List of Exsiccatae" (figure 13.6) is an accepted abbreviated method of citing all the collections examined. In revisionary treatments including several taxa the list of exsiccatae should be preceded by a numerical list of the taxa for easy reference. The information for each cited specimen is reduced to collector's name and number (or collection date in absence of a number), and the reference number to the taxon. The entries are listed alphabetically by collector's name without regard to sequence of taxa.

In a protologue the citation of the type specimen should include most or all available field data followed in parentheses by designation of the place of deposit of the holotype and isotypes (figure 13.7).

If a lectotype or neotype is selected, insert the words "here designated," e.g., "(Lectotype here designated: P!; isolectotypes: K!, NY!)."

Illustrations   The preparation of graphs and illustrations of various sorts is discussed in chapter 6, but the specialized aspects of technical botanical illustrations and distribution maps are mentioned here.

Line drawings   Nothing can take the place of an accurate, detailed line drawing in the presentation of morphological data. All new species should be illustrated.

Whenever an enlarged detail is illustrated its relationship to the plant

List of Exsiccatae

Numbers in parentheses refer to numbers used in the text for the taxa.

Allen 681 (3); *1557* (1); *4886* (4)

Almeda 551 (1); *705* (3)

Anderson & Mori 61 (2)

Barbour 1031 (2)

Biolleg. 86 (3)

Brenes s.n. [21 Jan 1906] (4); *24* [21 Jan 1906] (3); *9* [Dec 1912] (1); *592* [3 Jul 1925] (1); *372* [22 Jul 1926] (1); *4* [23 Jul 1932] (1); *61* [3 Nov 1932] (1); *9* [1 Jan 1933] (1); *12* [8 Dec 1933] (1)

Burch 4737 (2)

Burger 7948 (2); *8277* (2)

Burger & Gentry 8793 (1)

Burger & Gómez 8209A (4); *8209B* (2); *8209C* (2)

Burger & Liesner 6359 (2); *7426* (4); *7446* (2); *7453* (2); *7481* (2)

Burger & Matta 4585 (1)

Busy 451 (1)

Carlson 336 (1); *3416* (3); *3521* (2); *3543* (3)

Cooper 5873 (1)

Croat 13523 (1); *22317* (1)

Croat & Porter 16100 (1)

Cronquist & Moños 8826 (3)

Cruz 22 (2)

Cuatrecasas & León 26525 (3)

D'Arcy 10084 (4); *10685* (1); *10728* (1); *10795* (4); *11013* (4); *11049* (4)

D'Arcy & D'Arcy 6407 (1); *6524* (1)

Figure 13.6. A portion of a "List of Exsiccatae" (data taken from *Brittonia* 30:182–194; 1978). Initials should be added for collectors with the same surnames. Date of collection is given in absence of collector's sequential number.

Type: U.S.A., Utah, Kane Co., near N end of Coral Pink Sand Dunes, along road past Ponderosa Grove Campground, 10.6 km SW of jnct. with U.S Hwy. 89, T43S, R7W, S8, 1900 m elev., "locally common on sand dune with scattered *Wyethia scabra, Artemisia tridentata,* and *Juniperus osteosperma,* stems few to several from deep runners, corolla cream with a rose tinge in the middle, the column pale green, the hoods cream, the anther cells violet tinged," 20 Jun 1978 (fl), *N. & P. Holmgren 9009* (Holotype: NY; isotypes: BRY, UT, UTC).

Figure 13.7. An example of a type citation including all field data (for *Asclepias welshii,* modified from *Brittonia* 31:110–114; 1979).

should be made obvious. In an illustrated treatment of related species any diagnostic detail that is shown for more than one taxon should be drawn at one scale and in the same view.

A drawing made with a projection device attached to a microscope, such as the camera lucida, is accurate and easy to produce with little artistic talent. These devices are commonly used to illustrate microscopic details such as chromosomes and anatomical features.

The figure legend should include citation of the actual specimen(s) from which the artist made the drawing. The scale should be indicated either in the legend or preferably by bar scales in the illustration itself.

Photographs   A photograph of a herbarium specimen seldom illustrates more than vegetative form and branching patterns. It will not substitute for line drawings and should be avoided. Often details are lost in photographs due to obscuring vesture or overlapping parts or due to poor contrast. These are features that the pen-and-ink artist can adjust in a line drawing. However, a well-prepared photograph of a living plant showing its habit can enhance the information. The illustration of vegetation types, habitats, and scenery is best served by photographs.

In composite plates the individual photographs should be cut squarely and butted together in mounting so that no white space intervenes. The printer can border the individual photographs with a clean thin white line. The identifying numbers or letters should be placed inside the photographs, if necessary within a contrasting square or circle.

Distribution maps   A method often used to show geographical distribution of species is to enclose its range with a boundary line. This method is useful if overlapping distributions of few to several species are shown on a single map. The ranges of different species can be distinguished by different kinds of boundary lines, such as thick or thin solid lines, or lines that are broken, dotted, zigzag, dash-dot, or dash-dot-dot. Each species area can also be numbered, using the numbers given in the text.

A refinement on the boundary line method is to block in the area with shading patterns (*see* page 69). The distributional area then may be broken up into smaller ones to show known gaps.

The dot method is used most frequently and is superior to the boundary line and blocking-in methods.

A differentiated mark may be used to designate the type locality, plants that have been examined cytologically, collections with certain character combinations, and hybrids. Round dots, triangles, squares, diamonds, and stars can be further differentiated as solid or open shapes and triangles can be varied by orienting the points in different directions. Pictorialized dot maps can convey information on geographical variation of taxa. The use of dots and boundary lines on a map showing the range of more than one species combines the accuracy of the dot method with the ease of observation of the boundary line method.

The map should be detailed enough to allow precise location of the dots and is more effective when tailored to the particular distribution shown. A false economy is the use of a standard outline map, which rarely suits any specific purpose. An original base map should be drawn by direct tracing or by using various techniques of enlarging or reducing and tracing from existing maps. Excessive detail on a map should be avoided. Elaborate cartographic detail may overshadow the botanical information.

Lines such as those indicating coastlines, rivers, ponds, and political boundaries should be differentiated by varying widths or patterns of interruption. Natural features (except intermittent streams) are usually shown by continuous lines, political and artificial ones by dash or dash-dot patterns. Shading patterns can distinguish land from water.

The area projected should be immediately identifiable; sometimes it is necessary to include an inset map showing the placement of the detailed area. The addition of a legend box with a key to the symbols used for the taxa and the map scale improves the utility of a distribution map. The symbols should appear in the legend exactly as they appear on the map.

GENETICS AND CYTOGENETICS

A uniform system governing genetic and cytogenetic symbols and no-menclature for higher plants has not been established. However, com-

Table 13.2. Committees or organizations, and persons responsible for genetic and cytogenetic symbolization and nomenclature of higher plants (as of 1982)

Higher plant	Committee or organization	Responsible person	Reference
Barley	Barley Genetics Committee, American Barley Workers Conference	Dr. T. Tsuchiya Dept. of Agronomy Colorado State Univ. Fort Collins, CO 80523	Tsuchiya (31)
Cotton	S77-Regional Technical Committee, Genetics and Cytology of Cotton II	Dr. Russell Kohel Agronomy Field Laboratory College Station, TX 77840	Kohel (11)
Maize	Committee of Maize Genetics Cooperation	Dr. G. Fletcher Dept. of Agronomy Univ. of Illinois Urbana, IL 61801	Rhoades (21)
Oats	Committee for Standardizing Gene Nomenclature of Oats, National Oats Conference	Dr. M. D. Simons Dept. of Plant Pathology Iowa State Univ. Ames, IA 50011	Simons et al. (23)
Soybean	Soybean Genetics Committee	Dr. R. L. Bernard Davenport Hall Univ. of Illinois Urbana, IL 61801	Bernard et al. (4)
Tomato	Gene List Committee of Tomato Genetics Cooperative	Dr. E. C. Tigchelaar Dept. of Horticulture Purdue Univ. West Lafayette, IN 47907	Clayberg (6)
Wheat	Fifth International Wheat Genetics Symposium	Dr. R. A. McIntosh Dept. of Agricultural Botany Univ. of Sydney N.S.W. 2006, Australia	McIntosh (15)

Table 13.3. Reporting environmental conditions in controlled-environment studies

Variable*	Unit†
Radiation	
Photosynthetically active radiation (PAR)	
a) Photosynthetic photon flux density (PPFD), 400–700 nm with cosine correction	$\mu mol \cdot s^{-1} \cdot m^{-2}$ *or* $\mu E \cdot s^{-1} \cdot m^{-2}$
or	
b) Photosynthetic irradiance (PI), 400–700 nm with cosine correction	$W \cdot m^{-2}$
Total irradiance	$W \cdot m^{-2}$
With cosine correction	
Indicate bandwidth	
Spectral distribution	
a) Spectral photon flux density, $\lambda_1 - \lambda_2$ nm in <20 nm bandwidths with cosine correction	$\mu mol \cdot s^{-1} \cdot m^2 \cdot nm^{-1}$ ($\lambda_1 - \lambda_2$ nm) (quanta)
or	
b) Spectral irradiance (spectral energy flux density), $\lambda_1 - \lambda_2$ nm in <20 nm bandwidths with cosine correction	$W \cdot m^{-2} \cdot nm^{-1}$ ($\lambda_1 - \lambda_2$ nm)
Illuminance‡	klx
380–780 nm with cosine correction	
Temperature	
Air	
Shielded and aspirated ($\geq$3 m$\cdot$s^{-1}) device	°C
Soil or liquid	°C
Atmospheric moisture	
Shielded and aspirated ($\geq$3 m$\cdot$s^{-1}) psychrometer, dew point sensor, infrared analyzer	% RH, dewpoint temperature, *or* $g \cdot m^{-3}$
Air velocity	$m \cdot s^{-1}$
Carbon dioxide	$mmol \cdot m^{-3}$
Watering	ml per pot
Substrate	Specify
Nutrition	
Solid media	$mol \cdot m^{-3}$ *or* $mol \cdot kg^{-1}$
Liquid culture	$\mu mol \cdot l^{-1}$ *or* $mmol \cdot l^{-1}$
pH	pH units
Electrical conductivity§	$dS \cdot m^{-1}$

* Proposed by the North Central Region (NCR-101) Committee on Growth Chamber Use.

† Report in other subdivisions of indicated units if more convenient.

‡ Report with PAR reading only for historical comparison.

§ $dS \cdot m^{-1}$ = $mmho \cdot cm^{-1}$ (decisiemens per meter).

mittees of scientists interested in specific crop plants (table 13.2) have standardized the genetic symbols and nomenclature for each plant. The rules developed by those committees are modifications of the rules established by the International Committee on Genetic Symbols and Nomenclature (28). Scientists proposing new symbols and nomenclature should contact the person responsible for the nomenclature (table 13.2).

PLANT PHYSIOLOGY

Rules and conventions for terminology and symbols relating to plant physiology have not been standardized on a world-wide basis, although groups within several countries, including Australia, England, Sweden, and the United States, have strongly recommended the adoption of SI units. Journals such as *Plant Physiology*, *Physiologia Plantarum*, and the *Australian Journal of Plant Physiology* publish instructions for preparation of manuscripts for publication. The International Association for Plant Physiology has published recommendations for terminology (29); however, this document has not received international approval, and there is no international acceptance or conformity in usage.

CONTROLLED-ENVIRONMENT STUDIES

The proposed guidelines for reporting environmental conditions in controlled-environment studies were published initially in 1970 by the American Society for Horticultural Sciences (ASHS) Working Group on Growth Chambers and Controlled Environments and revised in 1972 and 1977 (2). The guidelines were later expanded by the North Central Region (NCR-101) Technical Committee on Growth Chamber Use, a committee formed under the Cooperative Regional Research Program of the State Agricultural Experiment Stations and the United States Department of Agriculture to include recommended procedures for making environmental measurements (30). These guidelines have been reviewed extensively by researchers and manufacturers and have been accepted widely.

Authors are urged to use the standardized terminology and SI units (3) listed in table 13.3 to characterize environmental conditions in controlled-environment studies. Widespread adoption should help greatly to improve the uniformity of studies conducted in controlled environments and to facilitate comparison of experimental results obtained world-wide. For further details *see* Krizek (12) and the sample paragraph published by ASHS (2).

MICROBIOLOGY

Microbiologic nomenclature is designed to achieve stability and universal acceptance of scientific names of microorganisms. Editors are obligated to accept the rules of nomenclature established by international committees (42, 44, 47, 63). Since the bacteriologic and virologic codes and practices differ substantially, they are discussed separately.

BACTERIOLOGIC NOMENCLATURE
Bacteriologic code   Editors who publish papers on bacteria should require that authors follow the rules and recommendations of the most

recent edition of the *International Code of Nomenclature of Bacteria* (49), hereafter referred to as the Bacteriologic Code. The names of bacterial species, genera, tribes, and families based on the Code are listed in *Bergey's Manual of Determinative Bacteriology* (38). The Code does not cover taxa lower than subspecies. Follow the rules and regulations outlined below to describe and name new species or to reclassify, or propose new names for, species, genera, tribes, and families.

The Bacteriologic Code stipulates that a new scientific name or combination originally must be published in the *International Journal of Systematic Bacteriology* to be validly published, and hence achieve standing in nomenclature. If the new name is first published elsewhere, a notice of the publication (citing name, nomenclatural type, author, title, and journal) must be published in the *International Journal of Systematic Bacteriology*. A description or a reference to a previously published description of the taxon and the designation of the nomenclatural type are also required for valid publication.

Descriptions of taxa should include the following information: 1) a list of the strains studied and their sources; 2) descriptions or references to descriptions of the methods used to characterize the strains; 3) characteristics necessary for membership in the taxon; 4) characteristics that qualify the taxon for membership in the next higher taxon; and 5) the diagnostic characteristics—those characteristics that distinguish the taxon from closely related taxa. For a species whose description is based on more than one strain, the following additional information is desirable: 6) the frequency of each characteristic expressed as the number of strains with the characteristic compared to the total number of strains studied (if the numbers are considered significant, they may be expressed as percentages); and 7) a separate description of the type (or neotype) strain (this is necessary for checking the authenticity of cultures of the type or neotype strain). Because few characteristics are completely invariant in taxa of bacteria, the characteristics that are most constant should be employed in requirements 3 through 5. When a new species or subspecies is described, include photomicrographs and, if necessary, electron micrographs with the description, to show any morphologic or anatomic characteristics pertinent to the classification or identification of the microorganism.

The *International Journal of Systematic Bacteriology* requires in taxonomic articles a list of all the strains studied and the presentation of all the strain data. The methods for presenting these data appear in the "Instructions to Authors" section of the January issues of the *International Journal of Systematic Bacteriology*.

A nomenclatural type is the constituent element of a taxon to which the name of the taxon is permanently attached. The type of a species or a subspecies is a strain and that of a genus is a species. The type of an order, suborder, family, subfamily, tribe, or subtribe is the genus on whose name the name of the higher taxon is based. For species and subspecies whose cells cannot be maintained in culture or for which cultures are not extant, the type strain may be represented by the original description and by illustrations and specimens.

A type strain is one of the strains on which the author who first published a name based the description of the organism and which that author or a subsequent author definitely designated as the type; if the description was based on a single strain, this strain is the type by monotypy. For species and subspecies that can be cultivated, the type strain should be described by itself and should be designated by the author's strain number as well as by the strain number under which it is held in at least one culture collection from which the strain is available.

A neotype strain may be designated if none of the cultures of the type strain possesses the original characters of the type strain, if cultures of the type strain are no longer extant, or if a type strain was never designated and none of the original strains on which the description of the species or subspecies was based is extant. A neotype strain is one that is accepted by international agreement to serve in place of a type strain. The neotype should possess the characteristics as given in the original description; explain any deviations. An author must propose a neotype strain in the *International Journal of Systematic Bacteriology* and must include a reference or references to the first description and name for the microorganism, a description (or reference to a description) of the proposed neotype strain, and a record of the author's designation for the neotype strain and of at least one culture collection from which cultures of the strain are available. The neotype strain becomes established from the date of publication in the *International Journal of Systematic Bacteriology*. Objections should be referred to the Judicial Commission of the International Committee on Systematic Bacteriology in care of the chairman of the Judicial Commission, Dr. L. G. Wayne, Veterans Administration Hospital, Long Beach, CA 90822. Subsequent discovery of an original strain should be immediately referred to the Judicial Commission.

To introduce new names, follow the rules of the Bacteriologic Code:
1) The name should be in the correct form. Generic and suprageneric names are single words in Latin form spelled with an initial capital letter. Names of species are binary combinations of words in Latin form consisting of a generic name and a single, specific epithet that has an initial lowercase letter. A subspecific name is a ternary combination consisting of the generic name and the specific epithet followed by the word "subspecies" (abbreviated ssp. or sspp.) and this in turn by a single, subspecific epithet. "Variety" (var.) is sometimes used in place of "subspecies," but the latter term is preferred. The gender of a specific or subspecific epithet must, if the epithet is an adjective, agree with the gender of the generic

name. The transfer of a species from one genus to another may necessitate a change in the ending of the specific epithet if the epithet is an adjective and if the gender of the name of the new genus is different from that of the name of the genus in which the species was previously placed. Thus, the transfer of a species *Bacillus albus* to *Clostridium* would require a change in the ending of the specific epithet, to give *Clostridium album.*

Names of taxa from the rank of order to subtribe, inclusive, are formed by adding a specified suffix to the stem of the name of the type genus.

Rank	Suffix	Example
Order	-ales	Pseudomonadales
Suborder	-ineae	Pseudomonadineae
Family	-aceae	Pseudomonadaceae
Subfamily	-oideae	Pseudomonadoideae
Tribe	-eae	Pseudomonadeae
Subtribe	-inae	Pseudomonadinae

2) The name should be clearly proposed as a new name or combination that is accepted by the author at the time of publication. Most authors append phrases such as "species nova" (abbreviated sp. nov.), "genus novum" (gen. nov.), "nomen novum" (nom. nov.), "combinatio nova" (comb. nov.) after the proposed new name or combination, or the author may state that a new name or combination is being introduced.

3) The name should not be a later (junior) homonym of a previously validly published name of a taxon of algae, bacteria, fungi, or protozoa. Authoritative publications list names for algae (41), bacteria (37), fungi (39, 59), and protozoa (47).

4) Give the derivation of the name. Consult *Bergey's Manual* for the style used in giving etymologies.

To form a complete citation of a scientific name, and to distinguish between scientific names that are homonyms, the name of the author who first validly published the scientific name should be given immediately after the scientific name (*Clostridium pasteurianum* Winogradsky). The author citation ordinarily needs to appear only once in an article, preferably in the text with the first mention of the name; usually it does not appear in the title. If there are three or more authors of the article in which the name was originally proposed, the author citation may consist of the name of the first author followed by "et al." The date of publication of the name follows the author's name, although inclusion of the date is not always important. Author citations may be especially important in taxonomic articles, but it is good practice to cite the author's name in any article dealing with unusual microorganisms.

When a species is transferred from the genus in which it was originally placed to another genus, the specific epithet in the first validly published name for this species must be used unless there is some obstacle to its use (for example, if there is a species in the genus with the same specific epithet). The name of the author who first validly published the name bearing the specific epithet is placed in parentheses after the scientific name, followed by the names of the authors who effected the change— for example, *Shigella dysenteriae* (Shiga) Castellani and Chalmers. Shiga was the first to validly publish a name (*Bacillus dysenteriae*) for the organism; Castellani and Chalmers subsequently transferred it to the genus *Shigella*. *Bacillus dysenteriae*, the original epithet-bearing synonym, is called the basonym.

Use only correct names of bacterial taxa. An organism may have a number of correct names, depending on the taxonomic placement of the organism. Use the nomenclature in the most recent edition of *Bergey's Manual* or, if you disagree with this nomenclature, place the name given in *Bergey's Manual* in parentheses after the first use of a scientific name in the article.

However, only those names that have standing in nomenclature should be used. For determining which names are currently available, consult the Approved Lists of Bacterial Names published in 1980 (34). The annual cumulative lists of newly validated names are published in the January issues of the *International Journal of Systematic Bacteriology*. For more recently published names, consult the subsequent quarterly issues of this journal.

Sometimes it is necessary to cite a name that does not have standing in nomenclature. In these cases, it is recommended that the name be enclosed in quotation marks and that mention be made in the text that such names do not have standing in nomenclature.

When strict adherence to the rules of nomenclature would only produce confusion and would undermine nomenclatural stability, "Opinions" allowing exceptions to the rules may be issued by the Judicial Commission of the International Committee on Systematic Bacteriology. Requests to the Judicial Commission (*see* page 172, this chapter) that are not supported by adequate, fully documented evidence will be returned to the author for revision. When an "Opinion" is challenged, the basis of the challenge should be stated and supported by documentation of the relevant facts.

Requests for "Opinions" or challenges of a proposed "Opinion" or of an "Issued Opinion" should be submitted to the Judicial Commission in such form that they can be published without delay in the *International Journal of Systematic Bacteriology*.

Abbreviations of scientific names   Names of genera and higher categories may stand by themselves to refer to their taxa; specific and subspecific epithets may not. A generic name that is followed by a specific epithet should be spelled out the first time it is used in the text; subsequently it may be abbreviated to its capitalized initial letter if the context makes the meaning clear—for example, *S. albus* for *Streptomyces albus*. If there are several generic names in the text with the same initial letter, the names preferably should be spelled out on each occasion. Since there are no international rules for forming abbreviations of more than one letter, if you must abbreviate use enough letters to avoid confusion (*Strep.* for *Streptococcus*, *Sal.* for *Salmonella*, *Sh.* for *Shigella*). A list of abbreviations with guidelines for constructing abbreviations of generic names for computer usage has recently been published (48).

Common names   Many microorganisms are known by their common (provincial, vernacular) names as well as by their scientific names—for example, gonococcus for *Neisseria gonorrheae*. The common name for an organism may differ from language to language or from place to place, even within the same country. There are no rules that govern the use of common names.

The *International Code of Nomenclature of Bacteria* gives the following advice for printing the names of taxa higher than genera: "For scientific names of taxa, conventions shall be used which are appropriate to the language of the country and to the relevant journal and publishing house concerned. These should preferably indicate scientific names by a different type face, e.g., italic, or by some other device to distinguish them from the rest of the text."

Adjectival forms and vernacular nouns derived from generic names   Internationally recognized rules do not exist for adjectival forms and nouns derived from generic names of bacteria. However, certain guidelines should be followed, as outlined below. Clarity is more important than general rules of grammar or word coinage.

Adjectival forms must not be derived from specific epithets, such as coli from *Escherichia coli* or aureus from *Staphylococcus aureus*. Thus, it is unacceptable to use the terms coli meningitis or aureus infection. In contrast, adjectival forms may be derived from generic names. Generic names, neither capitalized nor italicized, may be used as adjectives, in terms such as salmonella meningitis or pseudomonas infection. Alternatively, adjectival forms are derived from the generic names by the addition of a suffix, either "-ic" or "-al," as in streptococcic or streptococcal pneumonia. Adjectives can be derived also from common names, such as in pneumococcal pneumonia. Consult a medical dictionary for commonly used adjectival forms.

On strict etymologic grounds, the adjectival terms formed from names of Greek origin would have the Greek adjectival suffix "-ic." Thus, the proper adjectival forms for *Streptococcus* and *Leptospira* (both built from

Greek roots) would be constructed by adding "-ic" to the root term, to produce streptococcic and leptospiric, respectively. By the same rule, the adjectival form of *Proteus* would be proteic. Adjectives are formed from Latin-based names by adding the suffixes "-al" or "-ar" to the root. Thus, *Escherichia* becomes escherichial and *Brucella* becomes brucellar. Adjectives formed with Latin suffixes tend to become more euphonic than those with Greek suffixes, and, therefore, the Latin suffixes are frequently added to words with Greek roots. Adjectival generic names may be avoided by the use of established terms such as brucellosis and salmonellosis.

Use an initial lowercase letter and roman type to form vernacular nouns from generic names.

Generic name	Noun form	
	Singular	Plural
Escherichia	escherichia	escherichiae
Corynebacterium	corynebacterium	corynebacteria
Pseudomonas	pseudomonas, pseudomonad	pseudomonas, pseudomonads
Enterobacter	enterobacter	enterobacters
Vibrio	vibrio	vibrios

These terms should be used only if ambiguity does not arise; thus, the words "bacillus" and "bacilli" may be misinterpreted as either rod-shaped bacteria or members of the genus *Bacillus*. Occasionally more than one common name arises from a generic name, such as treponema (plural, treponemata or treponemas) and treponeme (plural, treponemes) from *Treponema*.

Some commonly used vernacular forms for names above the rank of genus include the terms actinomycete (plural, actinomycetes) for members of the order *Actinomycetales*, streptomycete (plural, streptomycetes) for members of the family *Streptomycetaceae*, and pseudomonad (plural, pseudomonads) for members of the family *Pseudomonadaceae*. For the appropriate terms, look at the journal to which the manuscript is to be submitted.

Synonyms   Two or more different scientific names based on the same nomenclature type are referred to as objective synonyms—for example, *Bacillus dysenteriae* and *Shigella dysenteriae*. The different names arose because the species was transferred from one genus to another. When two or more independently named taxa are regarded as belonging to the same taxon as a result of a comparison of their nomenclatural types, they are regarded as subjective synonyms—for example, *Photobacterium leiognathi* and *Photobacterium mandapamensis* (57). Even when the synonym is placed in parentheses, it is necessary to properly designate it as a synonym—for example, *Streptococcus pneumoniae* (syn. *Diplococcus pneumoniae*).

Infrasubspecific categories   The rules of the Bacteriologic Code do not apply to categories lower than subspecies. However, the Code does give recommendations on terms used for infrasubspecific categories. Examples of the preferred terms for commonly used taxa are biovar, chemoform or chemovar, morphovar, phagovar, and serovar (synonyms: biotype, chemotype, morphotype, phagotype, and serotype, respectively). Frequently it is logical and convenient to recognize clusters of strains or isolates as constituting an infrasubspecific taxon rather than a subspecies or species.

MYCOLOGIC NOMENCLATURE

The nomenclature of the fungi is governed by the rules of the *International Code of Botanical Nomenclature* (62), and much useful and timely information on their nomenclature appears in the journals *Taxon* and *Mycotaxon*. In 1948 bacteriologists published their first code of nomenclature. The Botanical Code no longer covers names of bacteria.

There are a number of minor differences between the Botanical and Bacteriologic Codes, particularly in terminology. The principal differences are as follows:

1) A Latin diagnosis (description) of a newly named taxon is required for the valid publication of the name of a fungus or other recent plant, but not of a bacterium.
2) In botany, the publication or announcement of new names is not restricted to any one journal. In contrast, new names and new combinations of bacteria must either be originally published in the *International Journal of Systematic Bacteriology* or, if published elsewhere, must be announced in the *International Journal of Systematic Bacteriology* as a requirement for valid publication.
3) The starting date for botanical nomenclature is 1 May 1753 (exceptions: Uredinales, Ustilaginales, and Gasteromycetes—31 December 1801; all other fungi—1 January 1821). The starting date for bacteria is 1 January 1980 (formerly, it was 1 May 1753).
4) The type of a plant name may not be a living culture.

VIROLOGIC NOMENCLATURE AND TAXONOMY

The International Committee on Nomenclature of Viruses meets regularly at the International Congresses for Virology and conducts mail ballots during intervals between meetings. The goal of the Committee is to develop a universal nomenclature for all viruses based on a latinized binomial system. Its subcommittee on bacteriophages, invertebrate viruses, plant viruses, and vertebrate viruses describes virus genera and subgenera, establishes their names, and designates their type species.

The code and data subcommittee deals with cryptograms for coding virus information. Because a number of the virus families now include agents that multiply in more than one of the four major kinds of hosts, a coordination subcommittee has been established to ensure that all possible members of a virus family are considered by the study group responsible for that family, regardless of the host class or classes that the viruses infect. Study groups make recommendations to the subcommittees regarding groups of viruses known or suspected to be taxonomically allied. Their early work is reviewed in the First Report of the International Committee on Nomenclature of Viruses (65).

Further decisions of the International Committee on Taxonomy of Viruses regarding family and generic names have been published in *Intervirology* (44), the official journal of the Virology Section of the International Association of Microbiological Societies. The Second and Third Reports of the International Committee on Taxonomy of Viruses (43, 53) present official decisions through the time of the most recent plenary meeting. Reports of study groups and subcommittees also appear in this journal before official consideration by the International Committee on Taxonomy of Viruses—for example, the report on Papovaviridae (55).

Much of the formal nomenclature in virology has been derived from the earlier common names of viruses and groups—for example, Picornaviridae from picornaviruses and Poxviridae from poxviruses, but the vernacular names or the informal group names still have more common usage.

Virologic taxonomy   Taxonomy for viruses has proceeded no higher than families, and in many instances only to generic and subgeneric groupings. Even the broad functional subdivisions based on major host categories (viruses of vertebrates, invertebrates, plants, and protists) are not mutually exclusive for the viruses themselves, because a number of genera and families of viruses include members infecting more than one of these host groupings.

Latin binomials have been assigned conservatively to viruses to avoid a false impression of levels of relatedness that further characterization may alter and to avoid fixing certain groupings at taxon levels that later may prove to be too low. Common names of groups, tentative designations of genera but without Latin species designations, and descriptive phrases for groups have been used to satisfy the need for practical consideration of related or similar viruses together, without prematurely naming formal taxa. The accepted practice is to state the generic or family name or both (if established) initially in a paper, followed by the common name or serotype designation or both—for example, a member of the genus *Herpesvirus*, human herpesvirus type 1 (HV-1); or a member of the *Enterovirus* genus, of the family Picornaviridae, echovirus type 6 (echovirus-6).

Almost exclusively, common names are used for plant viruses. Generally these are in English and are derived from the main host and major symptoms induced by the virus (tobacco mosaic virus, potato yellow dwarf virus). The Plant Virus Subcommittee is reluctant to designate family and genus, and at present prefers to retain the noncommittal taxon "group" for the plant viruses. Several group names for plant viruses have been latinized—for example, Tobamovirus for the tobacco mosaic virus group, Cucumovirus for the cucumber mosaic virus group, and Bromovirus for the group related to brome mosaic virus. These names have been endorsed by the International Committee on Taxonomy of Viruses.

Infraspecific categories   Infraspecific designations for viruses vary; a numbered serotype is the most common subdivision with viruses of vertebrates, but the specific name and history are also important because both serologic and other properties may differ within a serotype.

Cryptograms   The code and data subcommittee of the International Committee on Taxonomy of Viruses had chosen cryptograms to code information concerning viruses (43), but their views have not caught on and have now been abandoned.

KEYS TO THE IDENTIFICATION OF MICROORGANISMS

Bacteria   The major reference work for the identification of bacteria is *Bergey's Manual* (38). Examples of various kinds of keys are given below. The key to the genus *Streptococcus* (figure 13.8) is based on a dichotomous structure; the key to the differentiation of the species of the genus *Neisseria* (figure 13.9) provides information on the characteristics most useful for identification. Dichotomous keys are less suitable for identifying bacteria than for higher plants and animals because many of the characteristics used often are neither always present nor always absent in all of the strains of a species. For this reason, as illustrated in the key for the differentiation of members of the genus *Proteus* (figure 13.10), percentage figures based on the study of large numbers of strains are becoming more important. The Centers for Disease Control, Atlanta, Georgia, have developed helpful keys to the identification of unusual bacterial isolates.

DNA and RNA viruses   Tables of the current classification and nomenclature of both DNA and RNA viruses of vertebrates are given by Melnick (54). The classification table (figure 13.11) provides information on viruses with a DNA genome and is shown for illustrative purposes.

Portion of key to the species of the genus *Streptococcus*

I. Does not grow at 10 or 45°C (some exceptions in *S. sanguis*). Does not grow in 6.5% NaCl broth, at pH 9.6, or in 0.1% methylene blue milk.
   A. Does not hydrolyze sodium hippurate (some exceptions in *S. dysgalactiae*).
      1. Does not require a high CO_2 tension for rapid growth on blood agar. Cells and colonies not "minute." Ammonia produced from arginine.
         a. Does not ferment inulin.
            b. Fibrinolytic.
               c. Beta-hemolytic. Ferments trehalose but not sorbitol.
                  d. Does not ferment glycerol. Lancefield GROUP A.
                     1. *Streptococcus pyogenes*
                  dd. Ferments glycerol aerobically. Lancefield GROUP C.
                     2. *Streptococcus equisimilis*
            bb. Not fibrinolytic.
               c. Beta-hemolytic.
                  d. Ferments sorbitol but not trehalose. Ferments glycerol aerobically. Lancefield GROUP C.
                     3. *Streptococcus zooepidemicus*
                  dd. Does not ferment trehalose, sorbitol, or glycerol. Lancefield GROUP C.
                     4. *Streptococcus equi*
               cc. Not beta-hemolytic. Ferments trehalose. Usually ferments sorbitol. Does not ferment glycerol. Lancefield GROUP C.
                  5. *Streptococcus dysgalactiae*
         aa. Inulin usually fermented.
            b. May or may not be beta-hemolytic. Not bile soluble. Viscous polysaccharide may be produced in 5% sucrose broth. Lancefield GROUP H.
               6. *Streptococcus sanguis*
            bb. (Viscous polysaccharide not produced in 5% sucrose broth.) Alpha-reaction on blood agar. Bile soluble. No group antigen demonstrated.
               7. *Streptococcus pneumoniae*
      2. High CO_2 tension required for rapid growth on blood agar. "Minute" cells and colonies. Ammonia produced from arginine. Lancefield GROUP F and Type 1, GROUP G.
         8. *Streptococcus anginosus*
   B. Hydrolyzes sodium hippurate.
      1. Produces ammonia from arginine. Ferments glycerol aerobically. May be beta-hemolytic. Final pH in glucose broth 4.2–4.8. Lancefield GROUP B.
         9. *Streptococcus agalactiae*

Figure 13.8. Example of a dichotomous key. Adapted, with permission of the publisher, from Buchanan, R. E.; Gibbons, N. E., editors. Bergey's manual of determinative bacteriology. 8th ed. Baltimore: Williams & Wilkins Co.; 1974:491.

Characteristics differentiating the species of the genus *Neisseria* *

	1. *N. gon-orrhoeae*	2. *N. men-ingitidis*	3. *N. sicca*	4. *N. subflava*	5. *N. fla-vescens*	6. *N. mu-cosa*
Capsules	—	v	v	+	—	+
Acid from:						
Glucose	+	+	+	+	—	+
Maltose	—	+	+	+	—	+
Fructose	—	—	+	v	—	+
Sucrose	—	—	+	v	—	+
Starch	—	—	v	v	—	+
Polysaccharide pro-duced from 5% sucrose	0	0	+	d	+	+
Production of H_2S	—	—	+	+	+	+
Reduction of:						
Nitrate	—	—	—	—	—	+
Nitrite	—	d	+	+	+	+
Pigment	—	—	d	+	+	—
Extra CO_2	//	/	*	*	*	*
Growth at 22°C	—	—	d	d	+	+
G + C moles %	49.5–49.6	50.0–51.5	49.0–51.5	48.0–50.5	46.5–50.1	50.5–52.0

*+: Most strains positive (≧90%). −: Most strains negative (≧90%). d: Some strains positive, some negative. v: Character inconstant and in one strain may sometimes be positive, sometimes negative. 0: No growth on medium with 5% sucrose. G + C: Guanine + cytosine in the deoxyribonucleic acid. //: Very important. /: Important. *: not necessary.

Figure 13.9. Example of a key giving list of characteristics. Adapted, with permission of the publisher, from Buchanan, R. E.; Gibbons, N. E., editors. Bergey's manual of determinative bacteriology. 8th ed. Baltimore: Williams & Wilkins Co.; 1974:429.

GENETIC NOMENCLATURE AND SYMBOLS

Bacterial genetics   A system of uniform nomenclature and standard-ized symbols for bacterial genetics (40) gives rules for designation of genotypes (including loci, mutation sites, plasmids and episomes, and sex factors), phenotypes, and bacterial strains. Modifications of the system have been published (35, 36, 51, 56, 60, 61, 63).

Genotype symbols   In representing a genotype, each locus of a given wild-type strain of bacteria is designated by a symbol consisting of three lowercase italic letters. For example, *ara* refers to the loci in which occur mutations affecting the response of the cell to arabinose as a source of carbon and energy. Different loci, any one of which may carry mutations, are distinguished from one another by an italic capital letter added immediately after the three lowercase letters: Symbols *araA*, *araB*, and *araC* refer to loci that control arabinose utilization. Specific recommen-dations cover loci involved in genetic regulation, loci that govern resist-ance and sensitivity, and suppressor loci.

Designate a mutation site by a serial isolation number placed after the

Differentiation of *Proteus vulgaris* and *P. mirabilis**						
Test or substrate	*P. vulgaris*			*P. mirabilis*		
	Sign	%+	(%+)	Sign	%+	(%+)
Indol	+	98.2		−	1.9	
Voges-Proskauer						
37°C	−	0		− or +	15.6	
22°C	− or +	11.3		+ or −	51.6	
Citrate (Simmons')	d	10.5	(14.1)	+ or (+)	58.7	(37.1)
Ornithine decarboxylase	−	0		+	99.2	
Sucrose	+	94.7		d	18.9	(63.3)
Maltose	+	96.2	(1.9)	−	0.9	(0.4)
Salicin	d	58.2	(10.9)	d	0.8	(29.8)
Alpha methyl glucoside	d	79.5	(5.1)	−	0	
Esculin	d	59	(2.6)	−		(0.9)
DNase	+ or −	60		−	0	

* Figures in parentheses indicate percentage of delayed reactions (3 or more days).
+ Positive within 1 or 2 days' incubation (90% or more).
(+) Positive reaction after 3 or more days.
− No reaction (90% or more).
+ or − Majority of strains positive, occasional cultures negative.
− or + Majority of cultures negative, occasional strains positive.
(+) or + Majority of reactions delayed, some occur within 1 or 2 days.
d Different reactions: +, (+), −.

Figure 13.10. Example of key giving percentage figures. Adapted, with permission, from Edwards, P. R.; Ewing, W. H. Identification of Enterobacteriaceae. 3rd ed. Minneapolis: Burgess Publishing Co.; 1972:44.

locus symbol. If it is not known in which of several loci that govern related functions the mutation has occurred, substitute a hyphen for the capital letter—for example, the mutation sites that were previously designated *ara-1*, *ara-2*, and *ara-3* were designated *araB1*, *araA2*, and *araC3* after the altered enzymes had been identified.

The wild-type allele of a locus is designated by a plus sign; thus, *araB+* is the wild-type allele of the *araB* locus.

Designate plasmids and episomes by symbols clearly distinguished from those used for gene loci. The first letter of a symbol for a plasmid or an episome is a capital letter; the symbol is not italicized, and it is placed in parentheses (Col E1). Mutant loci and mutation sites on plasmids and episomes are designated by symbols of the same kind as those used for loci and sites on the chromosome. The description of a strain carrying an episome should include information on the state or the location of the episome, or both. Do not change a genotype symbol that has been published and that conforms to the recommended system; change one that does not conform to the system to agree with it; and note the change when the new symbol is first published. For yeast, *Chlamydomonas*, and

Table 17. Members of vertebrate virus families, with emphasis on viruses that infect human beings

Family and sub-family	Genus	Common species	No. of members
Picornaviridae	*Enterovirus*	polioviruses	3
		coxsackieviruses	23
		echoviruses	31
		enteroviruses 68–71	4
		viruses of other verte-brates	34
		possible member: hepatitis A virus	1
	Cardiovirus (EMC virus group)	encephalomyocarditis (EMC) virus and mengovirus murine encephalomyelitis	} 2
	Rhinovirus (common cold viruses)	virus types 1A–114	>115
		viruses of cattle	2
	Aphthovirus (foot-and-mouth dis-ease viruses)	aphthoviruses of cattle and other cloven-hoofed animals	7
	(Other picornaviruses not yet assigned to genera)	equine viruses	2
		viruses of invertebrates (including several vi-ruses of bees, and vi-ruses infecting Droso-phila, Gonometa, and other insects)	≥30
Caliciviridae	*Calicivirus*	vesicular exanthema of swine virus (VESV)	13
		viruses of cats, sea lions	many
		possible member: human calicivirus	

Figure 13.11. Example of classification of several viruses. Adapted, with permission, from Melnick, J. L. Taxonomy of viruses. Prog. Med. Virol. 26:214–232; 1980:221.

several fungal species, use symbols such as those given in *Handbook of Microbiology* (50).

Phenotype symbols Phenotype traits should be described in words or symbolically designated by abbreviations that are defined on first mention (40). The phenotype symbols should be clearly distinguishable from genotype symbols. Whereas a genotype symbol consists of three italic lowercase letters, a phenotype symbol consists of three roman letters, the first of which is capitalized. The same letters may be used for a genotype symbol and a phenotype symbol—for example, the phenotype Met is associated with a mutation in the *metA* locus.

Strain designations   Designate strains by simple serial numbers (40). To prevent duplication, each laboratory should use a letter prefix different from that of any other laboratory. Strains are not italicized. Do not change a designation that has been published and that conforms to the accepted recommendations. Change a designation that does not conform to agree with the recommendations; and note the change when the new designation is first published.

Viral genetics   There is no uniform system of nomenclature applicable to mutants of bacterial, plant, and animal viruses. Nomenclature for mutants has developed independently for each virus or group of viruses. Consequently, these systems reflect not only the unique properties of each virus group, but also the degree of complexity attained in the genetic analysis of a given virus.

Of the major groups of viruses, bacterial viruses—specifically λ and T4—have been studied most exhaustively. The efforts of investigators have produced a system that describes the mutants, genes, and recognition sites on the linkage map of λ (46). The genotype and phenotype designations on the linkage map of T4 have also been summarized (52).

Investigators in several laboratories have proposed schemes for uniform nomenclature for mutants of three groups of animal viruses. Because of unique properties of different virus systems, certain modifications of a general scheme are required for each virus group.

A nomenclatural scheme was first proposed for simian virus 40 (SV40) (58). The type of mutant is designated by two lowercase letters—for example, *ts* for temperature-sensitive, followed by the complementation group designated by a single capital letter, and then the mutant number (SV40 *tsA7*). Finally, the entire name is either italicized or underlined (*tsA7*).

The major modification of the above system required for adenovirus mutants (45) was necessary because there are numerous adenovirus species. The first term in the mutant name indicates the natural host and the immunologic type—for example, H5 = human adenovirus type 5.

A somewhat different scheme has been proposed for numbering the avian leukosis and sarcoma virus mutants (64). Two capital letters are used to designate the laboratory in which the mutant was isolated, followed by the number the investigator chooses to assign to that mutant. An italicized two-letter lowercase code designating the type of mutants— for example, *ts* = temperature-sensitive—precedes the laboratory code letters. Optionally, the mutant number may be followed by a two-letter capital letter code designating the wild-type virus, and the envelope subgroup may be appended with a hyphen to the mutant number. An example of a complete mutant designation is *ts*LA335PR-C (a temperature-sensitive virus, isolated in the Los Angeles laboratory, number 335, from the Prague strain of Rous sarcoma virus belonging to envelope subgroup C).

ANIMAL SCIENCES

NAMES AND KEYS

The rules and recommendations developed for giving an animal—or a taxonomic group of animals—a scientific name, with its proper reference of author and date, are systematized in the *International Code of Zoological Nomenclature* (74) and its amendments. The essential features of zoological nomenclature and taxonomy are explained in *Taxonomy* (67), in *Procedure in Taxonomy* (79), in *Principles of Systematic Zoology* (75), and in *Biological Systematics* (78); current developments are reported in *Systematic Zoology* (81). *Official Lists* of approved, and *Official Indexes* of rejected, names and works (publications) are produced by the International Commission on Zoological Nomenclature (77). Applications to the International Commission for approval of scientific names, and comments thereon, are published in the *Bulletin of Zoological Nomenclature* (68). Official decisions of the International Commission regarding names and works are also included in the *Bulletin of Zoological Nomenclature*.

Basic systematic and infraspecific categories   The basic systematic categories and groups (taxa; singular, taxon) in descending order are phylum or division, class, order, family, genus, and species. The scientific name of a species is a binomen and consists of the generic name followed by the specific name. The scientific names of all taxa are Latin or latinized forms.

Names of genera and higher categories may stand by themselves. When a generic name is followed by a specific name the generic name should be spelled out the first time it is used in the text, but subsequently it may be abbreviated to its initial letter (always capitalized) or letters if the context makes the meaning clear (*see also* page 174, this chapter). A specific name should be preceded by the generic name or its abbreviation except when used in a key, article, or section of an article devoted to a single genus.

The Zoological Code recognizes subspecies and will accept, as subspecific names, the names proposed for varieties or forms prior to 1961; it will not accept names within infrasubspecific categories proposed after 1960. The Code does not recognize any category below the subspecies level.

Authors of scientific names   The author of the scientific name in the family, genus, or species group is the person who first publishes it in a manner that satisfies the regulations on available names prescribed by the Code. In taxonomic articles the name of each genus, species, or subspecies mentioned should be supplemented with the name of its author: *Homo* Linnaeus; *Rana catesbeiana* Shaw; *Culex pipiens quinquefasciatus* Say. When several types of data are used to characterize taxa, many biologists (both authors and editors) recommend inclusion of the authority with the scientific name of any species mentioned, even in an article emphasizing physiology, embryology, or other biological aspect of the taxon. Some journals in the fields of physiology and biochemistry explicitly state that taxonomic author citations should be omitted; read the "Instructions to Authors" section of the journal for specific guidelines.

When a species or subspecies is transferred to a genus other than that in which it was first placed, the name of the author is placed in parentheses: *Lepomis gulosus* (Cuvier). The name of the original author is retained, but unlike the practice in botany and microbiology, the authority for the new combination is not added.

The author citation needs to appear only once in an article with the first mention of the taxon; usually it should not appear in the title. Inclusion of the year in which the name was proposed may be important in some articles, for comparison of name priority or for historical or other reasons, and should be written as follows: *Aphis gossypii* Clover 1877; if a species has been transferred to another genus, it should be written as *Blatella germanica* (Linnaeus 1767), but never as *Blatella germanica* (Linnaeus) 1767.

When a species is transferred from one genus to another, the ending of an adjectival specific name is changed if the generic names differ in gender: *Taeniothrips albus* (masculine) became *Frankliniella alba* (feminine) to agree in gender with the new genus.

Typography   The scientific name of a genus, subgenus, species, subspecies, or other subordinate taxon is italicized; the name of a higher taxon is set in roman type. When the name of a taxon proposed as new to science (new taxon, substitute name) appears in print for the first time, the abbreviation that designates its status may be set in boldface type—for example, **sp. nov.** or **comb. nov.** (*see* Abbreviations and Symbols, chapter 14). A generic name used as a common or vernacular name is neither italicized nor capitalized: *Gorilla*, gorilla; *Octopus*, octopus; *Python*, python. (Directions for marking words to indicate italic and boldface type are given in chapter 9.) The name of a genus or any higher taxon is written with a capital initial letter, but the specific or infraspecific name is written with a lowercase letter.

The Zoological Code (74) now requires the omission of all diacritical marks, apostrophes, diereses, and hyphens, except when hyphens are used to set off individual letters in a compound species-group name as in *c-album*. For names derived from German words, the standard replacement for the umlaut should be used (*kühniella* becomes *kuehniella*).

Common or vernacular names   Many plants and animals are known by their common (vernacular, provincial) names, as well as by their scientific names. The common name for an organism may vary from language to language, or from place to place, even within the same country.

The Entomological Society of America maintains standards for approving and publishing common names of insects. The most recent list published (70) contains more than 1900 names.

> In the case of names having two parts, one of them a group name . . ., the group name will be a separate word when used in a sense that is systematically correct as in "house fly" and "bed bug." If the group name used is not systematically correct, it should be combined in a single word with a modifier as in the examples "citrus whitefly" and "citrus mealybug."

The house fly is a true fly; the citrus whitefly is not. The bed bug is a true bug; the citrus mealybug is not. Because no insect larva is a true worm, the suffix *worm* is always written or printed as one word with the modifier: silkworm, *not* silk worm; striped cutworm, *not* striped cut worm.

The American Ornithologists' Union publishes a checklist of North American birds with scientific names for all taxa including species and subspecies (69). It recognizes vernacular names for species but not for subspecies. The American Fisheries Society maintains a list of common and scientific names of species, but not subspecies, of fishes in the United States and Canada. The list is published at irregular intervals as a report of the society's Committee on Names of Fishes (72). Lists have also been published for species of mammals (73), and, by the American Society of Ichthyologists and Herpetologists, for species and subspecies of amphibians and reptiles (71).

A common name may be formed from the scientific name of a family by making the initial letter lowercase and dropping the terminal "ae"— for example, sciurid from Sciuridae; chironomid from Chironomidae.

Keys for identifying organisms   The ideal key to a group of organisms presents rigorously selected information based on morphologic, ecologic, biochemical, or other characteristics in such a way that a series of choices leads the user step by step to the identification of one or more organisms. Identification should result if the key has been properly constructed, if the user interprets his or her material and the key correctly, and if the organisms to be identified have been included in the key. Metcalf (76) and Blackwelder (67) provide information on the construction and interpretation of keys.

Keys are useful and practical means of identifying organisms. They are not necessarily accurate pictures of phylogenetic lines or natural relationships. Some keys separate only two species; others separate as many as hundreds of taxa. The most useful keys have a dichotomous

---

Portion of key to species of the genus *Succinea*

1. Aperture round, not much higher than wide, occupying three-fifths length
    of shell . . . . *avara*, p. 124
    Aperture ovate, occupying three-fourths to four-fifths length of shell, p. 122
   2
2. Shell ovoid, somewhat inflated; aperture ovate, spire broad, p. 122 3
    Shell much elongated, narrow; aperture narrowly ovate, spire acute, p. 125.
   4
3. Aperture regularly ovate; color greenish or yellowish . . . . . . *ovalis*, p. 122
    Aperture obliquely ovate, expanded at lower part; color amber . . . .
    . . . . *concordialis*, p. 123
4. Aperture occupying three-fourths length of shell, little expanded at lower
    part . . . . *retusa*, p. 125
    Aperture occupying four-fifths length of shell, notably expanded at lower
    part . . . .*salleana*, p. 127

Figure 13.12. Example of style for a short key. Adapted from Baker, F. C.
Fieldbook of Illinois land snails. Ill. Nat. Hist. Surv. Man. 2; 1939: 121.

Portion of key to the American species of *Dictya*

1 (2). Second antennal segment shining on outer half or more, longer than high
        . . . . *abnormis* group
2 (1). Second antennal segment wholly pruinose, not longer than high.
3 (4). Terminalia in retracted condition well covered by elongated, scooplike
        sternite . . . .*ptyarion*
4 (3). Terminalia with at least tips of surstyli well exposed; no elongated sternite.
5 (8). Surstyli with dorsal tip furnished with long, apically directed, stiff bristles.
6 (7). Pregonite with well developed preterminal lobe . . . . *pictipes*
7 (6). Pregonite with no more than a minute terminal point . . . . *borealis*
8 (5). Surstylus with bristles of dorsal tip short, dorsally directed.

Figure 13.13. Example of style used for a long key. Adapted from Steyskal, G.
C. The American species of the genus *Dictya* Meigen (Diptera, Sciomyzidae).
Entomol. Soc. Am. Ann. 47:511–539; 1954.

---

construction in the form of couplets permitting only one correct choice.
Guiding principles for constructing a dichotomous key include the following (76):

1) Simplicity. Write entries in the key as simple, direct, and mutually
    exclusive couplets, thus constructing a dichotomous key.
2) Clarity. State the first member of a couplet in the positive and the
    second as a negative or contrasting statement of the character or
    characters displayed in the first.
3) Reversibility. Construct the key so that it can be used backward as

well as forward. Then if you have made an erroneous choice at one couplet you can retrace the steps and find the point of divergence. Figure 13.12 illustrates a common style especially popular for short keys. Figure 13.13 illustrates a style used for long keys, where a reversible-type key is definitely advantageous.

ANATOMY

The International Anatomical Nomenclature Committee (85) has published an official revised list of human gross anatomic terms in Latin. The International Committee on Veterinary Anatomical Nomenclature (87) has published a list of anatomic terms in Latin for cat, dog, swine, cattle, sheep, goat, and horse; anatomical terms for avian species are provided in *Nomina Anatomica Avium* (82). Standardized versions of embryologic terms for amniotes and histologic terms for humans were approved on an interim basis at the Ninth International Congress of Anatomists in Leningrad in 1970. *Nomina Embryologica* (83) and *Nomina Histologica* (84) were officially accepted by the Tenth Congress in 1975 in Tokyo, and both lists are included in the 4th edition of *Nomina Anatomica* (86). This new edition contains the internationally approved terms for macroanatomy, microanatomy, and developmental human anatomy.

For species other than humans and domestic mammals, terms based on the same principles are being prepared, but until an official list is available, these rules should be followed: Well-established terms should not be altered merely on pedantic or etymologic grounds; each structure should be designated by one term only; and differentiating terms should be arranged as opposites—for example, *major* and *minor.*

Anatomic terms derived from Latin are regarded as common nouns and consequently should not be capitalized or italicized. The Latin form of any term is the official term approved by the International Anatomical Nomenclature Committee, but English equivalents that either translate the Latin terms directly or provide common idiomatic substitutes may be used in biological writing. For example, "brachial plexus" could be used instead of "plexus brachialis," and "stomach" instead of "ventriculus." The form of some terms may or may not be changed (subcutaneous tissue or tela subcutanea), and some terms retain the Latin form because alternative, practical equivalents are lacking in English (femur; cisterna chyli). Avoid antiquated names and obsolete usage.

GENETICS AND CYTOGENETICS

In genetics and cytogenetics many rules of nomenclature have developed informally and have become established through wide use rather than by formal agreements among authorities. The number of symbols currently employed to designate genes and chromosomes is too large to permit complete description in this manual. General rules for genetic nomenclature and symbols were summarized by Y. Tanaka for the Tenth International Congress of Genetics and distributed privately; they have been supported and modified by resolutions of the Eleventh and Twelfth International Congresses of Genetics; several symbol systems are compared in table 13.4.

Compilations of gene symbols for many animals, with additional pertinent information, including linkages, can be found in the *Biology Data Book* (88) and *Handbook of Biochemistry and Molecular Biology* (96). The *Biology Data Book* covers *Bombyx mori* (silkworm moth), *Nasonia vitripennis* (parasitic wasp), *Drosophila melanogaster* (fruit fly), chicken, rabbit, rat, mouse, and guinea pig. The *Handbook of Biochemistry* also covers the fruit fly and mouse, and provides information on humans. The 63 chapters constituting volumes 3 and 4 of the *Handbook of Genetics* (100) are authoritative reviews and source guides to invertebrates and vertebrates of genetic interest.

Fruit fly   For descriptions of genetic variants of the fruit fly, *Drosophila melanogaster*, widely accepted conventions stipulate usage for symbolic representation of mutants and chromosome aberrations. A detailed account of these conventions, which should guide authors in the formation of new symbolic descriptions, is given by Lindsley and Grell (101). Symbols for both mutants and chromosome aberrations are italicized; they should not contain Greek letters, subscripts, or spaces. The spelled-out names of mutants are not italicized.

Symbols for mutant types are abbreviations of their characterizing names. Usually a symbol begins with the first letter of its name; the convention designates an initial capital letter for a dominant (*R* for roughened) and an initial lowercase letter for a recessive (*r* for rudimentary or *ry* for rosy).

Designations of genotypes with several mutant genes follow the rules outlined below.

Genes on same chromosome	Separate the gene symbols with spaces (*v w f B*)
Genes on homologous chromosomes	Separate symbols with slash mark (*y w f/B*)
Genes on nonhomologous chromosomes	Separate symbols with semicolons and spaces (*bw; e; ey*)

Alleles at a particular locus are represented by the same symbol (and name) but are differentiated by italicized superscripts: arbitrary numbers, experiment numbers, capitalized initials (representing finder or laboratory), or discovery date. Lindsley and Grell (101) should be consulted for conventions governing superscripts of a recessive allele of a prepon-

Table 13.4. Animal genetic conventions: comparative designations

Variable	Fruit fly and insect vectors of disease	Mouse, other rodents, cat, other mammals	Humans
Genotype			
Dominant	Capital italics	Capital italics	Capital italics
Recessive	Lowercase italics	Lowercase italics	Lowercase italics
Phenotype			
Dominant	Capital, roman type	Capital, roman type	Capital, roman type
Recessive	Lowercase, roman type	Lowercase, roman type	Lowercase, roman type
Name of mutant			
Dominant	Capital, roman type	Lowercase, roman type	Lowercase, roman type
Recessive	Lowercase, roman type	Lowercase, roman type	Lowercase, roman type (except proper nouns)
Linkage groups	Roman numerals	Roman numerals	Capital letters (chromosome groups)
Chromosomes			
Autosomes	Arabic numerals	Arabic numerals	Arabic numerals
Sex chromosomes	Capital, roman type	Capital, roman type	Capital, roman type
Wild-type alleles	Superior "+" after locus designation; or "+" on line if locus designated by context	Superior "+" after locus designation; or "+" on line if locus designated by context; or same symbol as mutant gene, but with capital italics for wild-type allele of recessive mutant gene, and lowercase italics for wild-type allele of dominant mutant gene	
Chromosome aberrations (translocation used as example; consult references for conventions of other types of aberrations)	*T* (signifying type of aberration) followed by italic chromosome numerals in parentheses, followed by italic letters or numerals (signifying symbol of mutant arising spontaneously with aberration or simply an experiment number): *T(1;Y;3)127*	*T* followed by boldface roman chromosome numbers in parentheses, followed by italic numbers and letters (signifying a series symbol): *T(**2;9**)138 Ca*	*See* table 13.5, pages 194–195

derantly recessive series; the normal allele; absence of a locus; or loci controlling electrophoretic mobility of proteins (including enzymes); and for conventions for designation of mimics, modifiers, and suppressor genes.

A wild-type allele is symbolized by a superscript plus sign after the locus designation (a^+), or by only a plus sign on the line (+) if the locus is identified by the context. A capital letter should not be used to designate the wild-type allele of a recessive mutation, as is often done in plant and mammalian genetics.

Chromosome aberrations are designated according to the elementary rearrangements: deficiency, duplication, inversion, ring, translocation, and transposition (abbreviated, respectively, *Df*, *Dp*, *In*, *R*, *T*, and *Tp*). Further details on symbols for the six types of rearrangements are given by Lindsley and Grell (101).

Insect vectors of disease   A code to be followed in designating different strains on a uniform basis has been proposed by a WHO Scientific Group on Standardized Strains of Insects of Public Health Importance (ref. 114; reprinted, 1967, ref. 115). Although the suggested nomenclature has not been formally adopted, workers are urged to use it in published reports.

Mouse   Rules for the symbolic designation of genes of the laboratory mouse have been published in a report of the Committee on Standardized Genetic Nomenclature for Mice (92) and by Lyon (102). With some exceptions, the rules are similar to those for *Drosophila*. The symbol for a gene is typically the abbreviation for the gene name (*d* for dilution, *ac* for absence of corpus callosum); the abbreviation, italicized, should begin with the same letter as the name. The name of a gene is written with a lowercase initial letter, whether the mutant is recessive or dominant, except where capitalization is normally used. The symbol for a recessive mutant gene has a lowercase initial letter (*a* for nonagouti) and that for a dominant gene has a capital initial letter (*Re* for rex). The symbol for a gene locus is the symbol of the first-named mutant gene, or allelic pair of genes, without superscript for a specific allele.

The wild-type may be designated by the locus symbol with a lowercase initial letter and a superscript plus (re^+); a plus sign alone if the context leaves no doubt as to the locus represented; or the same symbol as for the mutant gene but with a capital initial letter for a recessive mutant and a lowercase initial letter for a dominant mutant (*D* for the wild-type allele of *d*; *re* for the wild-type allele of *Re*). For most purposes, the first two methods of designation are preferred to the third.

Multiple alleles determining visible or other clear distinctions are represented by the locus symbol with a superscript, usually a lowercase letter, or letters, indicative of the name; the initial letter of the symbol is capitalized if the allele behaves as a dominant. Further details on these conventions and on those for mimics, variants of a series, indistinguishable alleles of independent origin, reversions to wild-type, and translocations are included in the 1963 report of the Committee (92).

The basic rules for naming any mutation have been extended to cover biochemical variants (94). Biochemical nomenclature should be in accord with the rules of the International Union of Biochemistry, Commission on Biochemical Nomenclature. Symbols for structural loci should be two- or three-letter abbreviations (italicized) of the official Commission name of the enzyme, protein, or other substance affected, unless such a symbol has been used for another locus. Further details are given in the 1973 report of the Committee (94).

All numbered linkage groups have now been assigned to chromosomes (113). Arabic chromosome numbers rather than roman linkage-group numbers should be used. Further details about the assignment of linkage groups to specific chromosomes are in a report of the Committee on Standardized Genetic Nomenclature for Mice (93), and in works of Miller and Miller (105). Special rules for nomenclature of inbred strains, with index lists of these strains and their clearly differentiated substrains, have been summarized by Staats (112).

Rodents other than *Mus musculus* The rules proposed by the Committee on Standardized Genetic Nomenclature for Mice (92, 94) should be used for guinea pigs, hamsters, rabbits, rats, and white-footed mice (*Peromyscus*). Lists of rat (98) and guinea pig (97) strains have been published.

Cat A list of standard gene names and symbols for known mutants of the cat has been published by the Committee on Standardized Genetic Nomenclature for Domestic Cats (95). The committee recommends that the rules governing genetic nomenclature for mice be adopted for cats. A procedure for grouping and numbering the chromosomes of the family Felidae was developed by scientists in 1964 at the Conference on Mammalian Cytology and Somatic Cell Genetics (99), and in 1982 the chromosome map of the domestic cat was published (106).

Humans Detailed rules for description of the human chromosome complement and its abnormalities, both numerical and structural, were established at the 1966 Chicago Conference (91) and the 1971 Paris Conference (107) on Standardization in Human Cytogenetics, and summarized in *An International System for Human Cytogenetic Nomenclature* at the 1977 Stockholm Conference (109). This system of description employs symbols (table 13.5) to be used in a prescribed sequence: The total

Table 13.5. Human chromosomes and their aberrations: recommended symbols and abbreviations (109)

Symbol or abbreviation	Explanation
AI	First meiotic anaphase
AII	Second meiotic anaphase
ace	Acentric fragment (see also f)
arrow ($\rightarrow$)	From–to
asterisk (*)	Used like a multiplication sign
b	Break
cen	Centromere
chi	Chimera
colon, single (:)	Break (in detailed descriptions)
colon, double (::)	Break and reunion (in detailed descriptions)
cs	Chromosome
ct	Chromatid
cx	Complex
del	Deletion
der	Derivative chromosome
dia	Diakinesis
dic	Dicentric
dip	Diplotene
dir	Direct
dis	Distal
dit	Dictyate
dmin	Double minute
dup	Duplication
e	Exchange
end	Endoreduplication
equal sign (=)	Sum of
f	Fragment (see also *ace*)
fem	Female
g	Gap
h	Secondary constriction
i	Isochromosome
ins	Insertion
inv	Inversion
lep	Leptotene
MI	First meiotic metaphase
MII	Second meiotic metaphase
mal	Male
mar	Marker chromosome
mat	Maternal origin
med	Median
min	Minute
minus (−)	Loss of
mn	Modal number
mos	Mosaic
oom	Oogonial metaphase
p	Short arm of chromosome
PI	First meiotic prophase
pac	Pachytene

Table 13.5. (Continued)

Symbol or abbreviation	Explanation
parentheses ()	Used to surround structurally altered chromosome(s)
pat	Paternal origin
pcc	Premature chromosome condensation
Ph¹	Philadelphia chromosome
plus (+)	Gain of
prx	Proximal
psu	Pseudo
pvz	Pulverization
q	Long arm of chromosome
qr	Quadriradial
question mark (?)	Indicates questionable identification of chromosome or chromosome structure
r	Ring chromosome
rcp	Reciprocal
rea	Rearrangement
rec	Recombinant chromosome
rob	Robertsonian translocation
s	Satellite
sce	Sister chromatid exchange
sdl	Side-line, sub-line
semicolon (;)	Separates chromosomes and chromosome regions in structural rearrangements involving more than one chromosome
sl	Stem-line
slant line, or solidus (/)	Separates cell lines in describing mosaics or chimeras
spm	Spermatogonial metaphase
t	Translocation
tan	Tandem translocation
ter	Terminal (end of chromosome)
tr	Triradial
tri	Tricentric
underline, double (=)	Used to distinguish homologous chromosomes
var	Variable chromosome region
xma	Chiasma(ta)
zyg	Zygotene

number of chromosomes is given first, the sex chromosome constitution next, and the designations for structural abnormalities last, written in a prescribed manner. The major change made at the Paris Conference, regarding recommendations originally agreed upon at the Chicago Conference, is in the position of the plus (+) and minus (−). These are now to be placed *before* the chromosome designation to mean an additional (for example, +21) or missing (for example, −13) chromosome, but *after* a structural designation to mean enlargement or reduction in size, such as p+, s+, h−, which, respectively, mean enlarged short arms (p), or satellites (s), or reduction in size of the secondary constriction or heterochromatic region (h).

The Paris Conference report gives a specific description of human chromosome bands and a numbering system for each band according to its position on the chromosome. The report also provides a detailed shorthand system for designating structural chromosome abnormalities by breakpoints and band composition—for example, a reciprocal translocation might be written 46,XX,t(4;13)(p21;q32) indicating a translocation between chromosome 4 and 13, with breakpoints in the short arm of chromosome 4 at band 21 and in the long arm of chromosome 13 at band 32. Examples of many other rearrangements are given in the report, which should be consulted for specific rules governing the correct use of the symbols in table 13.5. Other minor changes include the use of parentheses in describing structurally abnormal chromosomes, the recommended use of abbreviations for lengthy descriptions, and the terminology for interphase X and Y chromatin. The Paris Conference report also suggests a descriptive method for human meiotic chromosomes.

A 1975 supplemental report to the Paris Conference (108) amplifies some of the previous recommendations and provides a detailed code for the description of banding techniques as well as chromosome polymorphisms. The supplement also includes nomenclature, examples, and diagrams of chimpanzee, gorilla, and orangutan chromosomes, and recommends a three-letter code for abbreviated species designations.

At the Stockholm Conference in 1977, a report summarizing human chromosome nomenclature was produced for the purpose of facilitating communication of cytogenetic information and for eliminating former inconsistencies. New terms were added in areas where warranted. Thus, this report (109) supersedes previous nomenclature reports.

A gene map of human chromosomes was constructed by McKusick and Ruddle in 1977 (104) and was updated by McKusick in 1980 (103). It is a useful guide to the approximately 340 genes currently known to be located on specific chromosomes. These loci include at least one assigned to each chromosome (including the Y), about 230 assigned to specific autosomes, and about 110 to the X chromosome. For many loci, information on regional chromosomal localization is available as well. In addition, Shows and McAlpine (111) also have reviewed current human genetic nomenclature and genes that have been mapped in man, and Shows (110) has listed names and genetic symbols of isozyme systems in man as recommended by the International System for Human Cytogenetic Nomenclature.

At the Chicago Conference, requirements for complete and accurate descriptions of populations, families, and individuals were specified.

Typographic conventions should be carefully followed, including those for identifying persons studied and those for numbering generations and individuals in tables and pedigrees. Each person is to be clearly identified by initials, birth date, and any other necessary symbol. For example, John Smith born on 21 July 1954 is identified as JS210754. In tables and pedigrees, generations are numbered with roman numerals, beginning with I for the most senior generation. Members of each generation are numbered with arabic numerals, beginning with 1 for the most senior member (at the left in a pedigree).

In 1975, a catalog of chromosomal variations and anomalies (89) was published, and a Repository of Chromosomal Variants and Anomalies was established. The Repository issues periodic cumulative listings; the Fourth Listing (90) contains approximately one-third of the available karyotyping data from 200 laboratories.

IMMUNOLOGY

The formal conventions for terminology and symbols in human immunology may be useful guides for immunology of infrahuman species.

Human immunoglobulins   Recommendations for nomenclature and symbols for the immunoglobulins and their genetic factors have been prepared by drafting groups of The International Union of Immunological Societies and the World Health Organization (WHO) (126–129, 131), and have been briefly summarized by Rowe (121). The WHO memorandums of 1964, 1965, 1966, and 1969 have been reprinted in the *Handbook of Biochemistry and Molecular Biology* (118).

Abbreviated notations for classes of immunoglobulins are made up of the symbol Ig followed by a capital letter designating the specific class: IgG, IgA, IgM, IgD, and IgE. The Greek letter gamma (γ) may no longer be used, except to designate the heavy polypeptide chains of immunoglobulin G (IgG), according to the World Health Organization (132). The two major groups of polypeptide chains are known at present by the terms *light* (L) and *heavy* (H). The heavy chains are designated by lowercase Greek letters corresponding to the roman capital letters used for the immunoglobulin classes.

IgG	γ (gamma) as in "γ-chain"
IgA	α (alpha)
IgM	μ (mu)

Light polypeptide chains are of two types—kappa and lambda. The molecules or isolated light chains of these types are designated, respectively, as κ or kappa type and λ or lambda type (132). Recommendations for symbols to represent the variable and constant regions of the polypeptide chains and for formulas for immunoglobulin molecules are given in a WHO memorandum (131).

The general system for notation of immunoglobulin subclasses was described in a 1966 WHO memorandum (128). A subclass is indicated by an arabic numeral after the class letter—for example, IgG1, IgG2, and IgG3. A potential new subclass should be designated temporarily by a patient's initials, by a letter or letters representing a city, or by a similar symbol in parentheses—for example, IgG (Pr) for a potential new subclass identified in Prague (126). The final numerical notation should be assigned only after several laboratories have exchanged reagents and agreed on the categorization.

Development of a notation system for the genetic factors of human immunoglobulins has been hampered by insufficient information for precise correlation of genetic loci with the structures they influence. The symbols Gm and Inv are followed by arabic numerals within parentheses for the various factors—for example, Gm(1), Gm(2), Inv(1), and Inv(2). The phenotypes for an individual can be indicated in either of two ways: by recording the positive or negative result with each set of reagents— for example, Gm $(1, -2, 3, 4, 5)$ or by recording the positive results— for example, Gm $(1, 3, 4, 5)$, in which case the reagents used must be specified separately. Symbols for genes are set in italic type, and the factors determined by the gene are indicated by superscript digits: For example, for phenotype Gm(1, 5) the most probable genotype is presented as Gm^1/Gm^5.

Consult the 1964 WHO memorandum (126) and the pages on human immunoglobulins in the *Handbook of Biochemistry and Molecular Biology* (118) for recommendations for designation of immunoglobulin fragments and immunoglobulins in proliferative disorders of lymphocytic or plasmacytic cells.

Human complement   The system of symbols for components of human complement and related complexes is described in a 1968 WHO memorandum (130). The earlier system based on the symbol C' and subsidiary symbols has been replaced by the following symbols, in order of their reaction: C1 (with subcomponents C1q, C1r, and C1s), C4, C2, C3, C5, C6, C7, C8, and C9. (The anomalous place of C4 is a concession to previous usage.) Symbols for intermediate complexes are developed from E (erythrocyte), S (site of initiation of complement fixation), and A (antibody) in conjunction with C, followed by the numerals for the components that have interacted. EAC1423, for example, represents the intermediate complex produced by reaction of the first four components to yield sites SAC1423. The letters and numerals should not be subscript.

Two pathways for activation of the complement system are now recognized: the classical pathway mentioned above, and the alternative pathway. Both pathways utilize a single membrane attack pathway, i.e., the terminal six complement components, C3 through C9. A standard nomenclature for the alternative pathway has been adopted by a subcommittee of the IUIS/WHO Nomenclature Committee (135).

Five proteins of the alternative pathway are designated by capital letters B, D, P, H, and I, whereas C3 retains its original notation. Fragments of proteins that are produced during alternative pathway reactions are denoted by lowercase letters, "a" for the lesser fragment, "b" for the larger fragment, as Ba and Bb, for example. When a protein loses a defined activity without alteration of the primary polypeptide structure, it is denoted by the letter "i," as in Bbi, i.e., Bb that lost its peptide hydrolase activity. When a protein loses a defined activity as a consequence of peptide hydrolysis without fragmentation, it is preceded by "i," as in iC3b, i.e., the form of C3b whose α polypeptide has been hydrolyzed by I in the presence of H and is not capable of forming a C3 convertase. The WHO memorandums (130, 135) include descriptions of complement components showing altered activity, descriptions of fragments and chains, a table of previous designations in association with the proposed symbols, and a table of other factors reacting in the complement sequence.

Human histocompatibility leukocyte antigens   The major genetic complex for the system of leukocyte antigens related to human histocompatibility has been designated HLA and has been divided into loci designated as A, B, C, and D. Specific factors at each locus are indicated by numbers, such as HLA-A1 and HLA-B5. This official designation is awarded by the WHO Nomenclature Committee for Leukocyte Antigens. Before certification, putative HLA factors may be designated either by some local system (reflecting a particular laboratory) or by a w number—for example, HLA-Aw23. The w number refers to use in one or more of the Histocompatibility Testing Workshops, which are held about every 2 years. The w numbers may thus be considered as semiofficial. Factors at loci A, B, C, and DR (D related) are determined by serologic methods and at the D locus by means of the mixed lymphocyte reaction using homozygous typing cells.

Other details of this system of nomenclature, including recommendations for representation of genotype and phenotype, and a table showing the relationships of HLA factors, w numbers, and local or previous designations are given in the WHO-IUIS Terminology Committee report (125, 133, 134). The histocompatibility complex has been extensively reviewed in three successive issues of *The New England Journal of Medicine* (116).

Infrahuman histocompatibility   In addition to the well-known H-2 system of the mouse (119, 122), the DL-A system for the dog (123, 124) and the RHL-A system for the rhesus monkey (117, 120) have been characterized.

HEMATOLOGY

Symbols in hematology were developed first and most extensively for human blood and serum groups, clotting factors, and red cell enzymes. Some of these conventions have been used for infrahuman species also.

Blood and serum groups   Blood group antigens and serum factors in humans and other animals are conventionally represented by capital and lowercase roman letters. Usually letters have been arbitrarily assigned (as for the A-B-O blood groups in humans), but some stand for the name of the person (for example, Le for Lewis, Fy for Duffy) or animal that served as the identifying source. Genes corresponding to the antigens are usually represented by the same letters in italics. The antibody corresponding to a particular antigen is represented by the symbol for the antigen prefaced by "anti-."

Human blood groups   Symbols for human blood groups follow the pattern described in the preceding paragraph and are given in several sources (138, 147–149). The Rh system—Rh for antigen from the rhesus monkey—is represented by three different schemes of notation. The Fisher-Race (148) designations consist of capital letters C, D, and E for genes and lowercase letters c, d, and e for corresponding alleles. The Rh-Hr notation of Wiener (139, 147, 152, 153) uses italic type for symbols representing genes and genotypes, roman type for symbols representing agglutinogens and phenotypes, and boldface type for serologic specificities: For example, gene R^1 determines the corresponding agglutinogen Rh_1, having the serologic specificities **Rh₀**, **rh'**, **rh"**, **rh**ᵢ, **Rh**ᴬ, **Rh**ᴮ, **Rh**ᶜ, **Rh**ᴰ, and so forth. The Rosenfield-Allen (149) scheme of numerical nomenclature is based on observed serologic results with different antisera; positive reactions are indicated Rh1, Rh2, ..., and negative reactions are prefixed with a negative sign, Rh−3, Rh−4, ...

Infrahuman blood groups   There is no convention preventing the use of the same or similar alphabetical symbols in different species (136, 138); therefore, unless ambiguity is unlikely in a discussion of animal blood groups, the species to which a particular symbol refers should be mentioned. Give special attention to achieving a clear identification of a particular blood group system as an isoantigen-antibody system in a single species, or a system also existing or producible in a second, unstated species. Problems in symbolic representation of human-nonhuman interacting systems are discussed by Prokop and Uhlenbruck (147). The prerequisites for nomenclatural symbols as described by Swisher (150) are applicable to all infrahuman species. A nomenclatural change to fit Swisher's tenets has been introduced to eliminate confusion regarding symbols for the dog: Canine blood group A, B, ... has been changed to canine erythrocyte antigen (CEA-1, 2, . . .), and is described by Vriesen-dorp et al. (151)

Human serum groups   Symbols for serum-factor systems (such as the haptoglobin, Gm, Inv, Gc, and Ag systems) have developed informally on a basis similar to that of the blood groups (147). A WHO committee (154) has recommended a standardized system for the Gm and Inv systems (*see* page 198, this chapter).

Human clotting factors   By agreement among international authorities on blood coagulation, the various adequately characterized human clotting factors known by descriptive or eponymic terms are now designated by roman numerals—for example, factor IX for plasma thromboplastin component (PTC) or Christmas factor. This agreement, characterization of the factors, and a tabulation of the roman-numbered factors with their synonyms have been published by the International Committee (for) on (Nomenclature of) Blood Clotting Factors (140–143). Either the numbers or the eponymic names may be used, but the agreement recommends that both forms be used the first time a factor is mentioned in an article.

Hemoglobins   Human hemoglobins have been investigated far more extensively than those of lower animals; therefore, descriptive conventions have been developed in much more detail.

Human hemoglobins   The molecules of the three normal human hemoglobin fractions (hemoglobin A, hemoglobin A_2, and hemoglobin F) are composed of two pairs of globin chains, each chain having an attached heme group. These chains are designated by the Greek letters alpha (α), beta (β), gamma (γ), and delta (δ). The globin of the normal main human hemoglobin fraction, hemoglobin A (Hb A), is made up of two alpha and two beta chains ($\alpha_2\beta_2$), and the minor fraction, hemoglobin A_2, of two alpha and two delta chains ($\alpha_2\delta_2$). The normal fetal hemoglobin (Hb F) consists of two alpha and two gamma chains ($\alpha_2\gamma_2$); the gamma chain gene is duplicated, and the two chains differ in having glycine or alanine at position 136. Additional chains found in human embryonal hemoglobins are designated by the Greek letters epsilon (ϵ) and zeta (ζ). The terms for hemoglobins containing only non-α-chains are as follows (137): hemoglobin H (β_4), hemoglobin Bart's (γ_4), hemoglobin Gower 1 (ϵ_4), and hemoglobin Portland ($\gamma_2\zeta_2$). The abnormal hemoglobins that were first characterized by their electrophoretic mobility at pH 8.6 are designated by letters: C through Q, and S.

The recently described hemoglobins have been given names of places, laboratories, or hospitals representing the origin of the propositus or the place where the hemoglobin was identified—for example, Hb Chad and Hb Bart's. This convention should be used for newly discovered hemoglobins; do not repeat previously used labels—for example, Hb Hopkins-1 and Hb Hopkins-2; avoid using personal names.

Hemoglobins from a group with an identical property, such as electrophoretic mobility, may be identified by a letter and subscripts or suffixes. Thus, a new hemoglobin may be specified as to electrophoretic mobility, chain involved, and geographic label (Hb Gα Philadelphia, Hb Gα Norfolk).

Comparison of an apparently newly identified hemoglobin with previously known hemoglobins may or may not establish its identity as a "new" hemoglobin. If the hemoglobin appears identical to one previously described, it should not, of course, be given a new name; proof that it is a mutant hemoglobin not previously described, and that it should be given a new name, requires determination of the amino-acid substitution or other (primary) structural alterations.

Abnormal hemoglobins are more precisely described by indicating the specific locations of the amino acid differences in the polypeptide chains. Hb M Iwate, for example, differs from the normal Hb A by substitution of tyrosine for the heme-linked histidine at the 87th position in the alpha chain. This mutation is indicated as α87 His$\rightarrow$Tyr.

Most of the globins consist of an initial (amino-terminal) segment (NA), the helical amino acid segments (A-H), the interhelical segments (AB, BC, . . .), and a terminal sequence (HC). These symbols for the N- and C- termini do not correspond to those recommended by the IUPAC-IUB Commission on Biological Nomenclature for NH$_2$- and COOH-termini (*see* page 224, this chapter).

A mutation can be identified by its position in one of these segments, rather than in the entire amino acid sequence of the whole chain to reveal homologies of structure; thus, the amino acid substitution of Hb M Iwate is α87 His$\rightarrow$Tyr, and that of Hb M Hyde Park is β92 His$\rightarrow$Tyr. These hemoglobins have very similar properties, which can be signaled by use of helical notation, for each involves residue F8, the eighth amino acid in the F helical segment of the alpha chain. Alternative forms of complete description for the first of these hemoglobins are Hb M Iwate, α87 His$\rightarrow$Tyr; Hb M Iwate, αF8 His$\rightarrow$Tyr; or α87(F8)His$\rightarrow$Tyr. Superscript forms, with or without the replaced amino acid, are sometimes used in journals ($\alpha_2^{87\,His\rightarrow Tyr}\beta_2$ or $\alpha_2^{87\,Tyr}\beta_2$), but printing special characters as subscripts or superscripts is costly.

Hemoglobins resulting from unequal crossing over between chains are called fusion hemoglobins, and are designated by the chains involved and the proper name (137)—for example, ($\delta\beta$)Boston, ($\beta\delta$)Miyada, ($\gamma\beta$)Kenya.

Hemoglobins with other abnormalities have been described: hemoglobin C Harlem — $\alpha_2\beta_2^{(6\,Glu-Val,\,73\,Asp-Asn)}$ with two mutations in the same globin chain; hemoglobin Tochigi — $\alpha_2\beta_2^{(56-59\,deleted)}$ with a deletion; hemoglobin Constant Spring — $\alpha_2^{(142-172\,extended)}\beta_2$ with an extension; and hemoglobin Providence — $\alpha_2\beta_2^{(86\,Lys\rightarrow Asn,\,Asp)}$ with deamination.

The sources of the globin chains from which experimental hybrid hemoglobins are formed should be described. For example, a hemoglobin formed of alpha chains from Hb I and beta chains from Hb C should be designated as $Hb\alpha_2^I\beta_2^C$.

Other details for the descriptions of human hemoglobins and especially for those abnormalities involving minor components are described in a statement from the Tenth International Congress of Haematology (145), and in a paper by Perutz and Lehmann (146).

Infrahuman hemoglobins The main hemoglobin characteristic of an infrahuman species has customarily been designated Hb A with a preceding or following modifier to indicate genus—for example, canine Hb A or Hb A^{can}. Hemoglobins described subsequently have been designated by B, C, and so forth. This system is not adequate for more detailed or comparative descriptions. The system used for human hemoglobins can be employed in the description of newly discovered hemoglobins of animals, pending agreement on a widely accepted convention among veterinarians and comparative hematologists, but the author must explain the abbreviations and symbols.

Human glucose-6-phosphate dehydrogenase The phenotypic symbol for glucose-6-phosphate dehydrogenase (EC 1.1.1.49) is Gd; the symbol for the corresponding gene is *Gd*. The symbol Gd should be followed by indications of enzyme activity relative to the normal B enzyme. Normal activity is (+); various degrees of lesser and greater activity are indicated by (−), (±), (++), and similar graduated steps. The activity indicator should be followed by a comma and the specific symbol or name of the variant. The symbols B, A, and A− are retained for these widely recognized variants; other known variants have geographic or trivial names. Names for new variants should not contain broad geographic terms (such as continental or national names), or ethnic names, family names, further alphabetical designations, or numerals added to geographic names.

A name should not be definitely assigned to a supposedly new variant until it has been fully characterized by appropriate studies to distinguish it from known variants. Before such characterization, the name should be enclosed in quotation marks, which are dropped after the variant has been confirmed as new.

The genotypic symbol *Gd* is modified to indicate a specific allele with a superscript symbol or name set in smaller roman type. The two terms in the genotypic designation for a female heterozygote should be separated by a slant line. Additional details on nomenclature and symbolization, and recommendations for drafting the names of new variants, are in a report of a WHO scientific group (155).

Human blood coagulation The International Committee on Thrombosis and Haemostasis (144) adopted a system of genetic nomenclature for human blood coagulation, deemed necessary because of recent discoveries of numerous "variants" of hereditary blood coagulation factors. Taking advantage of the existing hemoglobin and glucose-6-phosphate dehydrogenase conventions, the new system is based on these general rules:

1) The roman numeral system I . . . XIII is used for the coagulation factors.
2) The phenotype of an individual with respect to a coagulation factor is recorded as F.I . . . F.XIII in ordinary roman letters.
3) The class of the locus responsible for an individual clotting factor is designated by the appropriate italicized roman numeral *I . . . XIII*.
4) The alleles at any locus are indicated by combining the proper roman numeral with a pair of italicized lowercase roman letters selected according to the following rules.

aa$^+$	"Usual" allele (most frequent allele in population under consideration).
aa$^-$	Class of allele characterized by no detectable product.
rr	Class of allele characterized by reduced coagulant activity.
ii	Class of allele characterized by increased coagulant activity.
ns	"Neutral" class of alleles characterized by "usual" activity but altered structure of product.

The full report of the International Committee on Thrombosis and Haemostasis gives examples of application of the rules. It also describes how to establish the presence of hereditary coagulation variants, and contains a glossary of descriptive terms.

PHYSIOLOGY

Symbols and abbreviations in most branches of physiology have developed informally but have gained wide acceptance. Many of these symbols and abbreviations are listed in chapter 14. Examples of their use can be found in authoritative textbooks and monographs, such as sections of the *Handbook of Physiology* (163). In thermal physiology and respiratory physiology coherent but independent systems of symbols have been formally proposed and published.

Thermal physiology   The system of symbols for thermal physiology is based on the International System of Units (SI), and was published after review by an international group of investigators (164). In 1973, the International Union of Physiological Sciences and its Commission for Thermal Physiology approved a glossary (158) designed to improve precision of meaning and uniformity in usage of technical terms in thermal physiology. The symbols used in the glossary appear in table

13.6. The same symbols are sometimes used for two different quantities; such usage is acceptable only when confusion is not likely to result. A dot over a symbol denotes time rate of change; a bar over a symbol denotes mean value of the quantity. Two-letter subscripts should be used in most instances to describe sites of physiological temperature measurements, e.g., T_{hy} for hypothalamic temperature, T_{es} for esophageal temperature, T_{or} for oral temperature, T_{re} for rectal temperature, T_{co} for core or colonic temperature (164). Additional derived symbols for special applications can be found in the sources cited in references 158 and 164.

Table 13.6. Thermal physiology: symbols and abbreviations (158)

Symbol or abbreviation	Term	SI unit*
A_b	Area, total body	m^2
A_D	Area, DuBois	m^2
A_p	Area, projected	m^2
A_r	Area, effective radiating	m^2
A_s	Area, solar radiation	m^2
A_w	Area, wetted	m^2
BMR	Metabolic rate, basal	W, $W \cdot m^{-2}$, $W \cdot kg^{-1}$, $W \cdot kg^{-3/4}$
C	Thermal conductance	$W \cdot m^{-2} \cdot {}^\circ C^{-1}$
C	Convective heat transfer	$W \cdot m^{-2}$
D	Diffusivity, mass	$m^2 \cdot s^{-1}$
E	Irradiance	$W \cdot m^{-2}$
E	Evaporative heat transfer	$W \cdot m^{-2}$
F	Radiation shape factor	ND
H	Body height	m
H	Metabolic heat production	$W \cdot m^{-2}$
H_r	Radiant flux, effective	$W \cdot m^{-2}$
I	Radiant intensity	$W \cdot sr^{-1}$
I_λ	Radiant intensity, spectral	$W \cdot sr^{-1} \cdot nm^{-1}$
I_{cl}	Thermal insulation, clothing	$m^2 \cdot {}^\circ C \cdot W^{-1}$
K	Conductive heat transfer	$W \cdot m^{-2}$
L_e	Radiance	$W \cdot sr^{-1} \cdot m^{-2}$
$L_{e,th}$	Radiance, thermal	$W \cdot sr^{-1} \cdot m^{-2}$
LOMR	Metabolic rate, least observed	W, $W \cdot m^{-2}$, $W \cdot kg^{-1}$, $W \cdot kg^{-3/4}$
M_e	Radiant exitance	$W \cdot m^{-2}$
$M_{e,s}$	Radiant exitance, self	$W \cdot m^{-2}$
$M_{e,th}$	Radiant exitance, thermal	$W \cdot m^{-2}$
M	Metabolic free energy production	$W \cdot m^{-2}$
MMR	Metabolic rate, maximum	W, $W \cdot m^{-2}$, $W \cdot kg^{-1}$, $W \cdot kg^{-3/4}$
MOMR	Metabolic rate, minimum observed	W, $W \cdot m^{-2}$, $W \cdot kg^{-1}$, $W \cdot kg^{-3/4}$
MR	Metabolic rate	W, $W \cdot m^{-2}$, $W \cdot kg^{-1}$, $W \cdot kg^{-3/4}$
NST	Thermogenesis, nonshivering	W, $W \cdot m^{-2}$
NST(O)	Thermogenesis, nonshivering (obligatory)	W, $W \cdot m^{-2}$
NST(T)	Thermogenesis, nonshivering (thermoregulatory)	W, $W \cdot m^{-2}$

Table 13.6 (Continued)

Symbol or abbreviation	Term	SI unit*
P	Pressure	Pa, bar, Torr
$P_{s,T}$	Pressure, vapor (saturated) at temperature T	Pa, bar, Torr
P_w	Pressure, water vapor	Pa, $N \cdot m^{-2}$, bar, Torr
PMR	Metabolic rate, peak	W, $W \cdot m^{-2}$, $W \cdot kg^{-1}$, $W \cdot kg^{-3/4}$
Q	Radiant energy	J
Q_λ	Radiant energy, spectral	$J \cdot nm^{-1}$
R_w	Gas constant (water vapor)	$3.47 \ m^3 \cdot Torr \cdot kg^{-1} \cdot K^{-1}$
R	Thermal resistance	$°C \cdot m^2 \cdot W^{-1}$
R	Radiant heat exchange	$W \cdot m^{-2}$
RMR	Metabolic rate, resting	W, $W \cdot m^{-2}$, $W \cdot kg^{-1}$, $W \cdot kg^{-3/4}$
S	Storage of body heat	$W \cdot m^{-2}$
SMR	Metabolic rate, standard	W, $W \cdot m^{-2}$, $W \cdot kg^{-1}$, $W \cdot kg^{-3/4}$
T_a	Temperature, ambient	°C
$\overline{T}_b$	Temperature, mean body	°C
T_{db}	Temperature, dry bulb	°C
T_{dp}	Temperature, dew-point	°C
T_{eff}	Temperature, effective	°C
T_g	Temperature, globe	°C
T_o	Temperature, operative	°C
$\overline{T}_r$	Temperature, mean radiant	°C
$\overline{T}_{sk}$	Temperature, mean skin	°C
T_{wb}	Temperature, wet bulb	°C
TNZ	Thermoneutral zone	°C
$\dot{V}_{O_2 \, max}$	Oxygen consumption, maximum	$ml \cdot s^{-1}$, $litre \cdot min^{-1}$
W	Body weight	kg
W	Work	W, $W \cdot m^{-2}$
c	Specific heat	$J \cdot kg^{-1} \cdot °C^{-1}$
h	Heat transfer coefficient, combined nonevaporative	$W \cdot m^{-2} \cdot °C^{-1}$
h_c	Heat transfer coefficient, convective	$W \cdot m^{-2} \cdot °C^{-1}$
h_D	Mass transfer coefficient (diffusion)	$m \cdot s^{-1}$
h_e	Heat transfer coefficient, evaporative	$W \cdot m^{-2} \cdot kPa^{-1}$, $W \cdot m^{-2} \cdot Torr^{-1}$
h_k	Heat transfer coefficient, conductive	$W \cdot m^{-2} \cdot °C^{-1}$
h_r	Heat transfer coefficient, radiative (linear)	$W \cdot m^{-2} \cdot °C^{-1}$
k	Thermal conductivity	$W \cdot m^{-1} \cdot °C^{-1}$
$\dot{m}$	Mass transfer rate	$kg \cdot s^{-1}$
rh	Humidity, relative	%
w	Wettedness, skin	ND
Φ	Radiant flux	W
Φ_λ	Radiant flux, spectral	$W \cdot nm^{-1}$
Ω	Solid angle	sr
α	Radiant absorptance, total	ND
α	Diffusivity, thermal	$m^2 \cdot s^{-1}$
β	Thermal expansion coefficient of volume	K^{-1}
γ	Humidity, absolute	$kg \cdot m^{-3}$
ϵ	Emissivity	ND

Table 13.6. (Continued)

Symbol or abbreviation	Term	SI unit*
$\epsilon_{(\theta,\Phi)}$	Emissivity, directional	ND
ϵ_λ	Emissivity, spectral	ND
ϵ_h	Emissivity, hemispherical	ND
ϵ_w	Emissivity, window	ND
η	Work efficiency	%
θ	Angular coordinate, vertical	rad
λ	Latent heat of vaporization	$J \cdot kg^{-1}$ (2.425×10^6 at 30°C)
λ	Wavelength	m, nm
ρ	Density	$kg \cdot m^{-3}$
ρ	Reflectance, radiation	ND
σ	Stefan-Boltzmann constant	$W \cdot m^{-2} \cdot K^{-4}$ (5.67×10^{-8})
τ	Transmittance, radiation	ND
ϕ	Angular coordinate, horizontal	rad
ϕ	Humidity, relative	ND

* ND = no dimensions.

Respiratory physiology   Symbols and abbreviations currently used in respiratory physiology were developed for descriptions of human pulmonary function; they are applicable also in respiratory physiology of other animals.

Symbols for specific variables and equations for interrelated variables should be based on table 13.7 derived from references 156, 163, 167, and 170. Capital letters (main symbols) denote general variables, such as volume and pressure; small-capital and lower-case symbols (modifiers) denote anatomic location, molecular species, or special conditions.

Anatomic site of a gas phase is denoted by small-capital letters after the general symbol: For example, pressure in alveolar gas should be designated by PA. The same arrangement is followed for the blood phase, but with lowercase letters—for example, Pa for pressure in arterial blood. The molecular species is designated with the chemical symbol in small-capital letters (P_{CO_2} is pressure of carbon dioxide), but, if both site and molecular species are to be given, the chemical symbol is subscript to the anatomic symbol (PA_{CO_2} is pressure of carbon dioxide in the alveolar gas phase). If use of the subscript is to be avoided (some journals), use the descriptive term and the symbol: For example, alveolar pressure of carbon dioxide can be written "alveolar P_{CO_2}" instead of PA_{CO_2}.

Somewhat different but related conventions are used in European journals to avoid confusion with SI symbols (157, 160, 161, 168). The major differences are in the use of italic letters, rather than roman capital letters, to denote general variables (physical quantities); in permitting use of lowercase letters, instead of small-capital letters, for gas variable

Table 13.7. Respiratory physiology: symbols for variables

Symbol	Definition	References
Main symbols used in gas exchange and pulmonary circulation:		
C	concentration (in liquid)	156, 167, 170
D	diffusing capacity	156, 167, 170
F	fractional concentration (in dry gas)	156, 167
P	pressure	156, 167, 170
Q	liquid volume	167
$\dot{Q}$	blood flow	156, 167, 170
R	respiratory exchange ratio	156, 170
S	saturation	156, 167, 170
V	gas volume	156, 167, 170
$\dot{V}$	gas flow	156, 167, 170
α	solubility coefficient	170
θ	reaction rate coefficient	156
Additional main symbols used in respiratory mechanics:		
C	compliance	170
E	elastance	170
G	conductance	156, 170
R	resistance	170
W	work	170
$\dot{W}$	rate of work	170
Additional main symbol used in control of breathing:		
T	duration (of respiration)	163
Modifiers—blood phase:		
a	arterial	156, 167, 170
b	blood in general	167
c	capillary	156, 167
c'	end-capillary	156
v	venous	156
$\bar{v}$	mixed venous	156, 170
va	venous admixture	163
Modifiers—gas phase:		
A	alveolar	156, 167, 170
B	barometric	156, 167
D	dead space	156, 167, 170
E	expired	156, 167
I	inspired	156, 167
T	tidal	156, 167, 170
Additional modifiers:		
aw	airway	156
awo	airway opening	156
bs	body surface	156
ds	downstream	156
dyn	dynamic	156
eff	effective	156
es	esophageal	156
L	transpulmonary	170
m	membrane	156
max	maximum	156

Table 13.7. (Continued)

Symbol	Definition	Reference
pl	pleural	156
s	shunt	156
T	total	163
ti	tissue	156
tm	transmural	156
us	upstream	156
w	chest wall	156
Additional symbols and abbreviations:		
‾ (overbar)	mean value	156, 167, 170
˙ (overdot)	time derivative	156, 167, 170
f	respiratory frequency	156, 167, 170
t	time	156, 163
STPD	standard temperature, pressure, dry (0° C, 760 mmHg)	167, 170
BTPS	body temperature, pressure, saturated with water vapor	167, 170
ATPD	ambient temperature, pressure, dry	167, 170
ATPS	ambient temperature, pressure, saturated with water vapor	167, 170

modifying symbols; and in separating anatomic and chemical symbols with a comma to avoid use of subscripts. In the European system, pressure of carbon dioxide in the alveolar gas phase would be Pal, CO_2.

Special abbreviations, which have come to serve as symbols, are available for many clinical indices of lung function as alternatives to the symbols listed in table 13.7 (157, 160, 162, 166). These abbreviations are printed in roman capital letters without spaces, periods, or commas—for example, total lung capacity (total V_L in table 13.7) is TLC, and tidal volume (V_T in table 13.7) is TV.

The American College of Chest Physicians–American Thoracic Society Joint Committee on Pulmonary Nomenclature (156) has attempted to clarify symbols and terms used in respiratory physiology. The fewest possible changes in existing conventions were made, while attempting to ease the problem of symbol presentation for typists and typesetters. Superscripts and subscripts should be used only when the meaning of the total symbol would be otherwise ambiguous. When small-capital letters are not available on typewriters or to printers, large-capital letters may be used as subscripts. The committee report covers general, gas phase, and blood phase symbols; tests and symbols for ventilation and lung mechanics, and for diffusing capacity; symbols for blood gas measurements and for pulmonary shunts; and terms describing pulmonary dysfunction.

Table 13.8. Units for reporting results of lung function tests

Quantity	Traditional unit (x)	SI derived working unit (y)	Conversion factor (f), $y = fx$
Volume rate:			
Average over time	litre·min^{-1}	m^3·s^{-1}	2.77×10^{-6}
Instantaneous	litre·min^{-1}	litre·s^{-1}	60^{-1}
Pressure	cm H$_2$O	kPa	0.098 at STP
	mm Hg (or Torr)	kPa	0.133
Compliance	litre·cm H$_2$O^{-1}	litre·kPa^{-1}	10.2
Resistance	cm H$_2$O·litre^{-1}·s	kPa·litre^{-1}·s	0.098
Conductance	litre·s^{-1}·cm H$_2$O^{-1}	litre·s^{-1}·kPa^{-1}	10.2
Gas uptake*	ml·min^{-1}	μmol·s^{-1}	22.4^{-1}
Diffusing capacity†	ml·min^{-1}·mm Hg^{-1} (or Torr)	mmol·min^{-1}·kPa^{-1}	0.335
Transfer coefficient (DL/VA)†	min^{-1}·mm Hg^{-1} (or Torr^{-1})	mmol·min^{-1}·kPa^{-1}· litre^{-1}	0.335
Ventilatory response to CO$_2$†	litre·min^{-1}·mm Hg^{-1} (or Torr^{-1})	litre·min^{-1}·kPa^{-1}	7.5
Energy	calorie	joule	4.18

* Conversion factor for O$_2$ and most other gases; for CO$_2$, the factor is 22.26^{-1}.

† In SI usage the time should be in seconds, but minutes may also be used for convenience.

The interrelations between the traditional and the SI units for indices used in respiratory physiology are given in table 13.8 (modified by Cotes, ref. 160). The SI system is based on the kilogram, the metre, and the second, but the minute and the hour are used where it is appropriate to do so—for example, for $\dot{V}$ (litre·min^{-1}), but never for $\dot{v}$ (litre·s^{-1}). A solidus may be used to separate two units—for example, for volume rate of expired gas ($\dot{V}$E)m^3/s; but for more than two units, the Newtonian notation should be employed—for example, for airways resistance (Raw) kPa·litre^{-1}·s, where Pa or pascal is the SI unit of pressure.

In 1971, the International Union of Physiological Sciences Committee on Nomenclature approved a glossary of terms used in respiratory and gas exchange physiology, thus reducing ambiguities and, through standardization, clarifying the nomenclature (170).

Cardiovascular physiology   Between 1967 and 1971, the Committee on Standardized Terminology of the American College of Cardiology and the American Heart Association (159) prepared a four-part glossary of terms used in the field of cardiology. The definitions standardized in the four parts are I. Heart Murmurs; II. Heart Sounds; III. Anterior Chest Movements: The Ventricles, the Atria, and the Great Vessels; and IV. Arterial Pulses.

The rationale for using the SI units for measurements that have particular relevance to cardiovascular studies is thoroughly explained by Kappagoda and Linden (165). The method of expressing the measurement in SI units is given for volume, concentration, cardiac output, pressure, peripheral resistance, work, viscosity, temperature, blood gases, and acid-base data.

Endocrine physiology   A special committee on nomenclature of the American Thyroid Association has developed an approved list of abbreviations, with accompanying definitions and comments (169).

EXPERIMENTAL MATERIALS

The use of animal materials in experimentation may require intact or surgically modified animals, or tissues or cells collected from them. The maintenance and care of experimental animals to provide humane treatment and to assure reliable results are described in the National Institutes of Health guidelines for use of laboratory animals (173). Experimenters are advised to comply with these guidelines and to acknowledge such compliance in their reports.

Animal materials used in experiments must be described precisely and completely. The ability of one investigator to confirm the findings of another may depend on the use of an identical kind of animal, tissue, or cell. Detailed recommendations for descriptions of experimental animals and of cell lines in animal tissue culture have been issued by several authorities.

Animals   In addition to common (vernacular) names for domesticated animals and scientific (binomial, or trinomial if appropriate) names for nondomesticated animals, the animals used in experiments should be clearly identified by descriptions that include stock source (or strain, if inbred) and other factors that determine their characteristics. Recommendations for full descriptions of outbred laboratory animal stocks by a literal-numerical symbol system have been published by the International Committee on Laboratory Animals (178).

The arrangement of characters in the description of an outbred animal begins with one capital letter and two or more lowercase letters to represent the name of the organization or individual that bred or supplied the animal. After these letters and a colon are symbols (one or more capitals and numerals) representing current and basic stock designations; these are followed by capital letters in parentheses to represent the original stock. Next come lowercase letters to indicate rearing by means other than natural mother (fostered, f; ova transplant, e; ovary transplant, o; hand-reared, h), and then capital letters for environmental factors (gnotobiote, GN; defined flora, DF; conventional rearing, CV; barrier rearing, BR). The following is a hypothetical example: The High Quality Farm produces A5 rats, of Sprague-Dawley descent, derived surgically, and hand-reared in isolators; offspring from these animals are made available to investigators as gnotobiotes, and are designated as Hqf:A5(SD)hGN. Abbreviations for names of suppliers and stocks are listed in *Animals for Research* (177); the stocks include common laboratory animals (lagomorphs, rodents, dogs, cats); domestic farm animals (fowl, cattle, sheep, goats, swine, horses, ponies, donkeys); and animals obtained from nature (protozoans through vertebrates).

The International Committee on Laboratory Animals (ICLA) does not encourage the inclusion of historical roots of stocks in the coded name because such references are frequently misinterpreted as indicating effective genetic relationship. Describe the historical origin of a stock separately from its name, in such a way that its true meaning can be explained and assessed. However, if a coded reference to stock origin must be included, use of the pertinent symbols proposed by the Committee on Nomenclature of the Institute of Laboratory Animal Resources (174) is compatible with the ICLA system.

Recommendations for similarly precise descriptions of farm animals have been issued by the British Society of Animal Production (172). They specify that each class of animal under discussion in an article must be clearly defined at first mention in terms of species, breed or cross, sex, age, physiologic state, and agricultural function; the class may be referred to in subsequent mention by a single descriptive term. Species may be designated by common terms (cattle, sheep, goat, pig or swine, horse, fowl, turkey, duck, goose). For English usage, give the full breed names as recommended by Mason (179)—for example, British Friesian or Holstein-Friesian, not Friesian.

Names of breeds of dogs are given in *The Complete Dog Book* (171), published by the American Kennel Club, and also in *The New Dog Encyclopedia* (184) which includes, in addition to breeds recognized by the American Kennel Club, those recognized by the United Kennel Club. *The Complete Cat Encyclopedia* (180) lists breeds of cats. Names of wild animals are given in *Mammals of the World* (185).

Special rules for nomenclature of inbred strains of mice and rats, with index lists of the strains and their clearly differentiated substrains, have been summarized by Staats (183) and by Festing and Staats (175).

Animal tissue culture   The Tissue Culture Association Committee on Terminology (182) has defined the following important terms for use in cell culture studies:

Cell line. A cell line arises from a primary culture at the time of first subculture. The term cell line implies that cultures from it consist of numerous lineages of cells originally present in the primary culture. The terms *finite* or *continuous* are used as prefixes if the status of the culture is known.

Cell strain. A cell strain is derived either from a primary culture or a cell line by the selection or cloning of cells having specific properties or markers. The properties or markers must persist during subsequent cultivation. In describing a cell strain its specific features must be described. The terms *finite* or *continuous* are to be used as prefixes if the status of the culture is known.

When cell lines are isolated and first described the following basic information should be provided: procedures for isolation, the species (and strain if known) of the donor animal, organ or tissue of origin, normal or neoplastic (benign or malignant), cell type isolated, and whether cloned. Characterization of the cells to complete the description should include the determination of specific properties or markers, tests for sterility, and information on the number of population doublings accrued since isolation, if appropriate (*see* bibliography on page 32 of ref. 176). Subsequent references to the use of previously described cell cultures should include the species and tissue of origin as well as the name of the cell culture (e.g., rabbit kidney cells LLC-RK$_1$).

Wherever possible, cell cultures should be obtained from recognized cell banks or from the culture's originator, who should be identified in the paper. Also, information should be provided regarding the number of passages since a complete characterization was done. The source and provenance of cells are critical because much confusion has resulted from mixed or contaminated cell lines (181).

The American Type Culture Collection, 12301 Parklawn Drive, Rockville, MD 20852, USA, and the Institute for Medical Research, Sheridan and Copewood Streets, Camden, NJ 08103, USA, provide many cell lines and strains that meet acceptable standards. Additionally, the ATCC maintains a Cell Source Information Bank containing information on sources of cells not within its collection but which are available upon request from originators of material.

There is no universally accepted nomenclature for cell lines and the literature attests to this fact. The Tissue Culture Association has recommended that not more than four letters designating the laboratory of origin, followed by arabic numerals indicating sequence of isolation, be used (e.g., NCTC 2071, IMR 381, NBL 6). Other systems employing numerical designation of the month, year, and sequence are being proposed and may find acceptance (e.g., NIH 10/81/33).

It is becoming obvious that some consistent principles are needed to avoid confusion and duplication. The growing use of cell fusion techniques to produce hybridomas and heterokaryons has resulted in many new cell strains, a number of which are the subject of patent applications. Therefore, it is particularly important that strain designations be unique and unambiguous.

CHEMISTRY AND BIOCHEMISTRY

The authority for the names of chemical and biochemical compounds is the International Union of Pure and Applied Chemistry (IUPAC), through the published rules of its several nomenclatural commissions. The International Union of Biochemistry has published a compendium of recommendations on biochemical nomenclature (197). An authoritative source for the names of chemical compounds is *Chemical Abstracts* and its indexes: the *Chemical Substance Index, General Subject Index, Formula Index*, and *Index of Ring Systems* published semiannually; the *Index Guide* (which helps the user to find subjects of interest in these indexes); the collective indexes, the most recent of which is the tenth (193); and the *Parent Compound Handbook* (192).

NONPROPRIETARY NAMES

The full chemical name of a complex substance, especially an organic compound, should be given the first time the substance is mentioned in an article, unless the generic or trivial name is well known and understood (for example, orotic acid for uracil-6-carboxylic acid, phenol for carbolic acid). The full name need not be repeated, but judgment is required in selecting another name, which should be nonproprietary. Usually, if no distinction between an organic acid and its salt is needed, the "-ate" form is correct and appropriate (orotate, citrate), and is recommended, especially in adjectival phrases (orotate-requiring, *not* orotic acid-requiring).

Many nonproprietary names, although not derived according to the rules of chemical nomenclature, are current and useful: trivial names, some of them derived from trade names (aspirin, DDT); source names, referring to the origin of the compounds (parathyroid hormone, digitalis); and coinages to suggest chemical structures (methoxychlor).

Principles that should be followed in devising nonproprietary names for pharmaceutical substances have been published by the Expert Committee on Nonproprietary Names for Pharmaceutical Preparations (195) and by the United States Adopted Names (USAN) Council (220). Names that are to be submitted to either the World Health Organization or the USAN Council for review and possible acceptance should be prepared in accord with the recommendations of the reviewing organization. Special criteria for names of antibiotics in the United States have been drafted by the American Society for Microbiology's Committee on Nomenclature of Antibiotics (186). Principles that should be followed for selection of common names for pest control chemicals and plant growth regulators have been published by the International Organization for Standardization (ISO) (196).

The recommended and official nonproprietary (chemical, generic, trivial, and source names) and proprietary (trade) names can be found in the most recent editions of *USAN and the USP Dictionary of Drug Names* (220), *The United States Pharmacopeia* (219), *Pharmacological and Chemical Synonyms* (213), *The Merck Index* (222), up-to-date computer printouts available from lists published by the World Health Organization (224), and *Pesticide Index* (223).

PROPRIETARY NAMES

Normally, a trade name is not to be used for a chemical compound; it is the official trademark of the registering manufacturer. If it is necessary for identifying the product used, spell it out and capitalize as specified in the registration (Vaseline, Adrenalin, Sephadex).

Confusion may occur when a registered trademark in one country is a nonproprietary name in another. Thus, "Adrenalin" is a trade name for epinephrine (generic name) in the United States, and "adrenaline" is the generic name in Great Britain.

ABBREVIATIONS

Avoid using nonstandard abbreviations where possible, and define any used. However, many abbreviations for long or complex names of organic compounds are acceptable—for example, NADP for nicotinamide adenine dinucleotide phosphate, and EDTA for ethylenediaminetetraacetate (207). *See* chapter 14 for lists of approved abbreviations and symbols, and authoritative sources. A compound can be referred to occasionally as *it, this compound*, or, in the examples above, *the cofactor* and *the chelator*. Symbols for atoms and for structural units are often used to create abbreviations (for example, EtOH, Me_2SO, Ado).

SYMBOLS AND FORMULAS

Refer to the *Handbook of Chemistry and Physics* (221) or *The Merck Index* (222) for confirmation of chemical symbols and formulas used in text, tables, or illustrations as shorthand designations (for example, Mg, Mn, HCl, CO_2, C_2H_5OH). When merely naming a salt or specifying its concentration in a solution, use its simplest formula (Na_2SO_4, KCl, $FeCl_3$); for quantities of ordinarily hydrated salts, indicate the full molecular formula ($BaCl_2 \cdot 2H_2O$ or $K_4Fe(CN)_6 \cdot 3H_2O$). Indicate ionic state by adding symbols for the charge (Mg^{2+}, SO_4^{2-}, H^+, Cl^-, CH_3COO^-). Denote molecules of gases by their formulas (H_2, O_2, N_2).

Give the oxidation number of an element in roman numerals on the line and in parentheses—for example, Cr(III). The proportions of the constituents in the formula of a compound also may be indicated indirectly by Stock's system—that is, by a roman numeral in parentheses immediately after the name: dilead(II) lead(IV) oxide. When used in conjunction with a symbol, the roman numeral is a superscript:

$Pb^{II}_2Pb^{IV}O_4$. For zeros and nonintegers, arabic numerals are substituted for roman numerals (201).

To denote an acid containing 18 carbon atoms, write C_{18} acid; to denote the carbon atom numbered 3, write C-3. Write $C_{18:1}$, $C_{18:2}$, $C_{18:3}$, and so forth to indicate the chain length and number of double bonds in an unsaturated acid.

Avoid using a chemical symbol if it can be mistaken for a word, particularly at the beginning of a sentence (*As* in these samples ... *He* was present in ... *I* was vaporized...). Avoid ambiguous formulas that indicate only composition; for example, C_2H_6O might be ethyl alcohol (C_2H_5OH) or methyl ether (CH_3OCH_3), and $C_4H_4O_2$ may be one of several structures.

For formulas that can be typewritten, include only the most important chemical bonds and indicate them by hyphens. Leucine, for example, may be written $(CH_3)_2$-CH-CH_2-CH(NH_2)-COOH. If there is no need to show linkages, the formula may be written without bond symbols: $(CH_3)_2CHCH_2CH(NH_2)COOH$.

Center each typed formula at an appropriate place between lines of text, leaving quadruple space above and below. Where structures of organic substances are important, type or draw the formulas to show every significant detail.

Formulas too complex to be typewritten are too complex to be set in type. For these formulas provide well-designed, black-ink drawings suitable for reproduction. Indicate the desired location of each drawing by a circled note in the margin of the manuscript.

If you refer frequently to substances with complex structures and difficult names, draw the structures, labeling each with its proper name and, for example, an arabic numeral, as in figure 13.14, and then refer to each one in the text by substance and number as labeled (acid 4, ketone 9).

NUCLIDES AND ISOTOPES

The ionic charge, number of atoms, atomic number, and mass number (atomic weight) characterizing the nuclide of an element are indicated by four indices placed around the symbol. Thus, $^{32}_{16}S^{2+}_2$ represents, in clockwise order, a molecule with two positive charges containing two atoms of sulfur, each having atomic number 16 and mass number 32 (ref. 201).

A nuclide is indicated by its mass number placed as a superscript to the left of the symbol—for example, ^{32}P; when spelled out, it should correspond to the spoken word (phosphorus-32). In an isotopically labeled compound, the isotopic prefix in brackets precedes and is attached directly to the part of the name to which it refers: sodium [^{14}C]formate; iodo[1,2-^{14}C]acetic acid; fructose 1,6-[1-^{32}P]bisphosphate. Terms such as

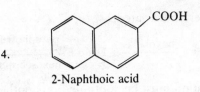

4.

2-Naphthoic acid

9. $(CH_3)_2N$-⟨ ⟩-CO-C_6H_5

p-Dimethylaminobenzophenone

Figure 13.14. Structural formulas. To prepare copy for such formulas, use a template for a ring; draw or hand-letter labels in black ink or type them.

"^{131}I-labeled albumin" should not be contracted to "[^{131}I]albumin" because native albumin does not contain iodine. The superscript mass number of an isotope must not be attached to a letter in an abbreviation, but precedes the entire abbreviation: [^{32}P]AMP, not AM^{32}P. When a substance is labeled by isotopes of more than one element, the symbols are arranged in alphabetical order (including ^{2}H and ^{3}H for deuterium and tritium, respectively). When more than one position in a substance is labeled by means of the same isotope, the number of labeled atoms is added as a subscript to the right, as in [^{14}C$_2$]glycolic acid. If the position of the labeled element is known, it is indicated by an arabic numeral or by an appropriate italic prefix: [1-^{14}C]acetic acid; [3-^{14}C; 2,3-^{2}H; ^{15}N]-serine; [*carboxy*-^{14}C]leucine; L-[*methyl*-^{14}C]methionine. If the position of labeling is unknown, the indication is omitted—for example, [^{14}C]glucose; if labeling is uniform or general, the indication is [U-^{14}C]glucose or [G-^{14}C]glucose, respectively. (*See* ref. 203 for more detailed information.)

EQUATIONS

Center a chemical equation between the right and left margins of the manuscript page, and leave quadruple space above and below it. If the equation represents an equilibrium, a double arrow is shown; if the reaction goes to completion, a single arrow is shown. In presenting biochemical reactions, authors frequently use the names of compounds rather than the complex formulas. Accepted abbreviations may be used. For indicating the course of an enzymatic reaction use the form shown in the example below.

$$\text{fructose} \xrightarrow{\text{hexokinase}} \text{fructose-6-}P \overset{\text{phosphofructokinase}}{\underset{\text{hexosebisphosphatase}}{\rightleftharpoons}} \text{fructose-1,6-}P_2$$

Or, further abbreviated:

$$Fru \xrightarrow{\text{hexokinase}} Fru\text{-}6\text{-}P \underset{\text{hexosebisphosphatase}}{\overset{\text{phosphofructokinase}}{\rightleftharpoons}} Fru\text{-}1,6\text{-}P_2$$

If an equation must be continued on another line, the arrow should be on the second line.

3'-phosphopolynucleotide + H_2O

$$\xrightarrow{\text{polynucleotide 3'-phosphatase}} \text{polynucleotide} + P_i$$

WATER OF HYDRATION

References to quantities of inorganic salts or hydrated organic substances should specify the number of molecules of water of hydration per molecule of compound—for example, copper sulfate pentahydrate ($CuSO_4 \cdot 5H_2O$).

CONFIGURATION AND ROTATION

Many names of organic substances include locant numbers and letters or syllables designating details of the chemical structure. Transcribe them accurately. Since there are several isomers of dinitrophenol, for example, the one used must be clearly identified.

In general, configurational relationships are indicated by capital italic letter prefixes R and S. This RS system is based on the actual three-dimensional formulas of the compound and can only be applied when the *absolute* configuration is certain (191, 202). In carbohydrate and amino acid nomenclature, configurational relationships are denoted by the small-capital prefixes D and L. Direction of optical rotation without regard to configuration is indicated by a plus or minus sign in parentheses or by the prefixes *d* for dextro or *l* for levo, in lowercase italic letters—for example, (+)-6-hydroxytryptophan or *d*-6-hydroxytryptophan (206).

Use italic type for the symbols of elements that occur as locants in the names of many organic compounds (*O*-methyltyrosine, *S*-benzyl-*N*-phthaloylcysteine).

SOLUTIONS

The concentration of a solution is preferably expressed in the International System of Units (SI) as mole per litre (mol/litre). The mole is the amount of substance of a system that contains as many elementary entities as there are atoms in 0.012 kg of carbon 12. When the mole is used, the elementary entities must be specified and may be atoms, molecules, ions, electrons, other particles, or specified groups of such particles (188). IUPAC has recognized the use of the abbreviation M for mole per litre. The M is preceded by a number (0.1 M NaCl). For dilute solutions, use, for example, 1.0 μM instead of 1×10^{-6} M.

Use of the term, normality (N, the number of gram-equivalents per litre), is discouraged by IUPAC because it lacks a universally accepted definition. Information about the amount of substance in solution can be conveyed equally well by the unit, mole, accompanied by a statement of the entity counted.

The distinction between mole (the molecular or formula weight in grams) and molar or molal (solution concentrations) should be clear. A molar (M) solution contains 1 mole of solute in 1000 ml of solution; a molal (mol/kg) solution contains 1 mole of solute dissolved in 1000 g of solvent.

The chemical definition of concentration should be used rather than percentage, an expression that is frequently ambiguous. If a percentage is used, specify the exact chemical substance weighed or measured, and whether the ratio is by weight and volume (wt/vol) or by volume only (vol/vol). Dilutions of ethyl alcohol, for example, are usually made from commercial alcohol of density 0.816, which has a concentration of 92.3% (wt/vol) and 94.9% (vol/vol).

MOLECULAR WEIGHT

The ratio of the mass of one molecule of a substance to one-twelfth the mass of an atom of carbon-12 is the molecular weight; it is the relative molecular mass of a substance. It is therefore a pure number and is dimensionless.

A dalton (symbol: Da) is a unit of mass equal to one-twelfth the mass of an atom of carbon-12 (refs. 194 and 218). Thus, 1 dalton equals N^{-1} g $= 1.663 \times 10^{-24}$ g, where N is Avogadro's number. Although many biologists use the dalton as a unit of mass, it has not been recognized by any international scientific union. One convenience of the dalton is that structures can be described for which the term "molecular weight" is inappropriate, such as ribosomes, mitochondria, and bacteriophages. It is incorrect to say that the molecular weight of a ribosome is 2.6×10^6 since a ribosome contains several kinds of protein and RNA molecules. The statement that the mass of a ribosome is 2.6×10^6 daltons avoids the implication that the ribosome is a molecule.

It is correct to say that the molecular weight of protein X is 30 000 or the molecular mass of protein X is 30 000 daltons. However, it is incorrect to say that the molecular weight of protein X is 30 000 daltons.

ANALYTICAL AND OTHER METHODS

If an analytical or procedural method that is not widely known was followed, cite the article in which the method was originally described. If an important modification of a fundamental method was used, name or explain it—for example, "I determined nitrogen by the Kjeldahl method as modified by Hiller et al. (1948)." If the modification was trivial, cite only the article describing the fundamental method. If the method was original, at least in part, describe it briefly, avoiding inconsequential details. Since analytical chemists invariably use distilled or deionized water, it need not be mentioned unless specially purified water was essential.

Report analytical results in the following conventional form: Analysis: calculated for $C_{17}H_{20}N_4O_4$ (344.2): C, 59.29; H, 5.85; N, 16.27. Found: C, 58.8; H, 6.03; N, 16.2. Note the punctuation, omission of the percentage symbol, and omission of a value for oxygen, which can be determined by adding the percentages for the known elements and subtracting from 100. Amino acid analyses (ratios) should be indicated as follows: $His_{0.9}Glu_{1.1}Val_{1.1}Leu_{1.9}$.

PHYSICAL PROPERTIES

Report the data on physical properties in the following standard form, indicating special conditions of measurement.

> Melting point: mp 140–142° C (unc), (cor), (copper block), (sealed tube)
> Boiling point: bp 120° C at 1.95 kPa
> Specific refractive index: $[n]_D^{16} = 1.476$
> Specific rotation: $[\alpha]_D^{22} = -20 \pm 2°$ (1.0 M in water).

In reporting specific rotation, record temperature, wavelength of light (λ), solvent, and concentration of solute used in the measurement. Molecular rotation may be obtained by multiplying the specific rotation by the molecular weight of the solute: $[M]_\lambda = $ (molecular weight/100) $[\alpha]_\lambda$. For macromolecules, the mean residue rotation (m) is often given: $[m]_\lambda = $ (mean residue weight/100) $[\alpha]_\lambda$.

Statements of melting points should indicate whether a correction for stem emergence of the thermometer was applied. If no statement about method is made, the reader will assume that the substance was heated in an open tube immersed in a suitable bath. It is assumed that boiling points are at atmospheric pressure unless stated otherwise.

SPECTROPHOTOMETRY

Spectrophotometric data are usually expressed in terms of absorbance, A, which is defined as $A = -\log_{10}T = \epsilon bc$. The transmittance, T, is the ratio of the radiant power transmitted by a sample to the radiant power transmitted by the solvent alone; ϵ is the molar absorption coefficient (molar absorptivity); b is the sample path length, usually given in centimetres; and c is the concentration of the absorbing substance in moles per litre. The wavelength (λ, expressed as micrometres or nanometres) of the radiation should always be specified. The value of A or ϵ at wavelength λ is written as A_λ or ϵ_λ, respectively (190).

CENTRIFUGATION

When conditions for centrifuging are critical, give sufficient information to enable another investigator to repeat the procedure; state the make of centrifuge, rotor used, temperature, time at maximum speed, and centrifugal force.

In reporting ultracentrifuge data, give sedimentation and diffusion measurements, including the temperatures at which they were made. The appropriate abbreviations are s, sedimentation coefficient; $s_{20,w}$, sedimentation coefficient corrected to 20° C in water; s^0, sedimentation coefficient at zero concentration; S, Svedberg unit of sedimentation coefficient (S = 0.1 picosecond or 10^{-13} second): $\bar{v}$, partial specific volume; D, $D_{20,w}$, D^0, diffusion coefficients corresponding to sedimentation coefficients.

CHROMATOGRAPHY

Chromatographic evidence for identity and purity should be presented by a photograph or by a smooth black-ink tracing of the chromatogram. Types of chromatography may be classified in several ways: according to phases used (gas or liquid chromatography), according to mechanisms (adsorption, partition, ion-exchange, or permeation chromatography), and according to techniques used (column, paper, or thin-layer chromatography). The type of chromatography should be stated. The American Society for Testing and Materials (187, 189) and IUPAC (200) have published recommended nomenclature for chromatography.

Gas chromatography   Specify the carrier gas (mobile phase); the liquid phase in gas-liquid chromatography or adsorbent in gas-solid chromatography (stationary phase); the amount of liquid phase in weight per weight of the solid support; the type and treatment of the solid support in gas-liquid chromatography; the size of support or adsorbent particles (usually in mesh units); the temperature of the oven in degrees Celsius; column material, length, and internal diameter (metric units); and the flow rate (in cubic centimetres per minute) of the carrier gas.

When temperature programming is used, describe the initial temperature and its duration, the rate of increase, and the upper limit of the temperature and its duration. State whether the stationary phase is chemically bonded to the support. Give the type of detector used—for example, thermal conductivity, flame ionization detector, electron capture detector. If splitting techniques are used, indicate the splitter ratio.

Retention of solutes is usually characterized by retention time, t_R (in minutes); total retention volume, V_R (in cubic centimetres); net retention volume, V_N (in cubic centimetres); specific retention volume, V_g (in cubic centimetres per weight of stationary phase); or Kovats retention index, I. Of these quantities, net retention volume (V_N), specific retention volume (V_g), or retention index (I) are preferred. The retention of solutes can also be given as the capacity ratio k; k is $(t_R - t_M)/t_M$, and t_M is the retention time of an inert solute.

When the solutes are quantitated, the method of measurement and calibration should be indicated; namely, peak height, peak height multiplied by width at base, integrators, and so forth. The efficiency of the column should be given either by the height equivalent to a theoretical plate, h (in centimetres), or by the number of plates, n, for the column length. The accepted notation for resolution is R_s. In temperature-programming gas chromatography, h and n as measured from the chromatogram have no meaning.

Column liquid chromatography   All operating and experimental conditions should be given. State the type of solvent (mobile phase) delivery: gravity flow or forced (pump) flow. The size of the support particles or the adsorbent is usually given in micrometres. Chromatograms can be described in terms of retention times, t_R (in minutes), or total retention (elution) volumes, V_R (cubic centimetres). When elution order is discussed, the capacity ratio k can also be used. In adsorption chromatography (liquid-solid chromatography) the stationary phase is an active solid, such as silica gel, alumina, or other solid matrix. In liquid-liquid chromatography a liquid stationary phase is deposited on the support; a chemical moiety can be chemically bonded to the support. In steric exclusion chromatography, the stationary phase is a noninteractive porous solid, usually silica or an organic gel, and sample molecules are separated by size. Clearly define the pretreatment of adsorbents in adsorption chromatography and the deposition process of the liquid phase. For gradient elution, the initial and final composition of the mobile phase and the type of gradient (concave, convex, or stepwise) should be given. The flow rate of the mobile phase (cubic centimetres per minute) should be specified. The term "reversed phase chromatography" indicates a chromatographic system in which the mobile phase is more polar than the stationary phase. The type of detector used should be indicated. Specify wavelength for an ultraviolet detector. The meanings and symbols for efficiency and resolution in liquid chromatography are identical to those in gas chromatography. Note that in gradient elution, h or n, as measured from the chromatogram, have no physical meaning.

Thin-layer chromatography and paper chromatography   The type of paper or thin layer (nature of stationary phases, active solid adsorbents, or ion exchangers) should be given. Specify any pretreatment of the paper or the thin layer. The nature of the mobile phase must be clearly indicated, including proportion of solvents, if more than one is used. Describe the condition in the developing chamber immediately before the chromatographic development. When two-dimensional chromatography is used, the developing time in each direction and the treatment of the chromatogram between changing direction and solvents should be included. The retention characteristics are given by R_f, the ratio of the movement of the solute to that of the solvent front. State the treatment of the thin-layer or paper chromatogram after development and the detection method (for example, type of reagent sprayed).

METABOLIC QUOTIENTS

The symbol Q_x represents metabolic quotient in microlitres of gas X per milligram dry weight of biological material per hour. Metabolic quotients in any other units of measurement (micromoles of X per milligram N per second) are symbolized by q_x. When first mentioned, the units for Q or q must be clearly defined. If the metabolite X is a solid or a liquid, it is conventionally considered a gas at normal temperature and pressure (NTP), 1 micromole of X being equivalent to 22.4 microlitres.

Superscript symbols should be used to indicate aerobic conditions, as $Q_{CO_2}^{O_2}$ or $q_{CO_2}^{O_2}$, and anaerobic conditions, as $Q_{CO_2}^{N_2}$ or $q_{CO_2}^{N_2}$. The substrate may be shown in parentheses—for example, $Q_{CO_2}^{N_2}$ (pyruvate), which written out would read, "microlitres of carbon dioxide produced anaerobically from pyruvate per milligram dry tissue per hour." Production or consumption can be indicated by adding + or − to the quotients—for example, $+Q_{CO_2}$.

The symbol Q_x or q_x may be omitted if the units of measurement are given whenever a quotient is mentioned.

ENZYMES

Names of enzymes and Enzyme Commission (EC) numbers are published in *Enzyme Nomenclature* and its supplements (214–217). An enzyme that is not the main subject of an article should be identified at first mention by its code number if one exists. When an enzyme is the main subject, its code number and systematic name (if such exist) or the reaction it catalyzes should be given at first mention of the enzyme; thereafter the recommended name may be used. For example, glucose-6-phosphate dehydrogenase is the recommended name for the enzyme D-glucose-6-phosphate:$NADP^+$ 1-oxidoreductase (EC 1.1.1.49). Both systematic and recommended enzyme names are listed in the index of *Enzyme Nomenclature*. If the enzyme is not listed, it should be reported to the Enzyme Commission.

RIBONUCLEIC ACIDS

Fractions or functions of ribonucleic acids are frequently designated by prefixes (mRNA for messenger RNA; rRNA for ribosomal RNA; nRNA for nuclear RNA; tRNA for transfer RNA; and cRNA for complementary RNA).

The tRNA that combines with a particular amino acid—glycine, for example—is written glycine tRNA (abbreviated tRNA^{Gly}). When the glycine tRNA has become attached to a glycyl residue, it is called glycyl-tRNA (abbreviated Gly-tRNA). Such a matched tRNA attached to its cognate amino acid is generally referred to as an aminoacyl-tRNA. A mismatch, such as glycine tRNA attaching to alanine, would be written Ala-tRNA^{Gly}.

If there is more than one specifying or accepting tRNA, each may be designated by a subscript arabic numeral tRNA$_1$^{Ala} and tRNA$_2$^{Ala}; these are "isoacceptors." The source of the tRNA is written tRNA^{Ala} (*Escherichia coli*) or (*Escherichia coli*) tRNA^{Ala}. Aminoacyl-tRNA's are familiarly referred to as "charged," and the specifying tRNA is called "stripped," but these terms should be avoided (209).

POLYPEPTIDES AND OTHER POLYMERS _____

In polypeptides and proteins, the constituent amino acid residues are designated by three-letter symbols, which are usually the first three letters of the trivial names. These symbols, which represent the names of the radicals and their structural formulas, should not be used in text as abbreviations for the free amino acids, but they are acceptable for this purpose in tables, diagrams, or figures, where space is limited. Their chief use is in structural representation of polypeptides and proteins. The recommended symbols for the common amino acids are given in chapter 14. An example of a tripeptide, glycyllysylalanine, in abbreviated form is Gly-Lys-Ala (each hyphen represents a peptide bond). Amino acid residues (except glycine) are assumed to be in the L configuration, unless the contrary is explicitly indicated.

The recommended abbreviation for a common amino acid is the same as the symbol for the residue; for example, Ala represents alanine, and, in polypeptides, it represents the residue, alanyl. Detailed discussions of designations of amino acid derivatives and peptides can be found in several sources (206, 211).

The left end of the polypeptide or protein is, by convention, the amino-terminal end and is written NH$_2$-terminal (rather than N-terminal). The right end is designated the carboxy-terminal end and is written COOH-terminal (rather than C-terminal). Amino acid residues in peptides or protein sequences are, by convention, numbered from left to right. A portion of a protein (partial sequence) might then be designated or identified by numbers and symbols—for example, His-23 to Ala-35. Further rules for peptides and polypeptides have been issued by the IUPAC-IUB Commission on Biochemical Nomenclature (208, 210).

Hyphens and commas between the symbols for amino acid residues have special meanings. Hyphens indicate a known sequence, as in Ala-Leu-Lys. Unknown sequences are enclosed in parentheses with the symbols separated by commas, as in (Gly,Phe,Tyr).

Special conventions are applied in characterizing the structures of synthetic polypeptides. The simple homopolymer, polyalanine, is designated poly(Ala) or (Ala)$_n$. For a linear copolymer of irregular sequence whose composition is unknown, write poly(DLAla,Lys) or (DLAla,Lys)$_n$. For a linear copolymer of alternating sequence and unknown composition, write poly(DLAla-Lys) or (DLAla-Lys)$_n$. For a linear sequence of unknown order with known composition, indicate the percentage of each with superscripts, poly(Glu^{56}Tyr^{44}) or (Glu^{56}Tyr^{44})$_n$; other information (Glu is DL, Tyr is L) may be added. Extensions of this usage to block polymers and graft polymers are given by the IUPAC-IUB Combined Commission on Biochemical Nomenclature (210).

Synthetic polyribonucleotides may also be designated by the "poly" system. For example, polyadenylate is poly(A); poly(adenylate-uridylate), alternating sequence, is poly(A-U); and poly(adenylate, uridylate), irregular sequence, is poly(A,U). For polydeoxyribonucleotides, poly(dN), the position of the deoxy- is optional; thus, poly(dA-dT) for poly(deoxyadenylate-deoxythymidylate) and poly[d(A-T)] are synonymous with each other and with (dA-dT)$_n$ and d(A-T)$_n$. Composition and size may be shown by appropriate subscripts as in (A$_2$,U$_1$)$_{50}$, which contains 100 A's and 50 U's in irregular sequence, and in d(A-T)$_{50}$, which contains 50 dA's and 50 dT's in regular alternating sequence.

Associated (noncovalently linked) polynucleotides are shown as, for example, poly(G)·poly(C), or as (G)$_n$·(C)$_n$. Similarly, base-paired nucleosides are shown with a raised period to indicate association (G·C), a hyphen to indicate a sequence (G-C), and a plus sign to indicate content (G+C content was 28%). Nucleotide sequences of codons may be written without separating punctuation (UAU or CAG or UGG).

The individual nucleoside symbols of a polynucleotide are written with a connecting hyphen, which represents the -OPO$_2$H-O- group. A lowercase p may be used on the left end of the sequence to indicate a terminal 5'-phosphate (pA-G-A) and on the right end to indicate a terminal 3'-phosphate (A-U-Gp). Left-to-right direction is implied, unless an arrow is used in place of the hyphen to indicate reverse direction: A-U-Gp can be written pG←U←A. Additional lists of abbreviations and symbols have been issued by the IUPAC-IUB Commission on Biochemical Nomenclature (209).

CARBOHYDRATES

Monosaccharide units and their residues in oligosaccharides and polysaccharides may be indicated in tables, lists, and figures by symbols created from the first three letters of their respective names, unless confusion with an existing symbol (Gly and Thr in the amino acid series) would result (*see* chapter 14).

A 2-deoxy sugar is designated by the symbol for its most common parent sugar with the prefix d (dRib for 2-deoxyribose). Other deoxy sugars may be designated similarly with a positional numeral (3-dGlc for 3-deoxyglucose).

Pyranose and furanose forms are designated where necessary by the suffixes p and f. Configurational symbols D and L (small-capital letters) and anomeric prefixes are shown where necessary as prefixes (Glc$p$ or αD-Glc$p$ for an α-D-glucopyranose unit; Fru$f$ or βD-Fru$f$ for a β-D-fructofuranose unit). Symbols thus formed are joined by hyphens to indicate the links between units. The position and nature of the links are shown by numerals and the anomeric symbols α and β.

> Maltose, Glc$p$(α1-4)Glc
> Lactose, Gal$p$(β1-4)Glc
> Stachyose, Gal$p$(α1-6)Gal$p$(α1-6)Gal$p$(α1-2β)Fru$f$

Arrows may be used to indicate the direction of the glycoside link, the arrow pointing away from the hemiacetal carbon of the link; for example, lactose may be represented as Gal$p$(β1→4)Glc. The hyphen in the examples above represents →.

Derived monosaccharide units may be designated by the addition of modifying suffixes (205, 207). To indicate an aldonic acid, add A (GlcA for gluconic acid); for uronic acids, add UA (GalUA for galacturonic acid). To indicate a 2-amino-2-deoxysaccharide, add the suffix N to the parent saccharide symbol (GalN for galactosamine); an N-acetyl derivative is shown by NAc (GalNAc for N-acetylgalactosamine).

For further details, the recommendations of the IUB-IUPAC Joint Commission on Biochemical Nomenclature should be consulted (198, 199).

LIPIDS

The rules for lipid nomenclature are too complex to be summarized here. The recommendations of the IUPAC-IUB Commission on Biochemical Nomenclature should be consulted (212).

STEROIDS

Likewise, the rules for steroid nomenclature are far too complex to be summarized. The official recommendations of the IUPAC Commission on the Nomenclature of Organic Chemistry and the IUPAC-IUB Commission on Biochemical Nomenclature should be consulted (204).

GEOGRAPHY AND GEOLOGY

For the accepted form and spelling of a place name, a geographic feature, or a geologic feature or stratigraphic unit (table 13.9), consult the *U.S. Government Printing Office Style Manual* (231), the lexicons published by the Geologic Names Committee of the U.S. Geological Survey (227–

Table 13.9. Stratigraphic and geologic time units (229)

Subdivisions (and their map symbols)					Beginning time*
Eon or eonothem	Era or erathem	Period or system	Subperiod or subsystem	Epoch or series	
Phanerozoic	Cenozoic (Cz)	Quaternary (Q)		Holocene	0.01
				Pleistocene	2
		Tertiary (T)	Neogene (N)	Pliocene	5
				Miocene	24
			Paleogene (Pɛ)	Oligocene	38
				Eocene	55
				Paleocene	63
	Mesozoic (Mz)	Cretaceous (K)		Late Cretaceous Epoch or Upper Cretaceous Series	96
				Early Cretaceous Epoch or Lower Cretaceous Series	138
		Jurassic (J)			205
		Triassic (Ṟ)			240
	Paleozoic (Pz)	Permian (P)			290
		Carboniferous (C)	Pennsylvanian Period or System (℗)		330
			Mississippian Period or System (M)		360
		Devonian (D)			410
		Silurian (S)			435
		Ordovician (O)			500
		Cambrian (Ꞓ)			570†
Proterozoic (P)	Proterozoic Z (Z)‡				800
	Proterozoic Y (Y)‡				1600
	Proterozoic X (X)‡				2500
Archean (A)				Oldest known rocks in U.S.	3600

* An approximation in millions of years.

† Rocks older than 570 million years also called Precambrian (pꞒ), a time term without specific rank.

‡ Time terms without specific rank.

229), or lists published by the Board on Geographic Names, U.S. Geological Survey, Reston, VA 22092. See also *Geowriting* (226) for problems and practices in geological nomenclature and *Suggestions to Authors of The Reports of The United States Geological Survey* (225, 230).

In capitalizing the names of features and units, the aim is to distinguish between formal accepted names and names that are informal, less specific, or used only locally. Obviously, the proper forms are "the Missouri River," "a Missouri river," and "the river." Less obviously, the Chugwater Group (capitalized) in Wyoming includes the Alcova Limestone and the Red Peak Formation, but another formation within that group might be called "the Branson formation." Upon acceptance as a formal name of a definite formation, it would become "the Branson Formation." Below are examples of terms that are formal (capitalized) or informal (lowercase).

Florida coast	Pittsburgh coal bed	Bedford stone
Dakota Sandstone	Orocopia Schist	Modelo Shale
Vermejo Park dome	Copley Greenstone	Sherwin Till
Franciscan chert	Franciscan Formation	Temescal gravel
Noonday Dolomite	Irvingtonian Stage	

Do not capitalize unit terms standing alone, such as "a granite" or "the conglomerate." Capitalize the words below, and similar ones, when they designate any of the great soil groups.

Alpine Meadow	Bog	Chernozem
Podsol	Tundra	Desert

Guidelines for abbreviating geographic names can be found in chapter 12, General Style Conventions.

LITERATURE CITED: Style in Special Fields

1. Jeffrey, C. Biological nomenclature. 2d ed. New York: Crane, Russak & Co., Inc.; 1977.

PLANT SCIENCES

2. American Society for Horticultural Sciences Special Committee on Growth Chamber Environments. Revised guidelines for reporting studies in controlled environment chambers. HortScience 12:309–310; 1977.
3. ASAE Engineering Practice: ASAE EP411, Guidelines for measuring and reporting environmental parameters for plant experiments in growth chambers. St. Joseph, MI: American Society of Agricultural Engineers; Agricultural Engineers Yearbook, 1982:406–409.
4. Bernard, R. L.; and others. Report of Soybean Genetics Committee. Soybean Genet. Newslett. 9:9–13; 1982.
5. Brickell, D. D., chairman. International code of nomenclature of cultivated plants. Regnum Veg. 104; 1980.

6. Clayberg, D. D. Rules for nomenclature in tomato genetics. Report of the Tomato Genetics Cooperative 20:3–5; 1970.

7. Davis, P. H.; Heywood, V. H. Principles of angiosperm taxonomy. New York: Van Nostrand Co., Inc.; 1963.

8. Farr, E. R.; Leussink, J. A.; Stafleu, F. A. Index nominum genericorum (plantarum). 3 vols. Regnum Veg. 100, 101, and 102:1979.

9. Hickey, L. J. Classification of the architecture of dicotyledonous leaves. Am. J. Bot. 60:17–33; 1973.

10. Holmgren, P. K.; Keuken, W.; Schofield, E. K. Index herbariorum. Part I: The herbaria of the world. 7th ed. Regnum Veg. 106; 1981.

11. Kohel, R. Genetic nomenclature in cotton. J. Hered. 64:291–295; 1973.

12. Krizek, D. T. Guidelines for measuring and reporting environmental conditions in controlled-environment studies. Physiol. Plant. 56:231–235; 1982.

13. Lawrence, G. H. M.; Bucheim, A. F. G.; Daniels, G. S.; Dolezal, H., editors. B-P-H, Botanico-Periodicum-Huntianum. Pittsburgh, PA: Hunt Botanical Library.

14. Leenhouts, P. W. A guide to the practice of herbarium taxonomy. Regnum Veg. 58:1–60; 1968.

15. McIntosh, R. A. Catalogue of gene symbols for wheat. Proceedings of the Fifth International Wheat Genetics Symposium. 2:1299–1309; 1979. Indian Society of Genetics and Plant Breeding, Indian Agricultural Research Institute, New Delhi-110012, India.

16. McVaugh, R.; Ross, R.; Stafleu, F. A. An annotated glossary of botanical nomenclature. Regnum Veg. 56:1–36; 1968.

17. Meikle, R. D. Draft index of author abbreviations compiled at the Herbarium, Royal Botanic Gardens, Kew. Basildon, England: Her Majesty's Stationery Office; 1980.

18. Payne, W. W. A glossary of plant hair terminology. Brittonia 30:239–255; 1978.

19. Porter, D. M.; Kiger, R. W.; Monahan, J. E. A guide for contributors to flora North America. Part II. An outline and glossary of terms for morphological and habitat description (provisional edition). FNA Report 66. Washington, DC: Dept. of Botany, Smithsonian Institution; 1973.

20. Radford, A. E.; Dickison, W. C.; Massey, J. R.; Bell, C. R. Vascular plant systematics. New York: Harper & Row; 1974.

21. Rhoades, M. M., editor. Revised genetic nomenclature for maize. Maize Genet. Coop. News Lett. 48:201–202; 1974.

22. Rickett, H. W. The English names of plants. Bull. Torrey Bot. Club 92:137–139; 1965.

23. Simons, M. D.; Martens, J. W.; McKenzie, R. I. H.; Nishiyama, I.; Sadanaga, K.; Sebesta, J.; Thomas, H. Oats: a standardized system of nomenclature for genes and chromosomes and catalog of genes governing characters. U. S. Department of Agriculture: Agriculture Handbook No. 509; 1978.

24. Stace, C. A. Plant taxonomy and biosystematics. Baltimore: University Park Press; 1980.

25. Stafleu, F. A.; Cowan, R. S. Taxonomic literature. 2nd ed. (TL-2). 1: A-G. Regnum Veg. 94; 1976. 2: H-Le. Regnum Veg. 98; 1979. 3: Lh-O. Regnum Veg. 105; 1981.

26. Stearn, W. T. Botanical Latin. New York: Hafner Publishing Co.; 1966.
27. Systematics Association Committee for Descriptive Terminology. Terminology of simple symmetrical plane shapes. Taxon 11:145–156, 245–247; 1962.
28. Tanaka, Y., chairman. Report of the International Committee on Genetic Symbols and Nomenclature. Union Internationale Sciences Biologiques, Serie B, Colloques No. 30; 1957.
29. Tentative recommendations of terminology, symbols and units in plant physiology. Lund: International Association for Plant Physiology; 1972.
30. Tibbitts, T. W.; Kozlowski, T. T. Controlled environment guidelines for plant research. New York: Academic Press; 1979.
31. Tsuchiya, T. Report of Barley Genetics Committee, American Barley Workers Conference. Barley Newslett. 15:2–6, 1972.
32. Voss, E. G., chairman. International code of botanical nomenclature. Regnum Veg. [In press]; 1983.
33. Willis, J. C. A dictionary of the flowering plants and ferns. 8th ed., revised by H. K. Airy Shaw. London: Cambridge Univ. Press; 1973.

MICROBIOLOGY

34. Approved lists of bacterial names. Int. J. Syst. Bacteriol. 30:225–240; 1980.
35. Bachmann, B. J. Pedigrees of some mutant strains of *Escherichia coli* K-12. Bacteriol. Rev. 36:525–557; 1972.
36. Bachmann, B. J.; Low, K. B.; Taylor, A. L. Recalibrated linkage map of *Escherichia coli* K-12. Bacteriol. Rev. 40:116–167; 1976.
37. Buchanan, R. E.; Holt, J. G.; Lessel, E. F., Jr. Index Bergeyana. Baltimore: Williams & Wilkins Co.; 1966.
38. Buchanan, R. E.; Gibbons, N. E., editors. Bergey's manual of determinative bacteriology. 8th ed. Baltimore: Williams & Wilkins Co.; 1974.
39. Clements, F. E.; Shear, C. L. The genera of fungi. New York: H. W. Wilson Co.; 1931.
40. Demerec, M.; Adelberg, E. A.; Clark, A. J.; Hartman, P. E. A proposal for a uniform nomenclature in bacterial genetics. Genetics 54:61–76; 1966.
41. De-Toni, J. B. Sylloge Algarum: Index Kewensis, 1895 to present. London: Royal Botanic Gardens; 1889.
42. Edwards, P. R.; Ewing, W. H. Identification of Enterobacteriaceae. 3d ed. Minneapolis: Burgess Publishing Co.; 1972.
43. Fenner, F. Classification and nomenclature of viruses. Second report of the International Committee on Taxonomy of Viruses. Intervirology 7:1–116; 1976.
44. Fenner, F.; Pereira, H. G.; Porterfield, J. S.; Joklik, W. K.; Downie, A. W. Family and generic names for viruses approved by the International Committee on Taxonomy of Viruses, June 1974. Intervirology 3:193–198; 1974.
45. Ginsberg, H. S.; Williams, J. F.; Doerfler, W. H.; Shimojo, H. Proposed nomenclature for mutants of adenoviruses. J. Virol. 12:663–664; 1973.
46. Hershey, A. D., editor. The bacteriophage Lambda. Cold Spring Harbor, NY: Cold Spring Harbor Laboratory; 1971.
47. Index zoologicus. 1902 to present. London: Zoological Society.

48. Kritchevsky, M. I.; Walczak, C. A.; Rogosa, M.; Johnson, R. Interchange of abbreviations and full generic names in computers. Int. J. Syst. Bacteriol. 30:585–593; 1980.

49. Lapage, S. P.; Sneath, P. H. A.; Lessel, E. F.; Skerman, V. B. D.; Seeliger, H. P. R.; Clark, W. A., editors. International code of nomenclature of bacteria. Bacteriological code. Washington, DC: American Society for Microbiology; 1976 rev.

50. Laskin, A. I.; Lechevalier, H. A., editors. Handbook of microbiology. Cleveland, OH: CRC Press; 1974; vol. 4, Microbial metabolism, genetics and immunology: 665–711.

51. Low, K. B. *Escherichia coli* K-12 F-prime factors, old and new. Bacteriol. Rev. 36:587–607; 1972.

52. Mathews, C. K. Bacteriophage biochemistry. ACS monograph. No. 166 New York: Van Nostrand Reinhold Co.; 1971.

53. Mathews, R. E. F. Classification and nomenclature of viruses. Third report of the International Committee on Taxonomy of Viruses. Intervirology 12:129–296; 1979.

54. Melnick, J. L. Taxonomy of viruses. Prog. Med. Virol. 26:214–232; 1980.

55. Melnick, J. L.; Allison, A. C.; Butel, J. S.; Eckhart, W., Eddy, B. E.; Kit, S.; Levine, A. J.; Miles, J. A. R.; Pagano, J. S.; Sachs, L.; Vonka, V. Papovaviridae. Intervirology 3:106–120; 1974.

56. Novick, R. P.; Clowes, R. C.; Cohen, S. N.; Curtiss, R., III; Datta, N.; Falkow, S. Uniform nomenclature for bacterial plasmids: a proposal. Bacteriol. Rev. 40:168–189; 1976.

57. Reichelt, J. L.; Baumann, P. *Photobacterium mandapamensis* Hendrie et al., a later subjective synonym of *Photobacterium leiognathi* Boisvert et al. Int. J. Syst. Bacteriol. 25:208–209; 1975.

58. Robb, J. A.; Tegtmeyer, P.; Martin, R. G.; Kit, S. Proposal for a uniform nomenclature for simian virus 40 mutants. J. Virol. 9:562–563; 1972.

59. Saccardo, P. A. 1882–1921, Sylloge Fungorum. Pavia. 25 vol.; index to fungi. 1940 to present. Kew, U. K.; Commonwealth Mycological Institute.

60. Sanderson, K. E. Linkage map of *Salmonella typhimurium*. Edition IV. Bacteriol. Rev. 36:558–586; 1972.

61. Sanderson, K. E. Current linkage map of *Salmonella typhimurium*. Bacteriol. Rev. 34:176–193: 1970.

62. Stafleu, F. A., chairman. International code of botanical nomenclature. Regnum Veg. 97:1–457; 1978.

63. Taylor, A. L.; Trotter, C. D. Linkage map of *Escherichia coli* strain K-12. Bacteriol. Rev. 36:504–524, 1972.

64. Vogt, P. K.; Weiss, R. A.; Hanafusa, H. Proposal for numbering mutants of avian leukosis and sarcoma viruses. J. Virol. 13:551–554; 1974.

65. Wildy, P. Classification and nomenclature of viruses. First report of the International Committee on Nomenclature of Viruses. Monographs in virology. Basel: S. Karger, Vol. 5; 1971.

ANIMAL SCIENCES

Names and keys

66. Baker, F. C. Fieldbook of Illinois land snails. Ill. Nat. Hist. Surv. Man. 2; 1939.

67. Blackwelder, R. E. Taxonomy: a text and reference book. New York: John Wiley & Sons; 1967.
68. Bulletin of zoological nomenclature. Published irregularly in four parts per volume by the International Trust for Zoological Nomenclature, c/o British Museum (Natural History), Cromwell Road, London, SW7 5BD, England.
69. Committee on Classification and Nomenclature. Check-list of North American birds. 5th ed. New York: American Ornithologists' Union; 1957.
70. Committee on Common Names of Insects. Common names of insects and related organisms approved by the Entomological Society of America. College Park, MD: Entomological Society of America; 1982.
71. Committee on Herpetological Common Names. Common names for North American amphibians and reptiles. Copeia: 172–185; 1956.
72. Committee on Names of Fishes. A list of common and scientific names of fishes from the United States and Canada. 4th ed. Bethesda, MD: American Fisheries Society; 1980.
73. Hall, E. R. Names of species of North American mammals north of Mexico. Univ. Kans. Mus. Nat. Hist. Misc. Publ. 43; 1965.
74. International Commission on Zoological Nomenclature. International code of zoological nomenclature adopted by the 16th International Congress of Zoology. London: International Trust for Zoological Nomenclature; 1964.
75. Mayr, E. Principles of systematic zoology. New York: McGraw-Hill Book Co.; 1969.
76. Metcalf, Z. P. The construction of keys. Syst. Zool. 3:38–45, 1954.
77. Official lists and official indexes. Published in two installments (1958 and 1966) by the International Trust for Zoological Nomenclature, c/o British Museum (Natural History), Cromwell Road, London, SW7 5BD, England.
78. Ross, H. H. Biological systematics. Reading, MA: Addison-Wesley Publishing Co.; 1974.
79. Schenk, E. T.; McMasters, J. H. Procedure in taxonomy. 3d ed. Stanford, CA: Stanford Univ. Press; 1956.
80. Steyskal, G. C. The American species of the genus *Dictya* Meigen (Diptera, Sciomyzidae). Entomol. Soc. Am. Ann. 47:511–539; 1954.
81. Systematic zoology. Published quarterly by the Society of Systematic Zoology, c/o National Museum of Natural History, Washington, DC 20560.

Anatomy

82. Baumel, J. J., et al., editors. Nomina anatomica avium: an annotated dictionary of birds. New York: Academic Press; 1979.
83. Embryology Subcommittee, International Anatomical Nomenclature Committee. Nomina embryologica. Bethesda, MD: Federation of American Societies for Experimental Biology; 1970.
84. Histology Subcommittee, International Anatomical Nomenclature Committee. Nomina histologica. Moscow; 1970.
85. International Anatomical Nomenclature Committee. Nomina anatomica. 3d ed. New York: Excerpta Medica Foundation; 1968.
86. International Anatomical Nomenclature Committee. Nomina anatomica. 4th ed. [together with Nomina histologica and Nomina embryologica] Amsterdam and Oxford: Excerpta Medica; 1977.

87. International Committee on Veterinary Anatomical Nomenclature. Nomina anatomica veterinaria. Ithaca, NY: New York State Veterinary College; 1973.

Genetics and cytogenetics

88. Altman, P. L.; Dittmer, D. S., editors. Biology data book. 2d ed. Vol. I. Bethesda, MD: Federation of American Societies for Experimental Biology; 1972:14–58.
89. Borgaonkar, D. S. Chromosomal variation in man: a catalog of chromosomal variants and anomalies. Baltimore, MD: The Johns Hopkins Univ. Press; 1975.
90. Borgaonkar, D. S.; Bolling, D. R., and others. Repository of chromosomal variants and anomalies in man: fourth listing. Baltimore, MD: The Johns Hopkins Univ. Press; 1977.
91. Chicago Conference (1966). Standardization in human cytogenetics: birth defects. Original article series, II:2. New York: The National Foundation; 1966.
92. Committee on Standardized Genetic Nomenclature for Mice. A revision of the standardized genetic nomenclature for mice. J. Hered. 54:159–162; 1963.
93. Committee on Standardized Genetic Nomenclature for Mice. Standard karyotype of the mouse, *Mus musculus*. J. Hered. 63:69–72; 1972.
94. Committee on Standardized Genetic Nomenclature for Mice. Guidelines for nomenclature of genetically determined biochemical variants in the house mouse, *Mus musculus*. Biochem. Genet. 9:369–374; 1973.
95. Committee on Standardized Nomenclature for Domestic Cats. Standardized genetic nomenclature for the domestic cat. J. Hered. 59:39–40; 1968.
96. Fasman, G. D., editor. Handbook of biochemistry and molecular biology. 3d ed. Cleveland, OH: CRC Press; 1976.
97. Festing, M. Inbred strains of guinea-pigs. Guinea-Pig News Lett. 7:3–8; 1973.
98. Festing, M.; Staats, J. Standardized nomenclature for inbred strains of rats: fourth listing. Transplantation 16:221–245; 1973.
99. Hsu, T. C.; Benirschke, K. An atlas of mammalian chromosomes. Vol. 1, Folio 31. New York: Springer-Verlag; 1967.
100. King, R. C., editor. Handbook of genetics. Vol. 3 and 4. New York: Plenum Press; 1975.
101. Lindsley, D. L.; Grell, E. H. Genetic variations of *Drosophila melanogaster*. Carnegie Inst. Wash. Publ. 627; 1968.
102. Lyon, M. Genetic nomenclature and nomenclatural rules in the mouse. Immunogenetics 5:393–403; 1977.
103. McKusick, V. A. The anatomy of the human genome. J. Hered. 71:370–391; 1980.
104. McKusick, V. A.; Ruddle, F. H. The status of the gene map of the human chromosome. Science 196:390–405; 1977.
105. Miller, D. A.; Miller, O. J. Chromosome mapping in the mouse. Science 178:949–955; 1972.
106. O'Brien, S. J.; Nash, W. G. Chromosome mapping in mammals: chromosome map of domestic cat. Science 216:257–265; 1982.

107. Paris Conference (1971). Standardization in human cytogenetics: birth defects. Original article series, VIII:7. New York: The National Foundation; 1972.
108. Paris Conference (1971), Supplement (1975): Standardization in human cytogenetics: birth defects. Original article series, XI:9. New York: The National Foundation; 1975.
109. Stockholm Conference (1977). An international system for human cytogenetic nomenclature: birth defects. Original article series, XIV: 8. New York: The National Foundation; 1978.
110. Shows, T. B. International system for human gene nomenclature. Cytogenet. Cell Genet. 25:96; 1979.
111. Shows, T. B.; McAlpine, P. J. The catalog of human genes and chromosome assignments: a report on human genetic nomenclature and genes that have been mapped in man. Cytogenet. Cell Genet. 22:132–145; 1978.
112. Staats, J. Standardized nomenclature for inbred strains of mice: seventh listing. Cancer Res. 40:2083–2128; 1980.
113. Womack, J. W. Mouse News Lett. 55:6; 1976.
114. World Health Organization. Standardized strains of insects of public health importance. Bull. WHO 34:452–453; 1966.
115. Wright, J. W.; Pal, R., editors. Genetics of insect vectors of disease. New York: American Elsevier Publishing Co.; 1967:722–724.

Immunology

116. Bach, F. H.; van Rood, J. J. The major histocompatibility complex—genetics and biology. N. Engl. J. Med. 295:806–812, 872–878, 927–936; 1976.
117. Balner, H.; Van Vreeswijk, W.; DeGroot, M. L.; D'Amaro, J. The major histocompatibility complex of rhesus monkeys. Transplant. Proc. 6:111–117; 1973.
118. Fasman, G. D., editor. Handbook of biochemistry and molecular biology. 3d ed. Vol. 2. Cleveland, OH: CRC Press; 1976.
119. Klein, J.; Bach, F. H.; Festenstein, F.; McDevitt, H. O.; Shreffler, D. C.; Snell, G. D.; Stimpt, J. H. Genetic nomenclature of the H-2 complex of the mouse. Immunogenetics 1:184–188; 1974.
120. Maurer, B. A.; Neefe, J. Definitions of 18 SD antigens and 2 LD antigens of the RhLA monkey histocompatibility complex. Transplant. Proc. 9:579–583; 1977.
121. Rowe, D. S. Nomenclature of immunoglobulins. Nature (London) 228:509–511; 1970.
122. Shreffler, D. C.; David, C. S. The H-2 major histocompatibility and the I immune response region: genetic variation, function and organization. Adv. Immunol. 20:125–195; 1975.
123. Vriesendorp, H. M. Major histocompatibility complex of the dog. Rotterdam, the Netherlands: Bronder Offset B.V.; 1973.
124. Vriesendorp, H. M.; Albert, E. D.; Templeton, J. W., and others. Joint report of the second international workshop on canine immunogenetics. Transplant. Proc. 8:289–314; 1976.
125. WHO-IUIS Terminology Committee. Nomenclature for factors of the HLA system. Transplantation 21:353–358; 1976.

126. World Health Organization. Nomenclature for human immunoglobulins. Bull. WHO 30:447–450; 1964.

127. World Health Organization. Notation for genetic factors of human immunoglobulins. Bull. WHO 33:721–724; 1965.

128. World Health Organization. Notation for human immunoglobulin subclasses. Bull. WHO 35:953; 1966.

129. World Health Organization. Immunoglobulin E, a new class of human immunoglobulin. Bull. WHO 38:151–152; 1968.

130. World Health Organization. Nomenclature of complement. Bull. WHO 39:935–938; 1968.

131. World Health Organization. An extension of the nomenclature for immunoglobulins. Bull. WHO 41:975–978; 1969.

132. World Health Organization. Nomenclature of human immunglobulins. Bull. WHO 48:373; 1973.

133. World Health Organization. Nomenclature for factors of the HLA system, 1977. Bull. WHO 56:461–465; 1978.

134. World Health Organization. Nomenclature for factors of the HLA system, 1980. Bull. WHO 58:945–948; 1980.

135. World Health Organization. Nomenclature of the alternative activating pathway of complement. Bull. WHO 59:489–491; 1981.

Hematology

136. Cohen, C., editor. Blood groups in infrahuman species. Ann. NY Acad Sci. 97:1–328; 1962.

137. Dayhoff, M. O., editor. Atlas of protein sequence and structure. Vol. 5. Washington, DC: National Biomedical Research Foundation; 1972.

138. Erskine, A. G. Other blood group systems and blood groups of nonhuman primates. Frankel, S.; Reitman, S.; Sonnenwirth, A. C., eds. Gradwohl's clinical laboratory methods and diagnosis. 7th ed. St. Louis, MO: C. V. Mosby Co.; 1970:820–846.

139. Erskine, A. G. Principles and practice of blood grouping. St. Louis, MO: C. V. Mosby Co.; 1973.

140. International Committee for the Nomenclature of Blood Clotting Factors. The nomenclature of blood clotting factors. J. Am. Med. Assoc. 180:733–735; 1962.

141. International Committee on Blood Clotting Factors. Thromboplastin [Conference on fibrinogen and fibrin turnover of clotting factors]. Thromb. Diath. Haemorrh. 13 (Suppl.):428–432; 1964.

142. International Committee on Nomenclature of Blood Clotting Factors. Nomenclature of blood clotting factors: four factors, their characterization and international number. J. Am. Med. Assoc. 170:325–328; 1959.

143. International Committee on Nomenclature of Blood Clotting Factors. New blood clotting factors: transactions of the conference held under the auspices of the International Committee on Blood Clotting Factors, Montreux, Switzerland, August 24–26, 1959. Thromb. Diath. Haemorrh. 4 (Suppl.):262–278; 1960.

144. International Committee on Thrombosis and Haemostasis. Genetic nomenclature for human blood coagulation. Thromb. Diath. Haemorrh. 30(1); 1973.

145. International Society of Haematology. Nomenclature of abnormal haemoglobins. [Recommendations unanimously accepted at the Tenth International Congress of Haematology, Stockholm, 1964.] Br. J. Haematol. 11:121; 1965.

146. Perutz, M. F.; Lehmann, H. Molecular pathology of human haemoglobin. Nature (London) 219:902–909; 1968.

147. Prokop, A.; Uhlenbruck, G. Human blood and serum groups (J. L. Raven, translator). New York: John Wiley & Sons; 1969.

148. Race, R. R.; Sanger, R. Blood groups in man. 6th ed. Oxford: Blackwell Scientific Publications; 1975.

149. Rosenfield, R. E.; Allen, F. H., Jr.; Swisher, S. N.; Kochwa, S. A review of Rh serology and presentation of a new terminology. Transfusion (Philadelphia) 2:287–312; 1962.

150. Swisher, S. N. Biochemical notation systems. J. Am. Med. Assoc. 185:21; 1963.

151. Vriesendorp, H. M.; Westbroek, D. L.; D'Amaro, J. Joint report of 1st international workshop on canine immunogenetics. Tissue Antigens 3:145–163; 1973.

152. Wiener, A. S. Elements of blood group nomenclature with special reference to the Rh-Hr blood types. J. Am. Med. Assoc. 199:985–989; 1967.

153. Wiener, A. S., editor. Advances in blood groupings. Vol. 3. New York: Grune & Stratton, Inc.; 1970.

154. World Health Organization. Notation for genetic factors of human immunoglobulins. Bull. WHO 33:721–724; 1965.

155. World Health Organization. Nomenclature of glucose-6-phosphate dehydrogenase in man. Bull. WHO 36:319–322; 1967.

Physiology

156. American College of Chest Physicians–American Thoracic Society Joint Committee on Pulmonary Nomenclature. Pulmonary terms and symbols. Chest 67:583–593; 1975.

157. Baron, D. N., editor. Units, symbols, and abbreviations: a guide for biological and medical editors and authors. 3d ed. London: Royal Society of Medicine; 1977.

158. Bligh, J.; Johnson, K. G. Glossary of terms for thermal physiology. J. Appl. Physiol. 35:941–961; 1973.

159. Committee on Standardized Terminology of the American College of Cardiology and the American Heart Association. Glossary of cardiologic terms related to physical diagnosis and history. Am. J. Cardiol. 20:286–287; 1967; 21:273–274; 1968; 24:444–445; 1969; 27:708–709; 1971.

160. Cotes, J. E. Lung function: assessment and application in medicine. 3d ed. Oxford: Blackwell Scientific Publications; 1975.

161. Douma, J. H.; Jacquemin, C.; Kamburoff, P. L.; Peslin, R.; Visser, B. F. Quantities and units in respiratory mechanics. Bull. Physiopathol. Respir. 9:1242–1243; 1973.

162. Gandevia, B.; Hugh-Jones, P. Terminology for measurements of ventilatory capacity: a report to the Thoracic Society. Thorax 12:290–293; 1957.

163. Handbook of physiology. Bethesda, MD: American Physiological Society; 1959–1983. [A continuing series of monographs published in sections, as

many as seven volumes in a section. Sections cover nervous system, circulation, respiration, environmental physiology, adipose tissue, alimentary canal, endocrinology, renal physiology.]

164. Hardy, J. D., chairman. Proposed standard system of symbols for thermal physiology. J. Appl. Physiol. 27:439–446; 1969.

165. Kappagoda, C. J.; Lindon, R. J. The use of SI units in cardiovascular studies. Cardiovasc. Res. 10:141–148; 1976.

166. Kory, R. C.; Rankin, J.; Snider, G. L.; Tomasefski, J. F. Clinical spirometry. Dis. Chest 43:214–219; 1963.

167. Pappenheimer, J. R., chairman. Standardization of definitions and symbols in respiratory physiology. Fed. Proc. 9:602–605; 1950.

168. Piiper, J.; Dejours, P.; Haab, P.; Rahn, H. Concepts and basic quantities in gas exchange physiology. Respir. Physiol. 13:292–304; 1971.

169. Solomon, D. H., chairman. A nomenclature for tests of thyroid hormones in serum: report of a committee of the American Thyroid Association. J. Clin. Endocrinol. Metab. 34:884–890; 1972.

170. Subcommittee for Respiration, IUPS Glossary Committee. Glossary on respiratory and gas exchange. J. Appl. Physiol. 34:549–558; 1973.

Experimental materials

171. American Kennel Club. The complete dog book. 15th ed. New York: Howell Book House; 1978.

172. British Society of Animal Production. The description of farm animals in scientific publications. Auchincruive, Ayr, Scotland: West of Scotland Agricultural College; 1967.

173. Committee on Care and Use of Laboratory Animals of the Institute of Laboratory Animal Resources, NRC. Guide for the care and use of laboratory animals. DHEW Publication No. (NIH) 78-23. Bethesda, MD: National Institutes of Health; 1978.

174. Committee on Nomenclature of the Institute of Laboratory Animal Resources, NAS-NRC. A nomenclatural system for outbred animals. Lab. Anim. Care 20:903–906; 1970.

175. Festing; M.; Staats, J. Standardized nomenclature for inbred strains of rats: fourth listing. Transplantation 16:221–245; 1973.

176. Hay, R.; Macy, M.; Shannon, J., editors. Catalogue of strains II. 3rd ed. Rockville, MD: American Type Culture Collection; 1981.

177. Institute of Laboratory Animal Resources, National Research Council. Animals for research: a directory of sources. 10th ed. rev. Washington, DC: National Academy of Sciences; 1979.

178. International Committee on Laboratory Animals. International standardized nomenclature for outbred stocks of laboratory animals. ICLA Bulletin No. 30; 1972.

179. Mason, I. L. A world dictionary of livestock breeds, types and varieties. Tech. Commun. 8 (rev. 1969) of the Commonwealth Bureaux of Animal Breeding and Genetics. Available from: Commonwealth Agricultural Bureaux, Farnham Royal, Slough, Bucks, England.

180. Pond, G., editor. The complete cat encyclopedia. New York: Crown Publishers, Inc.; 1972.

181. Nelson-Rees, W.; Daniels, D.; Flandermeyer, R. Cross contamination of cells in culture. Science 212:446–452; 1981.

182. Schaeffer, W. Proposed usage of animal tissue culture terms (revised 1978). In Vitro 15:649–653; 1979.

183. Staats, J. Standardized nomenclature for inbred strains of mice: seventh listing. Cancer Res. 40:2083–2128; 1980.

184. Stackpole Books. The new dog encyclopedia. Harrisburg, PA: Stackpole Books; 1970.

185. Walker, E. P. Mammals of the world, Vol. 1 & 2. Baltimore, MD: Johns Hopkins Univ. Press; 1975.

CHEMISTRY AND BIOCHEMISTRY

186. American Society for Microbiology. Committee on Nomenclature of Antibiotics. Statement concerning the use of names for antibiotics in the USA. Bull. WHO 37:151–152; 1967.

187. ASTM (American Society for Testing and Materials). Standard recommended practice for gas chromatography terms and relationships (ASTM E 355-77). Philadelphia: American Society for Testing and Materials; 1977.

188. ASTM (American Society for Testing and Materials). Standard for metric practice (ASTM E 380-77). Philadelphia: American Society for Testing and Materials; 1977.

189. ASTM (American Society for Testing and Materials). Standard practice for liquid chromatography terms and relationships (ASTM E 682-79). Philadelphia: American Society for Testing and Materials; 1979.

190. ASTM (American Society for Testing and Materials). Standard definitions of terms and symbols relating to molecular spectroscopy (ASTM E 131-81a). Philadelphia: American Society for Testing and Materials; 1981.

191. Cahn, R. S. An introduction to the sequence rule. A system for the specification of absolute configuration. J. Chem. Educ. 41:116–125; 1964.

192. Chemical Abstracts Service. Parent compound handbook. Columbus, OH: American Chemical Society; 1977.

193. Chemical Abstracts Service. Chemical Abstracts tenth collective index, Vol. 86–95, 1977–1981. Columbus, OH: American Chemical Society; 1982.

194. Edsall, J. T. Letter to the editor. Nature (London) 228: 888–889; 1970.

195. Expert Committee on Nonproprietary Names for Pharmaceutical Preparations. General principles for guidance in devising international nonproprietary names for pharmaceutical substances. WHO Chron. 24:141–142; 1970.

196. International Organization for Standardization (ISO). Pest control chemicals and plant growth regulators: Principles for the selection of common names (ISO 257-1976 (E)). International Organization for Standardization; 1976. Available from American National Standards Institute, New York.

197. International Union of Biochemistry. Biochemical nomenclature and related documents. London: The Biochemical Society; 1978. Available from The Biochemical Society, 7 Warwick Court, London WC1R 5DP, U.K.

198. IUB-IUPAC Joint Commission on Biochemical Nomenclature (JCBN). Abbreviated terminology of oligosaccharide chains: recommendations 1980. J. Biol. Chem. 257:3347–3351; 1982.

199. IUB-IUPAC Joint Commission on Biochemical Nomenclature (JCBN). Polysaccharide nomenclature: recommendations 1980. J. Biol. Chem. 257:3352–3354; 1982.

200. IUPAC Commission on Analytical Nomenclature. Recommendations on nomenclature for chromatography, 1973. Pure Appl. Chem. 37:447–462; 1974.

201. IUPAC Commission on the Nomenclature of Inorganic Chemistry. Nomenclature of inorganic chemistry 1970. 2nd ed. London: Butterworths; 1971.

202. IUPAC Commission on Nomenclature of Organic Chemistry. Rules for the nomenclature of organic chemistry. Section E: stereochemistry (recommendations 1974). Pure Appl. Chem. 45:11–30; 1976.

203. IUPAC Commission on the Nomenclature of Organic Chemistry. Nomenclature of organic chemistry. Section H: isotopically modified compounds—recommendations 1977. Eur. J. Biochem. 86:9–25; 1978.

204. IUPAC Commission on Nomenclature of Organic Chemistry and IUPAC-IUB Commission on Biochemical Nomenclature. IUPAC-IUB 1971 definitive rules for steroid nomenclature. Pure Appl. Chem. 31:285–322; 1972.

205. IUPAC Commission on Nomenclature of Organic Chemistry and IUPAC-IUB Commission on Biochemical Nomenclature. Tentative rules for carbohydrate nomenclature, Part 1. J. Biol. Chem. 247:613–635; 1972.

206. IUPAC Commission on the Nomenclature of Organic Chemistry and IUPAC-IUB Commission on Biochemical Nomenclature. Nomenclature of α-amino acids: recommendations. Biochemistry 14:449–462; 1975.

207. IUPAC-IUB Combined Commission on Biochemical Nomenclature. Abbreviations and symbols for chemical names of special interest in biological chemistry: revised tentative rules. J. Biol. Chem. 241:527–533; 1966.

208. IUPAC-IUB Commission on Biochemical Nomenclature. Rules for naming synthetic modifications of natural peptides. Tentative rules. J. Biol. Chem. 242:555–557; 1967.

209. IUPAC-IUB Commission on Biochemical Nomenclature. Abbreviations and symbols for nucleic acids, polynucleotides and their constituents. J. Biol. Chem. 245:5171–5176; 1970.

210. IUPAC-IUB Commission on Biochemical Nomenclature. Abbreviated nomenclature of synthetic polypeptides (polymerized amino acids): revised recommendations. J. Biol. Chem. 247:323–325; 1972.

211. IUPAC-IUB Commission on Biochemical Nomenclature. Symbols for amino-acid derivatives and peptides. J. Biol. Chem. 247:977–983; 1972.

212. IUPAC-IUB Commission on Biochemical Nomenclature. The nomenclature of lipids: recommendations (1976). Lipids 12:455–468; 1977.

213. Marler, E. E. Pharmacological and chemical synonyms: a paperback reprint of the 6th ed., updated and a supplement. New York: American Elsevier Publishing Co., Inc.; 1978.

214. Nomenclature Committee of the International Union of Biochemistry. Enzyme nomenclature 1978. New York: Academic Press; 1979.

215. Nomenclature Committee of the International Union of Biochemistry. Enzyme nomenclature—recommendations 1978. Supplement I: corrections and additions. Eur. J. Biochem. 104:1–4; 1980.

216. Nomenclature Committee of the International Union of Biochemistry. Enzyme nomenclature. Recommendations 1978. Supplement 2: corrections and additions. Eur. J. Biochem. 116:423–435; 1981.

217. Nomenclature Committee of the International Union of Biochemistry (NC-IUB). Enzyme nomenclature. Recommendations 1978. Supplement 3: Corrections and additions. Eur. J. Biochem. 125:1–13; 1982.

218. Nomenclature Committee of IUB (NC-IUB) and IUB-IUPAC Joint Commission on Biochemical Nomenclature (JCBN). Newsletter 1981. J. Biol. Chem. 256:12–14; 1981.

219. United States Pharmacopeial Convention. United States pharmacopeia: national formulary XV, 20th ed. Easton, PA: Mack Publishing Co.; 1980.

220. USAN Council (United States Adopted Names Council). USAN and the USP dictionary of drug names. Rockville, MD: United States Pharmacopeial Convention, Inc.; 1982.

221. Weast, R. C., editor. Handbook of chemistry and physics. 61st ed. Cleveland, OH: CRC Press; 1980.

222. Windholz, M., editor. The Merck index. 9th ed. Rahway, NJ: Merck and Co.; 1976.

223. Wiswesser, W. J., editor. Pesticide index. 5th ed. College Park, MD: Entomological Society of America; 1976.

224. World Health Organization (WHO). Expert Committee. Technical report series no. 581. Nonproprietary names for pharmaceutical substances. Geneva: World Health Organization; 1975.

GEOGRAPHY AND GEOLOGY

225. Bishop, E. E.; Eckel, E. B.; and others. Suggestions to authors of the reports of the United States geological survey. 6th ed. Washington, DC: U.S. Government Printing Office; 1978.

226. Cochran, W.; Hill, M.; Fenner, P., editors. Geowriting: a guide to writing, editing, and printing in earth science. 4th ed. Falls Church, VA: American Geological Institute; 1981.

227. Keroher, G. C., and others. Lexicon of geologic names of the United States for 1936–1960. U.S. Geological Survey Bulletin 1200. Washington, DC: U.S. Government Printing Office; 1966.

228. Keroher, G. C., and others. Lexicon of geologic names of the United States for 1961–1967. U.S. Geological Survey Bulletin 1350. Washington, DC: U.S. Government Printing Office; 1970.

229. Luttrell, G. W., and others. Lexicon of geologic names of the United States for 1968–1975; U.S. Geological Survey Bulletin 1950. Washington, DC: U.S. Government Printing Office; 1981.

230. U.S. Geological Survey. Suggestions to authors of the reports of the United States Geological Survey. 5th ed. Washington, DC: U.S. Government Printing Office; 1958.

231. U.S. Government Printing Office. Style manual. Rev. ed. Washington, DC: U.S. Government Printing Office; 1973.

Abbreviations and symbols

Two types of abbreviations and symbols are listed in this chapter: those established by internationally recognized authorities on units or nomenclature; and those not specifically endorsed by the first group of international authorities but generally used by U.S. standards organizations, international scientific bodies, and major U.S. scientific publishing groups.

Terms are listed in alphabetical order with prefixed arabic numerals, Greek letters, and italicized expressions disregarded in the alphabetization. Explanatory notes and cross-references are enclosed in parentheses.

Excluded from this list are abbreviations and symbols for chemical elements, genetic and taxonomic names, and structured coherent symbol systems other than the International System of Units (SI). Structured coherent systems are made up of interdependent symbols in a logically consistent relationship. Several systems are given in chapter 13, and the complete SI is given in chapter 12. The SI-derived units approved by the General Conference on Weights and Measures (CGPM) and those *frequently used* for length, mass, volume, molecular concentration, and in electrical studies are listed. References for non-SI units retained by the CGPM for general use with SI (because of their importance and wide use) are identified by a single asterisk (CGPM*). Non-SI units that have been designated by the CGPM for temporary use with SI are identified by a double asterisk (CGPM**). Additional units derived from SI, but which are cited only in the second group of sources, are also included.

USAGE NOTES

The lowercase l is the official SI symbol for litre (CGPM). However, the symbol L is being widely used among U.S. and Canadian scientific organizations, and it has been endorsed by the American Chemical Society, the National Bureau of Standards (The metric system of measurement: interpretation and modification of the International System of Units for the United States. Federal Register 41(239): 54018–54019; 1976), and the Canadian Standards Association (Metric practice guide,

CAN—Z2341-76. Rexdale, Ontario: Canadian Standards Association; 1976); it is also accepted by journals published by the American Institute of Physics. For this reason, L has been included in the list as an alternate symbol for litre.

Symbols for amino acids should not be used in written text as abbreviations for the free amino acids except in the restricted sense of sequence identification—for example, Glu-248 (*see* chapter 13, page 224). Other recommended practices for the use of abbreviations and symbols are given in chapter 12.

SOURCES FOR ABBREVIATIONS

INTERNATIONALLY RECOGNIZED AUTHORITIES

CGPM   Conférence Générales des Poids et Mesures [General Conference on Weights and Measures]. The International System of Units (SI). Washington, DC: National Bureau of Standards (Special Publication 330); 1981. [Joint translation by the National Physical Laboratory, U.K., and the National Bureau of Standards, USA, of Le Système International d'Unités. Parc de Saint-Cloud, France: International Bureau of Weights and Measures; rev 1981]. Available from: National Bureau of Standards, Washington DC 20234.

CGPM*   Non-SI units retained by the CGPM for general use with SI (because of their importance and wide use).

CGPM**   Non-SI units that have been designated by the CGPM for temporary use with SI.

CBN   International Union of Biochemistry (IUB). Biochemical nomenclature and related documents. London: The Biochemical Society; 1978.

CBNa   Nomenclature Committee of the International Union of Biochemistry (IUB). Enzyme nomenclature 1978. New York: Academic Press; 1979. Nomenclature Committee of the IUB. Enzyme nomenclature—recommendations 1978. Supplement 1: corrections and additions. Eur. J. Biochem. 104:1–4; 1980; supplement 2: corrections and additions. Eur. J. Biochem. 116:423–435; 1981; supplement 3: corrections and additions. Eur. J. Biochem. 125:1–13; 1982.

JCBN   IUB-IUPAC Joint Commission on Biochemical Nomenclature. Abbreviated terminology of oligosaccharide chains: recommendations 1980. J. Biol. Chem. 257:3347–3351; 1982.

OBN   Compilations from the Office of Biochemical Nomenclature, National Research Council, c/o Biology Division, Oak Ridge National Laboratory, Oak Ridge, TN; 1975.

OTHER SOURCES

ACS   American Chemical Society. Handbook for authors. Washington, DC: American Chemical Society Publications; 1978.

AIP American Institute of Physics. Style manual. New York: American Institute of Physics; 1978.

ASTM American Society for Testing and Materials. Standard for metric practice, ANSI/ASTM E 380-79. Philadelphia: American Society for Testing and Materials; 1979.

BIOSIS BioSciences Information Service. BIOSIS guide to abstracts—1978. Biol. Abst. 65(1): Jan. 1; 1978.

CAS Chemical Abstracts Service. Introduction to Chemical Abstracts. Columbus, OH: The American Chemical Society; [published in the first issue of the year of Chemical Abstracts].

ISO International Organization for Standardization. SI units and recommendations for the use of their multiples and of certain other units, ISO 1000-1981 (E). Geneva: International Organization for Standardization; 1981. Available from: American National Standards Institute, 1430 Broadway, New York, NY 10018.

WHO Lowe, D. A. (World Health Organization). A guide to international recommendations on names and symbols for quantities and on units of measurement. Geneva: World Health Organization; 1975. Available in the United States from: WHO Publications Centre, USA, 49 Sheridan Ave., Albany, NY 12210.

ABBREVIATIONS AND SYMBOLS WITH TERMS

a: arabinose (used only as substituent on nucleoside); (CBN)

a: are; (CGPM**, WHO)

a: atto- ($\times 10^{-18}$); (AIP, ASTM, CAS, CGPM, ISO, WHO)

A: ampere; (AIP, ASTM, BIOSIS, CAS, CGPM, ISO, WHO)

A_s: standard atmosphere; (AIP)

Å: ångström; (AIP, BIOSIS, CAS, CGPM**, WHO)

aa: amino acid (used only as substituent on nucleoside; (CBN)

AA: amino-acid residue; (ACS, CBN)

Aad: 2-aminoadipic acid; (ACS, CBN)

βAad: 3-aminoadipic acid; (ACS, CBN)

Abu: 2-aminobutyric acid; (ACS, OBN)

γAbu: γ-aminobutyric acid (4-aminobutyric acid); (ACS, CBN)

A_2bu: 2,4-diaminobutyric acid; (ACS, CBN)

ac: acetyl (used only as substituent on nucleoside); (CBN)

ac: alternating current; (AIP)

a.c.: alternating current; (CAS)

Ac: acetyl; (ACS, CAS, CBN)

AC: alternating current; (BIOSIS)

AcNeu: N-acetylneuraminic acid (acetylneuraminic acid); (CBN)

AcNHFln: acetylaminofluorene; (OBN)

AcO: acetoxy; (OBN)

εAcp: ε-aminocaproic acid (6-aminocaproic acid); (ACS, CBN)

ACTH: adrenocorticotropin (adrenocorticotropic hormone, corticotropin); (BIOSIS)

A.D.: anno Domini (with dates); (AIP, BIOSIS)

Ade: adenine; (CBN)

Ado: adenosine; (CBN)

AdoMet: S-adenosylmethionine; (CBN)

ADP: adenosine 5′-diphosphate (adenosine diphosphate); (BIOSIS, CBN)

ADPase: adenosine diphosphatase; (BIOSIS)

Aet: aminoethyl; (CBN)

af: audio-frequency; (AIP)

A h: ampere-hour; (AIP)

A·h: ampere-hour; (WHO)

εAhx: ε-aminohexanoic acid; (ACS, CBN)

Ala: alanyl; (ACS, CBN)

βAla: β-alanyl; (CBN)

βAla: 3-aminopropionic acid; (ACS, CBN)

All: allose; (JCBN)

Alt: altose; (JCBN)

a.m.: ante meridiem; (AIP, CAS)

AmLev: δ-aminolevulinic acid; (ACS, OBN)

AMP: adenosine 5′-monophosphate (adenosine monophosphate, adenylic acid); (BIOSIS, CBN)

AMPase: adenosine monophosphatase; (BIOSIS)

an: anisoyl (used only as substituent on nucleoside); (CBN)

A_2pm: 2,2′-diaminopimelic acid; (ACS, CBN)

A_2pr: 2,3-diaminopropionic acid; (ACS, CBN)

approx: approximate; (AIP)

approx.: approximate; (CAS)

Ara: arabinose; (ACS)

Arg: arginyl; (ACS, CBN)

Asn: asparaginyl; (ACS, CBN)

Asp: aspartyl; (ACS, CBN)

Asx: asparaginyl or aspartyl; (ACS, CBN)

atm: atmosphere, the unit (see also standard atmosphere); (AIP, BIOSIS, CAS)

atm: standard atmosphere; (WHO)

atm.: atmosphere, atmospheric; (CAS)

ATP: adenosine 5′-triphosphate (adenosine triphosphate); (BIOSIS, CBN)

ATPase: adenosine triphosphatase; (BIOSIS, CAS)

at. wt: atomic weight; (ACS, BIOSIS)

auct.: auctorum (of authors: taxonomy only); (BIOSIS)

b: barn; (AIP, ASTM, CGPM**, WHO)
bcc: body centered-cubic; (AIP)
bcc.: body centered-cubic; (CAS)
BCG: bacille Calmette-Guérin; (BIOSIS)
BeV or GeV: billion electron volts (*see also* giga-); (AIP, BIOSIS, CAS)
bh: benzhydryl (diphenylmethyl; used only as substituent on nucleoside); (CBN)
BHC: benzene hexachloride (hexachlorocyclohexane); (BIOSIS)
BMR: basal metabolic rate; (BIOSIS)
Boc: *t*-butoxycarbonyl; (CBN)
bp: boiling point; (ACS, AIP)
b.p.: boiling point; (CAS)
B.P.: before present (paleontology); (BIOSIS)
Bq: becquerel; (ASTM, CAS, CGPM, WHO)
br: bromo (used only as substituent on nucleoside); (CBN)
Btm: benzylthiomethyl; (CBN)
Btu: British thermal unit; (AIP, CAS, WHO)
BTU: British thermal unit; (BIOSIS)
bu: bushel; (BIOSIS, CAS)
Bu: butyl; (ACS, CAS, CBN)
bz: benzoyl (used only as substituent on nucleoside); (CBN)
Bz: benzoyl (PhCO-); (ACS, CAS, CBN)
Bza: benzimidazole or benzimidazolyl; (CBN)
BzAnth: benzanthracene; (OBN)
Bzh: benzhydryl (diphenylmethyl); (CBN)
bzl: benzyl (used only as substituent on nucleoside); (CBN)

c: centi- ($\times 10^{-2}$); (AIP, ASTM, BIOSIS, CAS, CGPM, ISO, WHO)
c: deaza (C replaces N; used only as substituent on nucleoside); (CBN)
C: coulomb; (AIP, ASTM, BIOSIS, CAS, CGPM, ISO, WHO)
°C: degree Celsius (centigrade); (AIP, ASTM, BIOSIS, CAS, CGPM, WHO)
cal: calorie (gram calorie; *see also* kilocalorie); (AIP, BIOSIS, CAS)
calc: calculated; (AIP)
calcd.: calculated; (CAS)
Cam: carbamoylmethyl; (CBN)
Cba: cobamide; (CBN)
Cbi: cobinamide; (CBN)
Cbl: cobalamin; (CBN)
Cby: cobyric acid; (CBN)
Cbz or Z: benzyloxycarbonyl; (CBN)
cd: candela; (AIP, ASTM, BIOSIS, CGPM, ISO, WHO)
CDP: cytidine 5'-diphosphate (cytidine diphosphate); (BIOSIS, CBN)
Cer: ceramide; (CBN)
cf: compare; (BIOSIS)
cf.: compare; (AIP, CAS)
cgs: centimetre-gram-second; (AIP)
Cho: choline; (CBN)
Chr: chorismic acid; (OBN)
Ci: curie; (AIP, ASTM, BIOSIS, CAS, CGPM**, WHO)
cl: chloro (used only as substituent on nucleoside); (CBN)
ClHgBzO: chloromercuribenzoate; (CBN)
cm: centimetre; (AIP, BIOSIS, CGPM)
cm³: cubic centimetre; (AIP, WHO)
Cm or Cme: carboxymethyl; (CBN)
>CMe₂ or Me₂C<: isopropylidene; (CBN)
CMP: cytidine 5'-monophosphate (cytidine monophosphate, cytidilic acid); (BIOSIS, CBN)
cms: carbodiimide residue (used only as substituent on nucleoside); (CBN)
CNS: central nervous system; (BIOSIS)
CoA: coenzyme A; (BIOSIS, CAS, CBN)
coef: coefficient; (AIP)
coeff.: coefficient; (CAS)

colog: cologarithm; (AIP)

comb. nov.: combinatio nova (new combination; taxonomy only); (BIOSIS)

const: constant; (AIP)

const.: constant; (CAS)

cos: cosine; (AIP)

cosh: hyperbolic cosine; (AIP)

cot: cotangent; (AIP)

coth: hyperbolic cotangent; (AIP)

cp: candlepower; (AIP)

cp: chemically pure; (AIP)

CP: chemically pure; (ACS, CAS)

cps: cycles per second (*see* hertz); (AIP, BIOSIS)

Crn: corrin; (CBN)

cRNA: complementary ribonucleic acid; (CBN)

c/s: cycles per second (*see* hertz); (WHO)

csc: cosecant; (AIP)

csch: hyperbolic cosecant; (AIP)

CTP: cytidine 5'-triphosphate (cytidine triphosphate); (BIOSIS, CBN)

cu: cubic; (AIP)

cv.: cultivar (only after a specific epithet); (BIOSIS)

cwt: hundred weight; (BIOSIS, CAS)

Cyd: cytidine; (CBN)

Cys: cysteinyl; (ACS, CBN)

Cyt: cytosine; (CBN)

d: day; (AIP, ASTM, CGPM*, WHO)

d: deci- ($\times 10^{-1}$); (AIP, ASTM, BIOSIS, CAS, CGPM, ISO, WHO)

d: diameter; (WHO)

d or (+): dextrorotatory (preceding a chemical name); (BIOSIS, CBN)

D: dextro (configuratio; preceding a chemical name); (CBN)

D: dextro (configuration: preceding a chemical name); (BIOSIS)

2,4-D: 2,4-dichlorophenoxyacetic acid; (BIOSIS)

da: deka- ($\times 10^1$); (ASTM, CAS, CGPM, ISO, WHO)

dADP: deoxyadenosine diphosphate; (BIOSIS, CBN)

dAMP: deoxyadenosine monophosphate; (BIOSIS, CBN)

dATP: deoxyadenosine triphosphate; (BIOSIS, CBN)

dB: decibel; (AIP, BIOSIS, WHO)

dc: direct current; (AIP)

d.c.: direct current; (CAS)

DC: direct current; (BIOSIS)

dCDP: deoxycytidine diphosphate; (BIOSIS, CBN)

dCMP: deoxycytidine monophosphate; (BIOSIS, CBN)

dCTP: deoxycytidine triphosphate; (BIOSIS, CBN)

DDD: dichlorodiphenyldichloroethane; (BIOSIS)

DDE: dichlorodiphenyldichloroethylene; (BIOSIS)

DDT: dichlorodiphenyltrichloroethane; (BIOSIS)

DDVP: dimethyldichlorovinyl phosphate; (BIOSIS)

DEAE-cellulose: diethylaminoethyl cellulose (*O*-diethylaminoethyl cellulose); (BIOSIS, CBN)

deg: degree; (AIP)

dGDP: deoxyguanosine diphosphate; (BIOSIS, CBN)

dGMP: deoxyguanosine monophosphate; (BIOSIS, CBN)

dGTP: deoxyguanosine triphosphate; (BIOSIS, CBN)

dHpuA: deoxyheptulosonic acid; (OBN)

diam: diameter; (AIP)

diam.: diameter; (CAS)

dIDP: deoxyinosine diphosphate; (BIOSIS, CBN)

dIMP: deoxyinosine monophosphate; (BIOSIS, CBN)

dis/sec: disintegrations per second; (AIP)

dITP: deoxyinosine triphosphate; (BIOSIS, CBN)

dl or DL: racemic (optical configuration, a mixture of dextro- and levo-; preceding a chemical name); (CBN) *dl* or DL: racemic (optical configuration, a mixture of dextro- and levo-; preceding a chemical name); (BIOSIS)

dmt: dimethoxytrityl (di-*p*-anisylphenylmethyl; used only as substituent on nucleoside); (CBN)

DNA: deoxyribonucleic acid (deoxyribonucleate; *see also* mitochondrial deoxyribonucleic acid); (AIP, BIOSIS, CBN)

DNase: deoxyribonuclease; (BIOSIS, CAS)

dns: dansyl (used only as substituent on nucleoside); (CBN)

Dns: dansyl (5-dimethylamino-naphthalene-1-sulfonyl); (CBN)

DodSO$_4$: dodecyl sulfate; (OBN)

dopa: 3,4-dihydroxyphenylalanine (dihydroxyphenylalanine); (BIOSIS, OBN)

dopamine: dihydroxyphenethylamine; (BIOSIS)

dpm: disintegrations per minute; (BIOSIS, CAS)

dTDP: deoxyribosylthymine diphosphate (thymidine 5'-diphosphate, thymidine diphosphate); (BIOSIS, CBN)

dThd: thymidine; (CBN)

dTMP: deoxyribosylthymine monophosphate (thymidine 5'-monophosphate, thymidine monophosphate); (BIOSIS, CBN)

dTTP: deoxyribosylthymine triphosphate (thymidine 5'-triphosphate, thymidine triphosphate); (BIOSIS, CBN)

dUDP: deoxyuridine diphosphate; (BIOSIS, CBN)

dUMP: deoxyuridine monophosphate; (BIOSIS, CBN)

dUTP: deoxyuridine triphosphate; (BIOSIS, CBN)

dXDP: deoxyxanthosine diphosphate; (BIOSIS, CBN)

dXMP: deoxyxanthosine monophosphate; (BIOSIS, CBN)

dXTP: deoxyxanthosine triphosphate; (BIOSIS, CBN)

dyn: dyne; (AIP, BIOSIS, WHO)

e: ethyl (used only as substituent on nucleoside); (CBN)

e: exponential; (AIP)

E: electromotive force; (WHO)

E: exa- ($\times 10^{18}$); (ASTM, CAS, CGPM, WHO)

ECG: electrocardiogram; (BIOSIS, CAS)

ECHO: enteric cytopathogenic human orphan (virus); (BIOSIS)

ED: effective dose; (BIOSIS, CAS)

ED$_{50}$: effective dose, 50%; (ACS, BIOSIS)

EDTA: ethylenediaminetetraacetate; (BIOSIS, CBN)

EEG: electroencephalogram; (BIOSIS, CAS)

emend.: emendation, emended (taxonomy only, change in spelling of a name); (BIOSIS)

emf: electromotive force; (AIP)

emf.: electromotive force; (CAS)

EPR: electron paramagnetic resonance; (AIP, BIOSIS)

eq: equation; (ACS)

μeq: microequivalent; (BIOSIS)

Eq.: equation; (AIP)

Eqs.: equations; (AIP)

equiv wt: equivalent weight; (ACS)

ESR: electron spin resonance; (ACS, AIP, BIOSIS)

Et: ethyl; (ACS, CAS, CBN)

EtdBr: ethidium bromide; (OBN)

Etn: ethanolamine; (CBN)

eV: electronvolt; (AIP, BIOSIS, CAS, CGPM*, WHO)

exp: exponential; (AIP)

expt: experiment(al); (AIP)

expt.: experiment(al); (CAS)

f: femto- ($\times 10^{-15}$); (AIP, ASTM, CAS, CGPM, ISO, WHO)

f: formyl (used only as substituent on nucleoside); (CBN)

f.: forma (form; only after a specific epithet); (BIOSIS)

f: furanose (suffix); (CBN)

F: farad; (AIP, ASTM, CAS, CGPM, ISO, WHO)

F: fermi; (AIP)

F_1: filial generation, first; (BIOSIS)

F_2: filial generation, second; (BIOSIS)

°F: degree Fahrenheit; (AIP, BIOSIS, CAS, WHO)

fa: formylaminoacyl (used only as substituent on nucleoside); (CBN)

FAD: flavin adenine dinucleotide; (BIOSIS, CBN)

$FADH_2$: flavin adenine dinucleotide, reduced; (BIOSIS, CBN)

fam. nov.: familia nova (new family; after a familial name only); (BIOSIS)

fc: foot-candle; (AIP, WHO)

fl: fluoro (used only as substituent on nucleoside); (CBN)

Fln: fluorene; (OBN)

fl oz: fluid ounce; (BIOSIS)

FM: frequency modulation; (AIP, BIOSIS)

FMN: flavin mononucleotide; (BIOSIS, CBN)

FMNH: flavin mononucleotide, reduced; (BIOSIS, CBN)

fp: freezing point; (ACS)

f.p.: freezing point; (CAS)

Fru: fructose; (CBN)

f.sp.: forma specialis (special form; only after a specific epithet); (BIOSIS)

ft: foot; (AIP, BIOSIS, CAS, WHO)

ft-c: foot candle; (BIOSIS)

ft lb: foot-pound; (AIP, CAS)

FSH: follicle stimulating hormone; (BIOSIS, CAS)

Fuc: fucose; (JCBN)

g: gram; (AIP, BIOSIS, CAS, CGPM, WHO)

μg: microgram; (BIOSIS)

g: gravity (gravitation constant); (BIOSIS, CAS)

G: gauss; (AIP, CAS)

G: giga- ($\times 10^9$); (AIP, ASTM, BIOSIS, CAS, CGPM, ISO, WHO)

GA: gibberellic acid; (BIOSIS)

gal: gallon; (AIP, BIOSIS, CAS, WHO)

Gal: galactose; CBN

GdmCl or Gdn·HCl: guanidinium chloride (guanidine hydrochloride); (OBN)

Gdn: guanidine; (OBN)

GDP: guanosine 5′-diphosphate (guanosine diphosphate); (BIOSIS, CBN)

gen. nov.: genus novum (new genus; only after a generic name); (BIOSIS)

GeV or BeV: billion electron volts (*see also* giga-); (AIP, BIOSIS, WHO)

Glc: glucose; (CBN)

GLC: gas-liquid chromatography; (ACS, BIOSIS)

GlcA: gluconic acid; (CBN)

GlcN: glucosamine; (CBN)

GlcNAc: *N*-acetylglucosamine; (CBN)

GlcUA: glucuronic acid; (CBN)

Gln: glutaminyl; (ACS, CBN)

Glu: glutamyl; (ACS, CBN)

<Glu: pyroglutamic acid; (ACS, CBN)

Glx: glutaminyl or glutamyl; (ACS, CBN)

Gly: glycyl; (ACS, CBN)

GMP: guanosine 5′-monophosphate (guanosine monophosphate, guanylic acid); (BIOSIS, CBN)

Gra: glyceraldehyde; (CBN)

Gri: glyceric acid; (CBN)

Grn: glycerone; (CBN)

Gro: glycerol; (CBN)

Gs: gauss; (WHO)

GSH: glutathione; (CBN)

GSSG: glutathione, oxidized; (CBN)

GTP: guanosine 5′-triphosphate (guanosine triphosphate); (BIOSIS, CBN)

Gua: guanine; (CBN)

Gul: gulose; (JCBN)

Guo: guanosine; (CBN)

Gy: gray; (ASTM, CAS, CGPM, WHO)

h: dihydro (used only as substituent on nucleoside); (CBN)

h: hecto- ($\times 10^2$); (ASTM, CAS, CGPM, ISO, WHO)

h: hour; (AIP, ASTM, BIOSIS, CAS, CGPM*, WHO)

H: henry; (AIP, ASTM, CAS, CGPM, ISO, WHO)

H_2: dihydro; (CBN)

H_4: tetrahydro; (CBN)

ha: hectare; (ASTM, BIOSIS, CAS, CGPM**, WHO)

Hb: hemoglobin; (BIOSIS, CAS, CBN)

HbO_2: hemoglobin, oxygenated; (BIOSIS, CBN)

hcp: hexagonal close-packed; (AIP)

Hcy: homocysteinyl; (ACS, CBN)

hep: hexagonal close-packed; (CAS)

hf: high-frequency; (AIP)

H_4folate: tetrahydrofolate; (CBN)

H_4furan: tetrahydrofuran; (CBN)

HgBzO: mercuribenzoate; (CBN)

His: histidyl; (ACS, CBN)

hm: hydroxymethyl (used only as substituent on nucleoside); (CBN)

ho or oh: hydroxy (used only as substituent on nucleoside); (CBN)

hp: horsepower; (AIP, BIOSIS, WHO)

Hp: heptyl; (OBN)

H_4pyran: tetrahydropyranyl; (CBN)

Hse: homoserinyl; (ACS, CBN)

Hse>: homoserine lactone; (ACS, CBN)

Hx: hexyl; (OBN)

Hyl: hydroxylysyl; (ACS, CBN)

αHyl: *allo*-hydroxylysine; (ACS, CBN)

Hyp: hydroxyprolyl; (ACS, CBN)

Hyp: hypoxanthine; (CBN)

Hz: hertz; (AIP, ASTM, BIOSIS, CAS, CGPM, ISO, WHO)

i: isopentenyl (used only as substituent on nucleoside); (CBN)

IAA: indoleacetic acid; (BIOSIS)

i.d.: inside diameter; (ACS, AIP)

ID_{50}: infective dose, 50%; (ACS)

Ido: idose; (JCBN)

IDP: inosine 5′-diphosphate (inosine diphosphate); (BIOSIS, CBN)

Ig: immunoglobulin; (ASM, BIOSIS, CAS)

Ile: isoleucyl; (ACS, CBN)

αIle: *allo*-isoleucine; (ACS, CBN)

i.m.: intramuscular; (BIOSIS, CAS)

IMP: inosine 5′-monophosphate (inosine monophosphate, inosinic acid); (BIOSIS, CBN)

in: inch; (WHO)

in.: inch; (AIP, BIOSIS, CAS)

inc. sed.: incertae sedis (uncertain position; taxonomy only); (BIOSIS)

Ino: inosine; (CBN)

Ins: inositol; (CBN)

io: iodo (used only as substituent on nucleoside); (CBN)

i.p.: intraperitoneal; (BIOSIS, CAS)

IQ: intelligence quotient; (BIOSIS)

iPr_2P-F: diisopropyl fluorophosphate (diisopropyl phosphofluoridate); (CBN)

Ips: *p*-iodophenylsulfonyl (pipsyl); (CBN)

IR: infrared; (ACS, AIP, BIOSIS, CAS)

ITP: inosine 5′-triphosphate (inosine triphosphate); (BIOSIS, CBN)

IU: international unit; (BIOSIS, CAS)

i.v.: intravenous; (BIOSIS, CAS)

J: joule; (AIP, ASTM, BIOSIS, CAS, CGPM, ISO, WHO)

k: kilo- ($\times 10^3$); (AIP, ASTM, BIOSIS, CAS, CGPM, ISO, WHO)

K: kelvin (use °K if risk of confusion with other symbols); (AIP, ASTM, CAS, CGPM, ISO, WHO)

K: phylloquinone; (CBN)

K_i: inhibitor constant (*see also* Michaelis constant and substrate constant); (CBNa)

K_m: Michaelis constant (*see also* inhibitor constant and substrate constant); (BIOSIS, CBNa, WHO)

K_s: substrate constant (*see also* inhibitor constant and Michaelis constant) (CBNa)

kat: katal; (CBNa, WHO)

kcal: kilocalorie (*see also* calorie); (AIP, BIOSIS)

KE: kinetic energy; (AIP)

kg: kilogram; (AIP, ASTM, BIOSIS, CGPM, ISO, WHO)

km: kilometre; (AIP, CGPM)

kx: crystallography unit; (ACS)

l: litre (write out if symbol may be confused with numeral 1); (ACS, AIP, ASTM, BIOSIS, CGPM*, WHO)

l: lyxose (used only as substituent on nucleoside); (CBN)

l or (−): levorotatory (preceding a chemical name); (BIOSIS, CBN)

L: levo- (configuration; preceding a chemical name); (CBN)

L: levo- (configuration; preceding a chemical name); (BIOSIS)

L: litre; (CAS)

lab: laboratory; (AIP)

lab.: laboratory; (CAS)

lb: pound (avoirdupois); (AIP, BIOSIS, CAS, WHO)

lb/in^2: pounds per square inch; (AIP, BIOSIS, WHO)

LC_{50}: lethal concentration, 50%: (BIOSIS)

LCAO: linear combination of atomic orbitals; (AIP, CAS)

LD: lethal dose; (BIOSIS, CAS)

LD_{50}: lethal dose, median; (ACS, BIOSIS)

Leu: leucyl; (ACS, CBN)

lim: limit; (AIP)

lm: lumen; (AIP, ASTM, CAS, CGPM, ISO, WHO)

ln: logarithm, natural; (AIP, BIOSIS)

log: logarithm (to base 10; common logarithm); (AIP, BIOSIS)

LSD: lysergic acid diethylamide; (BIOSIS)

lx: lux; (AIP, ASTM, BIOSIS, CAS, CGPM, ISO, WHO)

Lys: lysinyl; (ACS, CBN)

Lyx: lyxose; (JCBN)

m: methyl (used only as substituent on nucleoside); (CBN)

m: metre; (AIP, ASTM, BIOSIS, CAS, CGPM, ISO, WHO)

m: milli- ($\times 10^{-3}$); (AIP, ASTM, CAS, CGPM, ISO, WHO)

m.: morpha (form; only after a specific epithet); (BIOSIS)

μm: micrometre (micron); (AIP, BIOSIS, CGPM, WHO)

m: meta- (position; preceding a chemical name); (BIOSIS)

M: mega- ($\times 10^6$); (AIP, ASTM, BIOSIS, CAS, CGPM, ISO, WHO)

M: molar; (CAS)

M: molar; (BIOSIS)

mA: milliampere; (AIP, BIOSIS, CGPM)

Mal: maleyl; (CBN)

Mal < or -Mal-: maleoyl; (CBN)

MalN: maleimide; (CBN)

MalNEt: *N*-ethylmaleimide; (CBN)

Man: mannose; (CBN)

max: maximum; (AIP)

max.: maximum; (CAS)

Mb: myoglobin; (CBN)

Me: methyl; (ACS, CAS, CBN)

meq: milliequivalent; (BIOSIS)

Met: methionyl; (ACS, CBN)

MetHb: methemoglobin; (CBN)

Me_3Si: trimethylsilyl; (CBN)

Me_4Si: tetramethylsilane; (CBN)

Me_2SO: dimethyl sulfoxide; (CBN)

MeUmb: methylumbelliferyl; (OBN)

mg: milligram; (AIP, BIOSIS, CGPM)

mile/h: mile per hour; (WHO)

min: minimum; (AIP)

min: minute (time); (AIP, ASTM, BIOSIS, CAS, CGPM*, WHO)

min.: minimum; (CAS)

MK: menaquinone; (CBN)

mks: metre-kilogram-second system; (AIP)

ml: millilitre; (AIP, BIOSIS, CGPM)

MLD: minimum lethal dose; (BIOSIS)

mm: millimetre; (AIP, BIOSIS, CGPM)

mM: millimolar (concentration); (BIOSIS)

mmol: millimole (mass); (BIOSIS, CGPM)

mmp: mixture melting point; (ACS)

mmt: monomethoxytrityl (p-anisyldiphenylmethyl: used only as substituent on nucleoside); (CBN)

mo: month; (BIOSIS, CAS)

MO: molecular orbital; (AIP, CAS)

mol: mole; (AIP, ASTM, BIOSIS, CAS, CGPM, ISO, WHO)

μmol: micromole; (AIP, BIOSIS, CGPM)

mp: melting point; (ACS, AIP)

m.p.: melting point; (CAS)

mph: miles per hour; (AIP, BIOSIS, CAS)

M_r: molecular weight (relative); (AIP)

mRNA: messenger ribonucleic acid; (BIOSIS, CBN)

MSH: melanocyte stimulating hormone; (BIOSIS, CAS)

mtDNA: mitochondrial deoxyribonucleic acid; (CBN)

Mtc: methylthiocarbamoyl; (CBN)

Mur: muramic acid; (CBN)

mV: millivolt; (AIP, BIOSIS, CGPM)

Mz: methoxyphenylazobenzyloxycarbonyl; (CBN)

n: amino (N replaces H; used only as substituent on nucleoside); (CBN)

n: nano- ($\times 10^{-9}$); (AIP, ASTM, BIOSIS, CAS, CGPM, ISO, WHO)

n: normal (preceding a chemical name); (BIOSIS)

N: newton (*see also* nucleoside, unspecified); (AIP, ASTM, BIOSIS, CAS, CGPM, ISO, WHO)

N: nucleoside, unspecified (*see also* newton); (CBN)

N: normal (concentration); (BIOSIS, CAS)

N_2Ac: diazoacetyl; (CBN)

Nad: nitrosamide; (OBN)

NAD: nicotinamide adenine dinucleotide (diphosphopyridine nucleotide; coenzyme I; cozymase); (BIOSIS, CBN)

NADH: nicotinamide adenine dinucleotide, reduced (diphosphopyridine nucleotide, reduced); (BIOSIS, CBN)

NADP: nicotinamide adenine dinucleotide phosphate (triphosphopyridine nucleotide; coenzyme II); (BIOSIS, CBN)

NADPH: nicotinamide adenine dinucleotide phosphate, reduced (triphosphopyridine nucleotide, reduced); (BIOSIS, CBN)

Nan: nitrosamine; (OBN)

Nbs: 1-carboxy-2-nitrophenyl-5-thio; (CBN)

Nbs$_2$: 5,5′-dithiobis(2-nitrobenzoic acid); (CBN)

Neu: neuraminic acid; (CBN)

neut equiv: neutralization equivalent; (ACS)

Ngd: nitrosoguanidine; (OBN)

N$_2$gd: nitronitrosoguanidine; (OBN)

Nle: norleucyl; (ACS, CBN)

nm: nanometre; (CGPM)

NMN: nicotinamide mononucleotide; (BIOSIS, CBN)

NMR: nuclear magnetic resonance; (ACS, AIP, BIOSIS)

no.: number; (BIOSIS, CAS)

No.: number; (AIP)

nom. cons.: nomen conservandum (retained name; taxonomy only); (BIOSIS)

nom. dub.: nomen dubium (doubtful name; taxonomy only); (BIOSIS)

nom. nov.: nomen novum (new name; taxonomy only); (BIOSIS)

nom. nud.: nomen nudum (invalid name; taxonomy only); (BIOSIS)

nom. rej.: nomen rejiciendum (rejected name; taxonomy only); (BIOSIS)

N$_2$ph: dinitrophenyl; (CBN)

N$_2$ph-F: fluorodinitrobenzene; (CBN)

Nps: *o*-nitrophenylthio (*o*-nitrophenyl-

sulfonyl); (CBN)
Nuc: nucleoside; (CBN)
Nur: nitrosourea; (OBN)
Nva: norvaline; (ACS, CBN)

o: deamino (O replaces N; used only
as substituent on nucleoside);
(CBN)
o: ortho- (position; preceding a chemi-
cal name); (BIOSIS, CAS)
obs: observed; (AIP)
obsd.: observed; (CAS)
OBu^t: *t*-butoxy (*t*-butyl ester); (CBN)
OBzh: diphenylmethoxy (benzhydryl
ester); (CBN)
OBzl: benzyloxy (benzyl ester); (CBN)
Oc: octyl; (OBN)
o.d.: outside diameter; (ACS, AIP)
Oe: oersted; (AIP, CAS, WHO)
OEt: ethoxy (ethyl ester); (CBN)
OMe: methoxy (methyl ester); (CBN)
ONSu: succinimido-oxy; (CBN)
OPip: 1-piperidino-oxy; (CBN)
OQu: 8-quinolyloxy; (CBN)
Ord: orotidine; (CBN)
Orn: ornithyl; (ACS, CBN)
Oro: orotic acid (orotate); (CBN)
Ose: glycose; (CBN)
oz: ounce (avoirdupois); (AIP,
BIOSIS, CAS, WHO)

p: phosphoric residue (used only as
substituent on nucleoside); (CBN)
p: pico- ($\times 10^{-12}$); (AIP, ASTM,
BIOSIS, CAS, CGPM, ISO,
WHO)
p: para- (position; preceding a chemi-
cal name); (BIOSIS)
p: pyranose (suffix); (CBN)
P: peta- ($\times 10^{15}$); (ASTM, CAS,
CGPM, WHO)
P: probability; (BIOSIS, WHO)
P: phosphoric residue (phosphate);
(CBN)
P$_i$: inorganic phosphate (orthophos-
phate); (BIOSIS, CBN)
Pa: pascal; (AIP, ASTM, CAS,
CGPM, ISO, WHO)
p.d.: potential difference; (CAS)

PD: potential difference; (AIP)
pe: probable error; (AIP)
Pe: pentyl; (OBN)
pH: hydrogen ion concentration, neg-
ative logarithm of; (BIOSIS)
Ph: phenyl; (ACS, CAS, CBN)
Ph$_3$C or Trt: trityl; (CBN)
Phe: phenylalanyl; (ACS, CAS, CBN)
PhNCS: phenylisothiocyanate; (CBN)
> PhNCS: phenylthiohydantoin;
(CBN)
PhNHCS or Ptc: phenylthiocarbam-
oyl; (CBN)
Pht: phthaloyl; (CBN)
Pht < or -Pht-: phthalyl; (CBN)
pK: dissociation constant, negative
logarithm of; (BIOSIS)
p.m.: post meridiem; (AIP, CAS)
Poc: cyclopentyloxycarbonyl; (CBN)
poly: polymer of; (CBN)
PP$_i$: inorganic pyrophosphate;
(BIOSIS, CBN)
ppb: parts per billion; (ACS, BIOSIS,
CAS)
PPLO: pleuropneumonia-like orga-
nism; (BIOSIS)
ppm: parts per million; (ACS, AIP,
BIOSIS, CAS)
PQ: plastoquinone; (CBN)
Pr: propyl; (ACS, CAS)
preocc.: preoccupied (taxonomy only);
(BIOSIS)
Pro: prolyl; (ACS, CBN)
Prv: pyruvenol (for *enol*pyruvate; ab-
breviation may be prefixed by *e*
to distinguish from pyruvate);
(CBN)
psi or lb/in^2: pound per square inch;
(BIOSIS, CAS)
pt: pint; (BIOSIS, CAS)
Ptc or PhNHCS: phenylthiocarbam-
oyl; (CBN)
Ptd: phosphatidyl; (CBN)
Pte: pteroyl; (CBN)
Ptn: pterin (2-amino-4-hydroxypteri-
dine); (OBN)
Puo: purine nucleoside; (CBN)
Pur: purine; (CBN)
Pxd = or Pxd <: pyridoxylidene;

(CBN)
Pxl: pyridoxal; (OBN)
Pxm: pyridoxamine; (OBN)
Pxn: pyridoxine; (OBN)
Pxy: pyridoxyl; (CBN)
Pyd: pyrimidine nucleoside; (CBN)
Pyr: pyrimidine; (CBN)
Pz: *p*-phenylazobenzyloxycarbonyl;
    (CBN)

Q: ubiquinone; (CBN)
Q_{10}: rate change of a process with
    10° C increase; (BIOSIS)

R: roentgen; (AIP, ASTM, BIOSIS,
    CAS, CGPM**, WHO)
R_f: retardation factor (distance the
    unknown has traveled relative to
    the solvent front in chromatogra-
    phy); (BIOSIS)
rad: radian; (AIP, ASTM, CGPM,
    ISO, WHO)
rad: radiation (ionizing absorbed dose;
    use rd if risk of confusion with
    radian); (BIOSIS, CGPM**)
Rbu: ribulose; (OBN)
Rby: ribitol (ribityl); (OBN)
rd: radiation (ionizing absorbed dose;
    use if risk of confusion with ra-
    dian); (ASTM)
ψrd: pseudouridine; (CBN)
ref.: reference; (CAS)
Ref.: reference; (AIP)
rem: roentgen equivalent man;
    (BIOSIS, CAS, CGPM**)
RES: reticuloendothelial system;
    (BIOSIS)
Rib: ribose; (CBN)
r/min: revolutions per minute;
    (WHO)
RNA: ribonucleic acid (*see also* com-
    plementary, ribosomal, messen-
    ger, and transfer ribonucleic
    acids); (AIP, BIOSIS, CBN)
RNase: ribonuclease; (BIOSIS, CAS)
rpm: revolutions per minute; (AIP,
    BIOSIS, CAS)
rRNA: ribosomal ribonucleic acid;
    (BIOSIS, CBN)

RQ: respiratory quotient; (BIOSIS,
    CAS, WHO)

s: second (time); (AIP, ASTM,
    BIOSIS, CAS, CGPM, ISO,
    WHO)
s: thio (mercapto; used only as substi-
    tuent on nucleoside); (CBN)
s: symmetrical (preceding a chemical
    name); (BIOSIS)
S: siemens (conductance); (AIP,
    ASTM, CAS, CGPM, ISO,
    WHO)
Sar: sarcosyl (*N*-methylglycyl); (ACS,
    CBN)
s.c.: subcutaneous; (BIOSIS, CAS)
SD: standard deviation; (BIOSIS)
SE: standard error; (BIOSIS)
sec: secant; (AIP)
sec-: secondary (preceding a chemical
    name; as superscript use *s*, for ex-
    ample, Ba^s); (BIOSIS, CAS)
sect.: section (taxonomy only);
    (BIOSIS)
Ser: seryl; (ACS, CBN)
Shk: shikimic acid; (OBN)
Shy: 6-mercaptopurine; (CBN)
Sia: sialic acid; (CBN)
sin: sine; (AIP)
sinh: hyperbolic sine; (AIP)
s.l.: sensu lato (broad sense; taxonomy
    only); (BIOSIS)
Sno: 6-thioinosine; (CBN)
Snp: *p*-nitrophenylthio; (CBN)
sp. or spp.: species (only after a ge-
    neric name); (BIOSIS)
sp gr: specific gravity; (ACS, CAS)
Sph: sphingosine; (CBN)
SPh: phenylthio (phenylthiol ester);
    (CBN)
sp ht: specific heat; (ACS)
sp. nov.: species nova (new species;
    only after a specific epithet);
    (BIOSIS)
sp vol: specific volume; (ACS)
sq: square; (AIP)
sr: steradian; (AIP, ASTM, CAS,
    CGPM, ISO, WHO)
Srd: thiouridine; (CBN)

s.s.: sensu stricto (restricted sense; taxonomy only); (BIOSIS)

ssp. or sspp.: subspecies (only after a
specific epithet); (BIOSIS)

ssp. nov.: subspecies nova (new subspecies; only after a subspecific
epithet); (BIOSIS)

STP: standard temperature and pressure; (AIP)

Suc: succinoyl (3-carboxypropionyl);
(CBN)

Suc < or -Suc-: succinyl; (CBN)

Sur: thiouracil; (CBN)

Sv: sievert; (CGPM)

t: tonne (metric ton); (ASTM,
CGPM,* WHO)

t: tertiary (superscript with chemical
symbol); (BIOSIS)

T: tera- ($\times 10^{12}$); (AIP, ASTM, CAS,
CGPM, ISO, WHO)

T: tesla, (AIP, ASTM, CAS, CGPM,
ISO, WHO)

T: tocopherol; (CBN)

2,4,5,-T: 2,4,5-trichlorophenoxyacetic
acid; (BIOSIS)

Tal: talose; (JCBN)

tan: tangent; (AIP)

TDP: ribosylthymine 5'-diphosphate
(ribosylthymine diphosphate);
(BIOSIS, CBN)

TEAE-cellulose: triethylaminoethyl
cellulose (O-triethylaminoethyl
cellulose); (BIOSIS, CAS, CBN)

tert-: tertiary (preceding a chemical
name); (BIOSIS, CAS)

Thd: ribosylthymine; (CBN)

theor: theoretical(ly); (AIP)

theor.: theoretical(ly); (CAS)

thiotepa: triethylenethiophosphoramide; (BIOSIS)

thp: tetrahydropyranyl (used only as
substituent on nucleoside); (CBN)

Thr: threonyl; (ACS, CBN)

Thy: thymine (5-methyluracil); (CBN)

TLC: thin-layer chromatography;
(ACS, BIOSIS)

TMP: ribosylthymine 5'-monophos-
phate (ribosylthymine monophos-

phate); (BIOSIS, CBN)

tos: tosyl (p-tolylsulfonyl, toluenesulfonyl; used only as substituent on
nucleoside); (CBN)

TosArgOMe: N^{α}-tosylarginine methyl
ester; (CBN)

TosPheCH₂Cl: N^{α}-tosylphenylalanine
chloromethyl ketone; (CBN)

tr: trityl (used only as substituent on
nucleoside); (CBN)

tRNA: transfer ribonucleic acid;
(BIOSIS, CBN)

Trp: tryptophanyl; (ACS, CBN)

Trt or Ph₃C: trityl; (CBN)

TTP: ribosylthymine 5'-triphosphate
(ribosylthymine triphosphate);
(BIOSIS, CBN)

Tyr: tyrosinyl; (ACS, CBN)

u: atomic mass unit, unified; (CGPM*)

UDP: uridine 5'-diphosphate (uridine
diphosphate); (BIOSIS, CBN)

uhf: ultrahigh frequency; (AIP)

Umb: umbelliferyl; (OBN)

UMP: uridine 5'-monophosphate (uridine monophosphate; uridylic
acid); (BIOSIS, CBN)

Ura: uracil; (CBN)

Urd: uridine; (CBN)

UTP: uridine 5'-triphosphate (uridine
triphosphate); (BIOSIS, CBN)

uv: ultraviolet; (AIP)

UV: ultraviolet; (ACS, BIOSIS, CAS)

V: volt; (AIP, ASTM, BIOSIS, CAS,
CGPM, ISO, WHO)

V: volume; (WHO)

Val: valyl; (ACS, CBN)

var.: varietas (variety; only after a specific epithet); (BIOSIS)

var. nov.: varietas nova (new variety;
only after a varietal name);
(BIOSIS)

vol: volume; (ACS, BIOSIS)

vol.: volume (not volatile); (CAS)

vol/vol: volume ratio (volume per volume); (BIOSIS)

vs: versus; (AIP)

vs.: versus; (BIOSIS, CAS)

v/v: volume ratio (volume per volume); (ACS)

W: watt; (AIP, ASTM, BIOSIS, CAS, CGPM, ISO, WHO)
Wb: weber; (AIP, ASTM, CAS, CGPM, ISO, WHO)
wk: week; (BIOSIS, CAS)
wt: weight; (ACS, BIOSIS)
wt.: weight; (CAS)
wt/vol: weight per volume; (BIOSIS)
wt/wt: weight ratio (weight per weight); (BIOSIS)
w/w: weight per weight; (ACS)

x: xylose (used only as substituent on nucleoside); (CBN)
Xan: xanthine; (CBN)
Xao: xanthosine; (CBN)
XDP: xanthosine 5′-diphosphate (xanthosine diphosphate); (BIOSIS, CBN)
XMP: xanthosine 5′-monophosphate (xanthosine monophosphate; xanthylic acid); (BIOSIS, CBN)
XTP: xanthosine 5′-triphosphate (xanthosine triphosphate); (BIOSIS, CBN)
xu: x unit (x-ray unit); (AIP)

Xyl: xylose; (JCBN)

yd: yard; (BIOSIS, CAS)
yr: year; (AIP, BIOSIS, CAS)

z: aza (N replaces C; used only as substituent on nucleoside); (CBN)
Z: benzyloxycarbonyl; (CBN)

°: degree (angular); (ASTM, BIOSIS, CGPM*, WHO)
/: per; (BIOSIS)
%: percent; (ACS, BIOSIS)
‰: per mille; (BIOSIS)
π: *pros* (locant for the N of the imidazole ring of histidine nearer the alanine sidechain); (CBN)
τ: *tele* (locant for the N of the imidazole ring of histidine farther from the alanine sidechain); (CBN)
Ω: ohm; (AIP, ASTM, BIOSIS, CAS, CGPM, ISO, WHO)
>: cyclic (for example, A > or A > p; used only for nucleoside substituents); (CBN)
′: minute (angular); (ASTM, CGPM*, WHO)
″: second (angular); (ASTM, CGPM*, WHO)
μ: micro- ($\times 10^{-6}$); (AIP, ASTM, BIOSIS, CGPM, ISO, WHO)

TERMS WITH ABBREVIATIONS OR SYMBOLS

acetoxy: AcO; (OBN)

acetyl: Ac; (ACS, CAS, CBN)

acetyl (used only as substituent on nucleoside): ac; (CBN)

acetylaminofluorene: AcNHFln; (OBN)

N-acetylglucosamine: GlcNAc; (CBN)

N-acetylneuraminic acid (acetylneuraminic acid): AcNeu; (CBN)

adenine: Ade; (CBN)

adenosine: Ado; (CBN)

adenosine diphosphatase: ADPase; (BIOSIS)

adenosine 5′-diphosphate (adenosine diphosphate): ADP; (BIOSIS, CBN)

adenosine monophosphatase: AMPase; (BIOSIS)

adenosine 5′-monophosphate (adenosine monophosphate, adenylic acid): AMP; (BIOSIS, CBN)

adenosine triphosphatase: ATPase; (BIOSIS, CAS)

adenosine 5′-triphosphate (adenosine triphosphate): ATP; (BIOSIS, CBN)

S-adenosylmethionine: AdoMet; (CBN)

adenylic acid (see adenosine 5′-monophosphate)

adrenocorticotropin (adrenocorticotropic hormone, corticotropin): ACTH; (BIOSIS)

alanyl: Ala; (ACS, CBN)

β-alanyl: βAla; (CBN)

allose: All; (JCBN)

alternating current: ac; (AIP)

alternating current: a.c.; (CAS)

alternating current: AC; (BIOSIS)

altrose: Alt; (JCBN)

amino (N replaces H; used only as substituent on nucleoside): n; (CBN)

amino acid (used only as substituent on nucleoside): aa; (CBN)

amino acid residue: AA; (ACS, CBN)

2-aminoadipic acid: Aad; (ACS, CBN)

3-aminoadipic acid: βAad; (ACS, CBN)

2-aminobutyric acid: Abu; (ACS, OBN)

γ-aminobutyric acid (4-aminobutyric acid): γAbu; (ACS, CBN)

ε-aminocaproic acid (6-aminocaproic acid): εAcp; (ACS, CBN)

aminoethyl: Aet; (CBN)

ε-aminohexanoic acid: εAhx; (ACS, CBN)

2-amino-4-hydroxypteridine (see pterin)

δ-aminolevulinic acid: AmLev; (ACS, OBN)

3-aminopropionic acid: βAla; (ACS, CBN)

ampere: A; (AIP, ASTM, BIOSIS, CAS, CGPM, ISO, WHO)

ampere-hour: A h; (AIP)

ampere-hour: A·h; (WHO)

ångström: Å; (AIP, BIOSIS, CAS, CGPM**, WHO)

anisoyl (used only as substituent on nucleoside): an; (CBN)

p-anisyldiphenylmethyl (see monomethoxytrityl)

anno Domini (with dates): A.D.; (AIP, BIOSIS)

ante meridiem: a.m.; (AIP, CAS)

approximate(ly): approx; (AIP)

approximate(ly): approx.; (CAS)

arabinose: Ara; (ACS)

arabinose (used only as substituent on nucleoside): a; (CBN)

are: a; (CGPM**, WHO)

arginyl: Arg; (ACS, CBN)

asparaginyl: Asn; (ACS, CBN)

asparaginyl or aspartyl: Asx; (CBN)

aspartyl: Asp; (ACS, CBN)

atmosphere (see also standard atmosphere): atm; (AIP, BIOSIS, CAS)

atmosphere, atmospheric: atm.; (CAS)

atmosphere, normal (see standard atmosphere)

atmosphere, standard (see standard atmosphere)

atomic mass unit, unified: u; (CGPM*)
atomic weight: at. wt; (ACS, BIOSIS)
atto- ($\times 10^{-18}$): a; (AIP, ASTM, CAS, CGPM, ISO, WHO)
auctorum (of authors; taxonomy only): auct.; (BIOSIS)
audio-frequency: af; (AIP)
average: av; (AIP)
average: av.; (CAS)
aza (N replaces C; used only as substituent on nucleoside): z; (CBN)

bacille Calmette-Guérin: BCG; (BIOSIS)
barn: b; (AIP, ASTM, CGPM**, WHO)
basal metabolic rate: BMR; (BIOSIS)
becquerel: Bq; (ASTM, CAS, CGPM, WHO)
before present (paleontology): B.P.; (BIOSIS)
benzanthracene: BzAnth; (OBN)
benzene hexachloride (hexachlorocyclohexane): BHC; (BIOSIS)
benzhydryl (diphenylmethyl; used only as substituent on nucleoside): bh; (CBN)
benzhydryl (diphenylmethyl): Bzh; (CBN)
benzhydryl ester (*see* diphenylmethoxy)
benzimidazole or benzimidazolyl: Bza; (CBN)
benzoyl (PhCO-): Bz; (ACS, CAS, CBN)
benzoyl (used only as substituent on nucleoside): bz; (CBN)
benzyl (used only as substituent on nucleoside): bzl; (CBN)
benzyloxy (benzyl ester): OBzl; (CBN)
benzyloxycarbonyl: Cbz or Z; (CBN)
benzylthiomethyl: Btm; (CBN)
billion electron volts (*see also* giga-): BeV; (BIOSIS, CAS)
billion electron volts (*see also* giga-): GeV; (WHO, CAS)
biological oxygen demand (biochemical): BOD; (CAS)
body centered-cubic: bcc; (AIP)
body centered-cubic: bcc.; (CAS)

boiling point: bp; (ACS, AIP)
boiling point: b.p.; (CAS)
British thermal unit: Btu; (AIP, CAS, WHO)
British thermal unit: BTU; (BIOSIS)
bromo (used only as substituent on nucleoside): br; (CBN)
bushel: bu; (BIOSIS, CAS)
t-butoxy (*t*-butyl ester): OBu^t; (CBN)
t-butoxycarbonyl (butoxycarbonyl): Boc; (CBN)
butyl: Bu; (ACS, CAS, CBN)
t-butyl ester (*see t*-butoxy)

calculate: calc.; (CAS)
calculated: calc; (AIP)
calorie (gram calorie; *see also* kilocalorie): cal; (AIP, BIOSIS, CAS)
candela: cd; (AIP, ASTM, BIOSIS, CGPM, ISO, WHO)
candlepower: cp; (AIP)
carbamoylmethyl: Cam; (CBN)
carbobenzoxy (*see* benzyloxycarbonyl)
carbodiimide residue (used only as substituent on nucleoside): cms; (CBN)
carboxymethyl: Cm or Cme; (CBN)
1-carboxy-2-nitrophenyl-5-thio: Nbs; (CBN)
3-carboxypropionyl (*see* succinoyl)
Celsius (*see* degree Celsius)
centi- ($\times 10^{-2}$): c; (AIP, ASTM, BIOSIS, CAS, CGPM, ISO, WHO)
centigrade (*see* degree Celsius)
centimetre: cm; (AIP, BIOSIS, CGPM)
centimetre-gram-second: cgs; (AIP)
central nervous system: CNS; (BIOSIS)
ceramide: Cer; (CBN)
chemically pure: cp; (AIP)
chemically pure: CP; (ACS, CAS)
chloro (used only as substituent on nucleoside): cl; (CBN)
chloromercuribenzoate: ClHgBzO; (CBN)
choline: Cho; (CBN)
chorismic acid: Chr; (OBN)
cobalamin: Cbl; (CBN)

cobamide: Cba; (CBN)

cobinamide: Cbi; (CBN)

cobyric acid: Cby; (CBN)

coefficient: coef; (AIP)

coefficient: coeff.; (CAS)

coenzyme A: CoA; (BIOSIS, CAS, CBN)

coenzyme I (*see* nicotinamide adenine dinucleotide)

coenzyme II (*see* nicotinamide adenine dinucleotide phosphate)

cologarithm: colog; (AIP)

combinatio nova (new combination; taxonomy only): comb. nov.; (BIOSIS)

compare: cf; (BIOSIS)

compare: cf.; (AIP, CAS)

complementary ribonucleic acid: cRNA; (CBN)

conductance (*see* siemens)

constant: const.; (AIP, CAS)

corrin: Crn; (CBN)

corticotropin (*see* adrenocorticotropin)

cosecant: csc; (AIP)

cosine: cos; (AIP)

cotangent: cot; (AIP)

coulomb: C; (AIP, ASTM, BIOSIS, CAS, CGPM, ISO, WHO)

counts per second: counts/sec; (AIP)

cozymase (*see* nicotinamide adenine dinucleotide)

crystallographic unit: kx; (ACS)

cubic: cu; (AIP)

cubic centimetre: cm^3; (AIP, WHO)

cultivar (only after a specific epithet): cv.; (BIOSIS)

curie: Ci; (AIP, ASTM, BIOSIS, CAS, CGPM**, WHO)

cycles per second (*see also* hertz): c/s; (WHO)

cycles per second (*see also* hertz): cps; (AIP, BIOSIS)

cyclic (for example, A > or A > p; used only for nucleoside substituents): >; (CBN)

cyclopentyloxycarbonyl: Poc; (CBN)

cysteinyl: Cys; (ACS, CBN)

cytidilic acid (*see* cytidine 5′-monophosphate)

cytidine: Cyd; (CBN)

cytidine 5′-diphosphate (cytidine diphosphate): CDP; (BIOSIS, CBN)

cytidine 5′-monophosphate (cytidine monophosphate, cytidilic acid): CMP; (BIOSIS, CBN)

cytidine 5′-triphosphate (cytidine triphosphate): CTP; (BIOSIS, CBN)

cytosine: Cyt; (CBN)

dansyl (5-dimethylaminonaphthalene-1-sulfonyl): Dns; (CBN)

dansyl (used only as substituent on nucleoside): dns; (CBN)

day: d; (AIP, ASTM, CGPM*, WHO)

deamino (O replaces N; used only as substituent on nucleoside): o; (CBN)

deaza (C replaces N; used only as substituent on nucleoside): c; (CBN)

deca- (*see* deka-)

deci- ($\times 10^{-1}$): d; (AIP, ASTM, BIOSIS, CAS, CGPM, ISO, WHO)

decibel: dB; (AIP, BIOSIS, WHO)

degree (plane angle): °; (ASTM, BIOSIS, CGPM*, WHO)

degree (plane angle): deg; (AIP)

degree Celsius (centigrade): °C; (AIP, ASTM, BIOSIS, CAS, CGPM, WHO)

degree Fahrenheit: °F; (AIP, BIOSIS, CAS, WHO)

deka- ($\times 10^1$): da; (ASTM, CAS, CGPM, ISO, WHO)

deoxyadenosine diphosphate: dADP; (BIOSIS, CBN)

deoxyadenosine monophosphate: dAMP; (BIOSIS, CBN)

deoxyadenosine triphosphate: dATP; (BIOSIS, CBN)

deoxycytidine diphosphate dCDP; (BIOSIS, CBN)

deoxycytidine monophosphate: dCMP; (BIOSIS, CBN)

deoxycytidine triphosphate: dCTP; (BIOSIS, CBN)

deoxyguanosine diphosphate: dGDP; (BIOSIS, CBN)

deoxyguanosine monophosphate: dGMP; (BIOSIS, CBN)

deoxyguanosine triphosphate: dGTP;
(BIOSIS, CBN)

deoxyheptulosonic acid: dHpuA;
(OBN)

deoxyinosine diphosphate: dIDP;
(BIOSIS, CBN)

deoxyinosine monophosphate: dIMP;
(BIOSIS, CBN)

deoxyinosine triphosphate: dITP;
(BIOSIS, CBN)

deoxyribonuclease: DNase; (BIOSIS,
CAS)

deoxyribonucleate (*see* deoxyribonucleic acid)

deoxyribonucleic acid (deoxyribonucleate; *see also* mitochondrial deoxyribonucleic acid): DNA; (AIP,
BIOSIS, CBN)

deoxyribosylthymine diphosphate
(thymidine 5'-diphosphate, thymidine diphosphate): dTDP;
(BIOSIS, CBN)

deoxyribosylthymine monophosphate
(thymidine 5'-monophosphate,
thymidine monophosphate):
dTMP; (BIOSIS, CBN)

deoxyribosylthymine triphosphate
(thymidine 5'-triphosphate, thymidine triphosphate): dTTP;
(BIOSIS, CBN)

deoxyuridine diphosphate: dUDP;
(BIOSIS, CBN)

deoxyuridine monophosphate: dUMP;
(BIOSIS, CBN)

deoxyuridine triphosphate: dUTP;
(BIOSIS, CBN)

deoxyxanthosine diphosphate: dXDP;
(BIOSIS, CBN)

deoxyxanthosine monophosphate:
dXMP; (BIOSIS, CBN)

deoxyxanthosine triphosphate: dXTP;
(BIOSIS, CBN)

dextro (configuration; preceding a
chemical name): D; (CBN)

dextro (configuration; preceding a
chemical name): D; (BIOSIS)

dextrorotatory (preceding a chemical
name): *d* or (+); (BIOSIS, CBN)

diameter: d; (WHO)

diameter: diam; (AIP)

diameter: diam.; (CAS)

2,4-diaminobutyric acid: A_2bu; (ACS,
CBN)

2,2'-diaminopimelic acid: A_2pm;
(ACS, CBN)

2,3-diaminopropionic acid: A_2pr;
(ACS, CBN)

diazoacetyl: N_2Ac; (CBN)

dichlorodiphenyldichloroethane:
DDD; (BIOSIS)

dichlorodiphenyldichloroethylene:
DDE; (BIOSIS)

dichlorodiphenyltrichloroethane:
DDT; (BIOSIS)

2,4-dichlorophenoxyacetic acid:
2,4-D; (BIOSIS)

diethylaminoethyl cellulose (*O*-diethyl-
aminoethyl cellulose): DEAE-cellulose; (BIOSIS, CBN)

dihydro: H_2; (CBN)

dihydro (used only as substituent on
nucleoside): h; (CBN)

dihydroxyphenethylamine: dopamine;
(BIOSIS)

3,4-dihydroxyphenylalanine (dihydroxyphenylalanine): dopa;
(BIOSIS, OBN)

diisopropyl fluorophosphate (diisopropyl phosphofluoridate): DFP;
(BIOSIS)

diisopropyl fluorophosphate (diisopropyl phosphofluoridate): iPr_2P-F;
(CBN)

dimethoxytrityl (di-*p*-anisylphenyl-
methyl; used only as substituent
on nucleoside): dmt; (CBN)

5-dimethylaminonaphthalene-1-sulfo-
nyl (*see* dansyl)

dimethyldichlorovinyl phosphate:
DDVP; (BIOSIS)

dimethyl sulfoxide: Me_2SO; (CBN)

dinitrophenyl: N_2ph; (CBN)

diphenylmethoxy (benzhydryl ester):
OBzh; (CBN)

diphenylmethyl (*see* benzhydryl)

diphosphopyridine nucleotide: DPN;
(BIOSIS)

diphosphopyridine nucleotide (*see* nicotinamide adenine dinucleotide)

diphosphopyridine nucleotide, reduced (*see* nicotinamide adenine dinucleotide, reduced)

direct current: dc; (AIP)

direct current: d.c.; (CAS)

direct current: DC; (BIOSIS)

disintegrations per minute: dpm; (BIOSIS, CAS)

disintegrations per second: dis/sec; (AIP)

dissociation constant, negative logarithm of: pK; (BIOSIS)

5,5'-dithiobis(2-nitrobenzoic acid): Nbs_2; (CBN)

dodecyl sulfate: $DodSO_4$; (OBN)

dyne: dyn; (AIP, BIOSIS, WHO)

effective dose: ED; (BIOSIS, CAS)

effective dose, 50%: ED_{50}; (ACS, BIOSIS)

electrocardiogram: ECG; (BIOSIS, CAS)

electroencephalogram: EEG; (BIOSIS, CAS)

electromotive force: E; (WHO)

electromotive force: emf; (AIP)

electromotive force: emf.; (CAS)

electron paramagnetic resonance: EPR; (AIP, BIOSIS)

electron spin resonance: ESR; (ACS, AIP, BIOSIS)

electronvolt (or electron volt): eV; (AIP, BIOSIS, CAS, CGPM*, WHO)

emendation, emended (taxonomy only, change in spelling of a name): emend.; (BIOSIS)

enteric cytopathogenic human orphan (virus): ECHO; (BIOSIS)

equation: eq; (ACS)

equation: Eq.; (AIP)

equations: Eqs.; (AIP)

equivalent weight: equiv wt; (ACS)

ethanolamine: Etn; (CBN)

ethidium bromide: EtdBr; (OBN)

ethoxy (ethyl ester): OEt; (CBN)

ethyl: Et; (ACS, CAS, CBN)

ethyl (used only as substituent on nu-

cleoside): e; (CBN)

ethyl ester (*see* ethoxy)

ethylenediaminetetraacetate: EDTA; (BIOSIS, CBN)

N-ethylmaleimide: MalNEt; (CBN)

exa- ($\times 10^{18}$): E; (ASTM, CAS, CGPM, WHO)

experiment(al) (in subscript): expt; (AIP)

experiment(al) (in subscript): expt., exptl.; (CAS)

exponential: *e* or exp; (AIP)

Fahrenheit (*see* degree Fahrenheit)

face centered cubic: fcc; (AIP)

face centered cubic: fcc.; (CAS)

familia nova (new family; after a familial name only): fam. nov.; (BIOSIS)

farad: F; (AIP, ASTM, CAS, CGPM, ISO, WHO)

femto- ($\times 10^{-15}$): f; (AIP, ASTM, CAS, CGPM, ISO, WHO)

fermi: F; (AIP)

filial generation, first: F_1; (BIOSIS)

filial generation, second: F_2; (BIOSIS)

flavin adenine dinucleotide: FAD; (BIOSIS, CBN)

flavin adenine dinucleotide, reduced: $FADH_2$; (BIOSIS, CBN)

flavin mononucleotide: FMN; (BIOSIS, CBN)

flavin mononucleotide, reduced: FMNH; (BIOSIS, CBN)

fluid ounce: fl oz; (BIOSIS)

fluorene: Fln; (OBN)

fluoro (used only as substituent on nucleoside): fl; (CBN)

fluorodinitrobenzene: N_2ph-F; (CBN)

follicle stimulating hormone: FSH; (BIOSIS, CAS)

foot: ft; (AIP, BIOSIS, CAS, WHO)

foot-candle: fc; (AIP, WHO)

foot-candle: ft-c; (BIOSIS)

foot-pound: ft lb; (AIP)

foot-pound: ft-lb; (CAS)

for example: e.g.; (BIOSIS, CAS)

forma (form; only after a specific epithet): f.; (BIOSIS)

forma specialis (special form; only after a specific epithet): f.sp.; (BIOSIS)

formyl (used only as substituent on nucleoside): f; (CBN)

formylaminoacyl (used only as substituent on nucleoside): fa; (CBN)

freezing point: fp; (ACS)

freezing point: f.p.; (CAS)

frequency modulation: FM; (AIP, BIOSIS)

fructose: Fru; (CBN)

fucose: Fuc; (JCBN)

furanose (suffix): *f*; (CBN)

galactose: Gal; (CBN)

gallon: gal; (AIP, BIOSIS, CAS, WHO)

gas-liquid chromatography: GLC; (ACS, BIOSIS)

gauss: G; (AIP, CAS)

gauss: Gs; (WHO)

genus novum (new genus; only after a generic name): gen. nov.; (BIOSIS)

gibberellic acid: GA; (BIOSIS)

giga- ($\times 10^9$): G; (AIP, ASTM, BIOSIS, CAS, CGPM, ISO, WHO)

gluconic acid: GlcA; (CBN)

glucosamine: GlcN; (CBN)

glucose: Glc; (CBN)

glucuronic acid: GlcUA; (CBN)

glutaminyl: Gln; (ACS, CBN)

glutaminyl or glutamyl: Glx; (ACS, CBN)

glutamyl: Glu; (ACS, CBN)

glutathione: GSH; (CBN)

glutathione, oxidized: GSSG; (CBN)

glyceraldehyde: Gra; (CBN)

glyceric acid: Gri; (CBN)

glycerol: Gro; (CBN)

glycerone: Grn; (CBN)

glycose: Ose; (CBN)

glycyl: Gly; (ACS, CBN)

gram: g; (AIP, BIOSIS, CAS, CGPM, WHO)

gravity, standard acceleration of: *g*; (BIOSIS, CAS)

gray: Gy; (ASTM, CAS, CGPM, WHO)

guanidine: Gdn; (OBN)

guanidinium chloride (guanidine hydrochloride): GdmCl or Gdn·HCl; (OBN)

guanine: Gua; (CBN)

guanosine: Guo; (CBN)

guanosine 5′-diphosphate (guanosine diphosphate): GDP; (BIOSIS, CBN)

guanosine 5′-monophosphate (guanosine monophosphate, guanylic acid): GMP; (BIOSIS, CBN)

guanosine 5′-triphosphate (guanosine triphosphate): GTP; (BIOSIS, CBN)

guanylic acid (*see* guanosine 5′-monophosphate)

gulose: Gul; (JCBN)

hectare: ha; (ASTM, BIOSIS, CAS, CGPM**, WHO)

hecto- ($\times 10^2$): h; (ASTM, CAS, CGPM, ISO, WHO)

hemoglobin: Hb; (BIOSIS, CAS, CBN)

hemoglobin, oxygenated: HbO$_2$; (BIOSIS, CBN)

henry: H; (AIP, ASTM, CAS, CGPM, ISO, WHO)

heptyl: Hp; (OBN)

hertz: Hz; (AIP, ASTM, BIOSIS, CAS, CGPM, ISO, WHO)

hexachlorocyclohexane (*see* benzene hexachloride)

hexagonal close-packed: hcp; (AIP)

hexagonal close-packed: hep.; (CAS)

hexyl: Hx; (OBN)

histidyl: His; (ACS, CBN)

homocysteinyl: Hcy; (ACS, CBN)

homoserinyl: Hse; (ACS, CBN)

homoserine lactone: Hse>; (ACS, CBN)

horsepower: hp; (AIP, BIOSIS, WHO)

hour: h; (AIP, ASTM, BIOSIS, CAS, CGPM*, WHO)

hundred weight: cwt; (BIOSIS, CAS)

hydrogen ion concentration, negative logarithm of: pH; (BIOSIS)

hydroxy (used only as substituent on nucleoside): ho or oh; (CBN)

allo-hydroxylysine: αHyl; (ASC, CBN)

hydroxylysyl: Hyl; (ACS, CBN)

hydroxymethyl (used only as substituent on nucleoside): hm; (CBN)

hydroxyprolyl: Hyp; (ACS, CBN)

hyperbolic cosecant: csch; (AIP)

hyperbolic cosine: cosh; (AIP)

hyperbolic cotangent: coth; (AIP)

hyperbolic sine: sinh; (AIP)

hypoxanthine: Hyp; (CBN)

idose: Ido; (JCBN)

immunoglobulin: Ig; (BIOSIS, CAS)

incertae sedis (uncertain position; taxonomy only): inc. sed.; (BIOSIS)

inch: in; (WHO)

inch: in.; (AIP, BIOSIS, CAS)

indoleacetic acid: IAA; (BIOSIS)

infective dose, 50%: ID_{50}; (ACS)

infrared: IR; (ACS, AIP, BIOSIS, CAS)

inhibitor constant (*see also* Michaelis constant and substrate constant): K_i; (CBNa)

inorganic phosphate (orthophosphate): P_i; (BIOSIS, CBN)

inorganic pyrophosphate: PP_i; (BIOSIS, CBN)

inosine: Ino; (CBN)

inosine 5'-diphosphate (inosine diphosphate): IDP; (BIOSIS, CBN)

inosine 5'-monophosphate (inosine monophosphate, inosinic acid): IMP; (BIOSIS, CBN)

inosine 5'-triphosphate (inosine triphosphate): ITP; (BIOSIS, CBN)

inosinic acid (*see* inosine 5'-monophosphate)

inositol: Ins; (CBN)

inside diameter: i.d.; (ACS, AIP)

intelligence quotient: IQ; (BIOSIS)

international unit: IU; (BIOSIS, CAS)

intramuscular: i.m.; (BIOSIS, CAS)

intraperitoneal: i.p.; (BIOSIS, CAS)

intravenous: i.v.; (BIOSIS, CAS)

iodo (used only as substituent on nucleoside): io; (CBN)

p-iodophenylsulfonyl (pipsyl): Ips; (CBN)

allo-isoleucine: aIle; (ACS, CBN)

isoleucyl: Ile; (ACS, CBN)

isopentenyl (used only as substituent on nucleoside): i; (CBN)

isopropylidene: $>CMe_2$ or $Me_2C<$; (CBN)

joule: J; (AIP, ASTM, BIOSIS, CAS, CGPM, ISO, WHO)

katal: kat; (CBNa, WHO)

kelvin (use $°K$ if risk of confusion with other symbols): K; (AIP, ASTM, BIOSIS, CAS, CGPM, ISO, WHO)

kilo- ($\times 10^3$): k; (AIP, ASTM, BIOSIS, CAS, CGPM, ISO, WHO)

kilocalorie (*see also* calorie): kcal; (AIP, BIOSIS)

kilogram: kg; (AIP, ASTM, BIOSIS, CGPM, ISO, WHO)

kilometre: km; (AIP, CGPM)

kinetic energy: KE; (AIP)

laboratory: lab; (AIP)

laboratory: lab.; (CAS)

lethal concentration, 50%: LC_{50}; (BIOSIS)

lethal dose: LD; (BIOSIS, CAS)

lethal dose, median (lethal dose–fifty): LD_{50}; (ACS, BIOSIS)

leucyl: Leu; (ACS, CBN)

levo- (configuration; preceding a chemical name): L; (CBN)

levo- (configuration; preceding a chemical name): L; (BIOSIS)

levorotatory (preceding a chemical name): l or (–); (BIOSIS, CBN)

limit: lim; (AIP)

linear combination of atomic orbitals: LCAO; (AIP, CAS)

liter (*see* litre)

litre (write out if symbol may be confused with numeral 1): l; (AIP, ASTM, BIOSIS, CGPM*, WHO)

litre: L; (CAS)

logarithm (to base 10; common logarithm): log; (AIP, BIOSIS)

logarithm, natural (to base e): ln; (AIP, BIOSIS)

lumen: lm; (AIP, ASTM, CAS, CGPM, ISO, WHO)

lux: lx; (AIP, ASTM, BIOSIS, CAS, CGPM, ISO, WHO)

lysergic acid diethylamide: LSD; (BIOSIS)

lysinyl: Lys; (ACS, CBN)

lyxose (used only as substituent on nucleoside): l; (CBN)

lyxose: Lyx; (JCBN)

maleimide: MalN; (CBN)

maleoyl: Mal< or -Mal-; (CBN)

maleyl: Mal; (CBN)

mannose: Man; (CBN)

maximum: max; (AIP)

maximum: max.; (CAS)

mega- ($\times 10^6$): M; (AIP, ASTM, BIOSIS, CAS, CGPM, ISO, WHO)

melanocyte stimulating hormone: MSH; (BIOSIS, CAS)

melting point: mp; (ACS, AIP)

melting point: m.p.; (CAS)

menaquinone: MK; (CBN)

mercapto (*see* thio)

6-mercaptopurine: Shy; (CBN)

mercuribenzoate: HgBzO; (CBN)

messenger ribonucleic acid: mRNA; (BIOSIS, CBN)

meta- (position; preceding a chemical name): m; (BIOSIS)

meter (*see* metre)

methemoglobin: MetHb; (CBN)

methionyl: Met; (ACS, CBN)

methoxy (methyl ester): OMe; (CBN)

methoxyphenylazobenzyloxycarbonyl: Mz; (CBN)

methyl: Me; (ACS, CAS, CBN)

methyl (used only as substituent on nucleoside): m; (CBN)

methyl ester (*see* methoxy)

N-methylglycyl (*see* sarcosyl)

methylumbelliferyl: MeUmb; (OBN)

5-methyluracil (*see* thymine)

methylthiocarbamoyl: Mtc; (CBN)

metre: m; (AIP, ASTM, BIOSIS, CAS, CGPM, ISO, WHO)

metre-kilogram-second: mks; (AIP)

metric ton (*see* tonne)

Michaelis constant (*see also* inhibitor constant and substrate constant): K_m; (BIOSIS, CBNa, WHO)

micro- ($\times 10^{-6}$): μ; (AIP, ASTM, BIOSIS, CAS, CGPM, ISO, WHO)

microequivalent: μeq; (BIOSIS)

microgram: μg; (BIOSIS)

micrometre: μm; (AIP, BIOSIS, CGPM, WHO)

micromole: μmol; (AIP, BIOSIS, CGPM)

micron (*see* micrometre)

mile per hour: mile/h; (WHO)

mile per hour: mph; (AIP, BIOSIS, CAS)

milli- ($\times 10^{-3}$): m; (AIP, ASTM, BIOSIS, CAS, CGPM, ISO, WHO)

milliampere: mA; (AIP, BIOSIS, CGPM)

milliequivalent: meq; (BIOSIS)

milligram: mg; (AIP, BIOSIS, CGPM)

millilitre: ml; (AIP, BIOSIS, CGPM)

millimetre: mm; (AIP, BIOSIS, CGPM)

millimolar (concentration): mM; (BIOSIS)

millimole (mass): mmol; (BIOSIS, CGPM)

millivolt: mV; (AIP, BIOSIS, CGPM)

minimum: min; (AIP)

minimum: min.; (CAS)

minimum lethal dose: MLD; (BIOSIS)

minute (plane angle): '; (ASTM, CGPM*, WHO)

minute (time): min; (AIP, ASTM, BIOSIS, CAS, CGPM*, WHO)

mitochondrial deoxyribonucleic acid: mtDNA; (CBN)

mixture melting point: mmp; (ACS)

molar (concentration): M; (CAS)

molar (concentration): M; (BIOSIS)

mole: mol; (AIP, ASTM, BIOSIS, CAS, CGPM, ISO, WHO)

molecular orbital: MO; (AIP, CAS)

molecular weight (relative): M_r; (ACS)

monomethoxytrityl (p-anisyldiphenyl-methyl; used only as substituent on nucleoside): mmt; (CBN)

month: mo; (CAS)

month: mo.; (BIOSIS)

morpha (form; only after a specific epithet): m.; (BIOSIS)

muramic acid: Mur; (CBN)

myoglobin: Mb; (CBN)

nano- ($\times 10^{-9}$): n; (AIP, ASTM, BIOSIS, CAS, CGPM, ISO, WHO)

nanometre: nm; (CGPM)

neuraminic acid: Neu; (CBN)

neutralization equivalent: neut equiv; (ACS)

newton: N; (AIP, ASTM, BIOSIS, CAS, CGPM, ISO, WHO)

nicotinamide adenine dinucleotide (diphosphopyridine nucleotide; coenzyme I; cozymase): NAD; (BIOSIS, CBN)

nicotinamide adenine dinucleotide phosphate, reduced (triphosphopyridine nucleotide, reduced): NADPH; (BIOSIS, CBN)

nicotinamide adenine dinucleotide phosphate (triphosphopyridine nucleotide; coenzyme II): NADP; (BIOSIS, CBN)

nicotinamide adenine dinucleotide, reduced (diphosphopyridine nucleotide, reduced): NADH; (BIOSIS, CBN)

nicotinamide mononucleotide: NMN; (BIOSIS, CBN)

2-nitrobenzoic acid (see 5,5′-dithiobis-(2-nitrobenzoic acid))

nitronitrosoguanidine: N_2gd; (OBN)

o-nitrophenylsulfonyl (see o-nitrophenylthio)

o-nitrophenylthio (o-nitrophenylsul-fonyl): Nps; (CBN)

p-nitrophenylthio: Snp; (CBN)

nitrosamide: Nad; (OBN)

nitrosamine: Nan; (OBN)

nitrosoguanidine: Ngd; (OBN)

nitrosourea: Nur; (OBN)

nomen conservandum (retained name; taxonomy only): nom. cons.; (BIOSIS)

nomen dubium (doubtful name; taxonomy only): nom. dub.; (BIOSIS)

nomen novum (new name; taxonomy only): nom. nov.; (BIOSIS)

nomen nudum (invalid name; taxonomy only): nom. nud.; (BIOSIS)

nomen rejiciendum (rejected name; taxonomy only): nom. rej.; (BIOSIS)

norleucyl: Nle; (ACS, CBN)

normal (concentration): N; (BIOSIS)

normal (concentration): N; (CAS)

normal (preceding a chemical name): n; (BIOSIS)

normal atmosphere (see standard atmosphere)

norvaline: Nva; (ACS, CBN)

nuclear magnetic resonance: NMR; (ACS, AIP, BIOSIS)

nucleoside: Nuc; (CBN)

nucleoside, unspecified: N; (CBN)

number: no.; (BIOSIS, CAS)

number: No.; (AIP)

observed: obs; (AIP)

observed; obsd.; (CAS)

octyl: Oc; (OBN)

oersted: Oe; (AIP, CAS, WHO)

ohm: Ω; (AIP, ASTM, BIOSIS, CAS, CGPM, ISO, WHO)

optical configuration (see racemic)

ornithyl: Orn; (ACS, CBN)

orotate (see orotic acid)

orotic acid (orotate): Oro; (CBN)

orotidine: Ord; (CBN)

ortho- (position; preceding a chemical name): o; (BIOSIS)

orthophosphate (see inorganic phosphate)

ounce (avoirdupois): oz; (AIP,
    BIOSIS, CAS, WHO)
outside diameter: o.d.; (ACS, AIP)

para- (position; preceding a chemical
    name): *p*; (BIOSIS)
parts per billion: ppb; (ACS, BIOSIS,
    CAS)
parts per million: ppm; (BIOSIS,
    CAS)
pascal: Pa; (AIP, ASTM, CAS,
    CGPM, ISO, WHO)
pentyl: Pe; (OBN)
per: /; (BIOSIS)
percent: %; (ACS, BIOSIS)
per mille: ‰; (BIOSIS)
peta- ($\times 10^{15}$): P; (ASTM, CAS,
    CGPM, WHO)
phenyl: Ph; (ACS, CAS, CBN)
phenylalanyl: Phe; (ACS, CBN)
p-phenylazobenzyloxycarbonyl: Pz;
    (CBN)
phenylisothiocyanate: PhNCS; (CBN)
phenylthio (phenylthiol ester): SPh;
    (CBN)
phenylthiocarbamoyl: PhNHCS or
    Ptc; (CBN)
phenylthiohydantoin: >PhNCS;
    (CBN)
phenylthiol ester (*see* phenylthio)
phosphate (*see* inorganic phosphate)
phosphatidyl: Ptd; (CBN)
phosphoric residue (phosphate): *P*;
    (CBN)
phosphoric residue (used only as sub-
    stituent on nucleoside): p; (CBN)
phthaloyl: Pht; (CBN)
phthalyl: Pht< or -Pht-; (CBN)
phylloquinone: K; (CBN)
pico- ($\times 10^{-12}$): p; (AIP, ASTM,
    BIOSIS, CAS, CGPM, ISO,
    WHO)
pint: pt; (BIOSIS, CAS)
1-piperidino-oxy: OPip; (CBN)
pipsyl (*see p*-iodophenylsulfonyl)
plastoquinone: PQ; (CBN)
pleuropneumonia-like organism:
    PPLO; (BIOSIS)
polymer of: poly; (CBN)

post meridiem: p.m.; (AIP, CAS)
potential difference: p.d.; (CAS)
potential difference: PD; (AIP)
pound (avoirdupois): lb; (AIP,
    BIOSIS, CAS, WHO)
pounds per square inch: lb/in²; (AIP,
    BIOSIS, WHO)
pounds per square inch: psi; (BIOSIS,
    CAS)
preoccupied (taxonomy only): preocc.;
    (BIOSIS)
probability: *P*; (BIOSIS, WHO)
probable error: pe; (AIP)
prolyl: Pro; (ACS, CBN)
propyl: Pr; (ACS, CAS)
pros (locant for the N of the imidazole
    ring of histidine nearer the ala-
    nine sidechain): π; (CBN)
pseudouridine: Ψrd; (CBN)
pterin (2-amino-4-hydroxypteridine):
    Ptn; (OBN)
pteroyl: Pte; (CBN)
purine: Pur; (CBN)
purine nucleoside: Puo; (CBN)
pyranose (suffix): *p*; (CBN)
pyridoxal: Pxl; (OBN)
pyridoxamine: Pxm; (OBN)
pyridoxine: Pxn; (OBN)
pyridoxyl: Pxy; (CBN)
pyridoxylidene: Pxd= or Pxd<;
    (CBN)
pyrimidine: Pyr; (CBN)
pyrimidine nucleoside: Pyd; (CBN)
pyroglutamic acid: <Glu; (ACS, CBN)
pyrophosphate (*see* inorganic pyro-
    phosphate)
pyruvenol (for *enol*pyruvate; abbrevia-
    tion may be prefixed by *e* to dis-
    tinguish from pyruvate): Prv;
    (CBN)

8-quinolyloxy: OQu; (CBN)

racemic (optical configuration, a mix-
    ture of dextro- and levo-; preced-
    ing a chemical name): *dl* or DL;
    (CBN)
racemic: *dl* or DL; (BIOSIS)
radian (plane angle): rad; (AIP,

ASTM, CGPM, ISO, WHO)

radiation (ionizing absorbed dose; use rd if risk of confusion with radian): rad; (BIOSIS, CGPM**)

radiation: rd; (ASTM)

rate change of a process with 10° C increase: Q_{10}; (BIOSIS)

reference: ref.; (CAS)

reference: Ref.; (AIP)

respiratory quotient: RQ; (BIOSIS, CAS, WHO)

retardation factor (distance the unknown has traveled relative to the solvent front in chromatography): R_f; (BIOSIS)

reticuloendothelial system: RES; (BIOSIS)

revolutions per minute: r/min; (WHO)

revolutions per minute: rpm; (AIP, CAS, BIOSIS)

ribitol (ribityl): Rby; (OBN)

ribonuclease: RNase; (BIOSIS, CAS)

ribonucleic acid (*see also* complementary, ribosomal, messenger, and transfer ribonucleic acids): RNA; (AIP, BIOSIS, CBN)

ribose: Rib; (CBN)

ribosomal ribonucleic acid: rRNA; (BIOSIS, CBN)

ribosylthymine: Thd; (CBN)

ribosylthymine 5′-diphosphate (ribosylthymine diphosphate): TDP; (BIOSIS, CBN)

ribosylthymine 5′-monophosphate (ribosylthymine monophosphate): TMP; (BIOSIS, CBN)

ribosylthymine 5′-triphosphate (ribosylthymine triphosphate): TTP; (BIOSIS, CBN)

ribulose: Rbu; (OBN)

roentgen: R; (AIP, ASTM, BIOSIS, CAS, CGPM**, WHO)

roentgen equivalent man: rem; (BIOSIS, CAS, CGPM**)

sarcosyl (*N*-methylglycyl): Sar; (ACS, CBN)

secant: sec; (AIP)

second (plane angle): ″; (ASTM, CGPM*, WHO)

second (time): s; (AIP, ASTM, BIOSIS, CAS, CGPM, ISO, WHO)

secondary (preceding a chemical name; as superscript use *s*, for example, Ba^s): *sec*-; (BIOSIS, CAS)

section (taxonomy only): sect.; (BIOSIS)

sensu lato (broad sense; taxonomy only): s.l.; (BIOSIS)

sensu stricto (restricted sense; taxonomy only): s.s.; (BIOSIS)

seryl: Ser; (ACS, CBN)

shikimic acid: Shk; (OBN)

sialic acid: Sia; (CBN)

siemens (conductance): S; (AIP, ASTM, CAS, CGPM, ISO, WHO)

sievert: Sv; (CGPM)

sine: sin; (AIP)

species (only after a generic name): sp. or spp. (singular or plural); (BIOSIS)

species nova (new species; only after a specific epithet): sp. nov.; (BIOSIS)

specific gravity: sp gr; (ACS)

specific gravity: sp. gr.; (CAS)

specific heat: sp ht; (ACS)

specific volume: sp vol; (ACS)

sphingosine: Sph; (CBN)

square: sq; (AIP)

standard atmosphere: atm; (WHO)

standard atmosphere: A_s; (AIP)

standard deviation: SD; (BIOSIS)

standard error: SE; (BIOSIS)

standard temperature and pressure: STP; (AIP)

steradian (solid angle): sr; (AIP, ASTM, CAS, CGPM, ISO, WHO)

subcutaneous: s.c.; (BIOSIS, CAS)

subspecies (only after a specific epithet): ssp. or sspp. (singular or plural); (BIOSIS)

subspecies nova (new subspecies; only

after a subspecific epithet): ssp. nov.; (BIOSIS)

substrate constant (*see also* inhibitor constant and Michaelis constant): K_s; (CBNa)

succinimido-oxy: ONSu; (CBN)

succinoyl (3-carboxypropionyl): Suc; (CBN)

succinyl: Suc< or -Suc-; (CBN)

sulfhydryl: SH; (BIOSIS)

symmetrical (preceding a chemical name): *s*; (BIOSIS)

symmetrical (preceding a chemical name): sym.; (CAS)

talose: Tal; (JCBN)

tangent: tan; (AIP)

tele (locant for the N of the imidazole ring of histidine farther from the alanine sidechain): τ; (CBN)

tera- ($\times 10^{12}$): T; (AIP, ASTM, CAS, CGPM, ISO, WHO)

tertiary (preceding a chemical name): *tert*-; (BIOSIS, CAS)

tertiary (superscript with chemical symbol): *t*; (BIOSIS)

tesla: T; (AIP, ASTM, CAS, CGPM, ISO, WHO)

tetrahydro: H_4; (CBN)

tetrahydrofolate: H_4folate; (CBN)

tetrahydrofuran: H_4furan; (CBN)

tetrahydropyranyl: H_4pyran; (CBN)

tetrahydropyranyl (used only as substituent on nucleoside): thp; (CBN)

tetramethylsilane: Me_4Si; (CBN)

theoretical(ly): theor; (AIP)

theoretical(ly): theor.; (CAS)

thin-layer chromatography: TLC; (ACS, BIOSIS)

thio (mercapto; used only as substituent on nucleoside): s; (CBN)

6-thioinosine: Sno; (CBN)

thiouracil: Sur; (CBN)

thiouridine: Srd; (CBN)

threonyl: Thr; (ACS, CBN)

thymidine: dThd; (CBN)

thymidine 5′-diphosphate (*see* deoxyribosylthymine diphosphate)

thymidine 5′-monophosphate (*see* deoxyribosylthymine monophosphate)

thymidine 5′-triphosphate (*see* deoxyribosylthymine triphosphate)

thymine (5-methyluracil): Thy; (CBN)

tocopherol: T; (CBN)

tonne (metric ton): t; (ASTM, CGPM*, WHO)

toluenesulfonyl (*see* tosyl)

p-toluenesulfonyl (*see* tosyl)

tosyl (*p*-toluenesulfonyl; used only as substituent on nucleoside): tos; (CBN)

N^{α}-tosylarginine methyl ester: TosArgOMe; (CBN)

N^{α}-tosylphenylalanine chloromethyl ketone: $TosPheCH_2Cl$; (CBN)

transfer ribonucleic acid: tRNA; (BIOSIS, CBN)

2,4,5-trichlorophenoxyacetic acid: 2,4,5-T; (BIOSIS)

triethylaminoethyl cellulose (*O*-triethylaminoethyl cellulose): TEAE-cellulose; (BIOSIS, CAS, CBN)

triethylenethiophosphoramide: thiotepa; (BIOSIS)

trimethylsilyl: Me_3Si; (CBN)

triphenylmethyl (*see* trityl)

triphosphopyridine nucleotide (*see* nicotinamide adenine dinucleotide phosphate)

triphosphopyridine nucleotide, reduced (*see* nicotinamide adenine dinucleotide phosphate, reduced)

trityl: Trt or Ph_3C; (CBN)

trityl (used only as substituent on nucleoside): tr; (CBN)

tryptophanyl: Trp; (ACS, CBN)

tyrosinyl: Tyr; (ACS, CBN)

ubiquinone: Q; (CBN)

ultrahigh frequency: uhf; (AIP)

ultraviolet: uv; (AIP)

ultraviolet: UV; (ACS, BIOSIS, CAS)

umbelliferyl: Umb; (OBN)

United States Pharmacopeia: USP; (BIOSIS, CAS)

uracil: Ura; (CBN)

uridine: Urd; (CBN)

uridine 5'-diphosphate (uridine diphosphate): UDP; (BIOSIS, CBN)
uridine 5'-monophosphate (uridine
monophosphate; uridylic acid):
UMP; (BIOSIS, CBN)
uridine 5'-triphosphate (uridine triphosphate): UTP; (BIOSIS, CBN)
uridylic acid (*see* uridine 5'-monophos-
phate)

valyl: Val; (ACS, CBN)
varietas (variety; only after a specific
epithet): var.; (BIOSIS)
varietas nova (new variety; only after
a varietal name): var. nov.;
(BIOSIS)
versus: vs; (AIP)
versus: vs.; (BIOSIS, CAS)
volt: V; (AIP, ASTM, BIOSIS, CAS,
CGPM, ISO, WHO)
volume: *V*; (WHO)
volume: vol; (ACS, BIOSIS)
volume; vol.; (AIP, CAS)
volume ratio (volume per volume):
v/v; (ACS)
volume ratio (volume per volume):
vol/vol; (BIOSIS)

watt: W; (AIP, ASTM, BIOSIS, CAS,
CGPM, ISO, WHO)
weber: Wb; (AIP, ASTM, CAS,
CGPM, ISO, WHO)

week: wk; (BIOSIS, CAS)
weight: wt; (ACS, BIOSIS)
weight: wt.; (CAS)
weight per volume: wt/vol; (BIOSIS)
weight ratio (weight per weight):
wt/wt; (BIOSIS)
weight ratio (weight per weight):
w/w; (ACS)

xanthine: Xan; (CBN)
xanthosine: Xao; (CBN)
xanthosine 5'-diphosphate (xanthosine diphosphate): XDP; (BIOSIS,
CBN)
xanthosine 5'-monophosphate (xanthosine monophosphate; xanthylic acid): XMP; (BIOSIS,
CBN)
xanthosine 5'-triphosphate (xanthosine triphosphate): XTP;
(BIOSIS, CBN)
xanthylic acid (*see* xanthosine 5'-mon-
ophosphate)
x-ray unit (*see* x unit)
x unit (x-ray unit): xu; (AIP)
xylose (used only as substituent on nucleoside): x; (CBN)
xylose: Xyl; (JCBN)

yard: yd; (BIOSIS, CAS)
year: yr; (AIP, BIOSIS, CAS)

Word usage

In scientific writing, the shortest and most precise words should be chosen to convey the meaning; words used carelessly impede clear communication. Misspelled words distract the reader from the author's message. Although poor usage and misspellings may be corrected by an editor or a copy editor before the manuscript is sent to the printer, authors should make every effort to choose their own words carefully and accurately to avoid misinterpretation by readers.

The words listed below are frequently misused or confused with other words. Entry terms are in boldface, except for *Amoeba, Bacillus,* and Protozoa, which are given in the typographic style for taxonomic nomenclature (*see* chapter 13); example words that appear elsewhere in the list as entry terms are also in boldface. Additional guidance on precise usage and correct spelling can be found in standard general and scientific dictionaries and in other sources described in chapter 17, Useful References with Annotations.

CONFUSING PAIRS

Each word in the pairs in this section has been found to be misused where its companion would have been the correct choice. The close but not identical meanings and, for some pairs, similar spellings cause their erroneous use. The word more frequently used in error is given first. Because pairs are arranged alphabetically by the first word in the pair, cross-references are given for second words that do not follow alphabetical sequence.

absorption: an assimilation or taking up by capillary, osmotic, chemical, or solvent action.
adsorption: a taking up, through physical or chemical forces, by the surface of solids or liquids.

accuracy: degree of correctness of a measurement or a statement.
precision: degree of refinement with which a measurement is made or stated: *The number 3.43 shows more precision than 3.4, but it is not necessarily more accurate.* When applied to a statement, the qualities of definiteness, terseness, and specificity.

affect: *see* **effect/affect**

among: preposition, always applies to more than two objects.
between: preposition, literally applies to only two objects; may be used with more than two when each is treated individually, as *a treaty between three powers.*

analog: adjective, of or relating to an analog computer.
analogue: noun, something similar to something else.

axenic: adjective usually used to describe organisms maintained in isolation from all other living things, or to describe their environment.
gnotobiotic: adjective used to describe laboratory animals specifically reared to be germfree except for known microorganisms with which they have been inoculated.

between: *see* **among/between**

can: auxiliary verb meaning to know how to, to be able to.
may: auxiliary verb meaning to have permission to, to be in some degree likely to.

case: an episode or instance of illness or injury; do not use *case* to refer to a person.
patient: the ill or injured person.

cause: *see* **etiology/cause**

circadian: adjective meaning approximately 24 hours.
diurnal: adjective meaning repeated or recurring every 24 hours; also, occurring, or chiefly active, in the daylight hours.

compose: verb used after a plural subject to mean to form, to go together, to make up (an object), as in *composed of many ingredients.* In passive voice compose is synonymous with comprise.
comprise: verb meaning to include, to contain, to be made up of, as in *a district comprises three counties.*

connote: to imply a meaning beyond the usual specific, exact meaning.
denote: to indicate presence or existence of.

continual: going on in time without interruption or with only brief interruption.
continuous: going on in time or space without interruption.

denote: *see* **connote/denote**

diurnal: *see* **circadian/diurnal**

dosage: the amount of medicine to be taken by a patient in a given period of time, or the total amount. Also, especially in British usage, the regulation or gradation of doses; never the amount taken at one time.
dose: the amount of medicine to be taken by a patient at one time; sometimes the total amount taken.

effect: as a noun, the result of an action; as a verb, to bring about or to cause to come into being.
affect: as a noun in psychiatry and psychology, feeling tone accompanying an idea or mental representation, or a generic term for feeling, emotion, or mood; as a verb, to cause a change or an effect.

enable: to render able, to make possible.
permit: to allow, to give formal consent.

ensure: to make certain or guarantee.
insure: to assure against loss; to underwrite; to give, or take, or procure insurance.

etiology: the study or description of causes of a disease.
cause: the agent that brings about an effect, such as the agent that causes a disease or injury.

farther: more distant in space, time, or relationship.
further: as an adjective, going beyond what exists; as an adverb, in addition; as a verb, to move forward.

gnotobiotic: *see* **axenic/gnotobiotic**

homoeologous: adjective used to characterize partially homologous chromosomes.
homologous: in biology, corresponding in structure, position, origin, or other characteristics.

hypothesis: *see* **theory/hypothesis**

incidence: number of cases developing per unit of population per unit of time.
prevalence: number of cases existing per unit of population at a given time.

infer: to deduce or to conclude from facts or premises.
imply: to suggest a conclusion to be drawn from allusion or reference, in contrast to direct statement.

insure: *see* **ensure/insure**

may: *see* **can/may**

meiosis: cellular division resulting in production of cells with a haploid number of chromosomes.
miosis: excessive smallness of the ocular pupil.

patient: *see* **case/patient**

permit: *see* **enable/permit**

precision: *see* **accuracy/precision**

prevalence: *see* **incidence/prevalence**

theory: a working hypothesis given probable validity by experimental evidence (definition for experimental science; not to be used loosely for hypothesis, idea, concept).
hypothesis: a proposition set forth to be tested for validity by experiment or logical consistency with known facts.

that: *see* **which/that**

varying: that which is changing or causing to change.
various: of different kinds or aspects.

which: relative pronoun introducing a nonrestrictive clause (*these data, which I have discussed, were obtained at great cost*).
that: relative pronoun introducing a restrictive clause (*the information that we need is now available*).

WORDS OFTEN MISUSED OR MISSPELLED

abscissa, plural **abscissas:** horizontal coordinate.
absorbance: ability of a layer of a substance to absorb radiation; *see* **absorptance.**

absorbency: state or quality of being able to absorb.

absorbent: having the capacity or tendency to absorb.

absorptance: the proportion of radiant energy absorbed by a layer of the absorbing material.

absorption: *see* **absorption/adsorption** in "Confusing Pairs" above.

accuracy: *see* **accuracy/precision** in "Confusing Pairs" above.

Adrenalin: U.S. trade name for epinephrine.

adrenaline: British generic name for epinephrine.

adsorption: *see* **absorption/adsorption** in "Confusing Pairs" above.

affect: *see* **effect/affect** in "Confusing Pairs" above.

after: adverb, following in time or place; preferred to following.

albumen: white of an egg.

albumin: any of a large class of simple proteins.

alga: plural **algae**, adjective **algal**.

aliquot: verb meaning to divide (a number or quantity) into equal parts; noun, meaning equal portion.

alpha-toxin: not α-toxin.

ambience: noun, surrounding atmosphere or environment; in scientific usage preferred to *ambiance*.

ambient: as a noun, environment or encompassing atmosphere; as an adjective, surrounding or encompassing.

ameba (plural **amebas**) or **amoeba** (plural **amoebae**): common name.

amino acid: but **aminoaciduria.**

Amoeba: scientific name of a genus; name is capitalized and italicized.

among: *see* **among/between** in "Confusing Pairs" above.

analog: *see* **analog/analogue** in "Confusing Pairs" above.

analogous: not analagous.

analogue: *see* **analog/analogue** in "Confusing Pairs" above.

ante-: as prefix meaning before, earlier, or anterior, combines without hyphen, as in antemortem; distinguish from **anti-.**

anti-: against, opposed to; as prefix combines without hyphen (*anticholinesterase*) except before a base word beginning with a capital (*anti-Stokes line*) or an *i* (*anti-icer*); distinguish from **ante-.**

autoradiograph: *or* **radioautograph**; no preferred usage.

axenic: *see* **axenic/gnotobiotic** in "Confusing Pairs" above.

Bacillus: scientific name of a genus; name is capitalized and italicized.

bacillus, plural **bacilli**: common name.

base line: noun; **base-line**, adjective.

basis: plural **bases**.

between: *see* **among/between** in "Confusing Pairs" above.

biuret: a chemical compound: *biuret reaction; see* **burette, buret**.

brain stem: two words.

bromosulfalein: generic term is sulfobromophthalein sodium; also known by various trade names, including Bromsulphalein.

Büchner funnel: after Ernst Büchner.

Buchner hydraulic press: after Edward Buchner.

burette or **buret:** laboratory apparatus.

calix, plural **calices**: ecclesiastical chalice or chalices.

calyx, plural **calyxes** or **calyces**: part of a flower; *see* **calix, calices**.

can: *see* **can/may** in "Confusing Pairs" above.

cancel, canceled, canceling, but **cancellate, cancellus, cancelli, cancellous.**

cannot: one word.

carried out: experiments are not *carried out*; they are *conducted* or *performed*.

case: *see* **case/patient** in "Confusing Pairs" above.

cause: *see* **etiology/cause** in "Confusing Pairs" above.

chi-square: noun or adjective.

chloroacetic: preferred to *chloracetic.*

chromatography: not chromotography, but **chromotypography.**

circadian: *see* **circadian/diurnal** in "Confusing Pairs" above.

compare: verb; followed by *to* when a similarity is stated or suggested, as in *he compared Mendel to Washington* (one the father of genetics, the other the father of his country); followed by *with* when details of similarity or dissimilarity are stated or suggested, as in *he compared Mendel with Darwin,* that is, pointed out or suggested details in which the two scientists were similar or dissimilar.

connote: *see* **connote/denote** in "Confusing Pairs" above.

continual, continuous: *see* **continual/continuous** in "Confusing Pairs" above.

data: plural of **datum.**

demonstrate: *see* **exhibit.**

denote: *see* **connote/denote** in "Confusing Pairs" above.

deoxy: chemical prefix; **desoxy,** British spelling.

desiccate, desiccator.

determine: do not use as synonym for analyze, not *the chemist determined eight soil samples* but *the chemist determined the pH of eight soil samples.*

dialysate: product of **dialysis.**

dialysis: plural **dialyses.**

dialyze: to subject to **dialysis.**

dialyzer: apparatus for **dialysis.**

die: preferred to *expire, succumb,* and other euphemisms.

different from: preferred to *different than.*

dilatation: the act or anatomic result of dilating.

dilation: only the act of dilating.

disk: preferred to *disc* in American usage.

display: *see* **exhibit.**

drug: a *drug* is administered, given, taken, withdrawn; a *drug* is not "started" or "stopped." *Drug use, drug therapy, drug treatment* may be "started" or "stopped."

due to: correctly used with a preceding subject meaning *attributable to,* as in *her pneumonia is due to a virus,* not *due to a virus she contracted pneumonia.*

effect: *see* **effect/affect** in "Confusing Pairs" above.

effluent: something that flows out; **effluence:** usually a flowing out but sometimes that which flows out; **effluent** is preferred in technical and scientific writing.

eluate: washings obtainable by eluting.

eluent or **eluant:** solvent used in eluting.

enable: *see* **enable/permit** in "Confusing Pairs" above.

endemic: noun or adjective, refers to a human disease constantly present to some extent in an area; *see* **enphytotic** and **enzootic;** contrast with **epidemic.**

enphytotic: noun or adjective, refers to a disease of plants; analogous to **endemic** and **enzootic.**

ensure: *see* **ensure/insure** in "Confusing Pairs" above.

enzootic: noun or adjective, refers to a disease of infrahuman animals; analogous to **endemic.**

epidemic: noun or adjective, refers to a disease rapidly affecting many humans in an area at one time; *see* **epiphytotic** and **epizootic;** compare **endemic.**

epiphytotic: noun or adjective, refers to a disease simultaneously affecting many plants (usually of one kind) in an area.

epizootic: noun or adjective, refers to a disease simultaneously affecting many animals of the same kind in an area.

estrogen: noun; **oestrogen,** British spelling.

estrus: noun; **estrous,** adjective; **oestrus, oestrous,** British spelling.

etiology: *see* **etiology/cause** in "Confusing Pairs" above.

exhibit: one of a number of verbs (**demonstrate, display, visualize,** and others) used as elegant, pompous, or euphemistic substitutes for simpler words: *the patient exhibited anemia* is an elegant or pompous substitute for *the patient had anemia.*

expire: do not use as euphemism for **die.**

facilitative: do not confuse with facultative.

farther: *see* **farther/further** in "Confusing Pairs" above.

fasted: do not use as euphemism for starved, as in *the rats fasted,* or *the rats were fasted for 10 days;* fasting is usually considered a voluntary act.

female: use as adjective (not noun) in reference to an adult patient (*a jaundiced female patient,* not *a jaundiced female*); but girls and women may be referred to collectively as females.

fluoridate: to add a fluoride compound, as to drinking water.

fluoridize: to treat with a fluoride compound as in dentistry.

fluorinate: to introduce fluorine into a chemical compound in synthesis.

-fold: suffix that, with a spelled-out number, forms a solid word (*sevenfold*); that with an arabic numeral or numerals forms a hyphenated term (*14-fold*).

follow: verb meaning to go, proceed, or come after someone or something. Permissive meaning, to attend closely to. Do not overuse in this latter sense, as a shorthand for a more complex meaning in describing the course of an experiment or a physician-patient relationship.

following: *Webster's Third* (*see* chapter 4, page 45) recognizes this word as both an adjective and a preposition; Fowler (*see* chapter 17, page 293) discourages its use as a preposition; to avoid ambiguity, as in *following the lecture, the student ate his lunch,* substitute **after** for **following.**

Formalin: trade name; use *formaldehyde solution* unless reference is to the specific product.

further: *see* **farther/further** in "Confusing Pairs" above.

genus: plural **genera.**

germfree: specific laboratory connotation.

glycerol: preferred to glycerin.

gnotobiotic: *see* **axenic/gnotobiotic** in "Confusing Pairs" above.

gram-negative, gram-positive: adjectives, not capitalized.

Gram stain: after Hans C. J. Gram.

half-life: noun or adjective; plural **half-lives.**

half time: noun; **half-time,** adjective.

hemogram: clinical term referring to blood counts and other laboratory studies used to characterize a patient's hematologic condition; particular tests used should be specified.

homoeologous: *see* **homoeologous/homologous** in "Confusing Pairs" above.

human: noun or adjective; *human being* sometimes preferred as noun.

hydrolysate: product of **hydrolysis.**

hydrolysis: plural **hydrolyses.**

hydrolyze: to subject to **hydrolysis.**

hydrolyzer: apparatus for **hydrolysis.**

hypothecate: *see* **hypothesize** below.

hypothesis: *see* **theory/hypothesis** in "Confusing Pairs" above.

hypothesize: to form a **hypothesis;** to form a proposition to be tested by experiment. Preferred to *hypothecate,* which is primarily a legal term.

-ic, -ical: suffixes; endings used in adjectives; the *-ic* form is preferred (*microscopic examination, microscopical examination*); the two endings sometimes convey different meanings (*economic botany, economical process*).

identical: often followed by *with,* rarely by *to.*

imply: *see* **infer/imply** in "Confusing Pairs" above.

incidence: *see* **incidence/prevalence** in "Confusing Pairs" above.

index: noun and verb; plural **indexes** or **indices: indexes** for a book, **indices** for measurable quantities, as in *mitotic indices.*

infer: *see* **infer/imply** in "Confusing Pairs" above.

input: as verb, to enter as data into a computer or a data processing system; as noun, to describe something that is put in.

insanitary: adjective, not sanitary; in medical idiom, preferred to unsanitary, especially if the connotation *injurious to health* is intended.

insure: *see* **ensure/insure** in "Confusing Pairs" above.

interface: use as noun only; do not use as a verb, as in *the members interfaced with each other.*

juvenile: noun or adjective; **juvenal** sometimes preferred in wildlife research.

kill: preferred to *sacrifice.*

leukemia, leukocyte: preferred to *leucemia, leucocyte.*

-like: suffix; compound words formed with this suffix are solid (*lifelike, eellike*), unless the suffix follows a word ending in a double *el* (shell-like), a long compound word (*pleuropneumonia-like*), a proper name (*June-like*), or a hyphenated word (*half-ape-like*).

lipofuscin: frequently misspelled.

litre: preferred spelling in the International System of Units (*see* chapter 14).

lumen: plural **lumens** for units of luminous flux; plural **lumina** for cavities; adjectival form for both is **luminal.**

male: use as adjective (not noun) in reference to an adult patient (*a jaundiced male patient,* not *a jaundiced male*); but boys and men may be referred to collectively as males.

matrix: plural **matrixes;** in mathematics, plural **matrices.**

maximum: plural **maximums;** in mathematics, plural **maxima.**

may: *see* **can/may** in "Confusing Pairs" above.

media: plural of medium, as in *culture medium;* the word **media** is frequently misused as a singular noun, as in *television is a more effective advertising media than radio.*

media, plural **mediae:** middle layer of a blood or lymph vessel, or median vein of an insect's wing.

meiosis: *see* **meiosis/miosis** in "Confusing Pairs" above.

metre: preferred spelling in the International System of Units (*see* chapter 14).

microphotograph: a photograph on a greatly reduced scale, as on microfilm; do not confuse with **photomicrograph,** a photograph taken through a microscope.

migrate: do not use as a transitive verb; *the birds migrated,* not *the current migrated the bacteria.*

miosis: *see* **meiosis/miosis** in "Confusing Pairs" above.

mitosis, plural **mitoses:** a type of cell division.

molal, molar; molality, molarity: not synonymous; the *-al* forms refer to molecular concentration per 1000 g of solvent, the *-ar* forms to molecular concentration per 1000 ml of solution.

morphology: study of form or structure, not structure itself.

mucous: adjective; **mucus,** noun.

neuron: preferred to *neurone.*

optimum: plural **optimums;** in mathematics, plural **optima.**

osmolal, osmolar; osmolality, osmolarity: not synonymous; the *-al* forms refer to osmoles per 1000 g of solvent, the *-ar* forms to osmoles per 1000 ml of solution.

over: do not use for *more than* in describing quantities.

oxalacetic acid: preferred to *oxaloacetic acid*; but **oxalosuccinic acid.**

pandemic: widely **epidemic**; refers to disease in human beings.

panzootic: widely **epizootic**; refers to disease affecting animals.

paradigm: closest synonym is **ideal**, not *model* or *pattern*.

parameter: has a special meaning in mathematics and statistics; do not use loosely for variable, quantity, quality, determinant, or feature.

pathology: study and description of disease processes, abnormalities, and lesions; do not use in place of abnormalities or lesions.

patient: *see* **case/patient** in "Confusing Pairs" above.

percent: noun, adjective, or adverb; use symbol with numerals, as in 98%.

percentage: noun, part of a whole expressed in hundredths, as in *percentage of cells*; often misused as an adjective, *percent error*, not *percentage error*.

permit: *see* **enable/permit** in "Confusing Pairs" above.

phosphorus: noun, sometimes used attributively as in *phosphorus* research.

phosphorous: adjective, resembling *phosphorus* or used to designate a compound of *phosphorus* in which this element has a valence lower than that in phosphoric compounds.

photomicrograph: photograph taken through a microscope; do not confuse with **microphotograph.**

phylum: plural **phyla.**

plasmapheresis: method of plasma depletion by removing blood, centrifuging out cells, and returning them in a suitable liquid medium; preferred to plasmaphoresis.

precision: *see* **accuracy/precision** in "Confusing Pairs" above.

present, present with: do not use as shorthand verb to describe first chance to evaluate patient's signs and symptoms. Does not belong in formal writing.

prevalence: *see* **incidence/prevalence** in "Confusing Pairs" above.

preventive: preferred to *preventative*.

Protozoa: scientific name of a phylum of simple animals; note roman (not italic) type and capital letter.

protozoan, plural **protozoans**: common name; one of the Protozoa (preferred to *protozoon*, plural *protozoa*); **protozoan, protozoic,** adjectives.

proved: preferred to *proven* as past participle, as in *it was proved, it has been proved*.

proven: used in an attributive position, *a proven method*.

.radioautograph or **autoradiograph:** no preferred usage.

react: do not use as transitive verb, as in *he reacted the two reagents*.

roentgenograph: image made on photographic film by **x rays**; do not use **x ray** synonymously.

sacrifice: do not use as euphemism for **kill.**

septum, plural **septums** or **septa**: but *septum transversum*, plural *septa transversa*.

sequela, plural **sequelae**: aftereffect of disease or injury.

serology: science associated with sera; do not use to mean serologic test.

significant: in scientific papers, confine use to statistical judgment; do not use loosely for importance, notable, distinctive, major.

silica gel: but Silica Gel-G as trade name.

Student's *t* test: *Student* is the pseudonym for W. S. Gossett, British statistician, and is capitalized.

succumb: do not use as euphemism for **die.**

symptomatology: branch of science that deals with symptoms of diseases; not a synonym for symptoms and signs.

temperature: not equivalent to fever; *the patient had a fever*, not *the patient had a temperature*.

that: *see* **which/that** in "Confusing Pairs" above.

theory: *see* **theory/hypothesis** in "Confusing Pairs" above.

Tris buffer: trivial name for 2-amino-2-hydroxymethyl-1,3-propanediol; also known as tromethamine (USAN name), TRIS (code name); avoid use of TRIS alone as common noun.

-tropic, -trophic: adjectival suffixes; both *-trop* and *-troph*, combining forms used as suffixes or prefixes, are from Greek words; the first is from *trope*, a turning, affinity for, as in phototropism; the second is from *trophe*, food or nourishment, as in autotrophic. The *-tropic* form is recommended by the International Union of Pure and Applied Chemistry and the International Union of Biochemistry for hormone names such as *gonadotropin*, *corticotropin*; the *-trophin* form is used in some medical and endocrinologic journals.

Tween 80: trade name for polysorbate 80 or polyoxyethylene sorbitan monooleate.

under: do not use for *less than* in describing quantities.

various: see **varying/various** in "Confusing Pairs" above.

varying: see **varying/various** in "Confusing Pairs" above.

viral: adjective; **virus,** noun.

virial, virial coefficient: terms in physics.

visualize: to make or become visible, to picture mentally; not as synonym for *demonstrate* or *reveal*.

which: see **which/that** in "Confusing Pairs" above.

x ray: noun; **x-ray,** adjective; *x ray* is a jargon noun for *x-ray photograph* or *x-ray picture*; **radiograph** is preferred.

Secondary services for literature searching

Information is a valuable and important commodity. Proper sources of information yield a staggering abundance of knowledge when the correct doors are opened. Too often, individuals are satisfied to skim the surface of the literature for pertinent information by satisfying their needs from only familiar and comfortable sources, e.g., a small number of selected journals, personal communication, the invisible college or scientist-to-scientist information flow, and scholarly meetings. They ignore the vast wealth of pertinent and timely literature appropriate to their needs that would expand their horizons of knowledge.

Through the rapid growth of science and technological advances, an exciting era has opened. Data bases, containing millions of bits of information consolidated from many sources, both nationally and internationally, can be made available by the push of a button or input of a few words and phrases. Use of secondary services, both in hard copy and magnetic tape, opens a world of information far exceeding need or desire at times: it is the individual's obligation and option to take full advantage of these opportunities.

ABSTRACTING AND INDEXING SERVICES

Secondary services, usually known as abstracting and indexing services, have been in existence for many years, in fact centuries, because people have always desired precise and concise summarization of the most pertinent facts of a story rather than the multitudinous details. In order to become acquainted with the various systems and services available, the following documents are most valuable.

1) *Encyclopedia of Information Systems and Services* contains the name and address of each secondary service and a description of that system or service, the scope and subject matter, input source, holdings and storage media, publications, microform products and services, computer base products and services, clientele and availability, and person to contact.
2) *Abstracts and Indexes in Science and Technology* is a similar book, much smaller, that describes materials one would encounter doing a literature search in the areas of science and technology.

3) *Directory of Online Information Resources* contains three alphabetized data base indexes: a vendor index, a subject index, and a producer and vendor address index.

4) *Computer-Readable Data Bases: A Directory and Data Sourcebook* lists 528 data bases that meet the following criteria: they are in computer-readable form, are publicly available, and are used for information retrieval or available through the major online vendors of information retrieval services.

5) *Ulrich's International Periodical Directory* identifies the serials covered by abstracting and indexing services so that studies can be initiated with regard to overlap in coverage, identification of core serials, and development of an international network for control of serials. This book, together with the *Union List of Serials*, lists the primary journals and identifies the secondary services that abstract and index the journal articles.

The volumes above offer much information, but they do not convey to readers the importance of the interface between primary and secondary publications. Just as primary journals, such as the *New England Journal of Medicine* and the *Journal of Phytopathology*, provide access to original detailed research contributions, the secondary publications, such as *Biological Abstracts* and *Index Medicus*, provide access to the primary literature. The emphasis for the abstracting and indexing service is on accuracy of content and completeness of coverage. Primary and secondary publications do not compete: their services are complementary. Secondary services provide access to the primary literature, and the primary journals need to be abstracted and indexed in order to fulfill current awareness needs and their archival functions, and to provide readers with a method of retrieving the original articles. The two publications need each other and should aid each other. Through the efforts of international and national groups, such as the International Council of Scientific Unions Abstracting Board, the National Federation of Abstracting and Indexing Services, the Council of Biology Editors, the American National Standards Committee Z-39, and the International Standards Organization, editors and publishers have increased contact and greater opportunities for exchanging information and exploring ways of improving scientific communication. Their cooperative effort has resulted in the improvement of primary journals in standardizing abbreviations of journal titles, bibliographic citations, journal format, and placement of the abstract in the article and in encouraging more explicit and concise article titles and writing of a concise, informative abstract.

The modern scientist experiences difficulty in keeping up with the literature in the field. There is always an uneven distribution between the amount of literature and the time available for reading it. In view of the magnitude of the literature, the secondary service provides the reader with a specific tool—the abstract—in printed form and on magnetic computer tape. The time has come when scientists can use electronic equipment, in their own homes or laboratories, to search data bases. In order to proceed in the most efficient manner, it is important to understand the process used in searching data bases.

ONLINE SEARCHING

Online searching enables a researcher to access directly a computer-readable file usually at a remote location. It offers the opportunity for two-way interaction between the user and the machine.

Online technology is largely responsible for the remarkable growth in popularity of data base searching, for it allows users to locate and retrieve relevant data or information more rapidly, more easily, and less haphazardly than any other information retrieval method yet devised.

Most of the world's major computer-readable data bases in the sciences are currently searchable through today's online systems, and learning how to use online systems, and about the data bases available through these systems, should be a high priority for all scientists. Neglecting to become informed may result in real costs in terms of time wasted and information missed. Using an online system, a researcher can interrogate several multimillion-record bibliographic data bases in a matter of minutes. That same search might take weeks, even months, to complete manually.

Online searching is also more thorough. Not only can information be found online that is inaccessible through the printed indexes, but, more important, the online search can constantly be refined to reflect new information found at all stages of the search; computer programs are now being written that help the user to develop different strategy formulations to the same question, to see the answers immediately, to browse peripheral information, to use thesauri and other search aids during the search, and, in general, to participate in and change the search in progress. The final search strategy modification can easily be run back across the entire data base.

Online search techniques are particularly valuable in helping users to become familiar with the kinds of information in a particular file or data base. Much information can be discovered by looking at the data base structure and record fields.

DATA BASE STRUCTURE AND RECORD FIELDS

In most printed indexes, the full indexing and bibliographic records are not displayed in one place. In online files, full records are always available for viewing. Analysis of just a few full records from the same data base can give the user an immediate grasp of the bibliographic information available. It can also give a quick location of indexing conventions, abbreviation usage, foreign language usage, and other special features or characteristics. Many data bases have common characteristics, and the use of a number of different data bases by the researcher will improve his or her skill in searching as similar patterns become evident in different data bases.

In the bibliographic files for the life sciences there are a number of similarities. In their data base records, for example, one often finds the same basic fields. Fields used to group related information content usually are labeled to describe or define the information contained within the field. Some common field labels are: Record Accession Number, Title of Paper, Author Name(s), Author Affiliation, Index Terms, Descriptors, Abstract, and Source.

The concept of labeled fields is important because an expression located in one field can have a meaning different from the same expression located in another field. To take a simple example, the expression CARPENTER takes on one meaning in the author field (since it would be a surname) and another when located in the index term field. The field to which a particular word or expression belongs is so important to online searching that every word or expression is tagged with its field label (or qualifier) in the master alphabetized index content of the data base (the inverted file).

The inverted file is the key to online searching, and contains the following information: 1) the word by which the entry is alphabetized; 2) the field tag; 3) the record number; and 4) the position indicator. The inverted file display shown below contains all of these elements; however, the third and fourth elements are not usually displayed for viewing.

ANT/IT	12091,	22
CARPENTER/IT	12091,	21
CROW/IT	2886,	2
DATA/IT	8799,	7
DUST/IT	10765,	3

SEARCHING TECHNIQUES

Before going online, the researcher needs to consider which expressions to look up in the inverted file as well as which field tag or tags to use as qualifiers. Users also need to consider if certain relationships between expressions must be present in any one field. Perhaps a search on the word CARPENTER in the index term field is insufficient. If the search is for the expression CARPENTER ANT the user needs to retrieve those records in which the word CARPENTER is adjacent to the word ANT. Expressions derive information content not only from the fields in which they reside but also from the other words or expressions that are in the same field. In fact, all fields and expressions in the record work together to describe or clarify the content of the index paper.

Boolean operators   Users state their requirements by formulating a search strategy that specifies the expression(s) and the relationship between expressions that must be present in the record fields. When these requirements are met by the specified record fields, the record becomes a member of the retrieved set or a hit.

Online search strategies are most frequently formulated with the logical or Boolean operators: AND, OR, NOT. The AND operator indicates that two or more expressions must be present in the same designated field or fields. Those records that have the required expression(s) in the designated field or fields will be retrieved by the system. The operator OR indicates that if any one of several user-designated expressions exists in a particular field or fields, then the record will be retrieved by the system. The operator NOT eliminates records from the retrieval set by subtracting out those records that contain particular user-designated expressions.

Adjacency operator   Sometimes called ADJ, the adjacency operator is another important searching tool. Because most online systems link a numerical position indicator to every expression in the inverted field, a searcher can specify retrieval of only those records in which two expressions are adjacent to or close to each other.

Use of the operators   The following search strategy illustrations show the use of all four operators and two field tags: one for index term (IT) and one for author (AU). Note the use of parentheses to group search expressions into meaningful strategy units. The operations within the parentheses are executed first; operations outside the parentheses are executed next, in an order controlled by the search system.

1) ALLERGY/IT AND DUST/IT AND WALTON, J./AU

2) STREAM/IT OR RIVER/IT OR LAKE/IT

3) (CARPENTER/IT ADJ ANT/IT) NOT (ARMY/IT ADJ ANT/IT)

OTHER TECHNIQUES

In addition to logical operators (and parentheses), other features common to online search systems include truncation, a technique that allows root searching. Cross-file searching, which is often available, allows the user to formulate a strategy in one data base, to save the strategy, and then to apply it against another data base without having to input the search again. The basic or subject information index (in the inverted file) is another useful feature. Since most users do subject searching, the existence of a predetermined subject or basic index speeds strategy input. A search in the basic index could be entered as follows:

(SPILL OR SLICK) AND OIL AND ATLANTIC

No qualifiers are needed. When no qualifiers are specified, the system is programmed to direct the search to all subject information fields in the data base. These usually include the title, the index terms, and sometimes the abstract text.

New features are frequently added to online search systems in order to streamline search techniques. The future holds more user-friendly system innovations, simpler-to-use search strategy formulations, and even more online bibliographic and factual data bases in the sciences. Now that online systems can be used with microcomputers equipped with telecommunications modems, online search techniques are becoming commonplace tools of the research community.

SEARCH STRATEGY

When searching computer data bases for information, consider the scope of the search by building a vocabulary of terms. If *BIOSIS Previews* is to be searched, for example, use *BIOSIS Search Guide* and *Serials Sources for the BIOSIS Data Base.* Is the topic specific or broad? What is the time period to be accessed? How many documents should be perused? A preliminary search is often useful for strategy building.

The following can be considered in searching computer data bases for information:

Items Frequently to be Found in Data Bases
    Bibliographic Information
        Journal coden (a five-character, unambiguous identifier, the easiest
            and quickest way to retrieve from a particular journal)
        Journal name (may or may not use standard abbreviations)
        Book and other non-journal titles (may be in the original language,
            or in variant transliterations from non-Roman alphabet languages)
        Year of publication
        Language of publication
        Pagination (may or may not be inclusive)
        ISSN (International Standard Serial Number)
        ISBN (International Standard Book Number)
    Author Names
        Special treatment according to the data base
    Author's Affiliation (lack of standardization among data bases)
    Basic Index Terms
        Inverted file
        From title and additional indexing terms
        Weighting of terms

Unique Items Among Data Bases
　Special Coding Systems
　　MeSH trees (*Index Medicus*), EMclass (*Excerpta Medica*)
　　Concept and biosystematic codes (*Biological Abstracts* and *Biological Abstracts / Reports, Reviews and Meetings*)
　　Chemical Abstracts service registry numbers (the unambiguous identification of a chemical substance)
　　Classification codes
　Document Types
　Patents
　Accession Numbers
　Update Frequency and Size of Update (by the appropriate procedure, a stored search may be updated automatically)
Systems Features for Search
　Boolean Operators (AND, OR, NOT)
　Stop Words (of, by, for, the, with, an)
　Full Text Operators
　　Adjacency or proximity
　　Linking words within the same field
　　Stringsearching text lines
　Truncation (different symbols are used by different systems)
　If $ is truncation symbol:
　　Within a word (e.g., wom$n)
　　At the end of a word for all subsequent letters (e.g., mitochondr$)
　　At the end of a word limiting to X additional letters (e.g., cat$X; limited truncation of short character strings is important, because unlimited truncation of CAT would retrieve CATastrophe)
　Word Placement Within Basic Index
　　Check spelling (British and American English, as amoeba and ameba)
　　Foreign languages mixed with English (transliteration variation as from Russian and ideogram languages)
　　Expand, root, and neighbor functions of systems
　Saving Searches (reuse search in same or another data base)
　Cross Data Base Searching
　　Use one search statement of limited complexity
　　Help choose data base when contents of several data bases have been considered

When ready to search it is helpful to have a cue sheet of phone numbers, the LOGON sequence, the PASSWORD, and the specific format, including punctuation and spacing for the search system being used. In table 16.1 are formats for a search of *BIOSIS Previews* on three systems: System Development Corporation (SDC), DIALOG, and Bibliographic Retrieval Services (BRS).

Table 16.1. Formats for a search of *BIOSIS Previews*

Data element	System Development Corporation	DIALOG	Bibliographic Retrieval Services
Basic index	MONO(W)LAYER HYDRO(W)CARBON	MONO(W)LAYER HYDRO(W)CARBON	MONO ADJ LAYER HYDRO ADJ CARBON
Title	/TI MONO(W)LAYER	MONO(W)LAYER/TI	MONO ADJ LAYER.TI.
Index term	/IT CAN-DIDA(W)ALBICANS	CANDIDA(W)ALBI-CANS/DE	CANDIDA-ALBI-CANS
Abstract	/AB HYDROCARBON	HYDROCARBON/AB	Abstracts will be available soon
CODEN for a journal	JAMAA/JC	CO=JAMAA	..LIMIT/X CD EQ JAMAA (X is search statement number to be limited)
Author	BAKER C J/AU	AU=BAKER C J	BAKER ADJ C ADJ J
Language	EN/LA	TOXIC(C)LA=ENG-LISH*	..LIMIT/X LG EQ EN

* LA=ENGLISH is so highly posted that it is best limited by another term, in this example by TOXIC. This avoids overflow of the computer space available for an individual search. The C works like a Boolean AND.

Other access points not outlined in the table may be equally or more divergent. Not only is the query format dissimilar, but the appearance of the same document retrieved from these three systems is also different. An example is *Biological Abstracts* Volume 75 Abstract 15173, as retrieved from SDC (figure 16.1), DIALOG (figure 16.2), and BRS (figure 16.3)

Consult the information sheets published by DIALOG and SDC and the chapters published by BRS as aids to searching the various individual data bases.

There is no question that the availability of online searching as a tool in retrieving appropriate bibliographic references can contribute to the rapid retrieval of relevant information.

LITERATURE CITED: Secondary Services for Literature Searching

1. Abstracts and indexes in science and technology: a descriptive guide. Owen, D.; Hanchey, M. Metuchen, NJ: Scarecrow Press, Inc; 1974.
2. Computer readable data bases: a directory and data sourcebook. Williams, M. E., ed. Washington, DC: American Society for Information Science; 1982.
3. Directory of online information resources, 9th ed. Kensington, MD: CSG Press; 1982.
4. Encyclopedia of information systems and services. Kruzas, A. T., ed. Detroit, MI: Gale Research Company; 1981.
5. Ulrich's international periodicals directory, 20th ed. New York: R. R. Bowker Company; 1982.
6. Union list of serials in libraries of the United States and Canada, 3d ed. Titus, E. B., ed. New York: H. W. Wilson Company; 1965.

```
AN  - BA75-015173
TI  - EFFECTS OF PRE NATAL TRI PHENYL TIN EXPOSURE ON THE DEVELOPMENT OF
      BEHAVIOR AND CONDITIONED LEARNING IN RAT PUPS
AU  - LEHOTZKY K; SZEBERENYI J M; GONDA Z; HORKAY F; KISS A
OS  - NATL. INST. OCCUPATIONAL HEALTH, P.O.B. 22, 1450 BUDAPEST, HUNGARY.
SO  - NEUROBEHAV TOXICOL TERATOL (NTOTD), 4 (2). 1982., P. 247-250.
IT  - TINESTAN MORTALITY HYPERACTIVITY FUNGICIDE
AB  - Neurotoxic effects of triphenyl-tin acetate [the widely used fungicide
      tinestan] were examined in pups of mothers treated perorally on day 7-15
      of gestation. The gait and development of motor coordination did not
      differ from those of control animals in spite of the high mortality rate
      of control pups during the nursing period. Spontaneous locomotor activity
      of treated pups at 23 and 36 days was increased but by 90 days activity
      returned to control levels. Conditioned avoidance was acquired more
      rapidly but was also extinguished sooner in animals born from and nursed
      by poisoned mothers than in controls.
LA  - EN
BC  - 86375 (MURIDAE); 95000
CC  - *22501 (TOXICOLOGY-GENERAL/EXPERIMENTAL STUDIES,METHODS); *07003
      (BEHAVIOR BIOLOGY-ANIMAL BEHAVIOR); *07005 (BEHAVIOR
      BIOLOGY-CONDITIONING); 07508 (ECOLOGY-ANIMAL); 10069 (BIOCHEMICAL
      STUDIES-MINERALS); 12510 (PATHOLOGY-NECROSIS); *13010
      (METABOLISM-MINERALS); 16501 (REPRODUCTIVE SYSTEM-GENERAL
      STUDIES;METHODS); *17506 (MUSCLE SYSTEM-PATHOLOGY); 19001 (DENTAL/ORAL
      BIOLOGY-GENERAL STUDIES;METHODS); *20506 (NERVOUS SYSTEM-PATHOLOGY);
      21002 (PSYCHIATRY-PSYCHOPATHOLOGY;PSYCHODYNAMICS,THERAPY); 22100 (ROUTES
      OF IMMUNIZATION,INFECTION,THERAPY); *22506
      (TOXICOLOGY-ENVIRONMENTAL,INDUSTRIAL); 25000 (PEDIATRICS); *25503
      (DEVELOPMENTAL BIOLOGY-PATHOLOGICAL); *25504 (DEVELOPMENTAL
      BIOLOGY-EXPERIMENTAL); *25508 (DEVELOPMENTAL BIOLOGY-GENERAL
      MORPHOGENESIS); *25552 (DEVELOPMENTAL BIOLOGY-DESCRIPTIVE TERATOLOGY);
      *25554 (DEVELOPMENTAL BIOLOGY-EXPERIMENTAL TERATOLOGY); 37015
      (ENVIRONMENTAL HEALTH-AIR,WATER,SOIL POLLUTION); 51514 (PLANT
      PHYSIOLOGY/BIOCHEMISTRY/BIOPHYSICS-GROWTH SUBSTANCES); 54512
      (PHYTOPATHOLOGY-NONPARASITIC DISEASE); *54600 (PEST
      CONTROL,GENERAL/PESTICIDES/HERBICIDES)
```

Figure 16.1. Example of document retrieved from System Development Corporation (SDC).

```
75015173
   EFFECTS OF PRE NATAL TRI PHENYL TIN EXPOSURE ON THE DEVELOPMENT OF
BEHAVIOR AND CONDITIONED LEARNING IN RAT PUPS.
   LEHOTZKY K; SZEBERENYI J M; GONDA Z; HORKAY F; KISS A
   NATL. INST. OCCUPATIONAL HEALTH, P.O.B. 22, 1450 BUDAPEST, HUNGARY.
   NEUROBEHAV TOXICOL TERATOL   4 (2). 1982.  247-250.    CODEN: NTOTD
   LANGUAGE: ENGLISH
   NEUROTOXIC EFFECTS OF TRIPHENYL-TIN ACETATE [THE  WIDELY  USED  FUNGICIDE
TINESTAN] WERE EXAMINED IN PUPS OF MOTHERS TREATED PERORALLY ON DAY 7-15 OF
GESTATION.   THE  GAIT AND DEVELOPMENT OF MOTOR COORDINATION DID NOT DIFFER
FROM THOSE OF CONTROL ANIMALS IN  SPITE  OF  THE  HIGH  MORTALITY  RATE  OF
CONTROL  PUPS DURING THE NURSING PERIOD.  SPONTANEOUS LOCOMOTOR ACTIVITY OF
TREATED PUPS AT 23 AND 36 DAYS  WAS  INCREASED  BUT  BY  90  DAYS  ACTIVITY
RETURNED TO CONTROL LEVELS. CONDITIONED AVOIDANCE WAS ACQUIRED MORE RAPIDLY
BUT  WAS  ALSO  EXTINGUISHED  SOONER  IN  ANIMALS  BORN  FROM AND NURSED BY
POISONED MOTHERS THAN IN CONTROLS.
   DESCRIPTORS: TINESTAN MORTALITY HYPERACTIVITY FUNGICIDE
   CONCEPT  CODES:    BEHAVIOR    BIOL-ANIMAL   BEHAVIOR(◆07003);    BEHAVIOR
BIOL-CONDITIONING(◆07005);       ECOLOGY-ANIMAL(07508);      MINERALS(10069);
PATHOLOGY-NECROSIS(12510);      MINERALS(◆13010);      REPRODUCT    SYST-GENL
STUDS•METHS(16501);    MUSCLE SYST-PATHOLOGY(◆17506);    DENTAL/ORAL BIOL-GENL
STUD•METHS(19001); NERVOUS SYST-PATHOLOGY(◆20506); PSYCHIATRY-PSYCHPATH-DY-
NM•THERAP(21002); ROUTES OF IMMUNIZ,INFECT•THERAP(22100);  TOXICOL-GENL/EXP
STUDS•METHS(◆22501); TOXICOL-ENVIRONMNTL•INDUSTR(◆22506); PEDIATRICS(25000)
; DEVELOPMNTL BIOL-PATHOLOGICAL(◆25503); DEVELOPMNTL BIOL-EXPERIMENTAL(◆25-
504);   DEVELOPMNTL BIOL-GEN MORPHGENSIS(◆25508);   DEVELOPMNTL BIOL-DESCRIP
TERATOL(◆25552);     DEVELOPMNTL    BIOL-EXPER    TERATOL(◆25554);    ENVIRON
HEALTH-AIR•WATR•SL POLLN(37015);   PLANT PHYSIOL-GROWTH SUBSTANCES(51514);
PHYTOPATHOL-NONPARASITIC DISEASE(54512); PEST CONTRL GENL/PESTICS/HERBICS(-
◆54600)
   BIOSYSTEMATIC CODES: MURIDAE(86375); ABSTRACTS OF MYCOLOGY(95000)
```

Figure 16.2. Same document as in figure 16.1, retrieved from DIALOG.

```
AN 75015173.
AU LEHOTZKY K.  SZEBERENYI J M.  GONDA Z.  HORKAY F.  KISS A.
TI EFFECTS OF PRE NATAL TRI PHENYL TIN EXPOSURE ON THE DEVELOPMENT OF
   BEHAVIOR AND CONDITIONED LEARNING IN RAT PUPS.
SO NEUROBEHAV TOXICOL TERATOL. 4 (2). 1982. ◆ EN ◆ 247-250.
CD NTOTD.
DE TINESTAN MORTALITY HYPERACTIVITY FUNGICIDE.
PC 22501C.
SC 07003C 07005C 13010C 17506C 20506C 22506C 25503C 25504C 25508C 25552C
   25554C 54600C.
TC 07508T 10069T 12510T 16501T 19001T 21002T 22100T 25000T 37015T 51514T
   54512T.
BC 86375B 95000B.
IN NATL. INST. OCCUPATIONAL HEALTH, P.O.B. 22, 1450 BUDAPEST, HUNGARY.
```

Figure 16.3. Same document as in figures 16.1 and 16.2, retrieved from Bibliographic Retrieval Services (BRS).

17

Useful references
with annotations

This bibliography is extensive but not exhaustive; many books and documents that might be useful to writers and editors are not included, but this does not reflect against their quality or usefulness. References cited in chapters in this manual are listed at the end of those chapters; some of the cited references with broad use in scientific writing are also listed here. Authoritative sources for nomenclature and styles in specific disciplines within biology and closely related fields are given at the end of chapter 13.

STYLE MANUALS AND GUIDES

American Chemical Society. Handbook for authors. Washington, DC: American Chemical Society Publications; 1978.

Guide for authors submitting manuscripts to journals published by the American Chemical Society. Covers major aspects of manuscript preparation, including specified parts of text, preferred use of terms, illustrations, presentation of data, and typing of final copy.

American Institute of Physics. Style manual. New York: American Institute of Physics; 1978.

Guide for authors preparing articles for journals published by the American Institute of Physics and its member societies. Discusses preparation of a scientific paper, general style, presentation of mathematical expressions, special characters and signs, preparation of illustrations, steps in the printing of articles (including typesetting and correction of proof), and statements of editorial policies for journals.

American Medical Association, Scientific Publications Division. Style book: editorial manual. 6th ed. Acton, MA: Publishing Sciences Group, Inc.; 1976.

Detailed instructions for authors preparing articles for journals published by the American Medical Association. Some recommendations differ from those in the *CBE Style Manual*.

American Psychological Association. Publication manual. 3d ed. Washington, DC: American Psychological Association; 1983.

Specifies editorial style for manuscripts submitted to journals published by the American Psychological Association (APA) and other journals using the APA style. Includes publication procedures and policies for APA journals; citation and reference forms; and brief comments on theses, dissertations, and oral presentation of papers.

American Society of Agronomy, Crop Science Society of America, Soil Science Society of America. Handbook and style manual. Madison, WI; American Society of Agronomy, Crop Science Society of America, Soil Science Society of America; 1976.

Guide to writing, refereeing, and editing for the five journals and other publications of these societies. Editorial policies and procedures and specific details of style.

Andrews, D. C.; Blickle, M. D. Technical writing: principles and forms. New York: Macmillan Publishing Co., Inc.; 1978.

Guide to preparing scientific and technical reports and articles for professional and lay publications. Has particularly helpful discussions of sentence length and structure, paragraph structure and sequence, and errors in grammar and syntax.

BioSciences Information Service. BIOSIS guide to abstracts. Philadelphia: Biological Abstracts, Inc.; published in each January 1 issue of *Biological Abstracts.*

Format and appropriate content of abstracts, with special instructions for taxonomic style. List of acceptable symbols and abbreviations.

Butcher, J. Copy-editing: the Cambridge handbook. London: Cambridge Univ. Press; 1975.

Preparation of manuscripts of books, including estimating length, copy editing, and proof correction. Style for particular media and fields. Based on practices of Cambridge University Press.

Campbell, W. G.; Ballow, S. Form and style: theses, reports, term papers. 5th ed. Boston: Houghton Mifflin Co.; 1977.

Detailed instructions on typing and the construction of tables, including computer printouts.

Cochran, W.; Hill, M.; Fenner, P., editors. Geowriting: a guide to writing, editing, and printing in earth science. 3d ed. Falls Church, VA: American Geological Institute; 1979.

How to prepare typescripts, drawings, photographs, and maps for publications in geology and related sciences. Conventions and authorities for geologic names; proof correction. Refereeing of manuscripts and how authors can respond to referees' criticisms. The chapter, "Reference Shelf," gives useful annotations for works in the earth sciences.

CODATA Task Group on the Presentation of Biological Data in the Primary Literature. Biologists' guide for the presentation of numerical data in the primary literature: CODATA Bulletin 25. Paris, France: CODATA: 1977. Available from: CODATA Secretariat, 51 Boulevard de Montmorency; 75016 Paris, France.

Guide for authors, editors, and referees on reporting of numerical data in the biosciences. Recommendations are intended to facilitate use, evaluation, and comparison of data; cover description of experiments and observational procedures, treatment of data derived from them, and presentations of final numerical results.

Greenberg, L. P., compiler. A compilation of journal instructions to authors. Washington, DC: U.S. Government Printing Office; 1980.

Facsimiles of journal pages that specify manuscript form and style. Coverage includes many journals in the biomedical sciences.

Judd, K. Copyediting: a practical guide. Los Altos, CA: William Kaufmann, Inc.; 1982.

A guide to copy editing from the publisher's point of view. Provides information on copy editing and proofreading symbols, punctuation and grammar, style and word usage, numbers and abbreviations, notes and bibliographies, typemarking and keying, as well as specialized and other aspects of copy editing.

Manheimer, M. L. K. Style manual: a guide for the preparation of reports and dissertations. New York: Marcel Dekker, Inc.; 1973.

Notable for its detail on form and content of bibliographic references.

Nordic Publication Committee for Medicine. Nordic biomedical manuscripts: instructions and guidelines. Svartz-Malmberg. G.; Goldmann, R., eds. Oslo: Universitets forlaget; 1978.

Recommendations for preparation of manuscripts to be submitted to Nordic biomedical journals: title page; abstract page; bibliographic references; figures and tables; and use of abbreviations, quantities, symbols, and units. Guidelines for composition of articles, terminology, ethics, and language. Terminology in general, metrology—the use of the International System of Units (SI) in biomedicine—and terminology and units in medical statistics. Writing and spelling rules in Danish, Finnish, Norwegian, and Swedish; a list of the Nordic journals consulted during the standardization work; recommended correction marks.

The Royal Society. General notes on the preparation of scientific papers. Rev. ed. London: The Royal Society; 1974.

Short manual not specified for particular journals. Includes annotated references to authoritative sources on nomenclature, units, symbols, and abbreviations.

Skillin, M. E.; Gay, R. M.; and other authorities. Words into type. 3d ed. Englewood Cliffs, NJ: Prentice-Hall, Inc.; 1974.

Detailed guide to preparation of manuscripts, preparation of copy, correction of proof, typography and illustrations, style conventions, grammar, and word usage. Excellent index.

Smith, P. Proofreading manual and reference guide. Alexandria, VA: Editorial Experts, Inc.; 1981.

A comprehensive self-study text covering the fundamentals of proofreading.

U.S. Government Printing Office. Style manual. Rev. ed. Washington, DC: U.S. Government Printing Office; 1973.

Very comprehensive manual especially helpful on formation of compound words; capitalization; and foreign-language alphabets, abbreviations, and syllabification. Includes valuable compilations of scientific terms: geologic and geographic terms; plant names and adjectives; and insect names.

UNISIST Working Group on Bibliographic Data Interchange. UNISIST guide to standards for information handling. Paris: UNESCO; 1980.

Guide to international sources of information about standards, rules, guidelines, directives, and other documents of normative character relevant to communication interconnections. Covers intellectual preparation of documents and subject analysis, production of documents, reproduction of documents, representation of information, editing of documents, preparation of bibliographic records, interchange of machine-readable bibliographic data, management of document collections, and numerical data.

University of Chicago Press. The Chicago manual of style. 13th ed., rev. and expanded. Chicago: Univ. of Chicago Press; 1982.

A standard "how-to" reference work for authors, editors, and copywriters; clear guidelines for preparing and editing copy. Grammar, punctuation, illustrations, tables, abbreviations, quotations, documentation, and indexing covered in detail; cross-referenced. New technology; rights and permissions; technical aspects of design, printing, and binding included.

WRITING, PROSE STYLE, AND WORD USAGE

The American Heritage dictionary of the English language. Morris, W., editor. Boston: Houghton Mifflin Co.; 1976.

Notable among standard American dictionaries for its thorough and helpful discussion of usage and synonyms.

Barzun, J. Simple and direct: a rhetoric for writers. New York: Harper & Row Publishers, Inc.; 1975.

Thorough discussion of faults in prose and their remedies. Proceeds from word choice through sequence and linkage, tone, meaning, and structure, to revision. Main points are set forth in 20 principles. Test examples. Index to words, topics, and authors.

Booth, V. Writing a scientific paper. 4th ed. Colchester, Essex, U.K.: The Biochemical Society; 1979.

Pithy and often witty advice on how to write, defects in prose style, punctuation, and preparing a manuscript.

CBE Committee on Graduate Training in Scientific Writing. Scientific writing for graduate students: a manual on the teaching of scientific writing. Bethesda, MD: Council of Biology Editors, Inc.; 1968 [reprinted 1983].

Offers a logical scheme for organizing and writing research reports for publication in scientific journals.

Cremmins, E. T. The art of abstracting. Philadelphia: ISI Press; 1982.

A comprehensive guide to writing and editing abstracts of scientific and scholarly materials, focusing on the composition and content. Three major themes are developed: reading, rules (style and content), and relationships (cooperative and professional). An example of the fundamental cognitive skills involved in meaningful abstracting is presented.

Day, R. A. How to write and publish a scientific paper. Philadelphia: ISI Press; 1979.

A witty, easy-to-read, step-by-step guide to the preparation of a scientific article for publication. Includes information about submitting the manuscript, the review process, and reprints. Short, succinctly titled chapters and six appendixes help the reader to find specific information quickly and easily.

Follett, W. Modern American usage. New York: Warner Books; 1974.

Very much like Fowler and Gowers' *A Dictionary of Modern English Usage* but more permissive. Guide to desirable usage in American prose. "Edited and completed" by Jacques Barzun with a small group of writers and teachers of English.

Fowler, H. W.; Gowers, E. A dictionary of modern English usage. 2d ed. rev. New York: Oxford Univ. Press; 1965.

Detailed, precise, and often entertaining notes on prose style, grammar, and word meaning. Out of print, but still useful.

Harman, E.; Montagnes, I., editors. The thesis and the book. Toronto: Univ. of Toronto Press; 1976.

Chapters are articles from *Scholarly Publishing.* Illuminating and helpful discussion of differences in structure and style between the thesis (or dissertation) written to serve the needs of a highly specialized audience, and the book, usually published for a wider audience. Useful chapters entitled "Thesis to Book: What to Get Rid Of" and "Thesis to Book: What to Do With What is Left."

Hodges, J. C.; Whitten, M. E. Harbrace college handbook. 8th ed. New York: Harcourt, Brace Jovanovich; 1977.

A classic in the field of English language usage. Clearly organized, concise, and easy to use. Contains answers to most questions of grammar, mechanics of writing, and punctuation.

Huth, E. J. How to write and publish papers in the medical sciences. Philadelphia: ISI Press; 1982.

A guide to physicians and medical scientists for the preparation of clinical papers, research contributions, case reports, editorials, book reviews, together with information on literature search, reference citations, abbreviations and symbols for units of measure.

King, L. S. Why not say it clearly: a guide to scientific writing. Boston: Little, Brown and Co.; 1978.

Essays on such diverse subjects as parts of speech, the opening sentence, the outline, monotonous writing, and gross errors.

O'Connor, M.; Woodford, F. P. Writing scientific papers in English: an ELSE-Ciba Foundation guide for authors. Amsterdam: Associated Scientific Publishers; New York: American Elsevier Publishing Co., Inc.; 1975.

Concise summary of planning and writing a scientific article, with detailed instructions for typing a manuscript.

Partridge, E. Usage and abusage: a guide to good English. Baltimore: Penguin Books; 1963.

Short articles on aspects of vocabulary, grammar, syntax, and prose style, with comments on the meaning and use of particular words. Similar to Fowler and Gowers' *A Dictionary of Modern English Usage* (see above).

Sherman, T. J.; Johnson, S. Modern technical writing. 3d ed. Englewood Cliffs, NJ: Prentice-Hall, Inc.; 1975.

Sections on effective prose style, organizing materials, and preparing manuscripts; covers technical reports, proposals, and oral presentations.

Strunk, W., Jr.; White, E. B. The elements of style. 3d ed. New York: Macmillan Co.; 1978.

Exposition on attaining a graceful, clear prose style. Advice is practical and excellent.

Trelease, S. F. How to write scientific and technical papers. Cambridge, MA: M.I.T. Press; 1969.

Describes concisely and clearly the steps in planning and writing a scientific article and typing the manuscript. The sections "Logical Presentation of Ideas," "Revising the Manuscript," and "Graphs" are particularly recommended.

Turabian, K. L. A manual for writers of term papers, theses and dissertations. 4th ed. Chicago: Univ. of Chicago Press; 1973.

Designed for university students in all disciplines; includes a short section on scientific articles.

Webster's new dictionary of synonyms: a dictionary of discriminated synonyms with antonyms and analogous and contrasted words. Springfield, MA: G. & C. Merriam Co.; 1968.

Clarifies differences in meanings of words. Nuances of difference are generously illustrated by quotations from literature.

Williams, J. M. Style: ten lessons in clarity & grace. Glenview, IL: Scott, Foresman and Co.; 1981.

This book, written primarily for the mature writer, explains how to overcome the problem of an unnecessarily complex prose style. Exercises for the reader to do are scattered throughout the book and suggested answers are given in the back of the book.

ILLUSTRATION

Allen, A. Steps toward better scientific illustrations. 2d ed. Lawrence, KS; Allen Press, Inc.; 1977.

Characteristics, uses, and preparation of the two types of reproduction for illustrations in books and journals: line and halftone. Special problems of foldout illustrations, micropublications, color plates, 300-line illustrations, and mathematical equations and chemical formulas.

CBE Scientific Illustration Committee. Illustrating science: standards for publication. Bethesda, MD: Council of Biology Editors, Inc.: [in press].

A guide to standard practices in the preparation and production of scientific illustration for illustrators, authors, editors, publishers, and printers. Covers standards for camera-ready materials, graphs and maps, line copy, computer graphics, tone copy, and color. Models of guidelines for authors and illustrators are recommended. Includes annotated bibliography on all aspects of illustration and production. Available early 1984.

MacGregor, A. J. Graphics simplified. Toronto: Univ. of Toronto Press; 1979.

A guide for the planning and preparation of effective and attractive charts and graphs for authors, lecturers, and artists. Seven common types of graphs and their variations are described and the kinds of data each is best suited to are given.

Stone, B.; Eckstein, A. Preparing art for printing. New York: Van Nostrand Reinhold Co.; 1979.

The authors describe the equipment, tools, and materials, and give useful information on how these are used in preparing line and continuous tone art for the printer's camera. The book is aimed at the commercial artist, but hits near the mark for the scientific illustrator. The printing and plate-making processes are described, but this section is a little dated. The trade terminology is defined in a glossary.

Zweifel, F. W. A handbook of biological illustration. Chicago: Univ. of Chicago Press; 1961.

Very useful guide for artists, authors, and editors on preparing various kinds of illustrative materials for scientific publications.

SCIENCE DICTIONARIES

Butterworth's medical dictionary. 2d ed. London: Butterworths; 1978. [First edition published in 1961 as The British medical dictionary.]

Very comprehensive British dictionary concerned almost solely with vocabulary and names in human medicine. Drug names of the British Pharmacopeia are identified; official U.S. names are given but not identified as such. Preference is given to British spellings of terms such as oedema (edema) and oestrus (estrus).

Dorland's illustrated medical dictionary, 26th ed. Philadelphia: W. B. Saunders Co.; 1982.

Stedman's medical dictionary, 24th ed. Baltimore: Williams & Wilkins Co.; 1982.

These major American medical dictionaries include terms from clinical medicine and from the medical sciences (such as anatomy, biochemistry, embryology, microbiology), veterinary medicine, and dental medicine.

McGraw-Hill dictionary of the life sciences. New York: McGraw-Hill Book Co.; 1976.

Defines over 20 000 terms. Most definitions are from the earlier edition (1974) of the parent dictionary (*see* entry directly below); discipline in which each term is most widely used is given but not etymologic information and pronunciation. Appendixes give SI and U.S. customary units of measurement (with conversion factors); normal values for some hematologic, chemical, and other medical values; and taxonomic classifications for animals (to orders), bacteria (to genera), and plants (to orders).

McGraw-Hill dictionary of scientific and technical terms. 2d ed. New York: McGraw-Hill Book Co.; 1978.

Defines close to 100 000 terms from the sciences and the engineering fields. Entries do not include syllabification, pronunciation, or etymologic information. Appendixes include tables of SI and U.S. units of measurement (with conversion factors); chemical symbols and atomic numbers; mathematical signs, symbols, and notation; abbreviations for scientific and technical organizations; elementary particles; international graphic symbols; and bacterial taxonomy.

METRIC AND OTHER UNITS

American Society for Testing and Materials. Standard for metric practice, ANSI/ASTM E 380–79. Philadelphia: American Society for Testing and Materials; 1979.

Defines SI base units, supplementary units, and derived units; specifies their appropriate uses. Rules for SI style and for conversion and rounding of numbers. Appendixes give a history of SI, a comprehensive list of conversion factors, and other useful compilations.

Canadian Standards Association. Metric practice guide, CAN-3-Z234.1-76. Rexdale, Ontario: Canadian Standards Association; 1976.

The Canadian standard for metric practice.

Council of Ministers of Education. The metric guide. 2d ed. Toronto, Ontario: Ontario Institute for Studies in Education; 1976. Available from: OISE Publications Sales, 252 Bloor St. West, Toronto, Ontario, Canada M5S 1V6.

Thorough, well-illustrated discussion of metric units (SI and non-SI), their use, the structure of SI, and basic rules of metric style. Especially recommended for students and redactors who have not had a technical or scientific education.

International Commission on Radiation Units and Measurements. Radiation quantities and units: ICRU report 19. Washington, DC: International Commission on Radiation Units and Measurements; 1971.

Definitions of and symbols for quantities and units for use in the field of radiation protection; SI equivalent units; and special equivalent units.

Lippert, H.; Lehmann, H. P. SI units in medicine: an introduction to the International System of Units with conversion tables and normal ranges. Baltimore and Munich: Urban & Schwarzenberg; 1978.

Summary of SI and discussions of how changeovers to SI units will affect usage and style in clinical medicine and the medical sciences. Conversion factors and numerical tables for conversion of chemical, power, radiation, and temperature values into SI equivalent values, with normal ranges where appropriate.

Lowe, D. A. A guide to international recommendations on names and symbols for quantities and on units of measurements. Geneva: World Health Organization; 1975.

Supplement to *Bulletin of the World Health Organization*, volume 52. Comprehensive tabulation of quantities (including non-recommended equivalent terms), their symbols or abbreviations recommended by international organizations, appropriate SI units and symbols, and useful comments on the international authorities. Covers all scientific disciplines.

Metric units, conversion factors and nomenclature in nutritional and food sciences: report of the Subcommittee on Metrication of the British National Committee for Nutritional Sciences. London: The Royal Society; 1972.

Recommendations made to facilitate metric (SI) usage for units in nutrition and food sciences: conversion of imperial units to metric units; expressions of concentration; adoption of the joule to replace the calorie; appropriate terms to replace "calorie" and its derivatives; generic descriptors and quantities for vitamins.

Quantities, units, and symbols: a report by the Symbols Committee of the Royal Society. 2d ed. London: The Royal Society; 1975.

Recommendations on symbols, and their modifying subscripts and superscripts, for physical quantities. One section summarizes the SI. Shorter sections cover chemical symbols and the special use of symbols for mathematics, quantum states, nuclear physics, thermodynamics, and galvanic cells. Authorities for the recommendations and a bibliography of authoritative publications.

World Health Organization. The SI for the health professions: prepared at the request of the Thirtieth World Health Assembly. Geneva: World Health Organization; 1977.

Definitions of SI units as they apply to medical and allied professions. Tables of equivalent values in traditional units and SI units cover the more important tests for constituents of plasma, serum, spinal fluid, and urine. Tables of factors permit conversion of numerical values in traditional units to numerical values in SI units for cell concentrations ("counts") and related quantities, clinical chemistry determinations, quantities important in physiologic tests, and radiation quantities.

STANDARDS: NATIONAL AND INTERNATIONAL

Listed below are selected standards for publication and documentation that are likely to be useful to authors and editors. This listing does not imply endorsement by the Council of Biology Editors (CBE) of all these standards, but those published by the American National Standards Institute (ANSI) have been approved by CBE through its representative to ANSI Committee Z39, Standardization in the Field of Library Work, Documentation, and Related Publishing Practices.

The ANSI, British Standards Institution (BS), and International Organization for Standardization (ISO) standards can be ordered from the Sales Department, American National Standards Institute, 1430 Broadway, New York, NY 10018, USA.

Articles
Preparation of scientific papers for written or oral presentation, ANSI Z39.16-1972.

Abstracts
Documentation—abstracts for publication and documentation, ISO 214-1976.
Writing abstracts, ANSI Z39.14-1971.

Bibliographic references
Bibliographic references, ANSI Z39.29-1977.
Bibliographical references—abbreviations of typical words in bibliographical references, ISO 832-1975.
Bibliographical references—essential and supplementary elements, ISO 690-1975.
Recommendations for bibliographical references, BS 1629:1976.

Copy preparation and proof correction
Guide to copy preparation and proof corrections, BS 5261.
  Recommendations for the preparation of typescript copy for printing. BS 5261: Part 1: 1975.
  Specifications for typographic requirements, marks for copy preparation and proof correction, proofing procedure, BS 5261: Part 2: 1976.
Proof correction, ANSI Z39.22-1974.

Periodicals
Abbreviation of titles of periodicals, ANSI Z39.5-1969 (R1974).
Abbreviations of titles of periodicals, BS 4148.
  Principles, BS 4148: Part 1: 1970.
  Word-abbreviation list, BS 4148: Part 2: 1975.
Documentation—international code for the abbreviation of titles of periodicals, ISO 4-1972.
Documentation—international list of periodical title word abbreviations, ISO 833-1974.
Documentation—international standard serial numbering (ISSN), ISO 3297–1975.
Identification number for serial publications, ANSI Z39.9-1971.
Layout of periodicals, ISO 8-1974.

Periodicals: format and arrangement, ANSI Z39.1-1978.
Presentation of serial publications including periodicals, BS 2509:1970.

Books

Documentation—title-leaves of a book, ISO 1086-1975.
Title leaves of a book, ANSI Z39.15-1971.
Title leaves of a book, BS 4719:1971.

Reports

Guidelines for format and production of scientific and technical reports. ANSI Z39.18-1974.

Theses

Recommendations for presentation of theses, BS 4821:1972.

Translations

Documentation—presentation of translations, ISO 2384-1977.
Format for scientific and technical translations, ANSI Z39.31-1976.
Specifications for the presentation of translations, BS 4755:1971.

Thesauri

Documentation—guidelines for the establishment and development of mono-lingual thesauri, ISO 2788-1974.
Guidelines for thesaurus structure, construction, and use, ANSI Z39.19-1974.

Indexes

Basic criteria for indexes, ANSI Z39.4-1958 (R1974).
Documentation—index of a publication, ISO 999-1975.
Recommendations for the presentation of indexes and other publications, BS 3700:1976.

Subject index

Italic type is used for example terms and for terms properly italicized in scientific usage.